INTRODUCTION
TO COMPUTERS
AND
DATA PROCESSING

SHELLY & CASHMAN BOOKS

Introduction to Computers and Data Processing

Introduction To Computer Programming Structured COBOL

Advanced Structured COBOL Program Design and File Processing

Business Systems Analysis and Design

Computer Programming RPG II

Introduction To Computer Programming ANSI COBOL

ANSI COBOL Workbook

Advanced ANSI COBOL Disk/Tape Programming Efficiencies

Introduction To Computer Programming RPG

Introduction to Flowcharting and Computer Programming Logic

Introduction To Computer Programming IBM System/360 Assembler Language

IBM System/360 Assembler Language Workbook

IBM System/360 Assembler Language Disk/Tape Advanced Concepts

DOS Utilities Sort/Merge Multiprogramming

OS Job Control Language

DOS Job Control for Assembler Language Programmers

DOS Job Control for COBOL Programmers

Introduction to Computer Programming System/360 PL/I

INTRODUCTION TO COMPUTERS AND DATA PROCESSING

Gary B. Shelly
Educational Consultant
Fullerton, California

&

Thomas J. Cashman, CDP, B.A., M.A.
Long Beach City College
Long Beach, California

ANAHEIM PUBLISHING COMPANY
2632 Saturn St., Brea, CA 92621
(714) 879-7922

Library of Congress Catalog Card Number 79-57019

ISBN 0-88236-115-5

Printed in the United States of America

Table of Contents

3 Processing Data on a Computer System 3.1

4 The Processor Unit 4.1

5 Input to the Computer System 5.1

6 Obtaining Output From The Computer   6.1

7 Auxiliary Storage and File Organization   7.1

8 Data Communications 8.1

9 Data Base and Distributed Data Processing 9.1

10 Systems Analysis and Design   10.1

11 Program Design and Flowcharting   11.1

12 Programming Languages — Coding and Testing Programs 12.1

13 The Future of Computers in Society 13.1

Appendix A Programming in BASIC A.1

Appendix B The Coding of the 80 Column Card B.1

Appendix C Number Systems C.1

Glossary / Index

Preface

Introduction

The age of the computer is here. With increasing frequency, it is recognized that an understanding of the computer, how it works, and how it influences the daily lives of every citizen is a necessary part of the general education for all students who live and work in this technological society.

It is the purpose of this textbook to provide an introduction to computers and data processing for general education, business, and computer science students so that they are able to understand how computers operate and how they are used in all aspects of business and science.

This textbook, through the extensive use of color diagrams and photographs, is designed to teach not only the technical features of computers in an interesting and easy-to-understand fashion, but to also visually transport the student from the classroom into the world of data processing — into the computer center, the modern office, retail stores, banks, and manufacturing plants.

A result of almost two years of research, this book was produced with the cooperation of over 190 leading manufacturers and users of computer hardware and software. These companies very generously supplied technical material, slides, and photographs not only of their latest hardware but, more importantly, of the use of this hardware in actual operating environments.

The development of this textbook

In performing the research for the book, it became apparent that the material contained in most existing introductory texts reflected technology and processing methods of the late 1960's. Punched card and batch processing systems, which have served as the basis for much of the instructional material over the past years, are rapidly being augmented and replaced in industry by transaction-oriented processing systems using terminal input, data bases, and data communications. In the software area, it was evident that structured programming and structured design were having significant influence and should be included as the standard methods used.

As a result of this research, four goals were set for this book: 1) The book should reflect state of the art technology; 2) The book should present modern, up-to-date applications of computer systems in all areas of use; 3) The book should allow the student to see and understand the business, industrial, and scientific arenas in which the computer is used; 4) The textbook should move from an overview of a subject area to a detailed examination of the subject area.

To assist in reaching these goals and capturing the spirit and flavor of the data processing industry, an unprecedented committment was obtained from Anaheim Publishing Company to produce a four-color textbook with nearly 500 color photographs, drawings, and illustrations. The result is a very exciting, up-to-date introduction to the world of data processing.

Textbook approach

In presenting the material in the book, it was felt that computer hardware and software should not be treated as individual units of study. This approach never allows the student to view the entire picture of computers and data processing. Instead, these concepts should be integrated throughout each chapter. Therefore, the approach in this textbook is to integrate the subject areas by first presenting an overview of a subject and then, in subsequent chapters, proceding to more in-depth coverage.

For example, in Chapter 1 the student is provided with an overview of the profession of data processing; the basic concepts of computer hardware, software, and processing methods; and an introduction to computer systems of all sizes from microcomputers to large mainframes. Thus, the student is immediately immersed into the actual environment of the computer industry and gains an overall understanding of how a computer operates, what a data processing installation is, and an acquaintance with small, medium, and large computer systems.

Using this approach, even if the students complete but one week of class, they will have gained an overall understanding of the data processing profession and how a computer functions to solve problems.

Chapter 2 contains a discussion of the evolution of the electronic computer industry. Quite unlike other texts, the purpose of this chapter is not to identify dates when specific computer hardware was announced. Rather, the intent is to capture for the student the excitement, growth, and problems that the data processing profession faced as it emerged to become one of the world's largest industries. The chapter includes a discussion of not only computer hardware and software, but also personnel problems, social issues, and the impact of the minicomputer and microcomputer on the industry. The chapter concludes with a series of photographs showing state-of-the-art computer systems as they are used in the office, education, retailing, and manufacturing. Again it should be emphasized that at the end of Chapter 2, the student will have gained further insight into the entire spectrum of data processing and computer activities, including hardware, software, computer programming, and how computers are used in daily activities.

Having gained an overview of computers, their evolution, and their impact, the student is then exposed to a more detailed discussion of the types of processing which can occur on a computer system in Chapter 3. Included are diagrams and examples of input, processing, output, comparing, arithmetic operations, storing data on auxiliary storage, data retrieval from auxiliary storage, inquiries, updating, and other processing of data which can occur on a computer system. This chapter serves as an outline for the next four chapters.

Chapter 4 is dedicated to illustrating the storage of data in main computer storage and the processing that occurs internally in a computer system. Chapter 5 discusses in detail the process of entering data into a computer system for processing. In this chapter, the student is introduced to batch processing systems and transaction-oriented systems because a knowledge of these types of processing is necessary in order to understand the various means for entering data into a computer system. This chapter discusses not only hardware, but also the need for ensuring that valid data enters the system and the ways and formats that can be used for entering data. Thus, the entire spectrum of entering data is covered rather than just a discussion of hardware devices such as found in other textbooks. The student, therefore, can appreciate the problems and potential solutions to data entry on a computer system.

Chapter 6 explores all areas of output from a computer system. This includes printed output, output on CRT and other terminals, and output which is used for many types of reasons. It is concerned not only with the hardware, but with user interaction with the computer system, designing the format of output information, distributing output, and other similar concerns. Again, this is an integrated approach to the subject of output from the computer system.

In Chapter 7, the use of auxiliary storage is explained. Disk and tape hardware are illustrated, but the chapter also includes file access methods, file organization methods, and the software necessary to implement these organization and access methods.

The important subject of data communications is covered in Chapter 8. The use of remote communications and the method for implementing these systems is included. After studying the material in Chapter 8, the student will have gained an insight into how data communications takes place and how networks are established to utilize computers and data communications together.

Data bases and distributed data processing are covered in Chapter 9. Using the knowledge gained from Chapter 7 and Chapter 8, the student is exposed to the state-of-the-art methods for utilizing the power of the computer system.

Chapters 10, 11, and 12 are concerned with explaining how systems are actually implemented on computer systems. Chapter 10 explores in detail the design of a computer system. Chapter 11 discusses the most up-to-date methods for program design; while Chapter 12 examines the available programming languages and their uses. It also includes a discussion of operating systems and how these systems are used on a computer system.

The concluding chapter, Chapter 13, is designed to encourage the student to evaluate the influence that computer technology has, and will have, on the quality of life; and introduces some of the problems facing the profession and society because of rapid technological change.

Student learning aids

At the conclusion of each chapter except the last, a comprehensive summary is provided. Review questions are included to serve as the basis for testing one's knowledge of the concepts presented in the chapter.

An important aspect of the educational process is to encourage students to analyze and evaluate controversial issues in the subject matter being studied. For this purpose, a series of questions presenting these issues is included at the end of each chapter. The questions relate to the material presented in the chapter. Teachers are strongly urged to include a discussion of these issues as a part of the classroom activity, probing into these issues with students to assist in developing critical thinking about important issues in data processing.

In addition to these activities, research projects are included as a part of each chapter. Some projects require going into industry and gathering data, while others require academic research. It is strongly recommended that these research topics be included within the course work.

For additional student activities, a Study Guide and Workbook which accompanies this textbook is available. The material in the study guide is designed to further enhance the instructional materials in each chapter. In many cases, supplementary instructional material is contained in the study guide.

An additional feature of the study guide is a series of "simulation" projects which are designed to supplement classroom lectures with practical experience on computer terminals. These projects include word processing activities, inquiry applications, data entry, input editing, and similar activities that are commonly experienced by workers in all areas of business today. Thus, the opportunity is provided for the students, very early in their course work, to interact with the computer.

Learning to program

Many introductory courses introduce students to the principles and concepts of computer programming by requiring the students to write and execute a number of programs. Because of the wide usage of BASIC, Appendix A has been included in the text for those instructors desiring to teach BASIC programming.

The approach in this section of the text is much different from what has typically been taught in the past. In many introductory classes, students are taught a few of the widely used BASIC statements and then are allowed to write programs in any manner they see fit. Because of this approach, students develop poor programming habits, not only in terms of programming skills and techniques but in their general attitude and approach to the computer programming process.

To combat this problem, from the very first program the student is urged to develop a professional approach to programming; that is, the program should be carefully designed and properly coded and documented. Students should approach the problem solving process with the attitude that the program will execute properly the first time it is placed on the computer. It makes little difference whether the program is being written for home use, for games, or for business applications — programming is a serious business, and proper attitudes should be instilled in the students from the very beginning.

This does not mean that computer programming cannot be "fun." To the contrary, using a professional approach, programming no longer will be an activity of frustration and anxiety. The real joy in computer programming is not debugging a program; it is in producing useful output from the computer system.

Teachers are strongly urged to teach proper documentation and programming style in the introductory class and require students to complete programs in a professional manner.

Acknowledgements

A project of this size does not happen without the help of many people. We would like to thank the over 200 instructors who supplied us with information relative to what they would like to see in an introductory textbook. In addition, almost two hundred companies supplied us with pictures and source material. Without them, this book would not have happened.

We had the help of true professionals in putting together this book. Mr. Herb Grimm of Colormation, Inc., El Monte, California, was largely responsible for the high quality of the photographs which appear in this book. Ms. Sue Davis and Mr. Max Loftin of Quality Graphics, Santa Ana, California, undertook the difficult task of providing quality color separations and stripping for two very demanding authors. These people did a superior job and we thank them.

Our greatest appreciation, however, must be to our two colleagues at Anaheim Publishing Company — Mrs. Marilyn Martin and Mr. Michael Broussard. Michael developed and implemented the many unique diagrams and illustrations which so enhance the value of this textbook; while Marilyn typeset the "last" version of the manuscript many, many times. With words being inadequate to express our appreciation, we can merely say thank you, Marilyn and Mike, for a job well done.

Gary B. Shelly
Thomas J. Cashman

Picture Credits

The pictures contained in this book are courtesy of the following companies. We are most appreciative of their cooperation and help.

AM International Figure 5-29
American Airlines Company Figure 1-19
American Satellite Company Figure 8-7
Atchison, Topeka and Santa Fe Railway Company Figures 1-6, 1-12, 5-37
BASF Wyandotte Corporation Figures 7-29, 7-32
Basic Four Corporation Figure 3-21
Bell Laboratories Figure 8-8
Bergen Brunswig Corporation Figure 5-24
Bethlehem Steel Corporation Figure 2-44
Burroughs Corporation Figures 2-33, 5-23, 5-28, 7-4, 7-29
California Computer Products, Incorporated Figures 1-13, 6-31
Chromatics, Incorporated Figure 2-42
Communications Satellite Corporation Figures 8-31, 8-32, 8-33
CompuServe, Incorporated Figure 8-11
Computer Automation, Incorporated Figure 4-1
Computervision Corporation Figure 6-27
Computerworld Figures 2-1, 2-23, 2-26
Conrac Corporation Figure 6-29
Data General Corporation Cover, Figure 9-1
DatagraphiX, Incorporated Figure 6-25
Dataproducts Corporation Figures 6-4, 6-16, 6-17, 6-18, 6-20, 6-21, 6-22
Datatrol Incorporated Figure 5-30
Digital Equipment Corporation Figures 1-23, 2-30, 2-39, 2-45, 2-46, 8-12
Eastman Kodak Company Figures 6-24, 6-26, 10-1
Emhart Corporation Figure 6-33
Fairchild Camera and Instrument Corporation Figure 1-2
GRI Computer Corporation Figures 10-18, 10-19, 10-20
General Electric Company Figures 8-6, 8-30
General Instrument Corporation Figure 5-26
Georgia-Pacific Corporation Figures 1-11, 1-29
Goodyear Tire and Rubber Company Figure 2-35
Grace (W. R.) and Company Figure 7-5
Hazeltine Corporation Figure 5-13
Hewlett-Packard Company Figures 1-19, 1-22, 1-24, 2-22, 5-36, 6-9
Honeywell, Incorporated Figures 2-32, 2-48, 4-19
Intel Corporation Figure 4-19
International Business Machines Corporation Figures 1-10, 1-19, 1-25, 1-26, 2-9, 2-10, 2-11, 2-16, 2-18, 2-19, 2-29, 2-41, 2-47, 4-17, 5-6, 5-9, 5-10, 5-27, 5-31, 5-33, 6-32, 7-15, 7-16, 7-29, 10-5, 10-6

Interstate Electronics Corporation Figures 5-35, 6-28
Iowa State University Figures 2-2, 2-3
La Mantia Marketing Communications, Incorporated Figure 7-33
Lever Brothers Company Figures 1-15, 1-16, 1-18, 6-19, 8-5
Lockheed Aircraft Corporation Figure 2-43
3M Company Figure 7-31
MCAUTO (McDonnell Douglas Automation Company) Figures 1-17, 1-28, 6-5
Memorex Corporation Figure 7-30
Mohawk Data Sciences Corporation Figures 5-8, 5-12, 5-32, 5-34, 9-7
Motorola, Incorporated Figure 1-1
NCR Corporation Figures 2-34, 2-36, 3-19, 4-18
National CSS Incorporated Figure 6-1
National Semiconductor Corporation Figures 2-27, 4-19
Perkin-Elmer Corporation Figures 2-27, 6-30
Pertec Computer Corporation Figure 5-1
Princeton University Figure 2-5
Qume Figure 5-14
RCA Corporation Figure 5-15
Radio Shack, A Division of Tandy Corporation Figures 1-20, 1-21
Raytheon Company Figures 1-22, 2-38, 3-17, 4-21
Recognition Equipment Corporation Figure 5-25
Redifon Simulation Incorporated Figure 2-40
Siltec Corporation, Frank Wing Photographer Figure 4-19
Sperry Univac, A Division of Sperry Corporation Figures 1-9, 1-18, 2-8, 2-24, 4-19, 7-9, 8-3 13-1
Storage Technology Corporation Figure 7-1
Tektronix, Incorporated Figures 2-31, 2-43, 6-8
Trilog, Incorporated Figure 10-10
Tymshare, Incorporated Figures 1-27, 10-15
Union Pacific Railroad Company Figure 7-29
United Press International Figures 2-4, 2-7
United States Steel Company Figure 2-25
Universal Data Systems, Incorporated Figure 8-4
University of Pennsylvania Figure 2-6
Walgreen Company Figure 2-37
Wang Laboratories, Incorporated Figures 1-22, 2-28, 6-7, 7-34
Western Union Corporation Figures 8-1, 8-21
Xerox Corporation Figure 3-14
Zilog Figures 4-20, 4-21

Acknowledgements

The following companies donated materials used for research and photographs for use in the book. We thank them.

AEG–Telefunken; A. R. A. P. (drs); A. B. Dick Company; AM International; Advanced Micro Devices, Incorporated; American Airlines Company; American Microsystems, Incorporated; American Satellite Company; American Telephone and Telegraph; American Valuation Consultants, Incorporated; Anderson, Jacobson, Incorporated; Apple Computer Incorporated; Applied Data Research, Incorporated; Arcata National Corporation; Atchison, Topeka, and Santa Fe Railway Company; Avon Products; BASF Wyandotte Corporation; Bank of America; BayBanks, Incorporated; Basic Four Corporation; Beech Aircraft Corporation; Beehive International; Bell Laboratories; Bergen Brunswig Corporation; Bethlehem Steel Corporation; Borden, Incorporated; Bradford National Corporation; Bradford Trust Company; Bunker Ramo Corporation; Burroughs Corporation; CPT Corporation; CSP Incorporated; CW Communications, Incorporated; Cado Systems Corporation; California Computer Products, Incorporated; Chromatics, Incorporated; Cincom Systems, Incorporated; Cognitronics Corporation; Communications Satellite Corporation; Compugraphic Corporation; Compuscan Incorporated; CompuServe, Incorporated; Computer Associates, Incorporated (Trans American); Computer Automation, Incorporated; Computer Communications, Incorporated; Computer Horizons Corporation; Computer Products; Computer Sciences Corporation; Computer Usage Company; Computervision; Computerworld; Comshare Incorporated; Conrac Corporation; Continental Oil Company; Control Data Corporation; Crocker Bank; Cullinane Corporation; Data Electronics, Incorporated; Data General Corporation; Data Processing magazine; Data Specialties, Incorporated; DatagraphiX, Incorporated; Datamation; Dataproducts Corporation; Datapoint Corporation; Datatrol Incorporated; David R. McClurg, Consultant; Del Monte Corporation; Diebold, Incorporated; Digi-Log Systems, Incorporated; Digital Equipment Corporation; Digital Scientific Corporation; Dylakor Software Systems, Incorporated; EDP Industry Report; Eastman Kodak Company; Emhart Corporation; Esmark, Incorporated; Fairchild Camera and Instrument Corporation; Facit-Addo, Incorporated; Federal Reserve Bank of New York; Financial Technology Incorporated; Four-Phase Systems, Incorporated; GRI Computer Corporation; General Automation; General Electric Company; General Instrument Corporation; General Motors Research Laboratories; General Telephone; Genesco Incorporated; Genesee Computer Center, Incorporated; Georgia-Pacific Corporation; Goodyear Tire and Rubber Company; W. R. Grace and Company; Great Northern Nekoosa Corporation; Graham Magnetics; Hazeltine Corporation; Hewlett-Packard Company; Honeywell, Incorporated; Imperial Technology, Incorporated; Incoterm Corporation, A Subsidiary of Honeywell, Incorporated; Inforex, Incorporated; Information Magnetics Corporation; Information Processing Incorporated; Intel Corporation; International Business Machines Corporation; International Harvester Company; International Mathematical and Statistical Libraries, Incorporated; Interstate Electronics Corporation; Iowa State University; Johnson Systems, Incorporated; Keane Associates, Incorporated; Keydata Corporation; La Mantia Marketing Communications, Incorporated; Lever Brothers Company; Lexico Enterprises, Incorporated; Litton Industries, Incorporated; Lockheed Aircraft Corporation; 3M Company; MAI–Management Assistance Incorporated; MCAUTO (McDonnell Douglas Automation Company); MCI Communications Corporation; MRI Systems Corporation; MSI Data Corporation; Management Science American, Incorporated; McGraw-Hill, Incorporated; Medical Information Technology, Incorporated; Memorex Corporation; Microsoft; Mohawk Data Sciences Corporation; Modular Computer Systems, Incorporated; Monsanto Company; Motorola Incorporated; Muirhead, Incorporated; NCR Corporation; National Aeronautics and Space Administration; National Center for Atmospheric Research; National Computing Industries; National CSS Incorporated; National Data Corporation; National Semiconductor Corporation; Norden Systems, Subsidiary of United Technologies; Northern Telecom Limited; Owens/Corning Fiberglas; Pacific Gas and Electric Company; Perkin-Elmer Corporation; Pertec Computer Corporation; Pfizer Incorporated; POISE Company; Price Waterhouse and Company; Princeton University; Program Products Incorporated; Qantex (Peripherals Division of North Atlantic Industries, Incorporated); Qume; RCA Corporation; Radio Shack, A Division of Tandy Corporation; Raytheon Company; Recognition Equipment Incorporated; Redifon Simulation Incorporated; Rodriquez Graphics; St.Regis Paper Company; Shared Medical Systems Corporation; Sheller-Globe Corporation; Siltec Corporation, Frank Wing Photographer; Sorbus Incorporated; Southern California Edison Company; Southern Pacific Company; Sperry Rand Corporation; Sperry Univac, A Division of Sperry Corporation; Standard Oil Company of Indiana; Standard Register Company; Storage Technology Corporation; System Development Corporation; Tandem Computers, Incorporated; Technical Publishing Company; Tektronix, Incorporated; Teleram Communications Corporation; Threshold Technology Incorporated; Timplex, Incorporated; Tone Software Corporation; Trilog, Incorporated; Tymshare, Incorporated; U. S. Army ; Union Carbide Corporation; Union Pacific Railroad Company; United Press International; United States Steel Company; Universal Data Systems, Incorporated; University of Pennsylvania; Value Computing Incorporated; Walgreen Company; Wang Laboratories, Incorporated; Western Union Corporation; World Information Systems Incorporated; Xerox Corporation; Zilog.

Chapter 1
An Introduction to the Computer

Objectives

- Familiarization with the basic data processing cycle — input, process, and output

- Familiarization with the function of a computer program

- Familiarization with the types of equipment found in typical computer centers

- Familiarization with the roles played by computer operators, data entry operators, tape librarians, programmers, and systems analysts in typical computer centers

- Familiarization with different sizes and types of computers

Chapter 1

Figure 1-1 A microcomputer smaller than a thumbnail is stored on a single chip. This Motorola microcomputer contains the electronic circuitry to perform all the computations required of a computer, and it can store the data on which it will operate. It requires further components, however, to interface with other computers or with human operators.

An Introduction to the Computer

"The computer revolution is the most advertised revolution in world history. Yet one of the funny things about it is that we probably still underestimate its impact."[1]

Introduction

The statement above by Herman Kahn of the Hudson Institute identifies the importance of the study of computers and data processing. It is a rare individual who has not heard of a computer or, in some way, has not been affected by a computer. Yet an understanding of the computer and its impact on our society is not widely held by most persons. It is the purpose of this book to explain what a computer is, how it works, and how the computer is utilized to assist in solving problems, not only in business and science, but in our daily lives as well. Thus, as a result of reading this book, the reader should have an appreciation and understanding of the so-called "computer revolution."

What is a computer?

The most obvious question concerning the "computer revolution" is "What is a computer?". Although the term computer has come to mean a number of things, in actual fact a computer is a device which can perform computations, including arithmetic and logic operations, without intervention by a human being. A picture of a computer is illustrated in Figure 1–1. This device contains the electronic circuitry necessary to perform all of the functions required of a computer.

Even though the device illustrated in Figure 1–1 fulfills the definition of a computer, it is not the image of a computer which is imagined when one hears of the computer revolution. Instead, many people visualize a room full of strange looking machines, where lights flash, tapes spin, and people hurry about doing odd tasks. The whole aura is one of mystery and intrigue. This image is, perhaps, partially fulfilled by the picture of the world's most powerful computer illustrated on the following page.

---

1 "Computers and the Future of America," Hesh Weiner, COMPUTER DECISIONS, January, 1977.

Figure 1-2 The Cray-1 computer is the world's most powerful computer system. It can process 80 million instructions per second and can store over 1 million characters of data in its main storage. The Cray-1 pictured here is used at the National Center for Atmospheric Research in Boulder, Colorado, for analyzing atmospheric and weather information.

Disk Storage

CRAY-1

The answer to "what is a computer" lies somewhere between the awe-inspiring monster of the cartoons and the small device illustrated in Figure 1-1. A computer such as the Cray-1 shown in Figure 1-2 actually consists of a number of different devices which allow it to process data. These devices are interconnected to form a computer system. Thus, a computer system consists not only of the device which can perform computations without human intervention, but also devices which allow data to be made available for processing and devices on which data can be displayed or printed for use by human beings.

What does a computer do?

Although the results of computer processing can be marvelous indeed, such as controlling a lunar module landing on the surface of the moon or keeping track of airline reservations for thousands of flights and hundreds of thousands of passengers, any computer system, regardless of size, is capable of performing only a relatively few number of operations. These operations include:

1. Arithmetic operations, such as the addition, subtraction, multiplication and division of data.
2. Logical operations, such as determining whether one number is greater than another number.
3. Input/output operations, such as accepting data for processing or causing data to be printed on a report.

Even though these operations seem minimal, and in fact not very powerful, it is through the ability of the computer system to perform these operations quickly and reliably that the power of the computer system is derived. The operations are all carried out through the use of electronic circuits such as contained on the chip in Figure 1-1. Since electronic circuits rarely fail and the data flows along these circuits at close to the speed of light, the processing is accomplished quickly and reliably.

What is data?

In the three operations of a computer system just described, the common thread is that all three operations involve the processing of data. It is important, therefore, to have some concept of what data is.

Data is a representation of facts, concepts, or instructions in a formalized manner suitable for communication, interpretation, and processing by humans or automatic machines. For example, data is the grade a student receives for a course, the number of hours an employee worked during the week, or the flight number of an airplane flight from New York to Los Angeles. The purpose of a computer system is to accept data, process data, and as a result of the processing, produce output in the form of useful information.

Data input, processing, and output

The computer system is capable of processing data at very rapid speeds to produce results which are useful to people. In order to understand how a computer system can do this, it is necessary to examine the three primary units of the computer system (Figure 1-3). These units are:

1. Input units, which present data to the processor unit of the computer system for processing of the data.
2. Processor unit, which stores the data and contains the electronic circuitry necessary to carry out the processing of the stored data.
3. Output units, which can display, print, or otherwise make available to people the results of the processing of the data.

The processor unit of a computer system is normally composed of two distinct parts: the central processing unit (CPU) and main computer storage. The central processing unit contains the electronic circuits which actually cause processing to occur by interpreting instructions to the computer, performing calculations if necessary, and performing the input and output operations of the system.

The data which is to be processed must be stored in main computer storage before it can be processed. Main computer storage consists of components which can electronically store letters of the alphabet, numbers, and special characters such as decimal points or dollar signs. The data stored in main computer storage can be referenced by the CPU so that processing can occur.

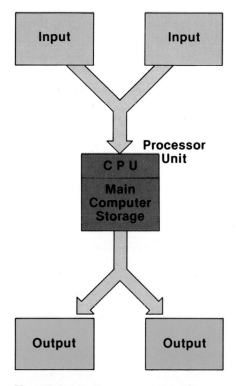

Figure 1-3 A basic computer system is composed of input units which make data available to the processor unit, the processor unit which stores data and processes the stored data, and output units on which the results of the processing are obtained.

Computer programs

The operations of input, process, and output which take place in a computer system must be controlled. These operations are controlled by a computer program. A computer program is a series of instructions which are stored in main computer storage and specify which processing operations are to occur in the computer system. For example, there are computer instructions to cause numbers to be added, to cause numbers to be multiplied, to cause data to be read into main computer storage from an input device, and to cause data to be printed. There are, of course, many more instructions.

Each of these instructions which cause the computer system to process data must be arranged in the proper sequence so that the correct processing will occur. Computer programmers write these instructions.

A typical application

To illustrate how these components work together in a computer system, assume that a program has been written to calculate the grade point average for students in a school. Data for each student is to be "read" into main computer storage. This data contains the name of the student, the number of units for each class, and the grade for each class. The program is to calculate the grade point average for the student and print the grade point average report (Figure 1-4). The following steps would occur in order to create this report (Figure 1-5).

Figure 1-4 The Grade Point Average Report contains the student name and the grade point average for each student.

GRADE POINT AVERAGE REPORT	
STUDENT NAME	G.P.A.
BECKER, JAMES	3.41
CARSON, NANCY	2.65
DELMON, ALICE	3.95
ELLIOT, DARYL	2.17
ESNON, CARL	2.75
FINGEL, NORMAN	1.79
HANSON, CAROLE	3.72
MOON, CHARLIE	2.90
NUNTON, PEARL	2.97
POPACA, KAY	2.10
RETTY, RITA	3.82

1. The information from a grading sheet concerning each student's grades would be recorded on some recording medium such as punched cards so that it can be read into main computer storage.

2. The data would be read into main computer storage through the use of an input device, such as a card reader.

3. The data which is stored in main computer storage would be processed under the control of the computer program also stored in main computer storage. In this processing, the grade point averages would be calculated.

4. As each grade point average is calculated, the results are printed on the grade point average report.

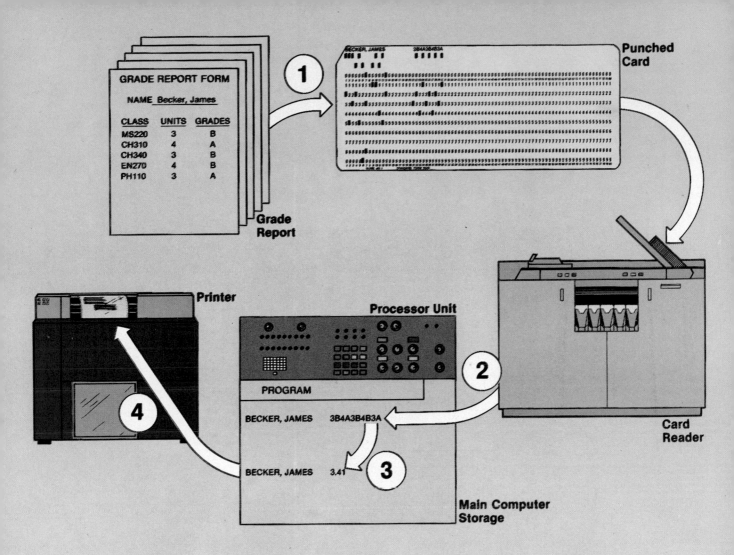

Figure 1-5 The cycle of input, process, and output is illustrated in this example of preparing a grade point average report. This basic cycle is found with all computer systems.

In the example just given, all of the elements of input, process, and output are used. Although this is a simplified example, virtually all computer systems have these capabilities and they are used together, under the control of the computer program, to cause meaningful processing to occur on the system.

A tour of a computer center

The computer center in most companies is used to house the processor unit and most or all of the input and output units which are utilized with the computer system. A typical computer center is pictured on the next page, followed by an explanation of the various pieces of equipment and the job duties usually found in a computer center.

Figure 1-6 A typical computer center contains the processor unit and many of the input and output devices utilized with the

computer system. The computer operators shown here are monitoring and responding to the needs of the computer system.

Figure 1-7 The computer console can contain lights and switches which indicate the processing status of the computer system. The lights and switches are not normally used by the computer operator.

Figure 1-8 A computer console terminal operator enters information into the computer system. The operator must respond to messages from the computer system in order to keep the system running.

Computer console

The image of flashing lights which has so often characterized a layman's view of a computer system normally comes from the computer console (Figure 1-7). The console and the housing of which it is a part usually contain the processor unit of the computer system. It may also contain electronic circuitry which allows the input and output devices to communicate with the processor unit. The lights, dials, and buttons which are found on the computer console indicate the status of the processor unit.

The computer operator communicates with the processor unit through a console terminal. The console terminal can be a typewriter-like device or a Cathode Ray Tube (CRT) device such as shown in Figure 1-8. The CRT terminal contains a television-like screen, which the operator can read and respond to, and a keyboard which can be used to enter data into main computer storage.

The computer operator is responsible for a number of different tasks when operating the computer. When the computer system is running, it will periodically send messages to the operator regarding different operations and needs. For example, the system may write a message to the operator on the CRT indicating that paper is required in the printer. The operator must respond to these messages in order to keep the computer system running.

The operator is also able to "quiz" the computer system to determine which jobs are currently running and which jobs will be run next. Thus, through the ability to communicate with the computer system on the console terminal, the operator is able to keep track of all processing on the computer system and respond to the needs of the computer system so that a maximum amount of work is accomplished.

Input devices

One of the more commonly found input devices on a computer system is a card reader (Figure 1-9). Punched cards, which contain holes representing data, are read by the card reader as input to main computer storage. Punched cards may be used to contain data indicating to the processor unit the tasks to be performed and may also be used to store data which is read into main computer storage for processing.

Figure 1-9 The card reader is commonly found in the computer center. It is used to read data stored on punched cards. The cards can contain control information for the computer system or data for programs which are being run on the computer system.

Another input device which may be found in the computer center is the "floppy disk" reader. A floppy disk is an oxide-coated plastic disk about the size of a 45 rpm record. Data is stored on the disk by electronic impulses recorded on the magnetic oxide. The reader shown in Figure 1–10 can read the electronic impulses and pass the data to main computer storage. Floppy disks (so-called because they are flexible like a phonograph record) are a widely used method for entering data into the computer system.

Output devices

The most commonly used output device in the computer center is the system printer (Figure 1–11). Printers produce printed reports which contain different information, depending upon the application which is being processed on the computer system. For example, printed reports can contain financial information for accounting applications, inventory information for manufacturing applications, or payroll checks for payroll applications.

Printers vary tremendously in their speed of printing. Some printers print 30 characters per second while others can print as many as 20,000 lines per minute with each line containing 132 characters. Most printers which are found in the computer room are fairly high-speed, with the ability to print 1,000–2,000 lines per minute common.

Figure 1–10 A floppy disk is loaded into a floppy disk reader by the computer operator. The floppy disk is oxide-coated and data is stored on the floppy disk by electronic impulses.

Figure 1–11 A computer operator checks the report alignment on a high-speed printer. Continuous forms are used on the printer to allow thousands of lines to be printed each minute.

Figure 1-12 Magnetic tape is commonly used for auxiliary storage. Here, the computer operator resets the tape drive after removing a reel of tape.

Auxiliary storage devices

In many applications which are processed on a computer system, data is prepared which must be stored so that it can be used at a later time. For example, in a grade reporting system, the grade point averages which are calculated may have to be saved so that they can be used when the next semester's grades are processed. In order to store this data, auxiliary storage devices are used.

The two most commonly used auxiliary storage devices are magnetic tape (Figure 1-12) and magnetic disk (Figure 1-13). With magnetic tape, the data to be stored is written on one-half inch magnetic tape (similar to audio cassette tape) as electronic impulses. This data can be written from main computer storage onto the tape and can also be read into main computer storage from the tape. Reels of magnetic tape are mounted on tape drives for reading and writing by the computer system.

When using magnetic disk, data is recorded on an oxide-coated disk as a series of electronic spots. Typical disk drives in larger installations have the capability of storing more than a billion characters of data. Multiple disk packs can be used on most disk drives and these packs are removable, allowing an unlimited amount of storage.

Figure 1-13 This magnetic disk storage device contains space for multiple disk packs on which data can be stored. Each disk pack is removable, allowing an unlimited amount of storage.

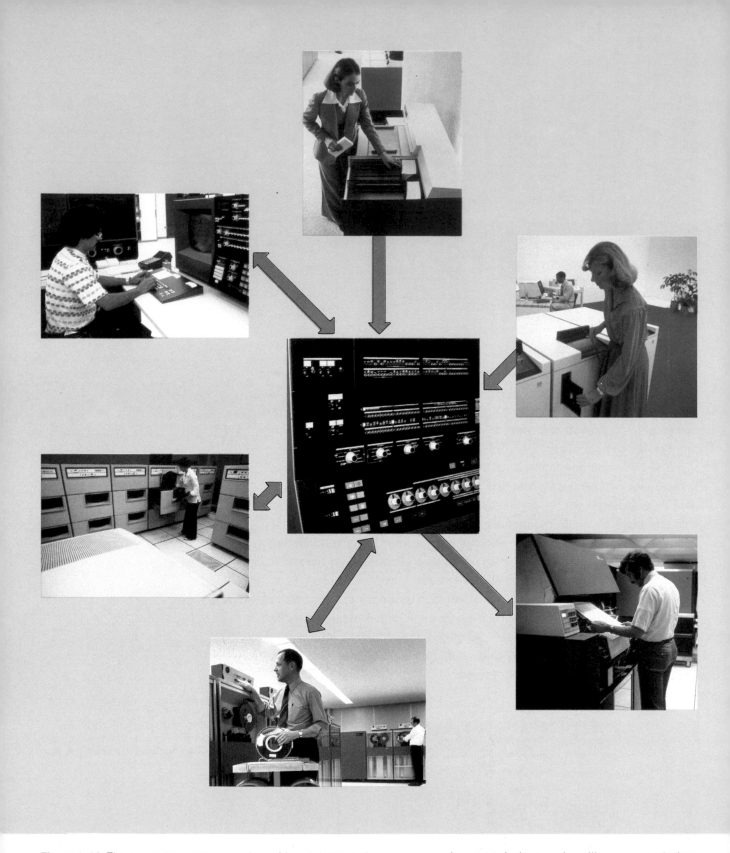

Figure 1-14 The computer system consists of input devices, the processor unit, output devices, and auxiliary storage devices.

The computer system

The computer system, then, consists of the processor unit which houses both the central processing unit and main computer storage, and connected to the processor unit via cables, the operator console, the input devices, the output devices, and the auxiliary storage devices (Figure 1-14). Under control of a computer program, these units are able to cause data to be processed with extremely high speeds and astounding reliability.

Tape library

In addition to the computer hardware found in the computer center, there are many support areas in the computer center which are necessary. One area which is important is the tape and disk library where tape reels and disk packs containing data are stored when not in use on the computer system (Figure 1-15). In large installations, thousands of reels of tape can contain data which is processed on the computer system. These reels must be catalogued and stored so that when they are required, the tape librarian can take them to the computer room for use.

The personnel in the tape library also have the responsibility of ensuring that the tapes and disks stored there are reliable and safe. Thus, they must clean tapes and disks so foreign dust particles or other contaminants do not appear on the magnetic surfaces and render the disk packs or tapes unusable. In addition, since tapes and disks are susceptible to heat, installations may have their tape libraries in fire-proof rooms and, in many cases, have more than one tape library so that a fire would not destroy the entire library of tapes and disks.

Figure 1-15 The tape library can contain thousands of reels of magnetic tape. Each tape must be labeled so it can be retrieved by the tape librarian for later processing.

Figure 1-16 The people in the data entry department prepare data to be processed on the computer system by using machines like the keypunch for punching cards or key-to-tape machines for placing data on magnetic tape.

Data entry department

Another critical support department is the data entry department (Figure 1-16). It is here that a good portion of the data to be processed on the computer system is prepared. Data entry operators, using machines, prepare the data to be processed by recording it on punched cards, magnetic tape, or disk. The cards, tape, or disk can then be taken to the computer room for processing on the system.

Bursting and decollating

Figure 1-17 Removing the carbon and separating the multiple pages of a report is called decollating. Here, the operators are using machines to decollate the reports.

When printed reports are prepared on the computer system, they are printed on continuous forms. In many cases, there are multiple copies made, with carbon paper between each copy. Before these reports are distributed to the users of the report, the carbon paper must be removed and the copies must be separated. This process is called decollating (Figure 1-17). In addition, it is sometimes desirable to separate each page of the report so that the pages can be placed in a binder. Separating each page of continuous forms is called "bursting" the report. In most computer centers, bursting and decollating is required.

Computer programmers and systems analysts

Two other groups of people play very important roles in the computer center — computer programmers and systems analysts (Figure 1-18).

Computer programmers design, write, test, and implement the programs which process data on the computer system. They utilize programming specifications, which are developed by systems analysts, to design computer programs. The programming specifications specify the data to be processed and the type of processing which is to take place.

Systems analysts design the "systems" which are required to properly process data. For example, a systems analyst may, after proper investigation, design a system which is responsible for a company's payroll processing. Included in this processing would be the writing of payroll checks, the preparation of W-2's, the preparation of required government reports, and the preparation of company payroll records. This payroll system would normally consist of a series of computer programs which would be written by computer programmers.

Figure 1-18 Computer programmers (above) can utilize CRT terminals to enter programs into the computer system. A systems analyst (below) confers with the user of a system to ensure the system design corresponds to the needs of the user.

Department management

A computer center is managed by management personnel at several levels. Generally, the operations manager will be responsible for computer system operation and data entry operations. Programming and systems managers oversee the activities in these areas. In many organizations, a data base administrator will be responsible for organizing and allowing access to the data which is used in the various applications within the company. The data processing manager is in charge of the entire department operation.

Figure 1-19 Many different people with different responsibilities within the company can be users of computer systems. Engineers (top), factory workers (left), management personnel (lower left), and office personnel can all use the power of a computer system to aid in performing their daily activities.

The computer user

The systems analyst also interacts with perhaps the most important people connected with the computer center — the users of the computer system (Figure 1–19). Users are those people who utilize the output from the computer system in their daily work. The applications which are run on the computer system must be designed so maximum use is received by the users. It is the responsibility of the systems analyst to investigate the needs of the users and to design application systems which are responsive to their needs. The users of computer systems are the reason for the existence of computers.

████████████████████████████████████

Computer Systems

Come in Many

Different Sizes

Although many computer systems are housed in computer centers such as previously illustrated, they are also found in many different areas of the company, in different sizes, and performing different tasks. The following pages contain some examples of different sizes, shapes, and functions of computer systems.

The Small

Computer Appears

Everywhere

In 1974, a small electronics firm in Albuquerque, New Mexico, named MITS startled the computer world by announcing that a "home, personal computer" could be purchased from their firm in kit form. The kit contained all the necessary parts to build a computer at a price of about $500.00. From this beginning, the small computer has progressed dramatically.

Most small computers which are purchased today come assembled with a Cathode Ray Tube (CRT) as the primary output device to display the results of the computer processing. A keyboard with typewriter-like keys is used as the primary means of input. Most also have an auxiliary storage device. In many cases, the auxiliary storage device is a cassette tape similar to that used for audio tape recorders.

Small computers also have optional equipment such as disk drives and printers which can be purchased.

Computers such as the Radio Shack TRS-80 illustrated on these pages have been put to use in a number of different applications and environments. For example, TRS-80's have been sold to small companies who are just beginning to use computers in their business. These small companies, by using the programs which are delivered with the computer or by developing or buying their own programs, have placed traditional accounting applications on the machines as well as more specialized applications such as matching potential buyers and homes by real estate companies.

The small computer has changed many people's conception of a computer; and as more of them are sold, at a price of $500.00 to $5,000, it will be common to find them in many environments.

Figure 1-20 The small computer (sometimes called a "microcomputer") is being utilized as a home, personal computer which can be used by the entire family. It is typically used for playing games, teaching computer programming, and performing personal accounting, such as balancing the checkbook or aiding in figuring income tax.

Figure 1-21 The microcomputer is being found in all areas of business and education. A small businessman (above) can generate accounting information such as the number of products which have been sold, and this information can be printed on the attached printer. In elementary schools (upper right), the computer is used for drill exercises in arithmetic, reading, and other skills. In the laboratory (right), scientists can use the microcomputer to record and analyze the results of experiments.

Desk Top Machines

Populate

The Office

The modern office of today contains desk top computers which can perform numerous tasks. These tasks include accounting operations, office management applications, and word processing. Word processing allows office personnel to store commonly used data and to include that data in letters, memos, or billing documents. These machines differ from the microcomputers illustrated previously by typically containing more main and auxiliary storage; and by costing more, usually $5,000.00 – $20,000.00.

Figure 1-22 The Wang desk top computer on the previous page includes disk auxiliary storage and a printer which can be used for word processing applications. The Hewlett-Packard 9835A computer above is used for high-speed computations in science and engineering applications, while the Lexitron system on the right is used for word processing.

Minicomputers Become Sophisticated Computers

When Digital Equipment Corporation announced in 1965, a machine smaller and less expensive than the typical large machines found at that time, a new term, "minicomputer," was added to the data processing vocabulary.

The first minicomputers were placed mostly in engineering and scientific installations, primarily because there was very little "software" offered with the machines. Software is a series of programs written by the computer manufacturer or others which aid in the running of the computer system. The first minicomputers, then, were used in applications where this software was not critical — which usually were scientific or engineering applications.

As the use of minicomputers increased, the computer manufacturers who were producing them realized that software was becoming a necessary product in order to continue their sales. Therefore, the software began to be produced, together with changes to the computer hardware, or equipment. Thus, minicomputers, with the accompanying software, began to be used for business applications as well as scientific and engineering applications.

Today, it is difficult to properly identify what a minicomputer is because computers range greatly in size, abilities, and cost. Thus, the term, "minicomputer," although still used, does not have the same importance as before.

Figure 1-24 The Hewlett-Packard 3000 computer (above) is typical of the many medium sized computers which are used for business and educational applications.

Figure 1-25 International Business Machines (IBM) entered the minicomputer market with the Series/1 Computer (below). IBM, the leader in larger computers, did not build a minicomputer until years after it had been introduced by DEC.

Figure 1-23 The ''minicomputer'' (left) from Digital Equipment Corp. (DEC) is a sophisticated computer that can be used for engineering, scientific, and business applications.

Figure 1-26 The IBM 4331 computer is one of the most current IBM computers. Its reduced price and increased processing characteristics led IBM to have a 3 year backlog on the machine two weeks after it was announced.

Figure 1-27 The IBM System/370-158 is one of IBM's larger machines. It is typically found with main computer storage of 1–2 million characters (megabytes) and 2 billion or more characters of data stored on auxiliary storage devices.

Whither Goest

The Dinosaurs?

Figure 1-28 Many computer installations with large machines require numerous input, output, and auxiliary storage devices to satisfy the processing needs. In the installation above, a row of printers is used for computer system output.

Large computers, sometimes called "mainframes," are capable of processing large amounts of data with very fast processing speeds.

These machines are also capable of accessing billions of characters of data stored on auxiliary storage devices such as magnetic disks. Large computers such as those pictured on these pages also have the capability of allowing other computers or terminals located at remote sites to communicate with them. This capability for "data communications" often requires the speed and sophistication of these computers.

Despite their capabilities, there are those in the data processing industry who support almost exclusive use of smaller computers; and these people have termed the large computers "dinosaurs" because they are large and, according to these people, will soon be extinct.

Despite these claims, however, it appears that large computers will continue to form the backbone of the business data processing community. The increased needs of business for storing large amounts of data and the increasing use of data communications in the business environment will require the large machines.

Special Computers

For

Special Chores

The computers illustrated on the previous pages are all called general purpose computers because they can perform any task required by changing the application program in main storage.

Computers are also developed to perform specific tasks. These computers are called special purpose computers. Special purpose computers are used for everything from guidance systems in missiles to controlling nuclear reactor facilities.

They are also finding their way into many consumer products in the recent years. The automobile industry has begun to experiment with computers in controlling the ignition in cars. Consumer appliances such as microwave ovens contain special purpose computers which control the oven.

As the size and price of computers decrease, it seems likely that more and more consumer products will take advantage of the power of the computer in their design.

Figure 1-29 This special purpose computer is used to control the chemical processes necessary to produce Polyvinyl Chloride (PVC). This computer controls the production of 425 million pounds of PVC per year for the Georgia-Pacific Corporation.

Chapter summary

The following points have been discussed and explained in this chapter.

1. A computer is a device which can perform computations, including arithmetic and logic operations, without intervention by a human being.

2. The Cray-1 is the world's most powerful computer system, with the ability to process 80 million instructions per second.

3. A computer system consists of the device which can perform computations without human intervention and also devices which allow data to be made available for processing and devices on which data can be displayed or printed for use by human beings.

4. A computer system can perform three basic operations: arithmetic operations, logical operations, and input/output operations.

5. Data is a representation of facts, concepts, or instructions in a formalized manner suitable for communication, interpretation, and processing by humans or automatic machines.

6. A computer system consists of input units, the processor unit, and output units.

7. The processor unit consists of the central processing unit (CPU) and main computer storage.

8. The central processing unit (CPU) contains the electronic circuitry which actually causes processing to occur on the computer system.

9. Main computer storage consists of components which can electronically store letters of the alphabet, numbers, and special characters.

10. The data stored in main computer storage is processed under the control of a computer program. A program is a series of instructions which are stored in main computer storage and that specify which processing operations are to occur in the computer system.

11. A computer operator communicates with the processor unit through the console terminal. The operator is responsible for keeping the computer system running.

12. Card readers and floppy disk readers are two of the more commonly found input devices in the computer center.

13. The high-speed printer is the most common output device. It can be used to produce printed reports for different applications.

14. Auxiliary storage devices are used to store data which must be used at a later time.

15. Magnetic tape and magnetic disk are devices for storing data to be used at a later time.

16. In addition to the computer hardware which is found in a computer center, there are many support areas which are necessary to keep the computer center functioning.

17. The tape library is used to store tape reels and disk packs when they are not being used on the computer system. Many installations have more than one tape library to avoid the danger of fire.

18. Many printed reports are printed on multi-part paper. They must be decollated prior to being distributed to users.

19. Much of the data used as input to the computer system is prepared in the data entry department. Using machines, data entry operators prepare the data to be processed by recording it on punched cards, magnetic tape, or disk.

20. Programmers design, write, test, and implement the programs which process data on the computer system.

21. Systems analysts design the "systems" which are required to properly process data. One of the most important roles an analyst plays is the interface between the data processing department and the user of the output of the computer system.

22. Many different people with different responsibilities within the company can be users of computer systems. These can include engineers, factory workers, management personnel, and office personnel. The users of computer systems are the reason for the existence of computers.

23. Small computers (microcomputers) are being used as personal computers, in business applications, in education, and in the laboratory. They are offered for sale in the price range of $500.00 to $5,000.00.

24. The modern office of today contains desk top computers which can perform numerous tasks. These tasks include accounting operations, office management applications, and word processing.

25. Word processing allows office personnel to store commonly used data and to include that data in letters, memos, and billing documents.

26. The first minicomputers were announced in 1965 and were used primarily for scientific and engineering applications. More recently, computer software has been developed for minicomputers, and they are used for business and other applications.

27. Large computers are used to store and process large amounts of data very quickly and also are used for data communications. Large computers are called dinosaurs by some people because the computers are large, and these people think they will soon be extinct.

28. Special purpose computers are used in many applications ranging from microwave ovens to large chemical processing machines. These computers are designed to perform one particular job.

Student Learning Exercises

Review questions

1. Specify some typical operations which a computer can perform.

2. What is the definition of data? Give some examples of data.

3. What three processes must take place in order for a computer to process data?

4. What is a computer program?

5. What is the purpose of a computer program?

6. Specify the steps required to create a grade report on the computer.

7. What does a computer operator do in the computer center?

8. What is the most common means of obtaining output from a computer system?

9. What are the two primary devices used for auxiliary storage on a computer system?

10. What are three important support areas in a computer center? What are their functions?

11. What is the role of a computer programmer in the computer center?

12. What is the role of the systems analyst in the computer center?

13. Why is the user of a computer system important? Who are some of the typical computer users?

14. What are four areas where small computers are being used?

15. Why is it difficult to define exactly what a minicomputer is?

16. What is a "dinosaur"? Is the name appropriate?

17. Specify some consumer products which utilize special purpose computers.

Controversial issues in data processing

1. Is the so-called "computer revolution" really a revolution or is it more a steady growth of a new industry? If we do not understand it even though it is clearly happening, what effects could this have on society?

2. Why is it that many people in society think the computer is a monster which can think and will eventually take over? Discuss several different approaches which can be taken to overcome this attitude.

Research projects

1. Write a report on three different small computers which can be purchased for home or personal use.

2. Write a report depicting at least five different views that people have of the computer. This could include the views of cartoonists, fiction writers, movies, and others.

3. Newspapers abound with articles on new developments in computer technology. Review the newspaper each day for these articles. Bring an article of interest to class and be prepared to give a brief summary of the article.

Picture credits

Figure 1-1   Motorola, Inc.
Figure 1-2   Fairchild Camera and Instrument Corp.
Figure 1-6   The Atchison, Topeka, and Santa Fe Railway Company
Figure 1-9   Sperry Univac
Figure 1-10 IBM*
Figure 1-11 Georgia-Pacific Corporation
Figure 1-12 The Atchison, Topeka and Santa Fe Railway Company
Figure 1-13 California Computer Products, Inc.
Figure 1-15 Lever Brothers Company
Figure 1-16 Lever Brothers Company
Figure 1-17 MCAUTO

Figure 1-18 Lever Brothers Company, Sperry Univac
Figure 1-19 IBM*, IBM*, American Airlines, Hewlett-Packard
Figure 1-20 Radio Shack
Figure 1-21 Radio Shack
Figure 1-22 Wang Laboratories Inc., Hewlett-Packard, Raytheon Company
Figure 1-23 Digital Equipment Corporation
Figure 1-24 Hewlett-Packard
Figure 1-25 IBM*
Figure 1-26 IBM*
Figure 1-27 Tymshare, Inc.
Figure 1-28 MCAUTO
Figure 1-29 Georgia-Pacific Corporation

* International Business Machines Corporation

Chapter 2
The Evolution of the Electronic Computer Industry

Objectives

- An understanding of the development of computer hardware which has led to modern computing devices

- An understanding of the role played by computer software in the history of the computing industry

- An understanding of the important contributions from people in the evolution of the electronic computer industry

- An appreciation of the major companies in the computer industry and the contributions they have made

- An appreciation of the excitement and vitality of the data processing industry

Chapter 2

Stock Trading Summary

COMPUTER SYSTEMS

A	AMDAHL CORP	23- 69	25 5/8	- 7/8	-3.3
N	BURROUGHS CORP	59- 87	69 1/4	-1 3/8	-1.9
O	COMPUTER AUTOMATION	11- 44	11	-2 1/2	-18.5
N	CONTROL DATA CORP	23- 44	39	- 5/8	-1.5
O	CRAY RESEARCH INC	8- 39	35	-1	-2.7
N	DATA GENERAL CORP	42- 74	66 5/8	-2 3/8	-3.4
N	DATAPOINT CORP	34- 82	73	-3 1/4	-4.2
N	DIGITAL EQUIPMENT	39- 58	54 5/8	-2 1/2	-4.3
N	ELECTRONIC ASSOC.	2- 13	6 1/4	- 1/8	-1.9
A	ELECTRONIC ENGINEER.	9- 19	10 1/2	- 7/8	-7.6
N	FOUR-PHASE SYSTEMS	19- 46	33	-1 1/4	-3.6
N	FOXBORO	28- 40	38	+2 3/8	+6.6
O	GENERAL AUTOMATION	7- 26	12 1/2	-1 1/8	-8.2
O	GRI COMPUTER CORP	1- 3	1 1/4	0	0.0
N	HEWLETT-PACKARD CO	62- 98	96	- 3/4	-0.7
N	HONEYWELL INC	43- 76	68 3/8	-1	-1.4
N	IBM	72-321	72 3/8	-1 1/8	-1.5
O	MANAGEMENT ASSIST	9- 29	16 5/8	-2 1/8	-11.3
O	MANUFACTURING DATA S	9- 26	25 1/2	- 3/4	-2.8
O	MICRODATA CORP	10- 31	30	+ 3/4	+2.5

SOFTWARE & EDP SERVICES

O	ADVANCED COMP TECH	1- 2	1 1/2	0	0.0
O	ANACOMP INC	8- 22	15 1/4	0	0.0
A	APPLIED DATA RES.	8- 17	9 3/8	-1 1/8	-10.7
N	AUTOMATIC DATA PROC	24- 36	32 1/2	- 1/4	-0.7
O	COMPU-SERV NETWORK	5- 16	14	-1 1/4	-8.1
O	COMPUTER HORIZONS	1- 9	4 1/4	0	0.0
O	COMPUTER NETWORK	5- 16	7 3/4	- 1/8	-1.5
N	COMPUTER SCIENCES	8- 17	11 5/8	- 1/2	-4.1
O	COMPUTER TASK GROUP	1- 7	7 1/2	0	0.0
O	COMPUTER USAGE	2- 4	2 1/4	+ 1/8	+5.8
O	COMPUT AUTO REP SVC	4- 10	7 3/8	+ 1/8	+1.7
O	COMSHARE	6- 26	20 1/4	-2	-8.9
O	CULL'NANE CORP	14- 33	20	0	0.0
O	DATA DIMENSIONS INC	3- 9	2 1/2	0	0.0
O	DATATAB	1- 4	2 3/4	0	0.0
N	ELECTRONIC DATA SYS.	15- 25	24	+ 5/8	+2.6
O	INSYTE CORP	1- 3	1 1/4	0	0.0
O	IPS COMPUTER MARKET.	2- 3	3	0	0.0
O	KEANE ASSOCIATES	3- 6	4 3/4	0	0.0

PERIPHERALS & SUBSYSTEMS

N	ADDRESSOGRAPH-MULT	13- 32	14 1/8	- 3/8	-2.5
N	AMPEX CORP	10- 19	14 7/8	- 3/4	-4.7
O	ANDERSON JACOBSON	5- 10	7 7/8	+ 1/8	+1.6
N	APPLIED DIG DATA SYS	8- 22	8 1/2	- 1/4	-2.8
O	BEEHIVE INT'L	3- 7	4 3/4	- 1/8	-2.5
A	BOLT,BERANEK & NEW	6- 14	13	- 1/2	-3.7
N	BUNKER-RAMO	10- 29	23 1/4	0	0.0
A	CALCOMP	3- 13	11 1/4	0	0.0
O	CAMBRIDGE MEMORIES	2- 9	2 1/8	- 1/8	-5.5
N	CENTRONICS DATA COMP	16- 48	46 3/8	+ 1/4	+0.5
O	COGNITRONICS	1- 4	2 1/4	- 1/4	-10.0
O	COMPUTER COMMUN.	6- 10	8 1/8	- 1/8	-1.5
O	COMPUTER CONSOLES	4- 16	12 3/4	- 1/4	-1.9
A	COMPUTER EQUIPMENT	3- 6	4 3/4	0	0.0
O	COMPUTER TRANSCEIVER	1- 5	2 5/8	+ 1/8	+5.0
O	COMPUTERVISION CORP	9- 61	54 3/8	-1	-1.8
N	CONRAC CORP	13- 26	14 3/4	+ 1/8	+0.8

Figure 2-1 The electronic computer industry consists of over 3,000 companies with revenues over $40 billion. These companies offer a wide variety of products and services.

The Evolution of the Electronic Computer Industry

"The importance of the study of history is to understand the forces which produce the events. Thus possibilities and prospects for the future may be better understood and evaluated."[1]

Introduction

Less than 40 years ago, no one had such a thing as a computer. Indeed, when Dr. George Stibitz, one of the early leaders in the development of modern computing devices, approached the management of the prestigious Bell Laboratories in 1937 and advised them that he had designed a calculator that could perform any general calculations, he was told "Who wants to spend $50,000.00 just to do calculations?"

Today the data processing and computational work done by the computers in the world could no longer be carried out by hand. It has been estimated that it would take 400 billion people, many times the world population, to tackle this workload.

The computer industry has truly developed "overnight" into one of the four largest in the world. This phenomenal growth has taken place because of the talents of many people and an industrial environment where the potential of the computer was recognized. Today, more than 3,000 companies with revenues over $40 billion comprise this exciting industry. Many of the companies are publicly held (Figure 2-1).

It is important to understand how the computer industry developed, for many of the events which have occurred on this short 40 year trip influence what is done today and what may be possible to do tomorrow.

---

1 Bauer, Walter F. and Rosenberg, Arthur M., "Software – Historical Perspectives and Current Trends," PROCEEDINGS – 1972 JOINT COMPUTER CONFERENCE, AFIPS Press, 1972.

How did it all begin?

Mankind has always responded to a problem with some type of solution. Although some solutions prove to be less acceptable than others, it is usually the search for a solution that leads to advances in man's knowledge and abilities. The birth of the electronic computer is no exception.

In the late 1930's, Dr. John V. Atanasoff, a mathematics professor at Iowa State College in Ames, Iowa, required a calculating device to perform mathematical operations for 20 masters and doctoral candidates. After examining various mechanical calculating devices then available, Atanasoff concluded that none of the devices was adequate for his needs. Instead, he felt the solution to his problem was in the development of a digital computing device based upon electronics.

Atanasoff, therefore, set about designing his own machine. He faced numerous problems in designing the logic circuitry for the machine. As with many inventors, some ideas were easier to come-by than others. In the winter of 1937-38, frustrated at not being able to complete the design, he drove across the Mississippi River into Illinois and settled in for a drink in a small roadside bar.

For some reason which he could not later identify, the ideas for computer memory and the associated logic which would not come to him in the laboratory came to him in the small roadside tavern. Thus, the basic concepts for the electronic digital computer were formulated that night.

Returning to the laboratory, Atanasoff, together with his assistant Clifford Berry, finished the design and began building the first electronic digital computer. They named this machine the Atanasoff-Berry-Computer, or simply the "ABC".

It is generally agreed that the design of the "ABC" and the use of electronics in the computer provided the foundation for the next advances which took place in the development of the electronic digital computer.

Mauchly and Eckert begin work

Atanasoff was not the only person who perceived the need for doing calculations faster and with more accuracy. Dr. John W. Mauchly, who had learned of the "ABC" in 1940, met several times with Atanasoff and Berry in Iowa during 1941.

Figure 2-2 Dr. John V. Atanasoff, shown lecturing on quantum-mechanics at Iowa State University, conceived of and designed the first electronic digital computer. For many years his invention was credited to others. In 1974 a federal judge ruled that Atanasoff was the true inventor of the concepts required for a working electronic digital computer.

Figure 2-3 The "Atanasoff-Berry-Computer" pictured above was the first electronic digital computer built. It used vacuum tubes as the logic elements within the machine.

Mauchly was shown the computer and was allowed to read much of the manuscript describing the principles of the "ABC", including the detailed design features. The principles of electronic computation described by Atanasoff were to have significant influence on the subsequent development of electronic digital computers by Mauchly and others.

In 1941 Mauchly also became acquainted with J. Presper Eckert, Jr., who was doing graduate work at the Moore School of Electrical Engineering at the University of Pennsylvania. The meeting of these two pioneers in electronic digital computers coincided with a war-time need of the United States.

With the outbreak of World War II, the United States Army had a need for calculating ballistic tables to produce trajectories for artillery and bombing. The Army, at the start of the war, was using "differential analyzers" to calculate the tables. These mechanical devices, together with some manual calculations, could compute a sixty-second trajectory in about 15 minutes. With the tremendous demand for these tables, 15 minutes was not fast enough.

On April 2, 1943, Mauchly and Eckert submitted a memo to the U.S. Army, describing an Electronic Difference Analyzer which would be able to do the calculations in 30 seconds, half the time of the projectile's flight. The really radical aspect of the idea was the proposal to build the machine using 18,000 vacuum tubes and requiring the simultaneous functioning of almost all of these tubes.

Nothing comparable had ever been attempted and there was considerable pessimism. Indeed, one mathematician noted that since "the average life of a vacuum tube is 3,000 hours, a tube failure would occur every 15 minutes. Since it would average more than 15 minutes to find the bad tube, no useful work could ever be done." Despite the pessimism, the Army funded Mauchly and Eckert in 1943 to begin the development of the machine.

ENIAC—The first large-scale electronic digital computer

In 1946, after spending about $400,000.00, Mauchly and Eckert completed the ENIAC (Electronic Numerical Integrator and Computer), the first large-scale electronic digital computer ever built. The ENIAC contained 18,000 vacuum tubes and could multiply two numbers in about 3 milliseconds (3/1000th of a second).

Figure 2-4 The co-inventors of the ENIAC, J. Presper Eckert, Jr. (left) and John W. Mauchly, are shown with the machine. The ENIAC weighed 30 tons, contained 18,000 vacuum tubes, and occupied a space 30 by 50 feet.

The ENIAC was programmed by connecting various wires between units of the computer and setting up to 6,000 switches in such a way that the program would be executed. Each time a program was changed, the wiring had to be completely redone.

When it was placed in operation in 1946, the New York Times stated, "It computes a mathematical problem 1,000 times faster than ever before... and has not a single moving part." Nine months after it had been in operation, Admiral Lord Mountbatten, President of the British Institute of Radio Engineers said of ENIAC, "the stage has now been set for the most Wellsian development of all — an electronic brain."

The ENIAC was moved from the Moore School of Electrical Engineering in Pennsylvania to the Aberdeen Proving Grounds in Aberdeen, Maryland. There it was used for not only ballistic tables, but also weather prediction, atomic energy calculations, cosmic ray studies, and random-number studies. On October 2, 1955, the machine which had led to the era of electronic digital computers was turned off for the last time.

The work of John von Neumann

In 1944, prior to the completion of the ENIAC, the Army asked the Moore School of Electrical Engineering of the University of Pennsylvania to build a more powerful computer than the ENIAC. In 1945, an Hungarian-born mathematician, Dr. John von Neumann, responded to that request. In a report for Contract No. W-670-ORD-4926 between the United States Ordnance Department and the University of Pennsylvania he described the EDVAC (Electronic Discrete Variable Automatic Computer). In addition to describing a number of new concepts for the computer hardware, this report contained the first written documentation of the "stored program concept" under which virtually all digital computers have since been built.

The stored program concept

Von Neumann proposed placing computer instructions, in the form of numbers, in main computer storage in a manner similar to the way data is stored in computer storage for processing. Thus, whenever a new program was to be executed on the computer, the program would be "read" into main computer storage rather than thousands of switches and wires being changed as required with the ENIAC.

Although accepted as "modus operandi" today, this concept was a brilliant breakthrough in 1945. The concept is largely credited to von Neumann because of his report. Several historians and colleagues who were present at the time have suggested, however, that J. Presper Eckert Jr. had mentioned the idea a year or two before von Neumann's paper.

Regardless of the originator of the stored program concept, the stage was now set for increased activity in the world of electronic digital computers.

Figure 2-5 Dr. John von Neumann, known to his contemporaries as "Johnnie," became interested in computers after a chance meeting with Herman Goldstine, an early designer on the ENIAC, at the railroad station in Aberdeen, Maryland. Because of his amazing ability to perform rapid mental calculations, one of his associates said, "Von Neumann was, of course, not human, but he had so carefully mastered the impersonation that most people believed him to be a member of the race."

Figure 2-6 This is the first page of the first program written for a modern stored program computer. Von Neumann, who wrote this program, foresaw the use of computers in business. Therefore, the first program he chose to write was a sort program, which is commonly found in business applications.

Figure 2-7 J. Presper Eckert, Jr., is seated at the console of the first UNIVAC I, delivered to the U.S. Bureau of the Census. This machine was the first commercially available electronic digital computer.

The first stored program computer actually built

In 1946, von Neumann and others conducted classes at the University of Pennsylvania on computer design and the von Neumann concept of stored program computers. One of the more attentive students was Maurice V. Wilkes from Cambridge University, England. Upon his return to England, Wilkes and his colleagues at Cambridge began work on the Electronic Delay Storage Automatic Calculator (EDSAC). Completed in May of 1949, it was the first computer which had operated using the stored program concept (the EDVAC, developed by von Neumann, was not to work until 1951). Wilkes said later that "the principles of the modern computer were then clear and the events of the last 25 years have been their logical working out. However, not everyone recognized this was the case and much energy had to be spent in countering the arguments of those who did not accept the stored program principle or who did not have sufficient faith that electronic technology would prove equal to the demands that would be made on it."[2]

The business of computers begins (1950–1955)

The work on the ENIAC, the EDVAC, the EDSAC, and other computer systems which were developed in the late 1940's was primarily experimental. The machines were used for scientific or engineering applications. It was evident to some pioneers, however, that electronic digital computers could have uses in more areas than just engineering. One of the first to recognize the potential of computers were the developers of the ENIAC, John W. Mauchly and J. Presper Eckert, Jr.

Accordingly, in 1947, not long after the ENIAC had become operational, they formed their own company, the Eckert-Mauchly Computer Corporation. Their intent was to design and build computers for use in government and industry.

Shortly after forming their company, they began the design of the UNIVersal Automatic Computer, called the UNIVAC I. In need of financial support, Eckert and Mauchly approached several major companies. Remington-Rand purchased their company and their talents. Thus, Remington-Rand was launched into the computer field with a product that was years ahead of its competitors.

2 Wilkes, Maurice V., "Historical Perspectives — Computer Architecture," PROCEEDINGS — 1972 JOINT COMPUTER CONFERENCE, AFIPS Press, 1972.

Their first major contract called for the delivery of a Univac I to the U. S. Bureau of the Census for use in the 1950 census. The first Univac I was delivered on June 14, 1951, marking this as the first computer system dedicated to data processing applications as opposed to scientific, military, or engineering processing (Figure 2-7). For almost five years following its installation, the Univac I was considered one of the best large-scale computer systems available.

A public becomes aware

The development of electronic digital computers took place in university laboratories, and as a consequence, the public was largely unaware of these machines. All that changed on November 4, 1952, when the Univac I computer predicted that Dwight D. Eisenhower would defeat Adlai E. Stevenson in the presidential election after analyzing only 5% of the tallied vote (Figure 2-8). CBS, fearful that the machine could not possibly be correct with such a small number of votes counted, withheld the information until it could be confirmed by actual votes. In a very short time, the public became aware of "giant brains" which "would be able to outthink man and take his jobs." This, of course, is not true, but it was the first impression of the computer which the general public seemed to acquire. To this day, many people still view the computer with apprehension and mistrust.

Figure 2-8 The Univac I computer system was used by CBS in 1952 to predict the outcome of the 1952 presidential election. Its accurate prediction of the results were at first distrusted by CBS.

Figure 2-9 Thomas J. Watson, Sr., a superb salesman and the guiding force behind IBM for forty years, reluctantly allowed IBM to enter the computer industry in the early 1950's.

Figure 2-10 Thomas J. Watson, Jr. led IBM during the time it became the world leader in electronic computers. He was one of the people at IBM who foresaw early the impact computers would have on business and science.

The giant awakens

Although the business world had not yet seen the need for the computer, businesses had, for almost 40 years, been using punched cards and electro-mechanical machines to process large volumes of data. Over 90 percent of these machines were built and marketed by the International Business Machines Corporation (IBM), under the leadership of Thomas J. Watson, Sr.

These machines were widely used in businesses to perform billing operations, process payrolls, and prepare sales reports. By 1950, IBM had a virtual monopoly on all such equipment.

Although the punched card machines produced by IBM were electro-mechanical, IBM was not unaware of the potential of more sophisticated computing devices. In 1937, IBM committed $500,000 and some of its most creative engineers to Howard H. Aiken of Harvard University to build a new kind of calculating machine. When it was completed in 1944, the Mark I calculator was donated to Harvard by IBM. The Mark I, which was electro-mechanical, followed a sequence of instructions stored on "paper tape."

Watson, Sr., however, did not want his company to devote much of its effort to something which would not prove commercially successful. Therefore, IBM did not enter the computer business with abandoned enthusiasm. In fact, shortly after forming their company, Mauchly and Eckert approached IBM to discuss the possibility of joining resources to put their new Univac I on the market. Their proposal was rejected by a memo from Watson, Sr. stating that "there can be no reasonable interaction possible between Eckert-Mauchly and IBM." Watson felt, as many did, that at most eight to ten of the large "brains" would be sufficient for the entire scientific community, and only a few businesses would be able to use these machines.

One person who did not share these ideas, however, was Thomas J. Watson, Jr., who had become president of IBM. Thus, Watson, Jr. was placed in the unenviable position of advocating a plunge into computers; while his father, the chairman of the board for IBM, did not want to rush headlong into a position which could seriously hurt IBM financially.

When, however, the Univac I computer was placed in the U. S. Bureau of the Census in 1951, IBM lost business because some of their punched card machines were displaced by the computer. It is in this period of time that the decision was made by IBM to become an active force in the computer industry. It was a decision which would lead to IBM becoming one of the four or five largest companies in the world and a dominant force in the computer industry.

A period of development and competition

During the early 1950's, while new hardware developments were taking place in both university laboratories and private industry, IBM and Remington-Rand emerged as the two leading computer companies. The Univac I computer had been installed in such companies as Sylvania and General Electric. IBM, the late entrant in the field, delivered its first computer, the 701 Data Processing System, to the government in late 1952. By the end of 1953, 13 companies were manufacturing computers. IBM and Remington-Rand led the field with a combined total of nine installations.

In 1953 IBM announced their 650 electronic computer, a medium-sized machine suitable for business applications (Figure 2–11). IBM's position in the punched card business data processing field gave them a tremendous marketing advantage because hundreds of businesses saw the 650 as the next step up from punched card accounting machines. IBM planned to produce only 50 of their 650 computers; instead, over 1,000 of the machines were leased in the ensuing years.

Until 1956, Remington-Rand computers outsold IBM computers; but by the end of 1956, IBM had delivered 76 machines compared to 46 for Remington-Rand and had firm orders for 193 machines as compared to Remington-Rand's 65.

IBM had taken the lead in the computer industry — a lead it would never relinquish.

Figure 2–11 IBM leased over 1,000 of their 650 computer systems after it was announced in 1953.

An emerging industry

It was apparent a new industry was developing. In 1947, an organization called the Association for Computing Machinery (ACM) was formed "to advance the science, development, construction, and application of the new machinery for computing, reasoning, and other handling of information." The first Joint Computer Conference was held in Philadelphia in 1951, marking the beginning of national conferences where computer professionals could gather to discuss events which they felt important in the development of the computer; and in 1951, Maurice V. Wilkes, David J. Wheeler, and Stanley Gill authored the first book on programming, The Preparation of Programs for an Electronic Digital Computer. Indeed, an industry was emerging.

The problem of programming

Although the stored program concept of von Neumann made a tremendous impact on the way computers were programmed, the programming process was nevertheless cumbersome, error-prone, and difficult. Indeed, von Neumann stated "I am not aware of any other human effort when the result really depends on a sequence of a billion steps ... and where furthermore it has the characteristic that each step really matters ... yet precisely this is true of computing machines."

The programmer who wrote a computer program had to write the instructions for the computer in a "language" that the computer hardware "understood" called machine language (Figure 2–12). Large amounts of time were required to write the program and most programs contained errors which could be traced back to the difficulty of writing instructions in the primitive language that had to be used.

The difficulty in using machine language was apparent to some in the early 1950's. In fact, some experimental work on "automatic programming" had been done in the late 1940's and early 1950's.

Automatic programming, as the term was used then, referred to writing a computer program in a notation other than machine language, thereby simplifying the programming process.

Step No.	Inst. Address	OP	A/I	B	Inst.	Data	Total
	5-7	12		19			
1	500	,	0 0 3		4		4
2	504	1			1		5
3	505	/	1 9 9		4		9
4	509	L	0 7 9	1 7 9	7		16
5	516	L	5 5 1	1 0 2	7		23
6	523	Y	0 8 0	1 0 1	7		30
7	530	C	0 7 9	1 7 9	7		37
8	537	B	5 4 6 /		5		42
9	542	5	5 0 5		4		46
10	546	.	5 0 5		4		50
11	551	4	1			2	52

Figure 2-12 With machine language programming, the programmer is required to write instructions by means of numbers, letters of the alphabet, and special characters, each of which has a special meaning when interpreted by the computer's electronic circuitry.

Symbolic programming becomes possible

One of the first steps toward automatic programming was the use of symbolic notation to represent operations to be performed (Figure 2-13). This somewhat improved the programming process, yet it was still necessary for each single step which had to be performed by the computer to be written as an instruction.

PG	LINE	TAG	OPERATION	NUM	OPERAND
02	01	START	SEL		100
	02		RD		WHSE INV
	03		TRA		ERROR
	04		RAD		RECEIPTS
	05		SUB		WITHDRAW
	06		ST		BALANCE
	07		TRP		ROUTINE 1
	08		TR		ROUTINE 2
	09	MOVE REC	RCV	0	OUTPUT BLK
	10		TMT	0	WHSE INV
	11		ADD	01	(+1)
	12		CMP	01	(5)
	13		TRE	01	WRITE
	14		AAM	02	MOVE REC
	15		TR		START
	16	WRITE	SEL		200
	17		WR		OUTPUT BLK
	18		TRA		ERROR
	19		TR		RESET
	20				

Figure 2-13 When using symbolic programming languages, simple words or abbreviations are substituted for the numbers, letters of the alphabet, and special characters required in machine language programming. These abbreviations must be translated into the machine language of the computer before the program can be executed.

High level programming languages are developed

To further improve automatic programming, a small group of IBM employees headed by John Backus began work in 1954 to develop a "high-level" automatic programming language for use by scientists, mathematicians, and engineers. This language was to be far removed from the internal characteristics of the machine. Instead of writing machine language, the programmer would write a statement in a mathematical notation. That statement would then be "translated" by the computer into the required machine language instructions.

Three years later, in April of 1957, FORTRAN was introduced. FORTRAN (FORmula TRANslation), which is still widely used today, allows the programmer to write a program in mathematical terms (Figure 2-14). A "translator" or "compiler" then interprets the program and converts it to machine language which the computer can execute.

It has been shown that the use of a high-level programming language such as FORTRAN can significantly reduce programming errors (although not to the extent predicted at the time when the first report on FORTRAN said, "FORTRAN should virtually eliminate coding and debugging . . ."). In addition, FORTRAN proved conclusively that languages could be developed which are not only easier to use than machine language, but that could also produce efficient programs for execution on computer systems.

STATEMENT NUMBER	CONT.	
C		LINEAR REGRESSION
		READ (2,2) N,XEST
2		FORMAT (I5,F1Ø.5)
		XSUM=Ø.Ø
		YSUM=Ø.Ø
		XXSUM=Ø.Ø
		XYSUM=Ø.Ø
		DO 6 I=1,N
		READ (2,4)X,Y
4		FORMAT (2F1Ø.5)
		XSUM=XSUM+X
		YSUM=YSUM+Y
		XXSUM=XXSUM+X*Y
6		XYSUM=XYSUM+X*Y
		FN=N
		XMEAN=XSUM/FN
		YMEAN=YSUM/FN
		A=YMEAN
		B=(XYSUM-FN*XMEAN*YMEAN)
		WRITE(3,8)A,B

Figure 2-14 The example of a FORTRAN program above shows that the program statements are written in a manner very similar to the notation used by mathematicians. These program statements must be translated into machine language in order to be executed on a computer system.

New programming languages appear

Other manufacturers began developing "automatic" programming languages for each new computer system they introduced. They were trying to provide an easy method for programming the computer, and at the same time, increase their sales with better languages than their competitors. By 1959, over 200 different programming languages had been developed in universities and by industry.

Flowmatic, FACT, Algol, Commercial Translator, and other programming languages were created in an attempt to make the process of writing instructions for the computer easier, faster, and less error-prone.

Business programming follows suit

Some members of the data processing community recognized all these computer languages as a potential problem. Programs written for one machine could not be executed on a different model machine from the same or different manufacturer. A group of concerned people from the academic world, computer users, and manufacturers met at the University of Pennsylvania in April, 1959, to explore solutions to the problem. Agreeing that a project to develop a single, machine-independent programming language for business applications was desirable, they approached the Department of Defense for sponsorship of the project.

On May 28-29, 1959, a meeting sponsored by the Department of Defense was held at the Pentagon. A committee was charged with the task of developing a programming language for business applications that would be machine-independent; that is, programs written in the language would be able to be executed on any computer made by any manufacturer.

This committee developed the programming language COBOL (COmmon Business Oriented Language), which was released in 1960 and is today one of the most widely used programming languages in the world (Figure 2–15). COBOL introduced several significant advances to the state of the art of programming languages, but perhaps its greatest contribution was that the programs could be written in English-like fashion and could be compiled and executed on computers made by different manufacturers.

With the advent of COBOL, FORTRAN, and the other high-level languages, significant steps had been made in the science of programming; significant advances were also being made in computer hardware in the late 1950's.

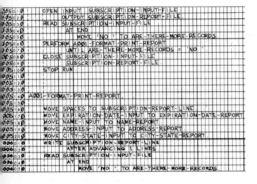

Figure 2-15 The COBOL program above illustrates the English-like phrases which are used in the language. The fact that COBOL programs could be executed on all makes of computers led to COBOL becoming one of the most widely used programming languages in the world.

The second generation is born (1958–1964)

In 1947, three scientists at Bell Laboratories, J. Bardeen, H. W. Brattain, and W. Shockley, invented a device called the transistor, for which they would later receive the Nobel Prize. As most people are aware, the invention of the transistor led to radios that could fit in their pockets. Less well known is that the invention of the transistor led to significant changes and advances in computer systems.

The computers of the early 1950's used vacuum tubes in their electronic circuitry. There were several significant disadvantages of vacuum tubes; among which were the tremendous heat they generated, the fact that they were not terribly reliable, the space which they required in a computer system, and perhaps most important, the speed at which they could process data. Even though computer systems were able to process data at faster rates than ever before, there was still a great deal of room for improvement. The transistor caused much of the improvement.

The first transistorized computer (TRADIC) was built in 1954 by Bell Laboratories, where the transistor was invented. It contained about 800 transistors. By December of 1955, it was reported that the Univac II, a newer model of the Univac I, contained 500 transistors. It soon became evident that transistors could replace vacuum tubes as the basis for the internal circuitry of computer systems.

Nineteen fifty-eight saw IBM announce the 7090 and the 7070 computer systems (Figure 2–16). Both of these machines used transistors exclusively. The business-oriented IBM 1401, another completely transistorized computer, was announced in 1959. These machines, together with others announced by various companies, ushered in the "second generation" of computers and signaled the death of vacuum tubes in the controlling circuitry of a computer system.

The second generation machines containing transistors were not only faster than their predecessors, they were also smaller and less costly. Thus, computers could now be afforded by many companies that could not consider the use of a computer for business applications only a few years prior to 1958.

To appreciate the impact of the transistorized computers, it is useful to examine the number of computer systems which were being used during the middle to late 1950's. In 1955, it is estimated that there were 244 computer systems in the United States. All of these computer systems together could perform 250,000 addition instructions in one second. This speed, incidentally, is equal to about one small computer today.

Figure 2-16 The IBM 7070 computer system is typical of "second generation" computers using transistors instead of vacuum tubes. The lower cost of these systems led to increased use of computers in business and industry.

By 1958, there were approximately 2,550 computer systems in the United States. A few years later in 1964, it is estimated there were 18,200 computers. This tremendous growth is attributable to the fact that transistorized computers such as the 7090 and the 1401 were less costly and more reliable than previous machines. Companies were finding that the computer could be helpful in performing activities critical to their operations. The "computer revolution" was well on its way in the early 1960's.

The people of the "computer revolution"

By the time the second generation computers were announced, the data processing industry was becoming quite active. Personnel were required in a number of areas, such as computer operations, computer programming, and systems analysis. The problem was that properly trained personnel in these areas were difficult to find.

Although some educators had become interested in computer education (called "an interesting new academic area" by one university president), most colleges and universities had not yet developed significant educational programs. Some training in computer programming was being offered by community colleges and private schools, but by and large, the people required by the industry were trained "on the job."

Thus, the data processing world of 1960 was populated mostly by people who had experience working with the punched card accounting machines produced by IBM. Punched card machine operators became computer operators and programmers; and accounting machine supervisors became data processing managers.

An aura of prestige descended upon those working in the new occupational area involving computers. The mystery and awe of the computer was transferred to those who had anything to do with computers. In many companies, the computer room became the showplace of the entire company, enclosed within glass walls so that visitors could marvel at the giant computer.

The industry was also beginning to become concerned with the quality and skills of the people in the industry. The National Machine Accountants Association, which later changed its name to the Data Processing Management Association (DPMA), conducted the first Certificate in Data Processing Examination in June of 1962 (Figure 2-17). This examination, which is still administered today, was designed to test the competency of data processing personnel in the industry. Although the examination has never reached the status of the Certified Public Accountants (CPA) examination, there are many in the industry who are proud to place the letters CDP after their name.

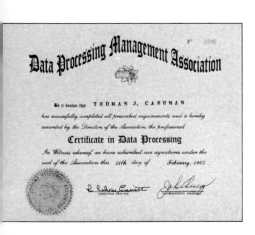

Figure 2-17 Successful candidates on the Certificate in Data Processing Examination are allowed to place the letters, CDP, following their name, indicating they have passed the industry's most important certifying examination.

A myriad of machines

By the beginning of 1964, the world of computers consisted of many different machines from a variety of manufacturers. The major manufacturers now included IBM, Sperry-Rand (formerly Remington-Rand), RCA, General Electric, Burroughs, Honeywell, NCR, and Control Data Corporation.

The striking thing about most of the computers produced by these manufacturers was that few of their computers were compatible with one another; that is, the internal designs of the various systems were each unique. Thus, computer instructions written in a symbolic programming language for one computer would not run on a computer from a different manufacturer; or, for that matter, on a different model computer from the same manufacturer. For example, a program written for an IBM 1401 computer would not run on a Burroughs computer; nor would the 1401 program run on an IBM 7090 computer.

One of the primary reasons for the incompatibilities was computers were viewed by both manufacturers and users as either scientific or business machines. Thus, IBM produced the 7090 series of computers for scientific applications and the 1401 series of computers for business applications. This concept of separate machines for business and scientific processing stemmed from the earliest days of computing. It was an attitude that, in 1964, was about to change forever.

A world of competition

For almost a decade, IBM had been the leading company in producing and installing computer systems. By 1964, over 70 percent of the computers installed were manufactured by IBM. The competition among IBM and the other manufacturers, however, was becoming more intense. In fact, it is widely acknowledged that many of the computer systems from other companies were at least equal to those from IBM. In particular, the Honeywell 200 computer system was significantly affecting the sales of the IBM 1401 computer by 1963, and Control Data had become a force in the development of large scale computer systems.

IBM, however, was aware of the problems it was facing in the computer systems market. Indeed, since 1960, development had been taking place on a computer system which IBM felt would change the way computing was done. In April, 1964, the world became aware of IBM's plans.

A most important announcement — the IBM System/360

April 7, 1964, may well go down as the most important product announcement date in the history of computers; for on that date, IBM announced the System/360 computer systems (Figure 2–18). When announced, the System/360 consisted of a "family" of six computers, all compatible, with 40 different input/output and auxiliary storage devices, and a variety of main computer storage sizes ranging from 16,000 to over one million storage positions.

The System/360 family of computers was designed for both scientific and business use. It is said that the new computers were called the "360" because they could be used for all types of processing, "encircling" the full range of both business and scientific applications.

This announcement tended to obsolete many existing computer systems, including those previously offered by IBM. IBM is reported to have expended nearly 5 billion dollars in the development of this new product line.

One IBM executive is purported to have called the System/360 computer system project, "You bet your company," for the success of the newly announced computer systems was vital to the continued success of IBM.

Figure 2–18 This half-acre room belonging to IBM is where much of the development of the System/360 took place. In the foreground is the console of one of the early models of the System/360. Tape and disk auxiliary storage devices can also be seen, as well as card readers and printers.

Solid logic technology

The System/360 offered a number of new features never before found on computer systems. For one, it incorporated what IBM called Solid Logic Technology (SLT). With this technology, the electronic components which make up the controlling circuitry of the computer system are stored on small chips rather than as discrete components such as transistors and diodes on a board (Figure 2–19).

A study of 10 billion hours of operation of the electronic components using solid logic technology revealed that such components rarely failed. Statistically, a failure would occur after 33 million hours of operation, a far cry from the prediction 19 years previously that said computers could not operate because vacuum tubes failed every 15 minutes. The circuitry in solid logic technology substantially improved the computer's internal processing speed; and in addition, the components could be mass produced at a low cost.

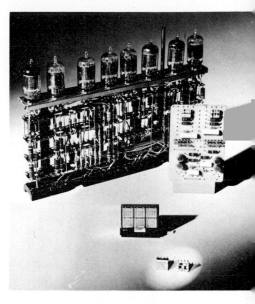

Figure 2-19 The three generations of computer components are shown in the picture above. The first generation needed vacuum tubes, the second generation used discrete components such as transistors and diodes on a board, and the third generation used solid logic technology and integrated circuits.

Only 10 years prior to the announcement of the System/360, some first generation computers could perform an estimated 2,500 computations per second at an estimated cost of $1.38 per 100,000 computations. The largest of the newly announced System/360 computers could perform 375,000 computations per second at a cost of 3½ cents for each 100,000 computations — a truly remarkable improvement in man's ability to process data.

The change in the method of designing and storing electronic components led to what most authorities call the "third generation" of computer systems. Thus, the computer industry took another step forward by producing computers that were smaller, faster, and less expensive.

Problems with the System/360 — program incompatibility

The internal design, or "architecture," of the System/360 was considerably different than previous generations of computer systems. Because of the new internal architecture, the programs written using symbolic programming languages for second generation computers would not run on the System/360 computers.

This condition potentially required System/360 users to rewrite thousands of programs which had been developed for other computers. In addition, users of the System/360 faced a tremendous education problem, for not only did the programs have to be rewritten, but the skills and knowledge of thousands of operators and programmers had to be significantly updated because of the changes in programming and operations methodologies required for the System/360 (Figure 2–20).

To ease the transition, IBM provided "emulators" which would allow 1401 programs to run on the System/360 computers, although not at maximum efficiency. These emulators, some of which are still in operation, solved certain incompatibility problems; but the transition from the second generation of computers to the third generation of computers created a period of considerable turmoil for managers, programmers, and operators within the industry.

```
0027E0  D5D640D5  C1D4C540  FF150007  EA002938
002810  00002858  00006FFF  00002800  6A0028C2
002840  00000000  00000000  00000000  00000000
002870  0000299C  0000296A  020029 9C  20000050
0028A0  00002BC8  08900909  000029EC  00000000
0028D0  00002890  0A02D259  412A4184  5810428E
002900  412840DA  D213413D  40DFD203  415840F3
002930  40F4F951  421E429A  4770409E  F342417B
002960  D22A4154  41DE47F0  40849240  412AD258
002990  00002858  00002890  0A020A0E  F1F0F0F0
0029C0  F3F0F040  40404040  40404040  40404040
0029F0  F0F04040  40404040  40404040  404040F0
002A20  F0404040  40404040  40404040  404040F0
002A50  40404040  40404040  40404040  4040C4C5
002A80  40404040  40404040  40C1D4D6  E4D5E340
002AB0  C1D5E3C9  E3E840C8  C1E5C540  C4C9E2C3
002AE0  00000C00  0A320000  0A320000  47F0F01A
002B10  F06058E0  10209101  10044780  F04858E0
002B40  5B58C2D6  D7C5D540  5B58C2C3  D306E2C5
002B70  C9D1C3C6  E9C9E9F0  F3F20A00  91801002
002BA0  F01A58E0  101C07FE  D501F05C  E0004770
002BD0  0A320000  47F0F01A  C9D1C4C6  E9E9E9E9
002C00  00000000  00000000  00000000  00000000
        --SAME--
006FE0  00000000  00000000  00000000  00000000
```

Figure 2-20 The report above is an example of a System/360 "core-dump," which is a listing of the contents of main computer storage. The data is represented in a "hexadecimal" format, which was new for programmers and operators. New ideas such as the hexadecimal representation of data caused a tremendous need for re-education in the computer industry.

Problems with operating systems

The users and IBM faced a greater problem, however; one which would be found in many subsequent product announcements from various manufacturers. It would become the major problem of the middle and late 1960's and 1970's — operating system and software reliability.

The term software refers to programs which are written for computer systems. There are two broad categories of software — system software and application software. Application software refers to programs which are written for certain applications, such as programs to process a company's payroll.

System software refers to programs written to aid in the operation of the computer system. When IBM announced the System/360, they also announced an "operating system." This system software consisted of a series of programs that were designed to control the input/output operations of the computer system, communicate with the computer operator, and schedule the resources of the computer system to allow for continuous operation of the computer with minimum manual intervention.

Approximately 2,000 programmers and support personnel were assigned by IBM to develop the operating system and related software at a budget of $125 million. Numerous difficulties arose as the software production fell behind schedule. One IBM executive, in explaining the problem, admitted, "We were trying to schedule invention, which is a dangerous thing to do on a committed project."

The operating system which was supposed to be available with the first System/360 was not completely operational when the machine was installed. Throughout the late 1960's, numerous "patches," changes, and additions were made to the programs comprising the operating system in an attempt to make it operate according to specifications. Indeed, it can be said that the period from 1965 to 1970 was characterized by problems concerning the reliability of operating systems and other software.

Despite the difficulties with software, however, the System/360 spurred rapid acceptance of the computer by users who had not considered the use of a computer before. Only three months after the initial announcement of the System/360, over $1.2 billion worth of orders had been received. By 1966, IBM was producing 400 System/360 computers per month and they had a two year backlog. Totally, over the next five years, more than 33,000 systems would be delivered.

The reaction to the System/360

Other manufacturers, such as RCA, Honeywell, Univac, and Control Data announced later in 1964 that they had machines which could compete with IBM's System/360. In December of 1964, RCA announced the Spectra 70 computer system, which adopted the instruction set and data representation of the System/360. This was the first example of other manufacturers using the same "machine architecture" as the System/360; but as the years progressed, it would become a common occurrence.

With the announcement of the System/360 and the many subsequent announcements from other companies, the "third generation" of computers was well underway. With the third generation came the most exciting, crazy, and sometimes frantic years the computing industry had yet seen.

The heydays of the late '60's (1965-1970)

By the end of 1965, approximately 26,000 computer systems were installed and in operation in the United States, with many thousands more on order. The increased power and reduced prices of third generation computers caused more and more companies to order and implement computer systems. Business systems were now readily available for approximately $2,000.00 per month rental.

The demand for trained personnel

This increase in the use of computers placed a premium on the people needed to implement data processing systems, particularly programmers and systems analysts. It was estimated that there were 100,000 programmers and analysts employed in the industry in 1967, with a need for an additional 50,000. Column after column of newspaper advertisements tempted specialists already in the field to move on to better jobs (Figure 2-21). It was common for programmers to change jobs every three to six months with substantial pay increases. Articles in popular magazines encouraged engineers, clerks, and anyone else who would listen to take up the calling and enter the exciting world of computers.

COMPUTER PERSONNEL

There has ***never*** been a better time to seek a position change. Our clients have immediate requirements for the following:

COMMERCIAL & SCIENTIFIC

Mgrs. of Data Processing	$14-25K
Asst. Mgrs. of Data Proc.	$14-18K
Tech. Assts. to the Mgr.	$10-14K
Mgrs. of Systems Analysis	$12-22K
Lead Systems Analysts	$10-20K
Sr. Systems Analysts	$10-14K
Jr. Systems Analysts	$ 8-10K
Mgrs. of Programming	$13-16K
Software Programmers	$10-15K
Lead Programmers	$11-14K
Sr. Programmers	$ 9-15K
Jr. Programmers	$ 8-11K
Mgrs. of Computer Oprns.	$10-20K
Lead Computer Operators	$ 9-12K
EDP Consultants	$12-15K
EDP Sales Reps.	$12-15K
Systems Reps.	$10-12K
Service Center Mgrs.	$18-20K
Service Center Sales Reps.	$10-12K

OPERATIONS RESEARCH

Lead O/R Analysts	$15-20K
Sr. O/R Analysts	$12-20K
Jr. O/R Analysts	$ 9-15K
O/R Consultants	$15-20K

Figure 2-21 Advertisements such as the one above encouraging computer personnel to "seek a position change" were found in magazines and newspapers everywhere during the middle and late 1960's.

An expanding industry

Programmers and analysts were not the only people cashing in on the "computer craze." It was said in the late 1960's if an engineer could draw a blueprint of a computing device and make a metal frame for it in his garage, he could approach the "venture capitalists" and receive a million dollars or more for his project. Venture capitalists give money to an inventor and, in turn, they own a part of the company which will produce the product.

Companies were formed to develop new computer-related peripheral devices, including computer terminals, graphic display devices, and optical character reading devices that could scan the shape of a printed character and transfer that data to the processor unit of the computer. Other more exotic pieces of equipment which had little chance of acceptance in the marketplace were developed as well. The only criteria was that the product had something to do with computers.

The software industry is born

Another new phase of the industry was born in this period of time. One of the distinct needs for computer systems is reliable software. Both reliable operating systems software and reliable computer programs to process the payroll, accounts receivable, and other business applications are required. Various individuals and companies recognized the need for software, and software and consulting firms were being formed to provide these services. Whereas in 1958, a few individuals who had become consultants were called "bold adventurers;" by 1968, consulting and software firms were a fact of life.

In 1968, Computer Sciences Corporation became the first software company to be listed on the New York Stock Exchange. Fletcher Jones, then president of C.S.C., predicted that at least one $100 million software company would emerge in the next few years.

His prediction was helped considerably in 1969 when IBM announced the "unbundling" of their software. Up to that point, IBM leased their computer hardware and their software as a package, at a single price. This stymied the software industry because, effectively, users were receiving IBM software at no cost. Under considerable pressure from the industry, IBM announced in 1969 that some of their software would be separately priced from the computer hardware. This allowed software firms to compete with IBM and opened up the software industry for considerable expansion in the 1970's.

The minicomputer emerges

The firm which had introduced the "minicomputer" in 1965, Digital Equipment Corporation (DEC), grew from a relatively small company in Massachusetts to a major manufacturer and supplier of computers during the late 1960's. Many other enterprising engineers and businessmen saw great opportunities in producing minicomputers as well.

Companies such as Hewlett-Packard, Data General, General Automation, and others began the development of a very important segment of the computer industry, centered around the manufacture of small computers, with processor units at that time costing as little as $5,000.00. These companies expanded their product line during the next decade so that today they are a significant factor within the industry.

Figure 2-22 The Hewlett-Packard 21mx minicomputer is only 17 inches high. When first introduced, minicomputers were noted for the small size of their processor units and low cost (hence, the name "minicomputers"). They are, however, very powerful computer systems.

Are computers really worth it?

Despite the fact that computers were becoming more widespread, the late 1960's found people asking whether the use of computer systems was economically a good choice for many companies.

A 1968 report by McKinsey and Company stated that of 27 companies they surveyed, two-thirds of them were making only limited use of their computers and were still a long way from covering current money outlays for the computers, much less recovering their initial investments in the machines.

Businesses had begun to take a closer look at the computer systems which they had unquestionably installed in the 1960's. Many companies did not like what they found.

Industry experts noted that a major reason for poor performance was computer specialists were ordering hardware and developing software without careful analysis by top-level management. It was at this time that management began to involve itself in the increasingly more important computer applications within their companies.

Unreliable programs

Another major reason computer systems were not fulfilling their promise for many businesses was the unreliability of computer programs. Programs which had been developed simply did not always process the data accurately and reliably. Newspaper articles such as "Water Bill Issued to Homeowner for $200,000.00" or "Voting System Felled by Programmer's Error" were all too commonly found.

As computer systems were used for more and more applications, these errors were increasingly affecting the general public. A problem which has not yet been solved — the safeguarding of public and private information and the proper processing of this information — had become apparent during the late 1960's.

Some did not survive

Even though the period from 1965 through 1970 was one of frantic growth, with many new products and services developed, some of the major manufacturers of computer systems did not survive the battle.

Expenditures in excess of $100 million for the research and development of both the hardware and software necessary to have a computer ready for market were not unusual. In addition, because of the rapidly changing technology, heavy expenditures for research and product improvement were necessary.

This, coupled with the difficulties in competing with IBM, led to the rather startling announcement in 1970 that General Electric was quitting the computer manufacturing business. That announcement was followed in 1972 with the news that RCA was leaving the computer business. In 1975, Xerox Corporation, which had entered the business in the mid-1960's, also announced that they would no longer manufacture and market computer systems. Although the computer business was extremely promising, it was also found that the competition was great, and the cost to remain in the business was high.

Welfare Recipients Receive $80,000 in Duplicate Checks

DETROIT – A computer in the state's Department of Social Services recently sent out $80,000 in duplicate checks to welfare clients throughout the state.

According to Gerrold Brockmyre, assistant deputy director of the state agency, the duplicate checks resulted when the same batch of supplemental emergency payments was fed into the computer on two separate days. The error was discovered when merchants who were asked to cash two checks grew suspicious.

Many of the 887 twice-paid recipients are cashing the second check under the mistaken impression that they are entitled to the money, but some clients "are sending the extra checks back," said Brockmyre.

"Those who have spent the money have received a rather strong letter suggesting they make an arrangement to repay the money," he added.

Figure 2-23 The error in using computers noted in the article above is typical of the publicity received by computers during the late 1960's and early 1970's. Although the majority of problems encountered could be traced to human error, the "computer" gained a reputation for mistakes and unreliability among the public.

Evolutionary growth (1970–1975)

By 1970, an estimated 100,000 computer systems were in operation. Although the growth of the data processing industry continued, the period of development from 1970–1975 may best be described as "evolutionary" rather than "revolutionary."

New product announcements continued from a variety of manufacturers. IBM announced the System/370, which used the same architecture as the System/360, but was faster, cheaper, and offered more main and auxiliary storage. Many System/370 computers were ordered with over one million positions in main computer storage and over a billion characters in auxiliary storage.

Smaller machines also gained prominence, with DEC continuing its inroads into the general purpose computer market. IBM announced the System/3 computer system, a relatively small system targeted for smaller companies than had previously been able to afford computers. The business computer system was becoming an indispensible management tool for both large and medium-sized companies.

The industry recognized that one of the least cost-effective areas within data processing operations was the data entry department, where data is placed in a machine-readable form to be processed. Accordingly, the punched card, which had been the primary means of entering data into a computer system since the inception of the computer, began to be replaced by magnetic tape and disk.

Data entry devices had been developed in the 1960's which could place data directly on tape or disk, thus saving time and money as well as increasing reliability. With the increased use of these machines in the early 1970's, it was predicted that the days of the punched card were numbered — some experts did not expect to see punched cards used by 1978. This forecast proved to be inaccurate, as punched cards are still an important way to enter data into computer systems; but key-to-tape and key-to-disk devices have become dominant in the data entry area.

Figure 2-24 The Sperry-Univac VDS 2000 is typical of modern data entry devices. It provides for data keyed on the keyboard to be stored on either floppy disks or magnetic tape.

Computers learn to communicate

During the 1970's, a major change took place relative to the way data was made available to a computer system for processing. Up to the early 1970's, most computer systems operated in a "batch" environment. In a batch environment, a given number of transactions are gathered over a period of time and then are processed together.

For example, to produce a sales report, all sales orders for a day would be accumulated and taken to the data entry department where the data would be prepared for machine processing. The sales orders would then be processed in a "batch" on the computer. Other applications would be processed in a similar manner.

With the added sophistication of both hardware and software, the 1970's saw increased use of another mode of processing data — a transaction-oriented mode. In this mode, data is entered into the computer system at the time a transaction occurs rather than "batching" the transactions. For example, when a sales order is received, it would be immediately entered into the system by a person using a computer terminal.

The ability to perform this type of processing depends largely on two capabilities which were developed during this time — the ability to store large amounts of data on auxiliary storage devices and data communications.

Most computers introduced in the early 1970's provided for large amounts of data to be stored on auxiliary storage devices. Software developed during this time provided a number of ways in which this data could be stored and retrieved for usage.

The second major factor was data communications, which allows a user to access a computer system through a terminal located at a remote site. The key to data communications is that the user can communicate with the computer system over telephone wires or other communication methods. That is, someone in Cleveland can communicate with a computer system which is located in Atlanta. This ability allowed transaction-oriented processing to occur.

Data communications became a reality for many companies in the early 1970's. Today, many experts have difficulty in separating the computer business from the communications business because they are so closely allied.

Figure 2-25 Transaction-oriented order entry systems use computer terminals at remote sites to process orders as they are received.

Social issues become a concern

During the early 1970's, leaders in the industry and many of the professional organizations were becoming increasingly concerned with what may be described as the social issues in computing.

With auxiliary storage devices capable of storing billions of characters, "data banks" containing information about thousands of individuals were being developed by credit reporting agencies, the Federal Bureau of Investigation, and other governmental and private organizations. The primary issue confronting data processing was whether the ability to obtain and store this information together with the ability to communicate this information through data communication lines and remote computer terminals would lead to an invasion of privacy.

Stories were written in newspapers and magazines concerning the so-called invasion of privacy acts committed by a number of agencies of the government and private industry (Figure 2-26). People reported losing driver's licenses, being arrested, and in one case, being shot by police, because of errors in the data stored in the "data banks."

The data processing organizations, private citizens, and increasingly, senators and congressmen, were asking what steps could be taken to ensure that "big brother" did not become a reality. There were three questions to be answered: first, was there a right for these data banks to exist; second, what could private citizens do to ensure that the data about themselves was accurate; and third, who could access the data.

After much debate, the Privacy Act of 1974 was passed by the United States Congress. This act provided that justification would have to be shown by federal agencies whenever a "data bank" was to be established or accessed. In addition, both governmental agencies and private industry would have to allow access by a citizen to the stored information concerning that citizen whenever it was requested. This act, although not without flaws, aided greatly in protecting the rights of citizens and demonstrated that the computing industry did indeed have a conscience.

Computer crime and fraud

Related to the social issues was the increased possibility of computer crime and fraud. With the ability to access large amounts of data, those with the inclination were able to obtain information which in the past was considered proprietary.

Top-Level Review Headed by Ford

Nixon Wants Privacy Shield for All

By E. Drake Lundell Jr.
Of the CW Staff

WASHINGTON, D.C. – Vice-President Gerald Ford has been tapped to head President Nixon's top-level review of the entire issue of personal privacy – particularly in relation to computerized data banks.

The review committee – made up entirely of administration functionaries –

posals, that could be acted on immediately.

Nixon, whose administration has been accused of violating personal privacy through wiretapping, concentrated most of his 15-minute radio address on the issue of privacy and problems with computer data banks, and specifically told the commission not to go into the issue of wiretapping which is being studied by another administration committee.

"Many things are necessary to lead a

zens' right to privacy fails to respect the citizens themselves," he added.

"Data banks affect nearly every man, woman and child in the U.S.," Nixon said, noting that computerized data banks "scattered across the country" now contain the names of over 150 million Americans.

Often the privacy of individuals has been "seriously damaged – sometimes beyond repair" by the operation of such systems, the President said.

Your Body May Be in MIB Information System Today

By E. Drake Lundell Jr.
CW Washington Bureau

WASHINGTON, D.C. – More than 12 million Americans "should have an absolute right to know what secret intelligence information about them lurks in the electronically controlled data banks of the Medical Information Bureau (MIB)," senators were told recently at a hearing on proposed amendments to the Fair Credit Reporting Act.

Furthermore, John E. Gregg of the Policyholders Protective Association told the Senate committee "Every A

William Proxmire (D-Wi bring medical info visions of th

Under th sumer wou denied credi medical repor to have "such licensed physici

In addition, t to be informed o information that that was the reaso

Secret White House Data Bank Uncovered

By E. Drake Lundell Jr.
CW Washington Bureau

WASHINGTON, D.C. – A secret dat bank on more than 5,000 individua accessible only to the White House ma be the "ultimate in governmental da banks," according to Sen. Sam J. Erv (D-N.C.).

The secret file was uncovered in a s vey of governmental data banks c ducted by Ervin's Subcommittee on C titutional Rights, but so far White Ho ficials have not delivered requeste 21- rmation to the committee about

Computer 'Accomplice' In Thefts

By Marvin Smallheiser
CW Correspondent

LOS ANGELES – The ar-old president of a ngeles communications ment firm was arrested la for allegedly stealing ne million worth of Pacif phone Co. supplies by de for the compa

Study to Probe the Evil Computer

CW Washington Bureau

WASHINGTON, D.C. – With the aid of a grant from the National Science Foundation, the Stanford Research Institute will conduct a study on how computers are – or could be – put to socially wrongful use.

The study u Donn B. just who of such cr opportuni the attitu and inv whether p procedures

In conducting the program, the investigators are to complete a coded inventory of more than 100 cases and catalog the research already documented in the stud such crimes.

Check Fraud Scheme Uncovered, 7 Charg

NEW YORK – Fraudulent checks s to be in excess of $1 million were app ently issued from 1969 through Janu computer operatic ouse Electric Cor n.

e U.S. attorney of New York, s Howard Hudgi r expert, allege iends of his, bo corporation. ere indicted w Westinghouse t house sales ass antique deal firm in Ne mployed tru

Is Fraud Possible?
Computerized Voting Under Investigation

LOS ANGELES – An investigation into the possibility that d could be committed has been

computer professionals are expected to be named. But Registrar-Recorder Ray E. Lee noted that the commission could computer experts if it

steps of the vote tabulation.
Action on computerized voting has also occurred on three other fronts in California:
• U.S. Sen. George Brown called on the California State to investigate com

---

Figure 2-26 The newspaper articles above are representative of the great concern for privacy and crime shown in the early 1970's.

One enterprising thief, using a computer terminal "tapped into" the phone lines, determined the method for ordering equipment that the telephone company used from their main computer to their warehouse. This clever fellow would then type in orders on his own terminal, which would be sent to the warehouse. The warehouse would gather the equipment together, not realizing that the order was from a thief, not from authorized personnel. The thief would then send his own trucks to pick up the equipment ordered. Larceny through the use of computer terminals and data communications equipment has become more common and is certainly a concern in today's modern computer society.

The economic slowdown

Even though there was a great deal of innovation and expansion in the data processing industry during the early 1970's, it was also a period of relaxation and reflection for the industry. The entire economy suffered a slowdown. With this slowdown, many computer installations re-examined their efforts with computers and the results they had obtained. It was clear the "heydays" of the '60's were over. Data processing specialists were held more accountable for their spending and results than they had previously been. It is said by some that this time will be marked as an important maturing point in the computing industry.

Following this moment of relaxation, the computer industry was to resume its exhilarating period of growth but a few years later with the introduction of a new era of microelectronics.

The development of microelectronics

Undoubtedly, one of the most revolutionary technological developments in the history of mankind has occurred in the field of electronics. Nearly unbelievable advances have taken place in the past 30 years. Shortly following the invention of the transistor in 1947 came a breakthrough in which electronic engineers learned to define transistors and related circuitry by "photolithography." Using this technique, circuits are drawn according to specifications. These circuits are then photographed and reduced. Through the use of sophisticated methodologies, the transistors are then "etched" on a thin wafer sliced from a large crystal of germanium or silicon (Figure 2–27).

Figure 2-27 The silicon "wafer" being held by tweezers (above) contains many circuits of the type illustrated at the right by the National Semiconductor INS 8900 microprocessor. Each small "square" on the wafer is the same as the square outline on the chip at the right. Hundreds and even thousands of circuits and transistors can be contained on these small chips.

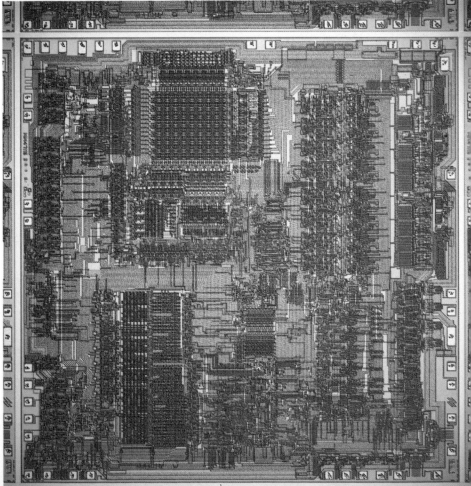

By 1965, each single "chip," approximately ¼" square, could contain as many as 1,000 circuit elements. By 1970, using what was called "large scale integration," or LSI, the number of elements which could be created on a single chip increased to over 15,000. It was this development which made feasible the hand electronic calculators which are so popular. Today, ¼" chips capable of storing over 70,000 transistors are possible, resulting in greatly reduced prices for modern computer systems.

The era of the microprocessor

In 1969, Dr. Ted Hoff, a young engineering graduate from Stanford University, obtained employment from Intel Corporation, an electronics manufacturing firm. Hoff was given the challenging assignment of designing the microelectronic components for a desk top calculator.

Using then-current design methodologies, a number of chips would be required to perform the various functions of the calculator. Hoff conceived the idea of placing the calculator's arithmetic and logic circuits on a single chip of silicon; resulting, effectively, in the creation of the central processing unit of a computer system on a single silicon chip.

This central processing unit, developed on a chip smaller than a fingernail and called a microprocessor, almost matched the power of the ENIAC with its 18,000 vacuum tubes. Intel's original announcement of this exciting new product proclaimed "a new era of integrated electronics . . . a computer on a chip." This small central processing unit, when combined with other chips to provide for main computer storage and other control functions, formed the basic electronics of a complete computer system — all stored on a printed circuit board less than one foot square.

The development of this microprocessor led to substantial changes in the design and use of computers. Smaller computer systems were developed for specialized applications. Computer terminals, which before had only been able to communicate with a larger computer, now became "intelligent," with the ability to process data without the power of the larger computer. The personal computer industry evolved and flourished.

And, of course, developments continued on these remarkable electronic circuits. Today, the circuitry for an entire computer can be contained on a single chip at a cost of less than $25.00. These "microcomputers" have many times more computing power than the original ENIAC, are a thousand times more reliable, occupy 1/2,000,000 the volume, and cost 1/16,000 as much.

The new world of computers (1975–present)

It is estimated that over 500,000 computers are now being used throughout the country, with sales in excess of $40 billion. Truly, the data processing industry has emerged as one of the nation's largest and fastest growing industries.

In the modern world of computers, the basic cycle of input, process, and output has not changed; however, the method of input, the speed of processing, and the variety of output devices has greatly altered the way in which computers are used.

An entire new vocabulary is now used to describe the modern computer environment. Personal computers, intelligent terminals, data communications, distributed data processing, and data base are terms found in the vocabulary of the new generation of computer specialists. These are topics to be discussed in subsequent chapters of this book.

The Application of the

Computer In

Modern Society

The development of the computer has led to its use in virtually all areas of business and science. The following pages illustrate but a few of the many applications where computer systems play a vital role in performing manual tasks and aiding in the decision-making processes which are so necessary in today's complex society.

The Office

Of Today

One of the more dramatic changes observed in the office of today is the conspicuous absence of the typewriter, the standard office tool for over a century.

Rapidly replacing the typewriter as a means of recording data and conveying facts essential to the world of business is the computer and related computer terminals. Many businesses have begun to use the computer terminal as the primary means of storing and communicating information.

With the ability of computer systems to communicate with one another, it has also been noted that many offices are utilizing these devices for "electronic mail," conferences between executives, and other communications needs.

Without doubt, the computer is an integral part of the modern business environment, and an understanding of the applications and use of computer systems Is an important part of the job skills for office employees.

Figure 2-28 Wang computers and terminals are utilized in this modern office to perform such tasks as letter writing, billing, order entry, credit checking, and the filing and retrieval of other information.

Will the Computer Replace the Teacher?

Probably not, but knowledge of the computer is becoming essential. Indeed, almost 20 years ago Dr. John J. Kemeny, now president of Dartmouth College, predicted that "In the next generation, knowing how to use a computer will be as important as reading and writing."

With the introduction of the microcomputer, inexpensive computing power is available to students at all levels of education. Today, in many schools from elementary to college, the use of the computer as an area of study, for problem solving, and as a teaching aid is becoming increasingly more important.

Figure 2-29 Computers are often used in elementary schools for Computer Assisted Instruction (CAI). When using CAI, problems (for example, math problems) are displayed on the computer terminal. The student is required to respond with the correct answer. A correct answer will result in a new question. An incorrect answer will result in a message indicating the wrong answer, followed by further instructions.

Figure 2-30 Most colleges in the United States offer a variety of classes in computers and data processing. During the 1960's, course work in business data processing and computer science became a standard part of many college and university curriculums.

Figure 2-31 Tektronix terminals are being used to teach circuit design. Note how the circuit on the chalkboard is duplicated on the terminals.

The World's Largest Paperwork Problem

One of the largest paperwork handling problems in existence is found in the banking industry. In the United States, over 25 billion checks are processed annually using the computer. At the current rate of growth, it is anticipated that by 1985 there will be a need to process 60 billion checks annually.

To combat this tremendous problem, banks have turned to computer systems. In addition to the applications illustrated on these pages, banks have instituted electronic funds transfer systems (EFT), whereby money is transferred from one account to another without the money ever being seen by the customer. For example, Social Security checks can be deposited directly into a person's account without that person ever receiving a check. It is safe to say that without computers, the banking industry could not cope with the needs of its customers.

Figure 2-32 Compact visual teller terminals from Incoterm Corporation, a Honeywell subsidiary, link Seattle First National Bank tellers state-wide with the bank's central computer. Terminals at 1,300 teller stations provide instant access to banking information.

Figure 2-33 Large-scale Burroughs computers (right) form the backbone of a data processing network at Midland Bank in the United Kingdom. Two centers, each with dual-processor systems, process some 2.3 million items each day. These computers are connected over communications lines to more than 2,600 terminals in one of the largest banking networks in the world.

Figure 2-34 Self-service automated teller terminals (below) are now widely used in the banking industry. These terminals, which are connected to the bank's main computer, allow the customer to insert an identifying bank card. After appropriate checks are performed by the computer, such as determining that there is money in the customer's account, the terminal will dispense actual cash to the customer. Upon dispensing the money, the computer will update the account by writing the new balance on the auxiliary storage devices used with the computer. Deposits to the account can also be made using the same terminals.

Computers in Retail Stores

Today, in modern retail stores, the stand-alone cash register is rapidly being replaced by computer terminals directly linked to a computer system. As a sale is made, a record of the sale is stored on the auxiliary storage of the computer system. In addition, inventory records are updated to reflect the fact that an item has been sold.

Besides keeping track of sales and inventory, computers allow sales personnel to validate personal checks used by customers, to verify a valid credit card purchase, and to more accurately determine the change in a cash transaction.

Retail stores have been able to use the power of computer systems to not only aid them in their businesses, but also to provide better service for their customers.

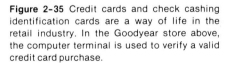

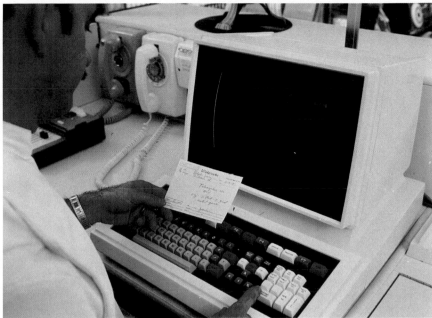

Figure 2-37 Pharmacists can use systems like the Intercom system to price prescriptions automatically, keep files on doctors, register patients and their prescriptions, keep track of any drug allergies of patients, and keep an inventory of all drugs dispensed and on hand.

Figure 2-35 Credit cards and check cashing identification cards are a way of life in the retail industry. In the Goodyear store above, the computer terminal is used to verify a valid credit card purchase.

Figure 2-36 Computerized grocery checkout stands (right) are being used to increase the efficiency with which groceries are checked. A bar code placed on the item is read by a "scanner." This data is passed to a computer which has the price for the item stored on auxiliary storage. A detailed grocery list is printed for the customer and the total for the sale is calculated.

Moving From

One Place

To Another

Moving people and goods over land, through the air, and on water demands tight scheduling, accurate counts of people and supplies, and close coordination of airplanes, ships, cars, and trucks. The computer is used by the transportation industry to aid in these requirements and others.

Airlines are particularly dependent upon the speed and accuracy of computer systems. For example, United Airlines maintains an average of 1.3 million reservations per day. On a typical day, 90,000 new tickets are sold, 30,000 changes to existing tickets must be made, and 30,000 tickets must be priced and printed. Every hour, airline personnel must answer questions from over a quarter million anxious travelers. Computers are also used to generate boarding passes, to calculate the weight and balance of aircraft, and to actually fly the aircraft from take-off to landing.

Figure 2-38 The travel agent using a computer terminal can, in a few seconds, confirm reservations for anywhere in the world.

Figure 2-39 A controller in a shipyard uses a computer terminal attached to a DEC computer system to aid in scheduling docking and unloading operations.

Figure 2-40 The realistic night scene of the runway below is not an actual photograph, but rather a computerized display from Redifon Simulation, Inc., that is used in flight training. Pilots will spend many hours using computer-controlled flight trainers and displays before touching the controls of an actual aircraft.

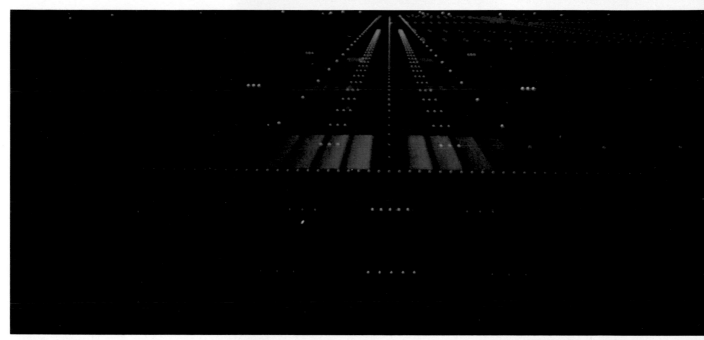

Figure 2-41 Engineers on the right are testing three IBM displays and five onboard IBM computers which are a part of the guidance system for NASA's space shuttle. Computers have played a major role in space flight since its inception, including the dramatic rescue of the Apollo 13 space mission. As man ventures into space in the future, the computer will be his constant companion.

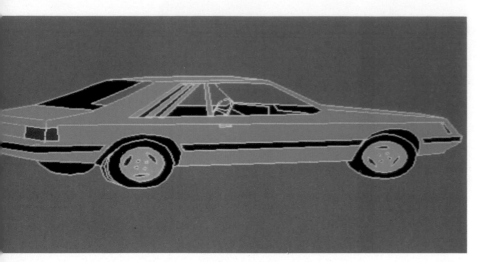

Figure 2-42 High resolution graphic display devices are used in product design to allow the proposed finished product to be viewed. In the photo at the left, the finished design of an automobile is displayed. Over 262,000 light "dots" are used on the CRT screen to create the picture. Through the use of this sophisticated device from Chromatics, the designer can also "zoom in" and display, for example, an enlarged picture of the front section of the car.

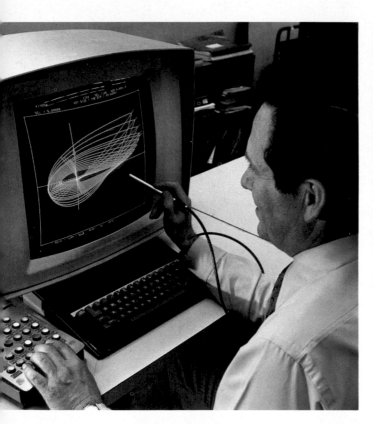

Figure 2-43 An important tool for the engineer is the "light pen" used with graphic display devices. The light pen, which the engineer is holding in the picture at the left, allows the designer to draw on the face of the display tube, adding or deleting lines. The new design is then stored on the computer's auxiliary storage for later retrieval. Prior to the use of the computer, a skilled draftsman would spend many hours redoing designs which required the slightest modification. "Hard copy," that is, printed documents, can be produced using plotters (right). These plotters will reproduce on paper the drawings which are displayed on the terminal.

Computerized

Manufacturing

and Design

While many computers are busy processing millions of business records each day, almost all large manufacturing companies also use computer systems to aid in the manufacturing process, including original design of the product, pro- duction of the tooling necessary to build the product, and control of the manufacturing process itself. The automobile industry, steel industry, textile plants, paper mills, and other manufacturing concerns operate under the control of one or more computer systems. One of the big- gest aids in the design process has been the increased development of graphic display devices and plotters. These new tools of the engineer have substantially altered the method of designing and testing new products.

Figure 2-44 Large manufacturing companies use sophisticated computer systems to con- trol their manufacturing processes and to keep track of the production from the processes. In the picture above, a steel worker monitors the production of steel. This mill in Bethlehem Steel's plant in Burns Harbor, Indiana, is con- trolled by a sophisticated process control com- puter system. The computer controls every phase of production—heating, rolling, and shearing. At the same time, another computer tracks the steel production from the slab yard through the shipping area, supplies schedul- ing information, and reports on the results of all processes.

The Everyday

Computers

Whether it be in a hospital, a library, a local bowling alley, or a shopping center, the computer is quickly becoming as common as the automobile or television. Indeed, with the increased use of home computers and the availability of affordable machines, some authorities have predicted that by 1995, there may be as many as 40 million computer systems of varying sizes throughout the United States.

The increase in the number of computers will lead to an increase in the ways computers are used. The applications shown on this and the previous pages illustrate a few of the ways in which computers are currently used. In the years to come, new and increased usage will affect every person in the country.

Figure 2-45 This Digital Equipment retail store in Manchester, New Hampshire, allows businessmen to browse and select

Figure 2-46 Patients in the Medical Intensive Care Unit at University Hospital in Cleveland (left) are under the watchful eye of a bedside monitoring system which transmits heart rate, blood pressure, and other vital signs to a central station where it is displayed on a terminal controlled by a DEC PDP-11 computer system. The system can monitor up to 20 patients simultaneously. It can provide immediate information on any patient and sounds an alarm if a medical emergency develops.

Figure 2-47 A librarian (right) uses a "wand" to read data encoded within a book. The data will include a code which can be used to reference the title of the book and also the number of days the book can be checked out. The librarian will also enter the date the book is checked out and the name of the borrower. This information will be saved on auxiliary storage so that other borrowers can be told when the book will be returned and also as follow-up in case the book is not returned.

computers for their particular needs.

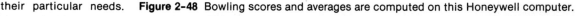

Figure 2-48 Bowling scores and averages are computed on this Honeywell computer.

Chapter summary

The following points have been discussed and explained in this chapter.

1. The computer industry has developed into one of the four largest industries in the world.

2. Dr. John V. Atanasoff and Clifford Berry designed the first electronic digital computer, called the Atanasoff-Berry-Computer.

3. Dr. John W. Mauchly and J. Presper Eckert, Jr. designed and built the ENIAC, the first large-scale electronic digital computer.

4. ENIAC, put into operation in 1946, was programmed by external wiring and switches.

5. Dr. John von Neumann is credited with originating the stored program concept. The first computer to use the stored program concept was EDSAC in 1949.

6. UNIVAC I, the first computer to be commercially available, was installed at the Bureau of the Census in 1951.

7. In the early 1950's, Remington-Rand and IBM emerged as the two leading computer companies. At the end of 1953, 13 companies were manufacturing computers.

8. By the end of 1956, IBM had taken a lead in the computer industry which it has yet to relinquish.

9. The first stored program computers were programmed in machine language.

10. Symbolic programming languages were devised, allowing symbolic notation to represent the operations to be performed by the computer.

11. In 1957, FORTRAN was announced by IBM. FORTRAN is a high-level programming language which allows the programmer to write a program in mathematical terms. A "translator" or "compiler" is required to convert a program written in FORTRAN to machine language.

12. COBOL (COmmon Business Oriented Language) was released in 1960. It allows programmers to write in an English-like fashion, and can be used on machines from different manufacturers.

13. In 1958, transistors became widely used in computer systems instead of vacuum tubes, ushering in the "second generation" of computers.

14. By 1958, there were an estimated 2,550 computer systems installed in the United States. By 1964, over 18,000 had been installed. This growth was largely due to the less costly transistorized computers.

15. Most programmers and operators in the early 1960's were trained on the job. Few schools had training programs.

16. The IBM System/360 family of computers, announced in 1964, brought in the "third generation" of computers. It used integrated circuits, was faster than most previous computers, and could be used for both scientific and business processing.

17. Symbolic language programs written for second generation computers would not run on the System/360, causing compatibility problems.

18. Operating systems for the System/360 were not complete nor reliable when the first computers were delivered. The period of 1965 to 1970 was characterized by problems concerning the reliability of operating systems and other software.

19. By the end of 1965, approximately 26,000 computers were installed in the U. S., with many more on order.

20. There was a shortage of trained personnel in the late 1960's. Many programmers and analysts changed jobs every few months with substantial pay increases.

21. Software companies became an important factor in the industry in the late 1960's.

22. The minicomputer, first introduced in 1965, gained importance as numerous companies began producing these machines.

23. The late 1960's found many companies not using their computer systems effectively. One reason was unreliable software.

24. Competition from IBM and the high cost of doing business caused RCA, General Electric, and Xerox to quit the computer business.

25. The early 1970's saw the development of data communications, which allowed users to communicate with computers at remote sites.

26. Invasion of privacy and computer crime were issues facing the computer industry in the early 1970's. The Privacy Act of 1974 was an attempt to lessen the invasion of privacy for private citizens.

27. The years since 1975 have been marked by the use and development of microelectronics.

28. The microprocessor and microcomputer have made a significant impact on the design and use of computer systems.

29. There are an estimated 500,000 computers now in use in the U. S. The forecast is for this number to grow rapidly.

30. Computer systems are used in the office, in schools, by banks, in retail establishments, in transportation, in manufacturing, and for a variety of other applications, all affecting our daily lives.

Student Learning Exercises

Review questions

1. Explain the significance of the Atanasoff-Berry-Computer.

2. Describe the characteristics of ENIAC. Who designed ENIAC, and when did it become operational?

3. Discuss the contributions of Dr. John von Neumann.

4. Explain the events in the early 1950's which led to IBM's becoming the dominant force in the industry.

5. What is the difference between machine language and symbolic programming languages?

6. What is a high-level language? What is the difference between FORTRAN and COBOL?

7. When did the "second generation" computers evolve? Why were they called second generation computers?

8. Why is the System/360 so important in the history of the computer industry? Explain some of its unique characteristics.

9. What were some of the problems with the System/360?

10. Briefly describe the data processing industry between 1965 and 1970.

11. What is meant by unreliable software? What effect did it have in the late 1960's?

12. Why did several major manufacturers leave the computing industry?

13. Briefly describe the data processing industry between 1970 and 1975.

14. What is data communications? What is its significance to the industry?

15. What major social issues were faced by the industry in the early 1970's? What was done to solve these problems?

16. What is microelectronics? What is its effect on the industry?

Controversial issues in data processing

1. Some people believe that large data banks containing information about private citizens would help raise the quality of life in our society. Others think they are an invasion of privacy and a threat to a democratic society. Discuss the positive and negative points in these arguments.

2. Some people argue that the use of the computer in all areas of business is bad because people are losing jobs, and society is too dependent on the computer. Others say it is good because tasks can be done which used to be impossible. Prepare an argument for one of these two positions.

Research projects

1. Fortune Magazine contains a number of excellent articles on computers. Select an era of interest and research an article from Fortune Magazine. Report to the class on the content of the article and also the feeling the article conveyed relative to the status of the industry when the article was written.

2. Many communities have retail computer stores. Visit one of these stores, and prepare a brief description of what was found in the store.

Picture credits

Figure 2-1 Computerworld	Figure 2-23 Computerworld	Figure 2-36 NCR
Figure 2-2 Iowa State University	Figure 2-24 Sperry Univac	Figure 2-37 Walgreen Company
Figure 2-3 Iowa State University	Figure 2-25 United States Steel Company	Figure 2-38 Raytheon Company
Figure 2-4 United Press International	Figure 2-26 Computerworld	Figure 2-39 Digital Equipment Corp.
Figure 2-5 Princeton University	Figure 2-27 Perkin-Elmer Corporation, National Semiconductor	Figure 2-40 Redifon Simulation Inc.
Figure 2-6 University of Pennsylvania		Figure 2-41 IBM
Figure 2-7 United Press International	Figure 2-28 Wang Laboratories, Inc.	Figure 2-42 Chromatics
Figure 2-8 Sperry Univac	Figure 2-29 IBM	Figure 2-43 Lockheed Aircraft Corp., Tektronix, Inc.
Figure 2-9 IBM	Figure 2-30 Digital Equipment Corp.	
Figure 2-10 IBM	Figure 2-31 Tektronix, Inc.	Figure 2-44 Bethlehem Steel Corp.
Figure 2-11 IBM	Figure 2-32 Honeywell	Figure 2-45 Digital Equipment Corp.
Figure 2-16 IBM	Figure 2-33 Burroughs Corporation	Figure 2-46 Digital Equipment Corp.
Figure 2-18 IBM	Figure 2-34 NCR	Figure 2-47 IBM
Figure 2-19 IBM	Figure 2-35 The Goodyear Tire and Rubber Company	Figure 2-48 Honeywell, Inc.
Figure 2-22 Hewlett-Packard		

Chapter 3
Processing Data
on a
Computer System

Objectives

- A detailed understanding of the input/process/output basic processing cycle

- An understanding of the operational capabilities of a computer system — input/output, arithmetic, and logical operations

- An understanding of the capability of a computer system to store data on auxiliary storage for access at a later time by the same or a different program

- An appreciation and understanding of data storage and retrieval, inquiry processing, update processing, and sorting

- An understanding of control break processing; classifying, selecting, and summarizing data; and the manipulation of data in a computer system for the production of useful information

Chapter 3

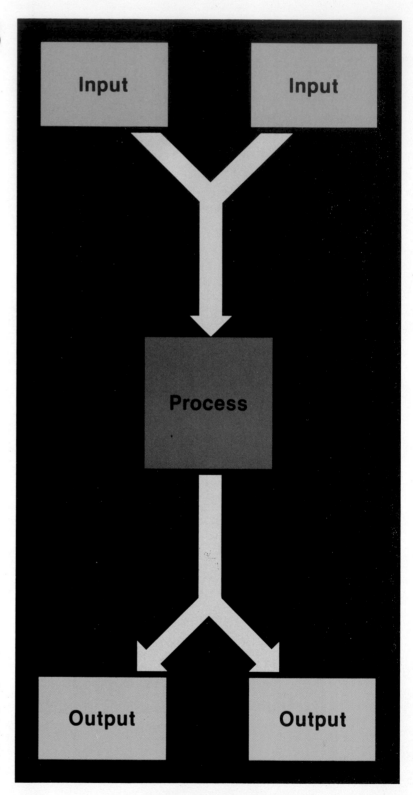

Figure 3-1 The basic processing cycle on a computer system consists of input, process, and output. The input operation causes data to be stored in main computer storage. The process operation manipulates the data, producing the information required. The output operation causes the results of the processing to be printed or displayed in a usable format.

Processing Data on A Computer System

"The faster the machine, the more nonsense it can produce in case of faulty operation. We are now asking for billions of correct arithmetic operations between errors — 1,000 people computing for a lifetime without an error."[1]

Introduction

Computer systems come in all sizes and are applied to the solution of problems in all areas of living. It is important, therefore, to gain an overall understanding of what computer systems really do in order to understand their capabilities and limitations.

The purpose of this chapter is to provide an overview of the basic processing cycle of input, process, and output common to all computer systems (Figure 3–1); and to illustrate the basic operations performed on a computer system, which include input/output operations, arithmetic operations, and logical operations.

Through the use of these operations, a wide variety of applications can be processed, including storing data on auxiliary storage devices, inquiry and updating of files, and sorting, selecting, classifying, and summarizing data. Examples of each of these activities as they are performed on the computer are illustrated in this chapter.

Data organization

The operations just described are all based upon the processing of data of some type. Data is defined as a representation of facts, concepts, or instructions in a formalized manner suitable for communication, interpretation, and processing by humans or automatic machines.

When data is to be processed on a computer system, it must normally be organized into logical entities called fields, records, and files.

---

1 Eckert, W. J., IBM Scientist, 1955.

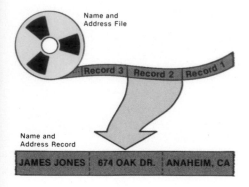

Figure 3-2 The name and address file is stored on magnetic tape. It consists of a number of name and address records. Each name and address record contains a name field, an address field, and a city/state field.

A field is defined as one unit of data. For example, in typing mailing labels, it may be necessary to type a name field, an address field, and a city/state field. Fields are commonly grouped together to form a record. A record is defined as a collection of fields related to a specific unit of information. Thus, there may be name and address records, with each record containing a name field, an address field, and a city/state field. Records are usually grouped together to form a file. A file is defined as a collection of related records. A name and address file, therefore, would consist of one or more name and address records. In Figure 3–2, there is a file of name and address records stored on magnetic tape. Each record contains a name field, an address field, and a city/state field.

Files of records are stored on some medium so that the data can be read into main computer storage. For example, files can be stored on punched cards, magnetic tape, and magnetic disk. These files can then be read, one record at a time, into main computer storage for processing.

It is important to realize that data is generally organized into files, records, and fields for processing on a computer system.

Input

The data which is organized in files, records, and fields is commonly stored on an external "medium" in a machine-readable format prior to being read into main computer storage for processing. Widely-used input media include punched cards, magnetic tape, and magnetic disk. Data stored on these media are read into main computer storage by devices such as floppy disk readers, magnetic tape readers, and punched card readers. Records may also be entered into a computer system through the use of computer terminals (Figure 3–3).

Figure 3-3 Typical input devices include terminals, floppy disk readers, tape readers, and card readers. Terminals can enter keyed data directly into main computer storage. The other devices read data stored on a medium in a machine-readable format into main computer storage.

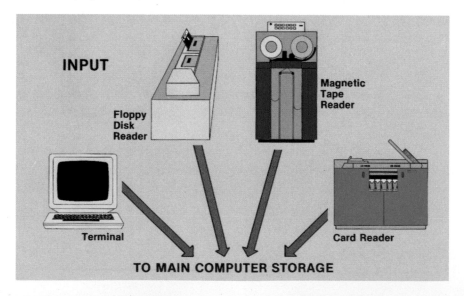

Processing data

Once the data is placed in main computer storage, it is processed under the control of a computer program which is also stored in main computer storage (Figure 3-4).

The computer program contains instructions which direct the computer system to process the data. The instructions in the program can direct the system to perform input/output operations, arithmetic operations, and logical operations. These operations can be carried out on each record which is read into main computer storage for processing.

The operations are accomplished by the electronic circuitry in the central processing unit (CPU). The instructions in the program direct the CPU to actually carry out the instruction. When execution is complete, the next instruction in the computer program will be executed in a similar manner.

Output

The reason for processing data on a computer is to produce useful information. This information is presented as output from the computer system. It can be produced in a number of different formats and on different devices. Two of the more popular forms of output are the printed report and the cathode ray tube (CRT) terminal (Figure 3-5).

Output is usually produced after a logical record has been processed on the computer system. For example, when an input record is read into main computer storage, the program will process the data so that the output record is in the proper format to be printed. This output record can then be written on the printed report. Another input record will then be read and processed.

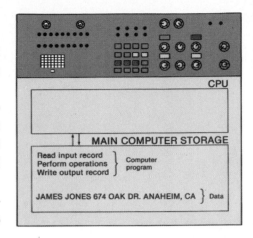

Figure 3-4 The processor unit contains the central processing unit and main computer storage. Data is read from an input device into main computer storage where a program, also in storage, will cause the data to be processed. The program illustrated above and in subsequent illustrations is shown as English statements for ease of understanding. Program instructions are actually stored in main computer storage in machine language.

Figure 3-5 On the left are pictured the two most popular devices for human-usable output — the CRT terminal and the printer. These devices can present output information in a displayed format (on the CRT) or as hard copy output (on the printer).

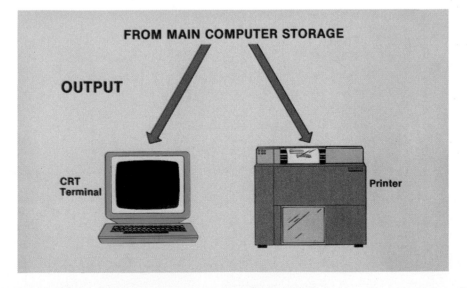

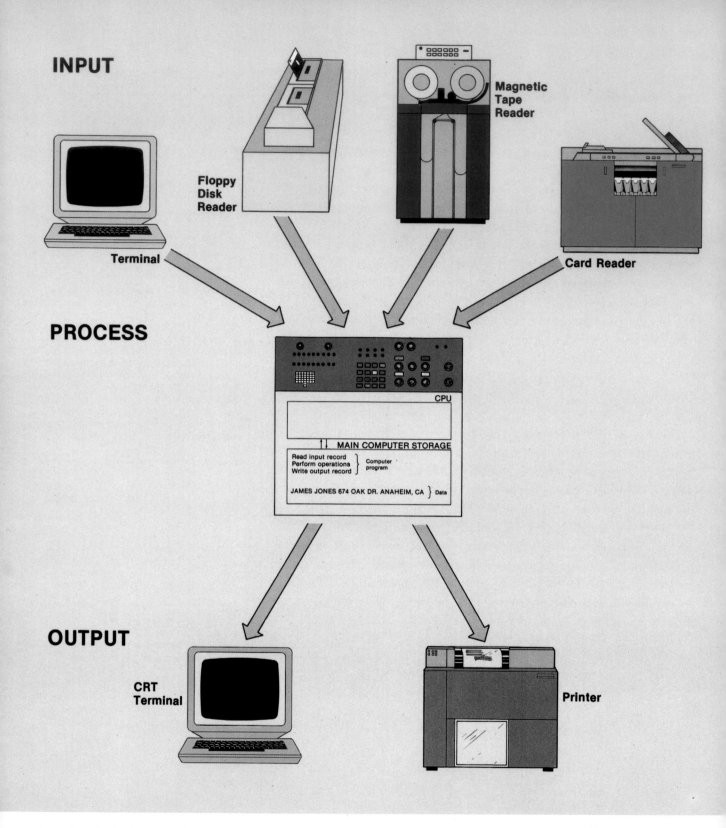

INPUT

Terminal

Floppy
Disk
Reader

Magnetic
Tape
Reader

Card Reader

PROCESS

CPU

MAIN COMPUTER STORAGE

Read input record
Perform operations } Computer
Write output record } program

JAMES JONES 674 OAK DR. ANAHEIM, CA } Data

OUTPUT

CRT
Terminal

Printer

Figure 3-6 The basic processing cycle of input, process, and output is the standard processing method on all computer systems.

The basic processing cycle

The basic processing cycle of input, process, and output is summarized in Figure 3-6, together with some of the typical devices used for input and output on a computer system.

BASIC PROCESSING CONCEPTS

Within the input/process/output processing cycle, computers are capable of performing three basic operations: 1) Input/output operations; 2) Arithmetic operations; and 3) Logical operations. It is important to understand how these three basic operations are performed within a computer system and their relationship to the processing cycle to appreciate how computers are able to solve problems.

INPUT/OUTPUT OPERATIONS

The preparation of an output report from a file of input records is one of the most fundamental input/output operations that can be performed on a computer system. The steps involved in the preparation of a report include: 1) Data from source documents is recorded on an input medium; 2) The data recorded on the input medium is read into main computer storage; 3) The data in main computer storage is processed; 4) The data which has been processed in main computer storage is printed on the report.

Prior to the data being processed to create the report, however, the computer program must be loaded into main computer storage. There are a number of ways to load a program into storage. The most common is to load it from an auxiliary storage device on which it has been stored. The important point, however, is that the program is placed in storage and controls the reading, processing, and writing of the data.

A sample application

To illustrate the input/process/output cycle when creating a report, a personnel report is to be prepared. The information for the report comes from a personnel file (Figure 3-7).

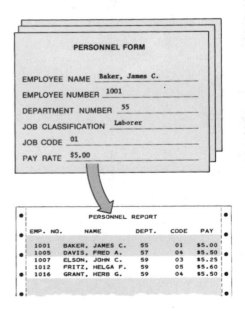

Figure 3-7 The personnel report is to be prepared from data contained on the personnel form. Data on the report includes the employee number, employee name, department number, job code, and pay rate.

3.5

The diagram in Figure 3-8 illustrates the steps that occur in the basic processing cycle when performing the operations necessary to prepare the printed personnel report. These input, process, and output steps are explained in the following paragraphs.

Input/process/output

In the sample application, the data on the source documents (personnel forms) is recorded on a diskette, or "floppy disk," by a device containing a keyboard, a CRT screen, and a disk drive on which the diskette is mounted. On the keyboard, the operator keys the data from the source documents. This data is recorded on the diskette. After the input file is built, the records on the diskette will be read into main computer storage under control of the computer program.

The records are read from the diskette one record at a time by the program stored in main computer storage. As each record is read, it will be processed by the program. In the example, the processing consists of moving the data from an input record area to an output record area. This processing is necessary to arrange the fields in the order in which they are to appear on the report prior to printing the record on the report.

The output step in the example consists of printing the line on the personnel report. Printing the line on the report completes the basic processing cycle for one record.

Processing the remaining records in the input file

After the first record has been read, processed, and printed on the report, the instructions in the computer program stored in main computer storage would be repeated. This would cause the second record in the input file to be read, processed, and printed. Thus, the input, process, and output cycle of reading an input record, processing the data, and writing an output record will continue so long as there are input records to process. When no more input records remain, the program is terminated. The process of repeating a sequence of instructions is called "looping."

It is important to carefully review the diagram in Figure 3-8 in order to gain an understanding of some of the basic concepts of processing data using a computer system.

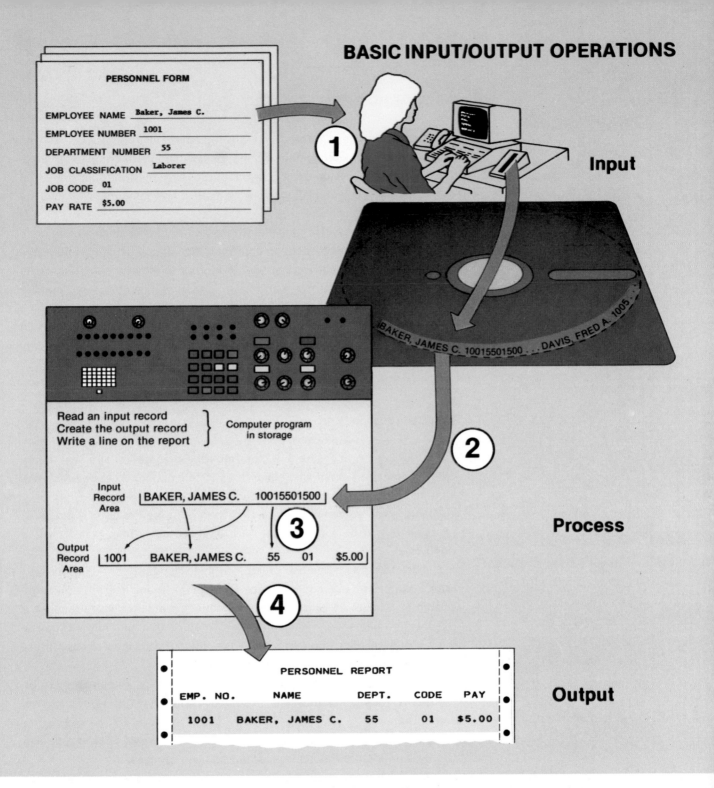

BASIC INPUT/OUTPUT OPERATIONS

PERSONNEL FORM

EMPLOYEE NAME Baker, James C.

EMPLOYEE NUMBER 1001

DEPARTMENT NUMBER 55

JOB CLASSIFICATION Laborer

JOB CODE 01

PAY RATE $5.00

Input

BAKER, JAMES C. 10015501500   DAVIS, FRED A. 1005

Read an input record
Create the output record
Write a line on the report

Computer program
in storage

Input
Record
Area

BAKER, JAMES C.   10015501500

Output
Record
Area

1001   BAKER, JAMES C.   55   01 $5.00

Process

PERSONNEL REPORT				
EMP. NO.	NAME	DEPT.	CODE	PAY
1001	BAKER, JAMES C.	55	01	$5.00

Output

Figure 3-8 The diagram above illustrates the preparation of a personnel report on a computer system. Input consists of a file of personnel records containing information about each employee in the company. To prepare the report, the following steps are taken: 1) The data on the personnel forms is recorded on a floppy disk; 2) The data stored in the personnel input file on the floppy disk is read into main computer storage, one record at a time; 3) The record read into main computer storage is processed, moving the fields from the input record area to the output record area in the proper arrangement for printing on the report; 4) A line is printed on the personnel report. The instructions in the computer program stored in main computer storage are then repeated until all records in the input file have been read, processed, and printed.

ARITHMETIC OPERATIONS

Basic input/output operations are fundamental to all operations performed on a computer system, no matter how simple or complex. In addition, many applications require arithmetic operations to be performed on data. Therefore, one of the important features of any computer system is the ability to perform calculations.

In a computer system, the electronic circuitry is designed so that once data has been placed in main computer storage, it can be used in addition, subtraction, multiplication, division, and other arithmetic operations. The resultant answers from these arithmetic operations can be stored in main computer storage for further processing.

Some modern computer systems can perform these calculations in less than a millionth of a second each. For both scientific and business applications, this ability to perform calculations rapidly is very important.

Input/process/output

The diagram in Figure 3-9 illustrates the preparation of a real estate sales commission report wherein arithmetic calculations must be performed as a part of the basic processing cycle.

The first step consists of placing the file of input data in a machine-readable format on a floppy disk. An input record is then read from the floppy disk.

After the record has been read into main computer storage, the next step is to perform the required processing. In the example, a multiplication operation is required to calculate a commission amount (sales amount X commission percentage = commission amount). In addition, the processing includes moving the fields from the input record area to the output record area to format the report.

After the data has been placed in the output area, a line is printed on the report, thus completing the basic processing cycle of input, process, and output.

As with most file processing, the instructions would be repeated over and over until all of the input records had been processed.

Although many applications involving arithmetic operations are much more complex than the application illustrated, an understanding of the internal operations of a computer system which occur when arithmetic applications are processed will provide an insight into the basic operations of computer systems.

BASIC ARITHMETIC OPERATIONS

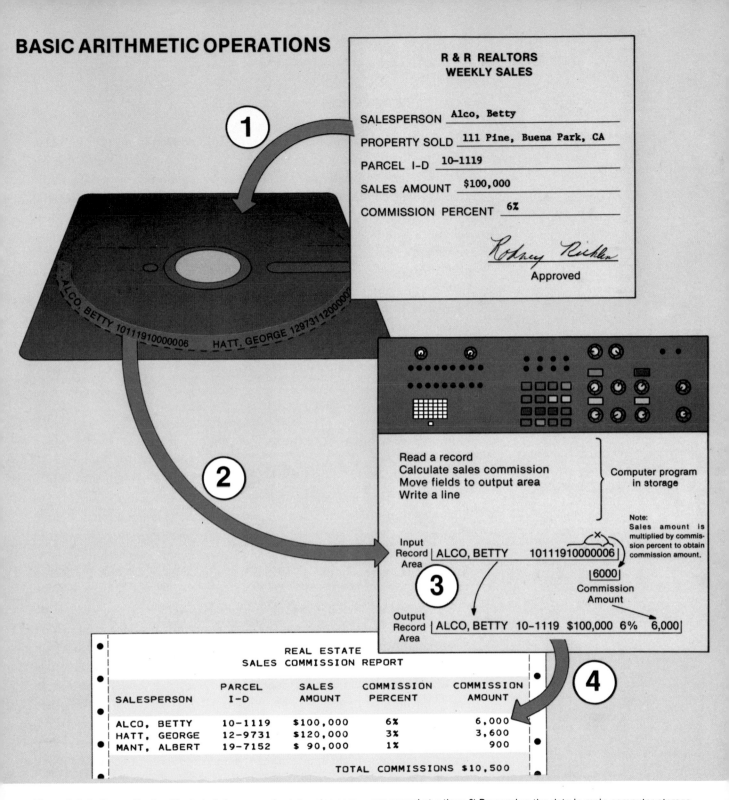

Figure 3-9 In the application illustrated above, a real estate commission report requiring arithmetic operations is prepared from data contained on a weekly sales sheet. The basic steps involve: 1) Recording the data from the weekly sales sheet on a diskette; 2) Under program control, reading the data from the diskette into main computer storage, one record at a time; 3) Processing the data in main computer storage, including calculating the sales commission by multiplying the sales amount by the commission percent and preparing the output record for printing; 4) Printing a line on the report. This sequence will be repeated for each record in the input file.

LOGICAL OPERATIONS

The real power of a computer system is derived from its third basic operation — the ability to compare numbers, letters of the alphabet, or special characters and perform alternative operations based upon the results of the comparison. It is this ability to perform logical operations that allows a computer system to carry out medical diagnoses, play chess, determine if a seat is available on an airplane, or generate the many types of reports required in businesses.

Three types of comparing operations are commonly performed: 1) Comparing to determine if the values in two fields are equal; 2) Comparing to determine if the value in one field is less than the value in another field; 3) Comparing to determine if the value in one field is greater than the value in another field. Based upon the results of these comparisons, the program in main computer storage can direct the computer system to take alternative actions.

Comparing — equal condition

Comparing to determine if the values in two different fields are equal is an important capability of a computer system. One example of comparing to determine if the value in one field is equal to the value in another field is found in educational applications where a grade point average report is to be prepared. The report is to contain a message identifying honor students. An honor student is defined as a student with a straight A average (grade point average = 4.0).

To create this report, the computer program would cause a record to be read into main computer storage. This record would, of course, be stored on a machine-readable medium such as punched cards. Once the record was in main computer storage, the program would compare the value in the grade point average field in the input record to the value 4.0 already stored in main computer storage by the program (Figure 3-10). If the value in the grade point average field in the input record was equal to 4.0, the computer program would cause the "HONOR STUDENT" message to be printed on the report. If the value in the grade point average field was not equal to 4.0, the message would not be printed on the report.

Thus, the computer program can direct the computer system to take alternative action based upon whether the value in one field is equal to the value in another field.

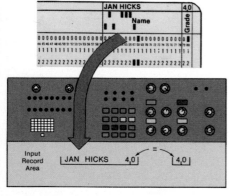

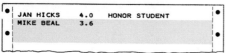

Figure 3-10 The grade point average contained in the input record stored in main computer storage is compared to the value 4.0, also stored in main computer storage. If the grade point average in the input record is equal to 4.0, the computer program will cause the message "HONOR STUDENT" to be printed on the report. If the grade point average in the input record area is not equal to 4.0, the message is not printed on the report.

Comparing — less than condition

Many applications require comparing fields to determine if the value in one field is less than the value in another field. If the value in one field is less than a value in another field, one sequence of operations in the computer program would take place; if the value in a field is equal to or greater than the value in another field, then a different sequence of operations in the program would occur.

Problems of this type are found in the insurance industry when insurance rates are based on age. For example, one insurance company bases its automobile insurance rates on the age of 25. If the applicant is less than 25, one set of insurance rates applies. If the applicant is 25 or more, another set of rates applies.

This example is shown in Figure 3-11. The input record containing the age of the applicant is read into main computer storage. Data can only be compared when it is stored in main computer storage. The age in the input record in storage is compared to the value 25 already stored in main computer storage by the program. If the age is less than 25, the cost of the policy is $700.00. Therefore, the computer program would cause this value to be printed on the report. If the age is 25 or more, the program would cause the value $400.00 to be printed on the report.

Thus, the basis of this comparison operation is to determine if the value in one field is less than the value in another field.

Comparing — greater than condition

Similarly, in many applications, it is necessary to determine if the value in one field is greater than the value in another field. For example, in a payroll application to determine if overtime is to be paid, the hours worked by an employee are compared to the value 40. If the hours worked are greater than 40, then overtime is calculated. If the hours are equal to or less than 40, regular pay is calculated.

In the example in Figure 3-12, the hours worked field for Larry Simms contains 41. Therefore, the computer program would cause the overtime pay to be calculated and printed. If the hours worked field contained 40 or less, overtime pay would not be calculated and printed.

The ability of a computer program to perform a comparing operation and take alternative action based on the result of the comparison is a basic function of all computer systems. It is this ability which gives the computer tremendous power in processing data.

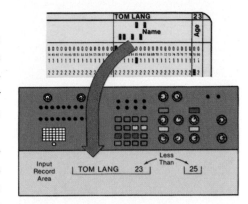
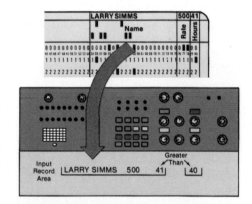

Figure 3-11 The age contained in the input record stored in main computer storage is compared to the value 25 also stored in main computer storage. If the age is less than 25, the high rate of $700.00 is printed. If the age is equal to or greater than 25, the lower rate of $400.00 is printed.

Figure 3-12 The hours field contained in the input record stored in main computer storage is compared to the value 40. If the hours in the input record are greater than 40, overtime pay is calculated and printed by the program. If the hours are equal to or less than 40, overtime pay is not calculated or printed.

It is important to realize that both the comparison operation and the alternative processing based upon the results of the comparison are accomplished by the program stored in main computer storage. Computer programs control the processing which occurs on a computer system.

STORING DATA

The basic processing cycle consists of input, process, and output. An additional element is many times necessary in this cycle — storing data for subsequent use.

When an input record is read into main computer storage and processed, output data is usually generated. In many instances, this output data, together with other data generated from the processing, may have to be used in a subsequent program. Data which is to be used in later programs must be stored on auxiliary storage. Data stored on auxiliary storage can be retrieved at a later time when a program needs it.

Magnetic tape and magnetic disk are the two primary media used for auxiliary storage.

The example in Figure 3–13 illustrates an application where a record is stored on auxiliary storage each time a new banking account is opened. Once the record is stored on auxiliary storage, it can be retrieved and processed by other programs.

The steps involved in building and storing the record on auxiliary storage are: 1) The input record containing the account number, name, and initial deposit is read into computer storage; 2) The auxiliary storage record is built. It contains the account number, name, balance, monthly deposits, and monthly withdrawals. As this is the first transaction for the account, the balance and monthly deposit will both contain 200.00. Since there were no withdrawals, the withdrawal field contains zeros; 3) The record is written on auxiliary storage; 4) A report is generated for the new account.

Figure 3-13 Auxiliary storage is used to store data for subsequent use. The bank account record stored on auxiliary storage contains the account number, name, balance, monthly deposits, and monthly withdrawals. When an additional deposit is made, an input record will indicate the amount. The record on auxiliary storage will then be updated to reflect the deposit and the new balance.

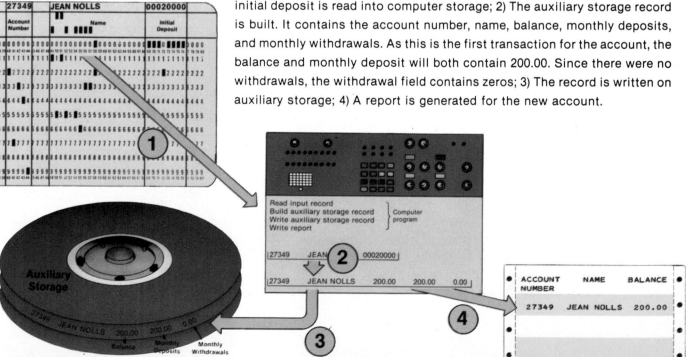

Once the record is stored on auxiliary storage, it is retained for subsequent use. For example, if Jean Nolls makes a deposit to her account, an input record would be prepared containing the amount of the deposit. This input record would be read by a program, and the record on auxiliary storage would also be read into computer storage. The deposit and balance fields would be updated by adding the deposit to them. The record, with the updated information, would then be rewritten onto auxiliary storage.

Storing data on auxiliary storage devices for subsequent processing by computer programs is an important part of processing data on a computer system. Through the ability to store data on auxiliary storage devices and the basic processing cycle of input, process, and output, computer systems can accomplish large amounts of processing accurately and quickly.

Processing

Applications on a

Computer System

The following pages illustrate many of the practical applications of data storage and retrieval, inquiry, updating, sorting, classifying and summarizing which are possible to accomplish on computer systems that use: 1) the basic processing cycle; 2) the three basic operations of input/output, arithmetic, and logical operations; and 3) the ability to store data on auxiliary storage.

The "Personalized" Letter From The Computer

One of the more widespread uses of the computer in the office is word processing. In word processing applications, repetitive data is stored on auxiliary storage and is retrieved as needed in the preparation of letters or reports. This is an example of a basic processing technique involving data storage and retrieval where data is stored on auxiliary storage for retrieval by later programs.

Word processing is justified in companies for a number of reasons. Two primary ones are the rising cost of labor in preparing paperwork and an increasing amount of reporting that must be done to governmental agencies.

Word processing machines come in several configurations. A stand-alone word processing system usually includes a CRT or hardcopy display device, an auxiliary storage device such as a floppy disk, and a fast printer which can print letter-quality type. These devices are under the control of a central processing unit with some main storage.

A shared-logic word processing system has several CRT's, auxiliary storage devices, and printers controlled by one central processing unit.

The use of word processing to create letters, reports, and other paperwork is increasing — it is estimated to be a $1 billion industry now with high growth predicted in the future.

The technology of word processing is increasing the efficiency of the modern office and allows businesses to keep up with their paperwork demands.

The ability to accomplish word processing depends on the basic processing cycle and on the operations of input/output, arithmetic, and logic. The example in Figure 3–15 illustrates how these operations are used to accomplish data storage and retrieval when producing a personalized letter.

Figure 3–14 The Xerox 850 display typing system is typical of word processing systems. The operator can display a full page on the CRT screen while the printer in the background prints a letter which has already been typed. Each letter can be stored on auxiliary storage for later use or modification.

DATA STORAGE AND RETRIEVAL

Figure 3-15 Generating personalized letters is a common word processing application and illustrates data storage and retrieval. Preparing the letter involves the following steps: 1) A series of letters is stored on auxiliary storage; 2) An operator enters a letter number on the terminal corresponding to a letter number stored on the disk; 3) Under program control, the proper letter is retrieved from auxiliary storage and placed in main computer storage; 4) The operator enters the name of the person to receive the letter. This name is placed in the letter by the program; 5) A personalized letter is written to the customer on the printer. The input/output capabilities of a computer system together with the system's logical capabilities are shown in this example of data storage and retrieval.

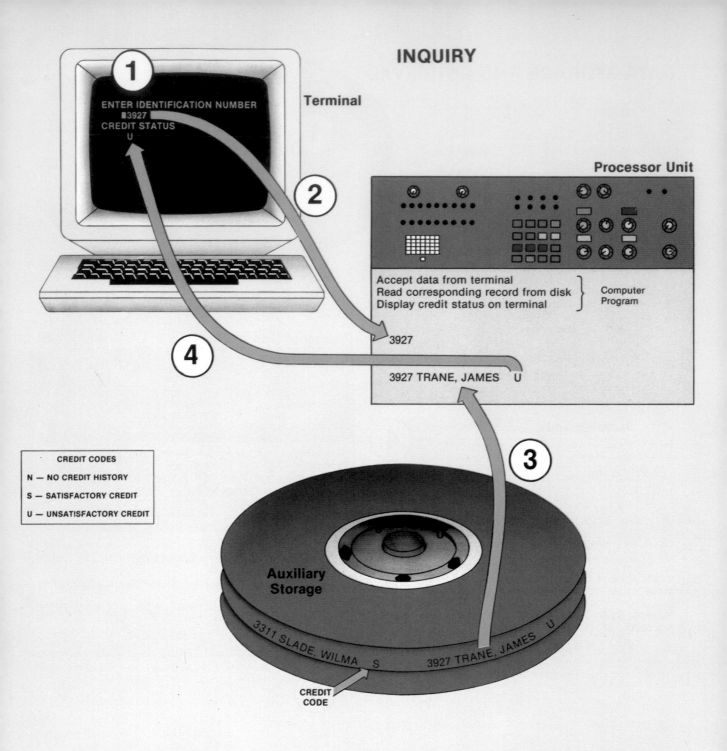

INQUIRY

Terminal

ENTER IDENTIFICATION NUMBER
▮3927
CREDIT STATUS
U

Processor Unit

Accept data from terminal
Read corresponding record from disk   } Computer
Display credit status on terminal   Program

3927

3927 TRANE, JAMES   U

CREDIT CODES

N — NO CREDIT HISTORY

S — SATISFACTORY CREDIT

U — UNSATISFACTORY CREDIT

Auxiliary Storage

3311 SLADE, WILMA   S   3927 TRANE, JAMES   U

CREDIT CODE

Figure 3-16 The procedure to perform an inquiry involves a number of steps: 1) The terminal operator enters an identification number (such as a customer number) into the terminal; 2) The identification number is transmitted and stored in main computer storage; 3) On the basis of the identification number (frequently called a "key"), the computer program reads the corresponding record from auxiliary storage into main computer storage; 4) The requested information from the disk record stored in main computer storage is transmitted back to the terminal. In the example, the information requested for customer 3927 is displayed on the CRT as "U," indicating an unsatisfactory credit rating. This cycle of inputting the customer number, retrieving the record from auxiliary storage and extracting the required information, and sending the information back to the operator can be done in less than one second on many systems.

Figure 3-17 Operators can enter inquiry data on a terminal to obtain information from the centrally located computer system. Under program control, the data is retrieved from auxiliary storage devices and sent over telephone lines to the terminal operator.

The Use

Of

"Data Banks"

With the widespread use of computer terminals and the ability to communicate over transmission lines, inquiry into files stored on auxiliary storage devices has become an important application area. Inquiries require the input/output and logical capabilities of a computer system.

When a purchase is made using a credit card, a computer terminal is likely to be used to perform an inquiry verifying the credit rating. An airline ticket agent usually uses a terminal to determine if there are any seats on an airplane flight. In many states, when a driver is stopped for a traffic violation, the police officer can make a direct inquiry into a file to determine if there are any unpaid traffic tickets or outstanding arrest warrants.

All of these applications involve storing data on auxiliary storage and using a computer terminal connected to a computer system to retrieve the information required. This process of accepting an inquiry, retrieving the data from auxiliary storage, and sending the answer take place under control of the computer program.

The processing of an inquiry is an application of the basic processing cycle of input, process, and output (Figure 3-16).

How Much

Is In My

Savings Account?

When files are created and stored on auxiliary storage, they will contain up-to-date information. As time passes, however, the data originally placed in the file will become obsolete. Therefore, it is necessary to "update" information stored on auxiliary storage with new data.

In some applications, this update processing will occur periodically. These applications do not require up-to-the-minute information.

In other applications, however, the data stored in files on auxiliary storage must be updated the moment a transaction occurs to change the data. Many banks find this type of updating is required.

Files are built which contain the balance in accounts in banks. Whenever a deposit or withdrawal is made, the balance in the file must be updated immediately so that it always reflects the correct amount.

When files are updated each time a transaction takes place, it is another example of the basic processing cycle of input (transaction entered), processing (retrieving proper record, changing it, and rewriting it), and output (notification to teller of new balance).

Figure 3–18 Updating customer account files is a common application in the banking industry.

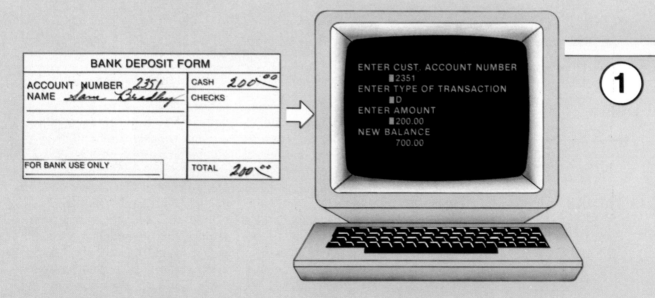

UPDATING

Step 1: The teller enters the customer's account number, the type of transaction ("W" for withdrawal, "D" for deposit), and the amount of the transaction. This data is then transmitted to main computer storage. After performing step 2 and step 3, the transaction is complete, and the new balance is transmitted back to the teller.

Figure 3-19 The use of terminals to update accounts in banking applications is common. Here, the teller is entering data on the terminal in order to update the account of a customer.

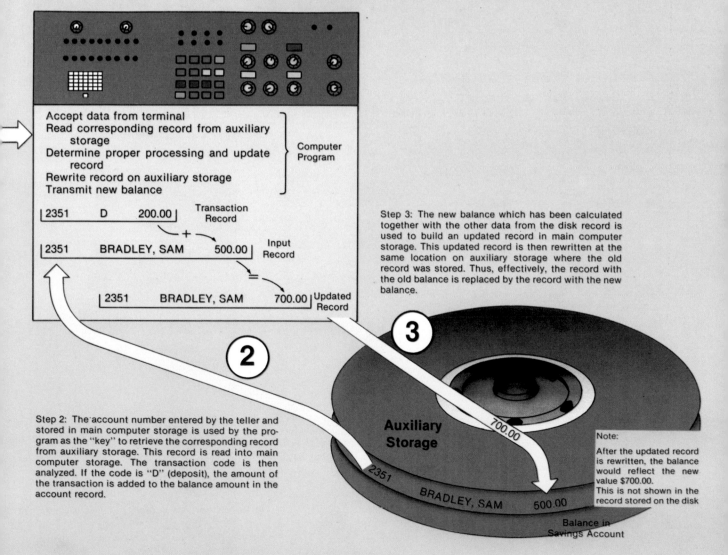

Accept data from terminal
Read corresponding record from auxiliary storage
Determine proper processing and update record
Rewrite record on auxiliary storage
Transmit new balance
} Computer Program

| 2351 | D | 200.00 | Transaction Record

+

| 2351 | BRADLEY, SAM | 500.00 | Input Record

=

| 2351 | BRADLEY, SAM | 700.00 | Updated Record

Step 3: The new balance which has been calculated together with the other data from the disk record is used to build an updated record in main computer storage. This updated record is then rewritten at the same location on auxiliary storage where the old record was stored. Thus, effectively, the record with the old balance is replaced by the record with the new balance.

Step 2: The account number entered by the teller and stored in main computer storage is used by the program as the "key" to retrieve the corresponding record from auxiliary storage. This record is read into main computer storage. The transaction code is then analyzed. If the code is "D" (deposit), the amount of the transaction is added to the balance amount in the account record.

Auxiliary Storage

700.00

2351

BRADLEY, SAM 500.00

Note:
After the updated record is rewritten, the balance would reflect the new value $700.00. This is not shown in the record stored on the disk

Balance in Savings Account

SORTING-ASCENDING SEQUENCE

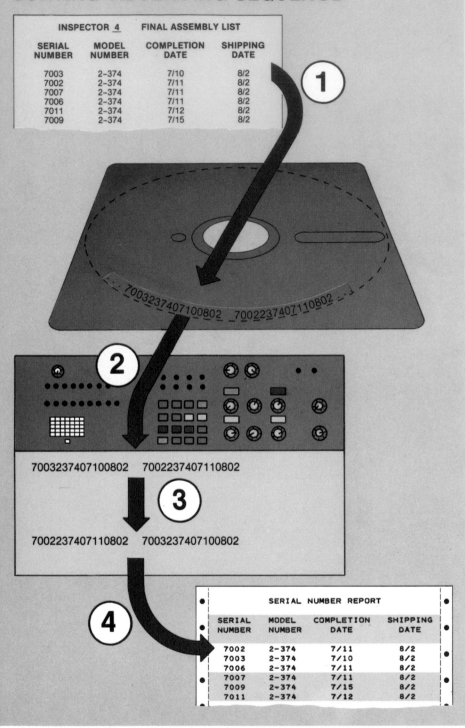

INSPECTOR 4		FINAL ASSEMBLY LIST	
SERIAL NUMBER	MODEL NUMBER	COMPLETION DATE	SHIPPING DATE
7003	2-374	7/10	8/2
7002	2-374	7/11	8/2
7007	2-374	7/11	8/2
7006	2-374	7/11	8/2
7011	2-374	7/12	8/2
7009	2-374	7/15	8/2

7003237407100802   7002237407110802

7002237407110802   7003237407100802

SERIAL NUMBER REPORT			
SERIAL NUMBER	MODEL NUMBER	COMPLETION DATE	SHIPPING DATE
7002	2-374	7/11	8/2
7003	2-374	7/10	8/2
7006	2-374	7/11	8/2
7007	2-374	7/11	8/2
7009	2-374	7/15	8/2
7011	2-374	7/12	8/2

Figure 3-20 The input data to the above application is captured from the final assembly list from each inspector. The serial number report is to be in ascending sequence by serial number. The following steps take place: 1) The data is recorded in a machine-readable format; 2) The input data is read into main computer storage; 3) The data is sorted by serial number. Although not shown, auxiliary storage is many times used for temporary storage during the sorting processing; 4) The sorted data is used to create the report.

Rearranging

Records

Data stored as input records or data stored on auxiliary storage can be arranged in an ascending or a descending sequence through sorting. For example, records can be sorted in an ascending sequence by serial number to produce a serial number report (Figure 3-20). Records can also be sorted in a descending sequence by quantity to produce a sales by quantity report (Figure 3-22).

Although sorting is used in many application areas, it is particularly useful in a manufacturing environment where parts and products are used and produced (Figure 3-21). For example, assembly lines which build computers and computer components require many thousands of

Figure 3-21 Assembly lines to build computer hardware such as illustrated below are commonly found in the computer industry. In most

ORDER SHEET

Date 8/15

SERIAL NUMBER	QUANTITY	BUYER
7473	15	McJones
7474	30	Hale
7475	1	Hanes
7476	3	Norass
7477	5	Shims
7478	13	Dilbert

parts. These parts must be at the proper place at the proper time so that the assembly line will keep moving. In addition, each part must be accounted for. By acquiring the data and then sorting the data in various sequences, the required information to schedule parts and report on them can be produced. This would be extremely difficult and time consuming without the use of a computer system.

It is the ability of the computer system to compare two values and determine that one is greater than the other which allows sorting to be accomplished rapidly and accurately. Sorting is accomplished by a program written specifically to sort data.

cases, computer systems are used to control and report on the manufacture of other computer systems.

① 747315MCJONES   747430HALE . . .

② 747315MCJONES   747430HALE . . .

③ 747430HALE   747315MCJONES . . .

SALES BY QUANTITY
DATE 8/15

SERIAL NUMBER	QUANTITY	BUYER
7474	30	HALE
7473	15	MCJONES
7478	13	DILBERT
7477	5	SHIMS
7476	3	NORASS
7475	1	HANES

④

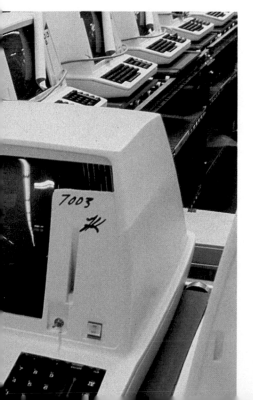

Figure 3-22 The sales by quantity report is created from data entered on an order sheet. The report is to be in a descending sequence by quantity, with the highest quantity first and the lowest quantity last. The following steps occur: 1) The serial number, quantity, and buyer name are recorded on magnetic tape for reading into storage; 2) The data is read into main computer storage; 3) The data is sorted by quantity, using auxiliary storage if required; 4) The report is created from the sorted data.

Manipulating Data And Records

Data can be manipulated in many ways by a program in a computer system to produce useful information which would many times be difficult, if not impossible, to obtain by other means. Four of the more common types of processing are: 1) Control break reporting; 2) Selecting; 3) Classifying; 4) Summarizing.

Control break reporting requires that the input data be grouped according to a control value. For example, input records can be grouped according to invoice number. When the invoice number changes, a control break has occurred. When a control break occurs, special processing can take place. For example, invoice totals can be printed.

Certain data can be selected for processing based upon some criteria. For example, all invoices with a value less than $20.00 can be printed while those with a value equal to or greater than $20.00 are not printed.

Classifying data occurs when data is separated into different classes according to some specification. For example, invoice records can be read; each food item on the invoice is printed on one report, and each non-food item is printed on another report.

Summarizing involves processing records and accumulating values contained in the records. For example, invoice records could be read and each salesman's sales could be accumulated. After all of the records are read, the total sales for each salesman can be printed.

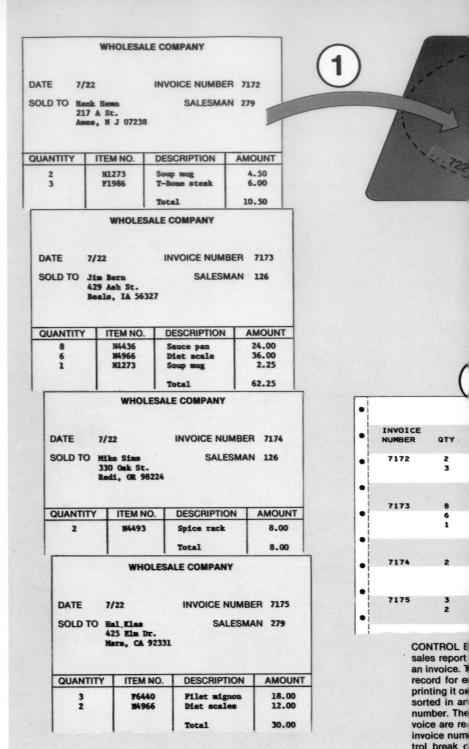

Figure 3-23 The applications above showing control break reporting, selecting, classifying, and summarizing involve the following steps: 1) The data on the source document is recorded on a machine-readable medium. In this case, a record for each item on an invoice is placed on a floppy disk; 2) After the data is recorded on the floppy disk, it will be read into main computer storage. The data will be read into storage, one record at a time. As the data

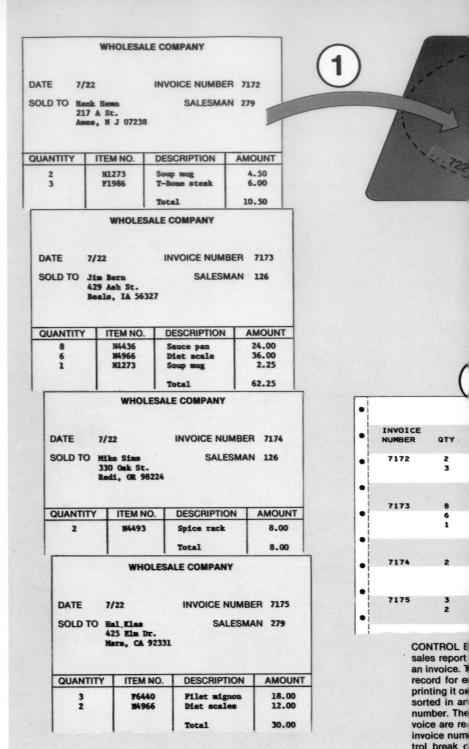

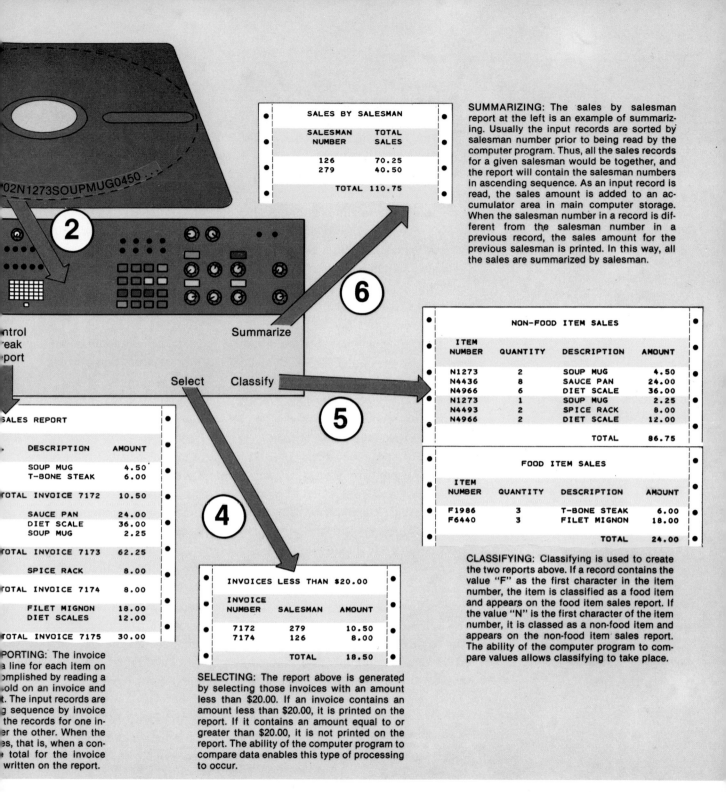

SALES BY SALESMAN

SALESMAN NUMBER	TOTAL SALES
126	70.25
279	40.50
TOTAL	110.75

SUMMARIZING: The sales by salesman report at the left is an example of summarizing. Usually the input records are sorted by salesman number prior to being read by the computer program. Thus, all the sales records for a given salesman would be together, and the report will contain the salesman numbers in ascending sequence. As an input record is read, the sales amount is added to an accumulator area in main computer storage. When the salesman number in a record is different from the salesman number in a previous record, the sales amount for the previous salesman is printed. In this way, all the sales are summarized by salesman.

ntrol
reak
port

Summarize

Select   Classify

NON-FOOD ITEM SALES

ITEM NUMBER	QUANTITY	DESCRIPTION	AMOUNT
N1273	2	SOUP MUG	4.50
N4436	8	SAUCE PAN	24.00
N4966	6	DIET SCALE	36.00
N1273	1	SOUP MUG	2.25
N4493	2	SPICE RACK	8.00
N4966	2	DIET SCALE	12.00
		TOTAL	86.75

FOOD ITEM SALES

ITEM NUMBER	QUANTITY	DESCRIPTION	AMOUNT
F1986	3	T-BONE STEAK	6.00
F6440	3	FILET MIGNON	18.00
		TOTAL	24.00

SALES REPORT

DESCRIPTION	AMOUNT
SOUP MUG	4.50
T-BONE STEAK	6.00
TOTAL INVOICE 7172	10.50
SAUCE PAN	24.00
DIET SCALE	36.00
SOUP MUG	2.25
TOTAL INVOICE 7173	62.25
SPICE RACK	8.00
TOTAL INVOICE 7174	8.00
FILET MIGNON	18.00
DIET SCALES	12.00
TOTAL INVOICE 7175	30.00

PORTING: The invoice
a line for each item on
omplished by reading a
old on an invoice and
. The input records are
g sequence by invoice
the records for one in-
er the other. When the
s, that is, when a con-
total for the invoice
written on the report.

INVOICES LESS THAN $20.00

INVOICE NUMBER	SALESMAN	AMOUNT
7172	279	10.50
7174	126	8.00
TOTAL		18.50

SELECTING: The report above is generated by selecting those invoices with an amount less than $20.00. If an invoice contains an amount less than $20.00, it is printed on the report. If it contains an amount equal to or greater than $20.00, it is not printed on the report. The ability of the computer program to compare data enables this type of processing to occur.

CLASSIFYING: Classifying is used to create the two reports above. If a record contains the value "F" as the first character in the item number, the item is classified as a food item and appears on the food item sales report. If the value "N" is the first character of the item number, it is classed as a non-food item and appears on the non-food item sales report. The ability of the computer program to compare values allows classifying to take place.

is read into storage, one of four reports can be prepared; 3) The control break report contains a detail list of each item on an invoice. When the invoice number changes (a control break occurs), the total for the invoice is printed; 4) The selection report contains any invoice with a total sales amount less than $20.00; 5) The classification processing produces two reports — one which contains all of the non-food items and one which contains all of the food items that have been sold; 6) The summarizing processing creates a report summarizing the sales by each salesman. The input records are usually sorted by salesman number to create this report.

Chapter summary

The following points have been discussed and explained in this chapter.

1. The basic operations of any computer system are input/output operations, arithmetic operations, and logic operations.

2. The basic processing cycle includes operations causing data to be placed in main computer storage (input), the processing of that data placed in main computer storage (processing), and operations causing the results of the processing to be placed in a format usable by other machines or by human beings (output).

3. Computers process data.

4. Data is a representation of facts, concepts, or instructions in a formalized manner suitable for communication, interpretation, and processing by humans or automatic machines.

5. Data to be processed on a computer system is usually organized into fields, records, and files.

6. A field is one unit of data.

7. A record is a collection of fields related to a specific unit of information.

8. Records are normally organized into a file.

9. A file is a collection of related records.

10. Logical records, normally organized as a file, are commonly stored on an external medium such as punched cards, magnetic tape, or magnetic disk prior to being read into main computer storage for processing.

11. The basic steps in performing input/output operations include: a) Converting data to a machine-processable form such as punched cards, magnetic tape, or magnetic disk; b) Reading the data into an input record area in main computer storage; c) Moving the data in the input record in main computer storage to an output record area in main computer storage; d) Writing the output record, commonly as a line on a printed report.

12. One of the important features of any computer system is the ability to perform calculations at a very rapid rate.

13. Once data is stored in main computer storage, the computer program can direct the electronic circuitry to add, subtract, multiply, and divide the data. If necessary, the answer can be stored in main computer storage for further processing.

14. Computer programs stored in main computer storage can compare numbers, letters of the alphabet, or special characters. Based upon the results of the comparisons, alternative operations in the program can be performed.

15. Three types of comparing operations are commonly performed: a) Comparing to determine if the values in two fields are equal; b) Comparing to determine if the value in one field is less than the value in another field; c) Comparing to determine if the value in one field is greater than the value in another field.

16. Storing data on auxiliary storage devices for subsequent use is often necessary in many computerized applications.

17. One of the more widespread uses of the computer in the office is word processing, where repetitive data is stored on auxiliary storage and retrieved as needed in the preparation of letters or reports.

18. Word processing machines are available in several configurations: Stand-alone word processing systems and shared-logic word processing systems.

19. Inquiry into files stored on auxiliary storage is a common computer system application.

20. The inquiry procedure involves the following steps: a) The terminal operator enters an identification number; b) The identification number is transmitted and stored in main computer storage; c) On the basis of the identification number, the corresponding record is retrieved from auxiliary storage and placed in main computer storage; d) The requested information from the retrieved record is sent back to the terminal.

21. When files are created and stored on auxiliary storage, they must be updated to contain the most current information.

22. Data stored as input records or on auxiliary storage devices can be arranged in an ascending or descending sequence through the use of sorting. This is accomplished through the ability of the computer system to compare two values and determine that one is greater than or less than the other.

23. Once data has been captured in the machine-readable format, it can be manipulated in ways which would many times be difficult, if not impossible, without computer systems. Four of the more common types of processing are: a) Control break reporting; b) Selecting; c) Classifying; d) Summarizing.

Student Learning Exercises

Review questions

1. List the basic operations which may be performed by a computer system.

2. Explain the basic processing cycle that occurs on every computer system.

3. Define the term "data."

4. Explain the relationship between files, records, and fields. Give an example of each.

5. Explain how input/output operations occur within a computer system. Draw a diagram of an application illustrating these operations.

6. Through the use of a diagram, explain how arithmetic operations occur on a computer system. The diagram should illustrate a typical application found on a computer system.

7. What are the three basic types of comparing operations that occur under the control of a computer program in a computer system?

8. What is a typical application that would use the processing concepts of storage and retrieval on a computer system? Illustrate this application through the use of step-by-step drawings.

9. Name three different application areas that might use the inquiry ability of a computer system. Choose one of the applications and draw a step-by-step illustration of the processing which would occur.

10. Explain what is meant by "file updating." Name five applications where updating is critical to the proper processing of the application.

11. Give an example where it is necessary to sort a file of records into three different sequences in order to obtain the information necessary for an application.

12. What is meant by a control break report? By selecting? By classifying? By summarizing?

Controversial issues in data processing

1. In computerized dating bureaus, applicants are given a psychological test to determine their likes, dislikes, personality, etc. Their data is then recorded on an input record, read into a computer system, and compared to other applicants to determine which applicants most nearly match one another. Their data will also be stored on auxiliary storage so that it can be matched to subsequent applicants. Because of the computer's rapid internal processing speed and storage, hundreds and even thousands of applicants can be compared. Is this a legitimate application for a computer system? Write a one page report supporting your position.

2. Medical diagnosis is an area where the ability of a computer program to compare data is used. In some hospitals, it is possible for patients to "tell" a computer their symptoms by answering a series of questions. The program stored in main computer storage then compares the symptoms to those retrieved from auxiliary storage and placed in main computer storage. When equal conditions are found, a diagnosis will be given and, perhaps, medication prescribed. Does this process take away the proper role of a doctor? Is the computer system doing the same type of "thinking" that a doctor does when analyzing symptoms? Defend your answer.

Research projects

1. Visit a local store, hospital, bank, or manufacturing plant and determine what type of computer inquiry systems they use. Write a report and present it to class. Supplement the report by means of diagrams illustrating the processing that occurs in the application selected.

2. Bring a "personalized" computer-generated letter to class. Explain the contents of the letter and discuss your reaction upon receiving the letter.

Picture credits

Figure 3–14	Xerox Corporation	Figure 3–19	NCR Corporation
Figure 3–17	Raytheon Company	Figure 3–21	Basic Four Corporation

Chapter 4
The Processor Unit

Objectives

- An understanding of how data is stored in main computer storage

- An understanding of the EBCDIC coding scheme

- An understanding of storing and referencing characters and fields stored in addressable main computer storage

- An understanding of the elements comprising a computer instruction and the method used by the central processing unit to execute an instruction

- An understanding of variable word length machines and fixed word length machines

- An understanding of the history, manufacture, and types of main computer storage

Chapter 4

Figure 4-1 The Computer Automation NAKED MINI[R] Family 4/10 series processor is stored on a single board. The entire processor unit, including the central processing unit and some main computer storage, is included. Input/output units and a few other components are required to complete the computer system.

The Processor Unit

"Before the end of the century, 100 billion gates will be put on a chip — roughly equal to the number of neurons in the human brain."[1]

Introduction

The basic processing cycle of input, process, and output requires that data be read into main computer storage from an input device prior to being processed. Once the data has been stored in main computer storage, the computer system, under control of a computer program, can process the data and create output.

Whenever data is to be processed, it must first be stored in main computer storage. The electronics in the central processing unit (CPU) then can interpret computer instructions in the program and cause the processing to occur. Both main computer storage and the central processing unit are contained in the processor unit of the computer system. Processor units can vary from very large devices to "computers on a board" (Figure 4–1). Regardless of their size, they perform basically the same functions — store data to be processed and, under control of the computer program, process the data.

It is the purpose of this chapter to examine the way in which data is stored in main computer storage, to explain the concept of addressable storage, and to follow the events which occur when instructions are executed on a computer system.

How is data stored?

Modern computer systems store data electronically. Through various methods and electronic components, the circuitry of a computer system can sense the presence or absence of electronic impulses. It is this ability to sense these impulses that allows data to be stored in main computer storage.

---

1 Dr. Earl Joseph in "Future of Technology: Fact Eerier Than Fiction," E. Drake Lundell, Jr., COMPUTERWORLD, Vol. XIII, No. 32, August 6, 1979, p.1.

"ON" "OFF"

Figure 4-2 A bit (binary digit) in main computer storage can assume one of two possible values — "on" or "off." This is symbolically represented by a darkened circle indicating the bit is "on," and an open circle indicating the bit is "off."

The basic unit for storing data in main computer storage is the "bit" (binary digit). This single unit in storage can assume one of two possible values. It can either be considered "on," or it can be considered "off" (Figure 4–2). The determination of whether a bit is "on" or "off" is made by the electronics in the computer hardware. Some computers make this determination by the polarity of magnetized material, while others determine the status of a bit by whether or not electricity is flowing along a circuit.

Regardless of the electronic means used to detect whether a bit is "on" or "off," it is the ability of the computer electronics to identify the status of a bit which is the basis for storing data in main computer storage.

A single bit with only the ability to be "on" or "off" is not sufficient to store all the numbers, letters of the alphabet, and special characters needed to process data on a computer system. Therefore, computer designers decided that the way to represent actual data in main computer storage was to utilize a series of bits. Codes are assigned to the various combinations which can be obtained from the series of bits being "on" or "off." The various combinations represent letters of the alphabet, numbers, and special characters.

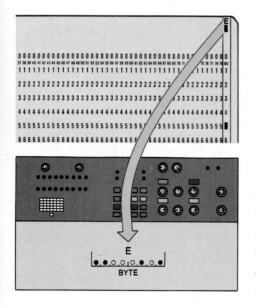

Figure 4-3 When a character is read from a punched card into main computer storage, the electronic circuitry converts the holes in the punched card to a combination of "on" and "off" bits in a byte of main storage. These "on" and "off" bits in the byte represent the character read. Here, the letter of the alphabet "E" is shown as it would be stored in a byte of main computer storage after being read from a punched card.

Extended binary coded decimal interchange code (EBCDIC)

One of the most commonly used coding schemes, called the Extended Binary Coded Decimal Interchange Code (EBCDIC), uses eight bits to store a letter of the alphabet, number, or special character. These eight bits together are called a "byte." Thus, as a character is read into main computer storage, it is stored in a byte of storage (Figure 4–3). The electronics of the computer system interpret the character which is read from an input device and form the correct bit pattern to represent the character. This bit pattern is stored in a byte, and when the byte is referenced in a computer instruction, the correct character will be processed.

With EBCDIC, each byte is divided into two portions — the zone portion of the byte and the digit portion of the byte (Figure 4–4). The bits in both the zone portion of the byte and the digit portion of the byte are assigned numeric values based upon the binary number system, forming the basis for a logical representation of data in storage (for a detailed explanation of the binary number system, see Appendix C).

Representing numeric values in storage

Numeric values are represented in EBCDIC with all the zone bits "on," and the proper combination of bits in the digit portion of the byte "on" to represent the particular numeric value.

In Figure 4-5, the value zero is represented by all of the bits in the zone portion of the byte being "on," and all of the bits in the digit portion of the byte being "off." The value one is represented by the bits in the zone portion of the byte being "on" and the bit with the place value of 1 in the digit portion of the byte being "on."

The digit portion of the byte to represent the value 2 has the bit with the place value 2 "on." The digit portion of the byte representing the value 3 has the bit with the place value 2 and the bit with the place value 1 "on." The numbers 4-9 are represented in a similar manner.

It is the proper combination of bits "on" in the digit portion of the byte, together with all of the bits in the zone portion of the byte being "on," which represents numeric values in main computer storage with the EBCDIC coding format.

Each decimal digit is stored in a single byte when using EBCDIC. Therefore, numbers such as 10, 11, or 12 require two bytes of storage — one for each digit.

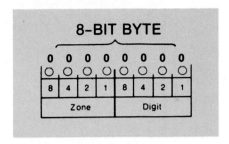

Figure 4-4 Each bit in the zone portion of the byte and each bit in the digit portion of the byte are assigned a value based on the binary number system. It is a particular combination of these bits being "on" or "off" that represents data in storage. There are 256 possible code combinations in an 8-bit byte.

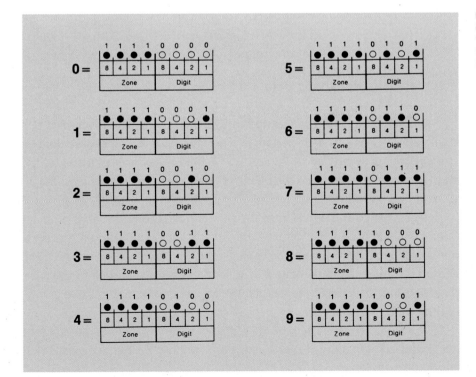

Figure 4-5 Numbers are represented in EBCDIC by all of the zone bits "on," and the digit bits "on" that represent the particular number. Bits that are "on" are represented by a "1." Bits that are "off" are represented by a "0."

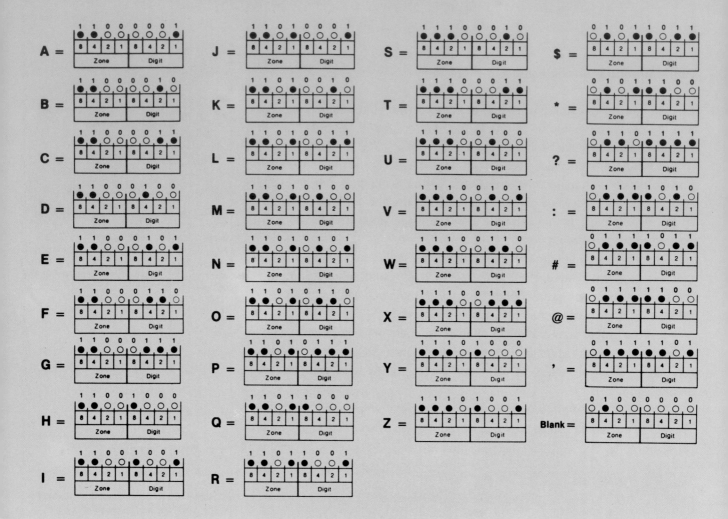

Figure 4-6 The letters of the alphabet and the special characters each have a unique bit configuration when using EBCDIC. EBCDIC gained prominence on the System/360. It is used for most computers manufactured by IBM.

Representing alphabetic data in storage

Alphabetic data is represented in EBCDIC with a combination of bits "on" and "off" (Figure 4-6). Letters of the alphabet A through I have the bits corresponding to the 8 and 4 values "on" in the zone portion of the byte. The digit portion of the byte has the bit corresponding to 1 "on" for an A, the bit corresponding to 2 "on" for a B, and so on.

The letters J through R have the bits corresponding to the 8, 4, and 1 values "on" in the zone portion of the byte. In the digit portion of the byte, the value 1 bit is "on" for a J, the value 2 bit is "on" for the K, and so on. The letters S through Z contain bits 8, 4, 2 "on" in the zone portion of the byte. The digit portion of the byte has the bit corresponding to the value 2 "on" for the letter S, and so on.

Thus, each of the letters of the alphabet is represented in storage by a particular combination of bits being "on" or "off" in the zone and digit portion of a byte.

Storing special characters

The special characters illustrated in Figure 4-6 each contain a special bit configuration to represent the character. It might be noted that the character blank has the bit with the place value 4 "on" in the zone portion of the byte and all bits "off" in the digit portion of byte. Thus, even a blank has a unique bit configuration.

Size of main computer storage

Main computer storage is composed of numerous bytes. Computers are found with as few as 4,096 bytes (known as 4K, for 4 thousand), and as many as 16 million bytes (known as 16 megabytes — "mega" meaning million). Typically, microcomputers will contain somewhere between 4K and 64K bytes in main computer storage. Minicomputers may contain between 64K and 1 megabyte. Larger computers typically have main computer storage with between 512K bytes and 16 megabytes. The amount of computer storage obtained in a computer system is normally related to the size and complexity of the applications to be processed.

Addressable storage

When data is read into main computer storage from a punched card, a floppy disk, or a terminal, it is interpreted by the electronic circuitry and stored in a byte with the proper bits "on" and "off." In order for the data to be processed, the computer program must be able to indicate to the electronic circuitry in the CPU where the data is located in main computer storage. Therefore, each byte in main computer storage has a unique address associated with it.

An address in main computer storage identifies each byte. It is a unique number which is assigned when the storage is wired into the computer system. When a computer program causes a character to be read into main computer storage, the program specifies where in storage the character is to be placed by specifying the address. In Figure 4-7, the program directs that the page number entered from the terminal is to be stored at address 2000.

This ability to store data at unique addresses within main computer storage allows the use of the data in subsequent operations such as arithmetic, logical, and input/output operations.

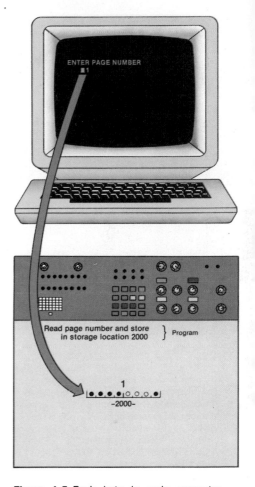

Figure 4-7 Each byte in main computer storage has a unique address so that the computer program can reference the address and process the data stored in the byte at that address. In the illustration above, the program directs the computer system to place the page number entered by the terminal operator at storage location 2000. After the page number is stored at location 2000, subsequent instructions in the program can reference storage location 2000 and process the value stored in the byte.

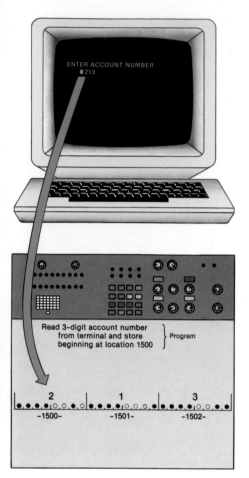

Figure 4-8 In the illustration above, the program specifies that the 3-digit account number is to be read from the terminal into main computer storage beginning at location 1500. Therefore, the first digit of the account number (2) is stored at location 1500. The second digit of the account number (1) is placed in the next adjacent location (1501). The third digit is stored in location 1502. It should be noted that when the computer programmer writes the program, the exact storage locations will usually not be specified. They will be generated when the program is translated to machine language.

Storing fields

Numbers or letters of the alphabet stored as a field in an input record are recorded in main computer storage in adjacent, addressable storage locations. In Figure 4–8, for example, the account number 213 is entered into storage locations 1500, 1501, and 1502. Once in storage, this data can be processed as a field — the account number field.

When a field is processed, computer instructions must specify not only the location of the field in storage, but also the number of characters in the field to be processed. Typically, the instruction will contain the address of the first byte of the field and the length of the field. In this way, the electronics of the computer system can reference the correct data. For example, to reference the account number in storage, a computer instruction must indicate that the account number is stored beginning at storage location 1500 and is 3 bytes in length.

Alphabetic data is entered into main computer storage in the same manner as numeric data. The only difference is that different bit configurations are used to represent letters of the alphabet. Each letter of the alphabet is placed in a byte at a given address within main computer storage.

In summary, as input records are read into main computer storage, each character in the input record is stored at an addressable storage location. Thus, a punched card containing 80 characters would require 80 bytes of storage. Each character and field in the record that is in storage can be referenced by a unique address.

Manipulating data in main computer storage

Once data has been recorded in main computer storage, it can be referenced and manipulated. It can be moved to other locations in main computer storage, used in arithmetic operations, compared to other data in storage, or otherwise be processed to prepare the desired output information. This is possible because of the ability of the computer program to direct the electronic circuitry to extract data located at a specific address and use the data for processing.

In Figure 4–9, a segment of the operations required to produce a printed report from data contained in punched cards is shown. Under control of the computer program, the data from the input record is read into main computer storage at a specific address. The fields in the input record area are then moved to the fields in the output area. The instructions causing this to happen will reference both the address of the input fields and the address of the output fields in main computer storage. The fields in the output record area are then written on the report.

The ability to address data stored in main computer storage and process it after it is addressed form the basis of the internal operations in a computer system.

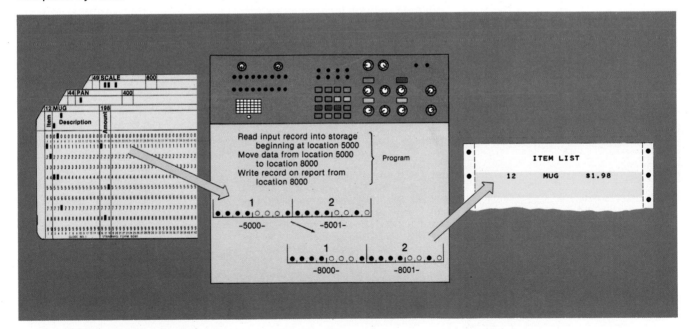

Figure 4-9 In the example above, only the item number field is illustrated in main computer storage. In reality, the entire record would be stored in adjacent storage locations when the record is read into main computer storage. After the data is read into an area in main computer storage reserved for the input record, it can be moved to an output area for printing on a report. The item number is moved from locations 5000-5001 to locations 8000-8001. After the data is moved from locations 5000-5001 to locations 8000-8001, it is still available for processing in locations 5000-5001. Thus, data is essentially duplicated in main computer storage when it is moved from one location to another.

Use of main computer storage

When a number, letter of the alphabet, or special character is read from an input device into main computer storage or is moved from one location to another, the character is stored using its assigned bit configuration. Once a character or bit configuration has been stored in a location in main computer storage, it will remain in that location until another character is placed in the same location.

This feature of main computer storage has two important consequences. First, once data is placed in a location in storage, it will remain there until changed. This allows the program to reference the data for any processing which might be required while the program is being executed.

Second, since data which is moved to or read into a particular location in storage replaces the data which was stored there, a single set of instructions in a computer program which reference particular locations in main computer storage can be used to process many different records which would each be stored in the same storage locations as they are processed. This ability enables a computer programmer to write one sequence of instructions which can process hundreds or thousands of different records.

Figure 4-10 illustrates the processing that occurs as a series of area codes are entered into computer storage from a computer terminal. The first area code, 212, is entered from the terminal and is stored at storage locations 6000, 6001, and 6002. The field, once in storage, would then be processed as required.

When the second area code, 714, is entered from the terminal, it is also stored in storage locations 6000, 6001, and 6002. It replaces the value 212 which was previously stored in these locations. Area code 714 can then be processed by the same instructions which processed area code 212.

STORAGE — AFTER READING THE FIRST ENTRY

Read area code from terminal and store beginning at location 6000

```
    2           1           2
-6000-      -6001-      -6002-
```

STORAGE — AFTER READING THE SECOND ENTRY

Read area code from terminal and store beginning at location 6000

```
    7           1           4
-6000-      -6001-      -6002-
```

Figure 4-10 The instruction in the computer program specifies that the area code is to be read into main computer storage beginning with location 6000. The next 2 digits are placed in storage locations 6001 and 6002. This field would then be processed by the computer program. The same read instruction would then be repeated. When the read instruction is executed a second time, the value "714" entered by the terminal operator is stored in storage locations 6000, 6001, and 6002. This concept is sometimes referred to as "destructive read in."

Computer instructions

The operations performed by a computer are controlled by a computer program. A computer program consists of instructions to the electronics of the computer system to process data in some manner. Program instructions are stored in main computer storage as machine language instructions which the electronic circuits of the computer system can interpret and execute. A knowledge of the basic characteristics of machine language instructions is useful in understanding how a computer operates.

A machine language instruction is composed of: 1) An operation code; 2) Values indicating the number of characters to be processed by the instruction; 3) The addresses of the data to be used in the processing (Figure 4-11).

The operation code is a unique value which is typically stored in a single byte. This unique value indicates to the computer electronics what operation is to occur. For example, the letter of the alphabet "A" stored as the operation code might indicate that an addition operation is to occur. The letter "D" might mean that division is to take place.

The number of characters to be processed must be included in a computer instruction so that the electronic circuitry of the processor unit will reference the proper number of digits in the field to be processed. For example, if a four digit field were to be added to another four digit field, the number of characters specified in the instruction for each field would be four.

The locations of the fields involved in the operation must be specified in the instruction. This enables the circuitry to identify where in storage the data to be processed is located.

Although the formats of computer instructions vary a great deal between different computer systems, the basic elements of operation code, number of characters to process, and the addresses of the data to be processed will almost always be present.

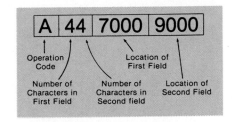

Figure 4-11 The instruction illustrated above is representative of machine-language instructions. The exact format of the instructions varies among different types of computers. The instruction above contains an operation code (A) which indicates it is used to add two numbers. The number of characters for the first and second fields specifies the number of digits in each field to be added. The location of the first field (7000) specifies the address of the first field to be added. The location of the second field (9000) specifies the address of the second field to be added. The answer will typically be stored in the location of the first field. When the instruction is executed, the four digits located at address 9000-9003 will be added to the four digits stored at address 7000-7003 and the answer will be stored at location 7000-7003.

The central processing unit

Instructions stored in main computer storage control the operations which occur within the central processing unit. The central processing unit (CPU) is the heart of the computer system. It contains the electronic circuitry which actually causes processing to occur. The CPU interprets the instructions in a computer program, performs the calculations and the moving of data as specified by the program, and controls the input/output operations of the system.

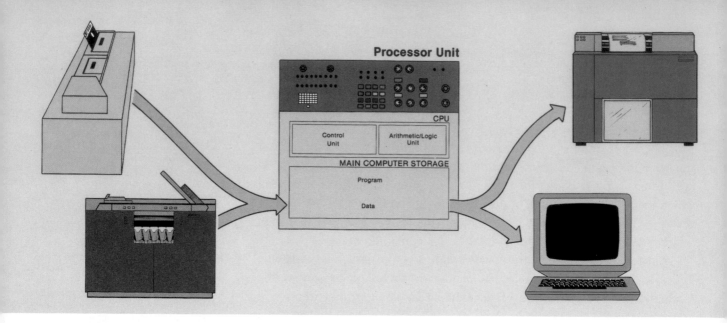

Processor Unit

CPU

Control Unit

Arithmetic/Logic Unit

MAIN COMPUTER STORAGE

Program

Data

Figure 4-12 The central processing unit consists of the control unit and the arithmetic/logic unit. The control unit coordinates and controls the entire computer system, including the input/output operations to main computer storage. The arithmetic/logic unit performs arithmetic and logical operations on data.

The central processing unit, of course, is a part of the processor unit (Figure 4-12). The CPU consists of two major components: the arithmetic/logic unit and the control unit.

The arithmetic/logic unit contains the electronic circuitry necessary to perform arithmetic operations such as addition, subtraction, multiplication, and division. It also contains the circuitry required to perform logical operations such as comparing one number to another and indicating the results of that comparison.

The control unit directs and coordinates the entire computer system. Its tasks include controlling the input/output units, controlling the operations of the arithmetic/logic unit in the CPU, and transferring data to and from main computer storage.

Executing instructions on a computer

The execution of an instruction on the computer system involves the control unit of the CPU "fetching," or obtaining, the instruction from main computer storage and placing the instruction in an instruction register. An instruction register is nothing more than a storage area within the control unit of the CPU which can store a single instruction at a time.

The control unit will also fetch any data required for the execution of the instruction and place the data in special "registers" which can be referenced by the arithmetic/logic unit of the CPU.

The arithmetic/logic unit of the CPU is then given control. It will perform the actual execution of the instruction and store the answer in another register.

The control unit will then place the answer into main computer storage.

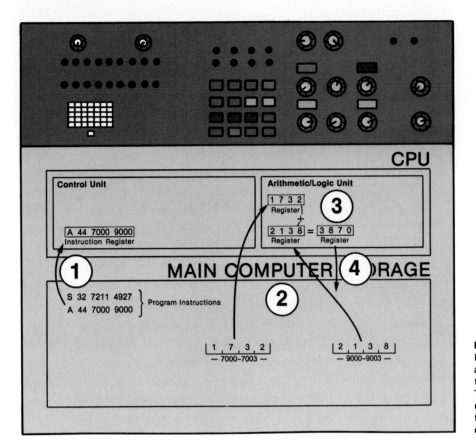

Figure 4-13 The control unit and arithmetic/logic unit of the central processing unit actually execute computer program instructions. Here, the add instruction is executed. The answer from the add instruction would usually be stored in the address for the first field. This is not explicitly shown in the diagram.

The illustration in Figure 4-13 shows the steps involved in executing a computer instruction on a typical computer system. The computer instructions are stored in main computer storage. The control unit keeps track of the next instruction to be executed. When an instruction is to be executed, the following steps occur: 1) The instruction is "fetched" from main computer storage and placed in an instruction register. In Figure 4-13, the instruction A 44 7000 9000 indicates that two fields, each four digits in length, are to be added together; 2) After the control unit has analyzed the instruction, it causes the data stored at the two addresses specified in the instruction to be fetched and placed in registers available to the arithmetic/logic unit in the CPU; 3) The arithmetic/logic unit executes the actual instruction. In the example in Figure 4-13, the two numbers obtained from main computer storage are added. The sum is stored in a different register; 4) The control unit would then move the answer from the register back to main computer storage.

Although this process appears to be cumbersome and time-consuming, large computer systems can perform millions of these operations in one second. This basic sequence of fetch the instruction, fetch the data, execute the instruction, and store the results is fundamental to most computer systems.

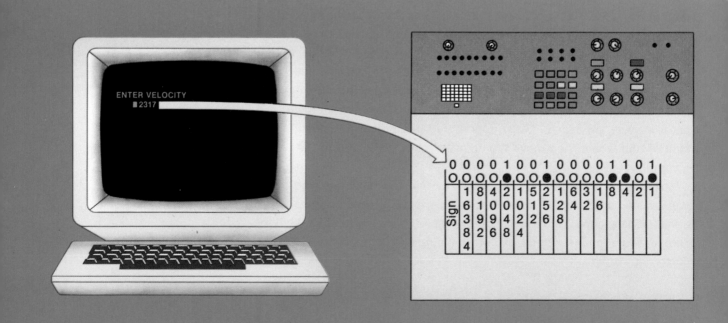

Sign	16384	8192	4096	2048	1024	512	256	128	64	32	16	8	4	2	1

Figure 4–14 A sixteen-bit word is illustrated above. Each bit corresponds to the values shown. The high-order (leftmost) bit is effectively used as the sign of the number, so that both positive and negative numbers can be stored in the word.

Figure 4–15 The value stored in the word below is 2317. This is computed by adding together the values represented by the bits which are "on." Thus, the value in the word is obtained by 2048 + 256 + 8 + 4 + 1 = 2317. In fixed word length machines, numbers are not represented by unique bit configurations. Rather, they are stored as binary numbers in main computer storage.

Fixed word length machines

The previous examples of the storage of data have shown a single character stored in a single addressable location in main computer storage. The length of the fields being processed varied. Machines which use storage organized in this manner are called variable word length machines.

Another technique for representing data in storage is often found in minicomputers and machines used for scientific and engineering processing. Machines using this technique are called fixed word length machines.

With fixed word length machines, a word is defined as a number of consecutive bits within main computer storage. For example, there are 12-bit word machines, 16-bit word machines, 32-bit word machines, and so on (Figure 4–14). Each word in storage is addressable in a manner similar to that used for bytes in variable word length machines.

Numeric data is stored in fixed word length machines not as a representation of the number with zone bits and digit bits but rather as the number itself in a binary format. Each bit in the word is assigned a value based upon the binary number system (see Appendix C). If a bit in the word is "on," then the decimal equivalent of that bit, added to the values of other bits which are "on," will determine the value of the number stored in the word.

In Figure 4–15, the value 2317 is stored in a sixteen-bit word. The binary number corresponding to the decimal value 2317 is 0000100100001101.

Alphabetic data is stored as a single character in a single word of storage on some machines; and on others, several alphabetic characters are stored in one word of storage.

Fixed word length machines are commonly found where the processing to be performed on the machine requires a great deal of arithmetic calculations, such as engineering and scientific applications. Fixed word length computer systems are generally used in these application areas because, due to the way numeric data is stored, they can perform the calculations faster than can variable word length machines.

On the other hand, fixed word length machines do not offer the flexibility in processing alphanumeric data that variable word length machines do.

Some computers have the ability to operate in either a fixed word length mode or a variable word length mode, depending upon the needs of the application.

The History, Manufacture, and Types of Storage

Over the years, various means have been used to store data in main computer storage. In addition, sophisticated manufacturing techniques have been employed to build memories for computer systems. And, different types of memories have been developed for specific purposes. These subjects are explored in the following pages.

The Search

For Main

Computer Storage

Electronic components are required to store data in main computer storage. Each bit in storage must be sensed as either "on" or "off." The search for electronic components to store data has taken engineers and designers up many paths.

The components for main computer storage should be reliable, should not generate much heat, should be relatively compact, and should be fast.

Vacuum tubes, one of the first methods for storing data, failed in most of these areas. They generated a great deal of heat, they failed with regularity, and were very bulky. The positive factor was that they worked. Therefore, they were used in the earliest computer systems as main computer storage.

There were many attempts to find better components for main computer storage. Mercury delay lines, cathode ray tubes, the "Williams" tube, and other devices were all used for storage.

The most successful, however, was magnetic core storage developed at MIT by Jay W. Forrester and his group in the early 1950's. Magnetic core storage was the dominant storage method for two decades and is still used today.

As microelectronics assumed more importance, the use of semiconductor memory became more apparent. Today, much of the storage used on computer systems is semiconductor memory. It is fast, inexpensive, cool, reliable, and compact. Major breakthroughs in storage prices and capabilities are attributable to semiconductor technology.

Figure 4-16 The first electronic components used for main computer storage were vacuum tubes. Although they worked, there were significant disadvantages — tubes were bulky, delicate, and expensive. They generated much heat, were unreliable, and used a lot of current. The module of tubes illustrated at the right was used in an early IBM computer called the Selective Sequence Electronic Calculator. The machine had 12,500 tubes that were used for both the arithmetic/logic unit of the CPU and main computer storage.

Figure 4-18 Semiconductor memory (below) has increased the speed and decreased the price of storage substantially. Whereas access to data stored in core was measured in microseconds (millionths of a second), access to data stored in semiconductor memory is measured in nanoseconds (billionths of a second). In addition, 1 million bytes of magnetic core memory could cost as much as $2 million in 1964, but the price for 1 million bytes of semiconductor memory in 1979 was $15,000.00. One of the reasons for the drop in price is that the chips required for semiconductor memory can be mass produced economically and reliably. Semiconductor memory has one major disadvantage as compared to magnetic core memory. It requires constant electric current in order to represent bits, but core memory does not. Thus, whenever current is dropped for semiconductor memory, the data stored will be lost; with core memory the data will be retained. The photo below shows 32 transistors on an NCR chip that is used for memory. The transistors are enlarged 600 times their actual size.

Figure 4-17 Magnetic cores (above) were, for two decades, the most popular means for storing data in main computer storage. A magnetic core is a small ring-shaped piece of material which can be magnetized, or polarized, in one of two directions. The polarity indicates whether the core is "on" or "off." Wires on which the cores are strung are able to sense the polarity of the core.

Making

Computer Storage

Semiconductor memory is used in most computer systems today for main computer storage. Its use has coincided with the unbelievable technological growth which has occurred in the electronics field.

The trend toward miniaturization began soon after the development of the transistor. By the mid-1960's, as many as 1,000 different circuit elements could be stored on a small chip. By the mid-1970's, this number had grown to over 15,000 circuit elements. It is predicted that in the 1980's, over one million circuit elements will be stored on a chip less than ¼" square; and by the year 2000, 100 billion elements may be

Figure 4-19 The production of a circuit chip includes a number of technically sophisticated steps. Some of these steps are summarized by the following: 1) The circuits which are produced are etched on silicon wafers. The first step to make a wafer is to develop very pure silicon crystals; 2) These crystals are then heated to a temperature of 1420° C., where they become liquified. While the liquid is turning in the crucible on the heating machine, a small "seed" is dipped into the liquid and then is pulled out. Each time the seed is dipped, a little more of the crystal grows on it. Eventually, an ingot about 4 inches in diameter and about 30 inches long is grown; 3) The ingot, after being smoothed, is taken to a diamond saw where it is cut into "wafers." The wafers vary in thickness from 1/91" to 1/50". The wafers are then polished to a very smooth surface on one side. They are now ready for a circuit to be etched on them; 4) Circuits which are placed on the wafers must be designed by engineers. While some circuits take a month or two to design, others have taken over two years to design. Using light pens and sophisticated terminals, the designers design each of the circuits which will be etched on the chip. Most chips will have 4–6 layers on them in order to completely perform the function for which they are designed.

stored on a small chip.

One of the reasons for this phenomenal growth is the sophisticated production capabilities developed to build the circuits on these small chips. Whereas twenty years ago circuits were almost completely hand built, today machines such as electron microscopes, diamond saws, heating chambers controlled to ½° C., and other devices allow the chips to be mass-produced cheaply and reliably.

As shown by the pictures on these pages, the manufacturing process requires sophisticated machines to keep the tolerances required by these amazing devices.

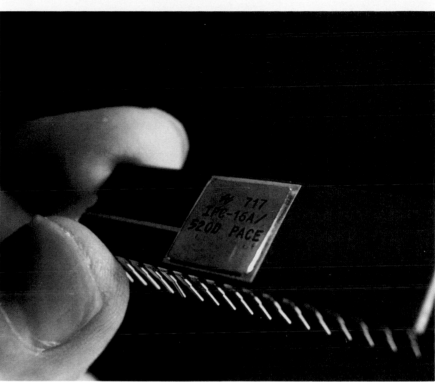

8

After the circuits are designed, a photomask which is up to 500 times larger than the actual circuit is developed. The engineer can closely scrutinize the mask to be sure it is absolutely correct. The mask is then photographically or electronically reduced to the size of the circuit on the actual chip; 5) The wafer of silicon must be placed in ovens at specific temperatures to form oxide and other layers of minerals on it. It is these layers which are "etched" to form the

circuits; 6) After the layers are on the wafer, the photomask for the circuit is carefully placed on the wafer. The registration for the different layers must be within 1 micrometer, so high-powered microscopes are used to ensure proper registration. After ensuring the mask is on properly, the layers on the wafer are exposed to ultraviolet light and then are "washed" in an acid. The portions of the layers not exposed to the ultraviolet light are washed away, leaving a

circuit; 7) The process of oxidizing, masking, exposing to ultraviolet light, and washing continues until all levels are on the wafer and the chip is complete. Each chip is then cut apart from the wafer and placed in a package. The wires connecting the circuit to the "outside world" are connected to the chip; 8) The final circuit is contained in a hard plastic covering with a number of pins to be used for connecting the device to other devices.

5

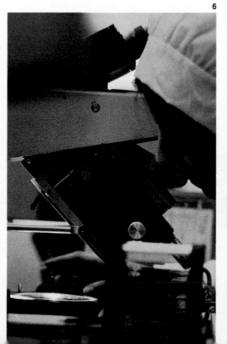

6

7

Figure 4-20 The Z-80 microprocessor unit (MPU) contains the circuitry necessary to control the computer system.

4.18

ROM,

RAM

And The MPU

Although all storage used with computer systems store data in the form of bits, there are a number of different types of storage.

The most commonly used storage is Random Access Memory (RAM). RAM is the type of storage described in the text of this chapter. Data can be written in the storage and data can be read from the storage. RAM is used as main computer storage for most machines.

ROM is the term for Read Only Memory. With ROM, data is recorded in the memory when it is manufactured. The data which is stored in ROM can be read and used, but it cannot be altered. ROM is typically used to store programs which will not be altered, such as BASIC interpreters used with microcomputers.

A variation on ROM is Programmable Read Only Memory (PROM). PROM acts the same as ROM when it is part of the computer system; that is, it can be read, but its contents cannot be altered when it is used on the computer system. With PROM, however, the data is not stored in the memory when it is manufactured. Instead, the user of the PROM can store data in the memory prior to assemblying it with the computer system.

The microprocessor unit is sometimes called the MPU. It performs many of the same tasks as the central processing units described in the text.

Figure 4-21 Memory which is used in a computer system is mounted on a printed circuit board (above). The memory chips enclosed in their plastic packages are wired together on the board. Microcomputers usually contain both RAM and ROM memory systems (right). The memory chips, together with the microprocessor unit (MPU) are mounted on the printed circuit board and are placed in the microcomputer housing (below). The housing contains a power supply and other electronics to communicate with outside devices such as the keyboard or floppy disk device shown. Together, these elements constitute the microcomputer.

Chapter summary

The following points have been discussed and explained in this chapter.

1. The basic processing cycle of input, process, and output requires that data be read into main computer storage from an input device prior to being processed.

2. The computer system, under the control of a computer program, processes data stored in main computer storage and creates output.

3. Whenever data is to be processed, it must first be stored in main computer storage.

4. Both main computer storage and the central processing unit are contained in the processor unit of the computer system.

5. The basic unit for storing data in main computer storage is the bit (binary digit).

6. Data is represented in main computer storage by a series of bits being "on" or "off."

7. The extended binary coded decimal interchange code (EBCDIC) uses 8 bits in combination to store a letter of the alphabet, a number, or a special character.

8. The 8 bits together in EBCDIC are called a byte.

9. Each byte is divided into two portions — the zone portion of the byte and the digit portion of the byte.

10. Numeric values are represented in EBCDIC with all of the zone bits "on" and the proper combination of bits in the digit portion of the byte "on" to represent the particular numeric value.

11. Each decimal digit is stored in a single byte when using EBCDIC.

12. Alphabetic data is represented in EBCDIC with a combination of bits "on" and "off."

13. Computers are found with as few as 4,096 bytes and as many as 16 million bytes of main computer storage.

14. Each byte in main computer storage has a unique address associated with it. The address in main computer storage identifies each byte.

15. The ability to store data at unique addresses within main computer storage allows the use of the data in subsequent operations, such as arithmetic, logical, and input/output operations.

16. Characters stored in a field in an input record are recorded in main computer storage in adjacent, addressable locations when they are read.

17. As input records are read into main computer storage, each character in the input record is stored at an addressable storage location.

18. Once data has been recorded in main computer storage, it can be referenced and manipulated. This is possible because of the ability of the computer program to direct the electronic circuitry to extract data located at a specific address and use the data for processing.

19. The ability to address data stored in main computer storage and process it after it is addressed forms the basis of internal operations in a computer system.

20. Once a character has been stored in a location in main computer storage, it will remain in that location until another character is moved to the same location.

21. When a program reads data into storage or moves data into a storage location, it destroys what has previously been stored at that location. This is sometimes called "destructive read in." It allows programs to use the same sequence of instructions to process many records.

22. Computer programs consist of instructions to the electronics of the computer system to process data in some manner. An instruction is composed of: a) An operation code; b) Values indicating the number of characters to be processed by the instruction; c) The main storage addresses of the data to be used in the processing.

23. The central processing unit (CPU) is the heart of the computer system. It consists of the arithmetic/logic unit and the control unit.

24. The arithmetic/logic unit performs arithmetic and logic operations. The control unit directs and coordinates the entire computer system.

25. The execution of an instruction on a computer system consists of the following steps: a) The instruction is fetched by the control unit and is placed in an instruction register; b) The data is fetched and placed in registers available to the arithmetic/logic unit; c) The instruction is executed by the arithmetic/logic unit; d) The answer is placed in main computer storage by the control unit.

26. Machines where each number or letter of the alphabet is stored in main computer storage in a single addressable location are called variable word length machines.

27. A fixed word length machine contains addressable words of information. A word is defined as a number of consecutive bits in main storage.

28. Numeric values are stored in fixed word length machines as binary numbers.

29. The three "generations" of main computer storage are vacuum tubes, core memory, and semiconductor memory.

30. Random access memory (RAM) is used for writing, reading, and then rewriting data in storage. Read Only Memory (ROM) has values stored in it when the memory is manufactured, and the values cannot be changed.

Student Learning Exercises

Review questions

1. What is meant by the term "bit"?

2. What is EBCDIC? How is data represented in EBCDIC?

3. Define the term "byte."

4. Explain the basic structure of a byte. Illustrate the byte by means of a diagram.

5. Explain how numeric data is stored in a byte.

6. Illustrate by means of a diagram how the number 15 would be recorded in storage using EBCDIC.

7. Illustrate by means of a series of "0's" and "1's" how the letters of the alphabet ARZ would be recorded in storage when using EBCDIC.

8. What is meant by the term 4K bytes of storage? 16 megabytes?

9. Explain the concept of addressable storage.

10. When data is moved from an input area to an output area in storage, what is contained in the input area after the move operation?

11. What is meant by "destructive read in"?

12. What are the basic elements of a computer instruction. Illustrate, by means of an example, each of the elements.

13. What are the two major components of the central processing unit.

14. Briefly explain the steps that occur when executing an instruction.

15. What is meant by the terms variable word length computer? Fixed word length computer.

16. Discuss the advantages and disadvantages of vacuum tubes, magnetic core and semiconductor memory.

17. Explain the terms RAM, ROM, and PROM.

Controversial issues in data processing

1. Main computer storage is often called computer "memory." Some authorities feel that the term memory implies a human quality which tends to threaten the general public. Write an argument which indicates the best choice of terms — "main computer storage" or "main computer memory."

2. "Computers may have a memory, but they can't think." Defend this statement.

3. Computers have been programmed to "play" a wide variety of games such as tic-tac-toe, checkers, and chess. If a computer wins a game, has not the computer outthought its human opponent? In fact, have not humans been "programmed" to play these games in exactly the same way as a computer? Take a position on this issue and defend your answer.

Research projects

1. Scientific American frequently contains current technical and general interest articles on computer technology. Using it as one possible source, prepare a research paper on the latest developments in computer storage and related circuitry.

2. Define the term "think." Document the definition by referencing authorities in the fields of philosophy, psychology, and computer science.

Chapter 5
Input to the Computer System

Objectives

- An understanding of the differences between batch processing systems and transaction-oriented processing systems

- An understanding of punched cards, magnetic tape, and magnetic disk as input media for batch processing systems

- An understanding of dumb and intelligent terminals as input devices for transaction-oriented processing systems

- An understanding of the processing cycles for batch processing systems and transaction-oriented processing systems

- An appreciation of and introduction to the need for editing input data prior to processing the data on computer systems

Chapter 5

Figure 5-1 The data entry department shown here contains a number of keystations in a key-to-disk shared processor system. These data entry devices are used to record data on tape and disk so the data can be entered into main computer storage. Increasingly sophisticated hardware and software are being used in data entry departments to increase the reliability and decrease the costs of preparing data for input to a computer system.

Input to the Computer System

"GIGO — Garbage In, Garbage Out"[1]

Introduction

In the basic data processing cycle, the input step must occur before any data can be processed and any information produced. Without valid input data, a computer system is not capable of producing any useful information.

It is important, therefore, to understand how data is prepared for processing on a computer and to be aware of some of the techniques used to ensure that only valid data enters the computer for processing. As noted above, GIGO is a truism of computer systems; that is, if the data which is entered into the computer is not valid, the information received in the form of output from the computer system cannot be trustworthy.

Source data

Before data is entered into main computer storage for processing, the data must be obtained. Data can be obtained from numerous sources. The facts, figures, and operating data within an organization provide a large amount of the data entered for processing.

For example, timecards for payroll applications, merchandise tags for retail applications, invoices for accounts payable applications, and other documents reflecting the business activity occurring within an organization provide input data.

Input data can also be obtained from sources outside the company, such as sales orders from customers.

Depending on the method used to process the data, it is either recorded from a source document onto a machine-readable medium for entry into storage (Figure 5–1), or the data is entered directly into main computer storage. The methods for preparing and entering input data will be discussed in this chapter.

---

1 Anonymous

Entering data into the computer

Two basic processing systems are used when entering data into a computer. These systems are called: 1) transaction-oriented processing systems; 2) batch processing systems. Historically, batch processing systems have been widely used for processing data on a computer. Today, however, with the widespread use of computer terminals, transaction-oriented processing systems are very effective for many applications.

In a transaction-oriented processing system (also known as interactive processing), data is entered directly into main computer storage for immediate processing as the transaction occurs. For example, ticket agencies that issue tickets for entertainment events through the use of computers use a transaction-oriented processing system. When an individual purchases a ticket for an event, the terminal operator enters the required information (event, date, price of ticket). This information is transmitted to the computer for immediate processing, and a ticket is issued to the purchaser. Thus, data is processed as the transaction occurs.

In a batch processing system, source documents containing the data to be processed are gathered together as a group (batch). The data is then recorded on an input medium, such as punched cards, and is processed as a group or batch of data. For example, the preparation of the company payroll is normally accomplished using batch processing.

In a payroll application, the employee timecards are gathered at the end of each pay period. The timecards serve as the source documents for the payroll application. The number of hours worked, days worked, and related data are recorded on some input medium (such as punched cards) and the input records are then entered into the computer system to be processed. This processing produces, among other things, the paychecks at the end of payroll period.

Whether a transaction-oriented processing system or a batch processing system is used is largely dependent upon the type of application. Although many applications readily lend themselves to transaction-oriented processing systems, other applications lend themselves to the processing of data in groups in a batch processing mode.

Reliability of input data

Regardless of whether data is entered into a computer system for transaction-oriented processing or batch processing, it is critical that the data being entered for processing is accurate.

Inaccurate data may originate from two primary sources. First, an error may be made when recording data on source documents; and second, data, through operator error, may be incorrectly entered into a computer terminal or erroneously recorded on an input medium.

For example, if the date on which a document is being prepared is January 9, 1980, and the person preparing the document records the date as 9/1/80 (the format is month/day/year), an error has been made when entering the data on the source document. Unless corrected at some point in the processing cycle, this data can result in incorrect processing and invalid output from the computer system.

The second type of mistake is made when input data is prepared for entry into the computer system. These errors commonly occur when an operator enters data into a terminal or data is recorded in a machine-readable format. For example, in a transaction-oriented system, an error can be made by the terminal operator when the data is keyed into the system on the keyboard of the terminal. In a batch system, errors can be made when the data is recorded from the source documents to a machine-readable medium such as punched cards.

In either case, it is essential that these types of errors be detected prior to reading and processing the data on the computer system. Otherwise, incorrect output will result. In the discussion of the means for entering data into a computer system which follows, error detection and correction methods will be included.

BATCH PROCESSING

Batch processing of input records involves gathering and transcribing the source data, as a group, onto a medium which can be read into main computer storage for processing. The input records are then processed in a batch under the control of a computer program.

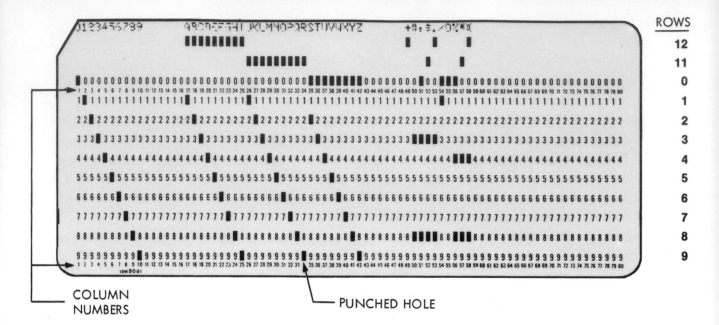

COLUMN
NUMBERS

PUNCHED HOLE

Figure 5-2 A punched card contains holes to represent data. One or more holes in a vertical column represents one character. Each column has 12 rows. Numeric data (0-9) is represented by a single punch in the row corresponding to the numeric value. Alphabetic data is represented by a combination of two punches — one in the 12, 11, or 0 row (also called zone punches), and one in the 1-9 row. Special characters are represented by two or more punches in a column. Since one character is stored in one column, an 80-column card can contain 80 characters of data.

Punched cards

One of the earliest means of storing data for input to machines was the punched card. The punched card was developed in the late 1880's by Dr. Herman Hollerith for use in recording and processing data to be used in tabulating the 1890 census. Since that time, the punched card has been widely used as input to a variety of data processing machines, including computer systems.

A punched card is nothing more than a piece of lightweight cardboard capable of storing data in the form of punched holes recorded in predefined locations. Although a number of different formats for punched cards have been developed since Hollerith first introduced the card, by far the most dominant is the 80-column card introduced by IBM in 1928. This card provides for the storing of numbers, letters of the alphabet, and special characters through the use of holes punched in one of the eighty vertical columns on the card (Figure 5-2).

Card and input record design

The data which is recorded on a punched card is normally prepared from data stored on source documents. This process of obtaining data from source documents for recording in input records is illustrated in Figure 5-3. The source documents consist of invoices which have been prepared as a result of sales. An input record stored on a punched card will be prepared for each line item on the invoice. This will allow subsequent processing of the data on the computer to produce any required output.

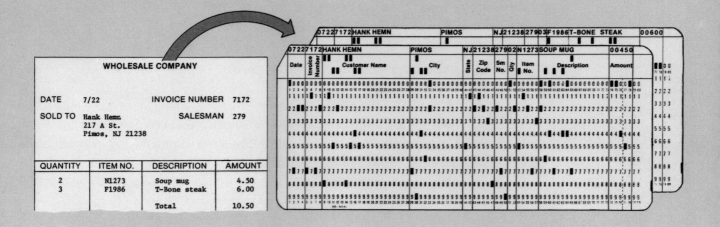

Designing an input record

When designing an input record for recording on a punched card or other medium, the record is "subdivided" into fields when it is prepared from the source documents. The length of the fields in the record is dependent upon the maximum number of digits or characters which will ever be found in the field on the source document. For example, the date field, which contains a two-digit number representing the month and a two-digit number representing the day would require four columns in the input record. Thus, in Figure 5–3, the date field is stored in columns 1–4 of the card. Similarly, the salesman number, which is three digits in length, requires three card columns (in the example, columns 48-50).

Special characters are not normally placed in an input record. For example, the date field on the source document contains a slash (/) separating the month from the day. This character is not recorded in the input record. Similarly, characters such as a decimal point, comma, or dollar sign would not be included in the input record. If such characters are to be printed on a report, they are printed under the control of the computer program.

The placement of the field in the input record depends on the design of the record by a systems analyst. Generally, an input record is designed so that the transcription from the source document to the record Is as simple as possible. In this way, the chance for error is reduced. Thus, the record format in Figure 5–3 corresponds to a left-to-right, top-to-bottom reading of the source document.

The data recorded in the input record is usually directly related to the processing to be performed on the record. Thus, not all fields on a source document are necessarily included in the input record. In the example in Figure 5–3, the customer name and city/state are included in the record but the address is not. This is because subsequent processing by the program reading these input records does not require the address field.

Figure 5–3 The data in the fields on the source documents is recorded into the fields on the card. The fields on the card are identified by columns. Thus, the date field is in columns 1–4, the invoice number field is in columns 5–8, the customer name field is in columns 9–28, and so on. If a field on the source document is not required when the input data is processed, it will not be contained in the input record. In this example, the street address contained on the source document Is not included in the punched card input record.

Recording data on a punched card

Data is recorded on a punched card by punching holes representing the data in the card. When punched cards were first used, this was a laborious task because each hole was punched by hand using a manual card punching device (Figure 5-4). Since that time, card punching devices have been developed which greatly facilitate the punching of large volumes of input data for processing on computer systems.

Figure 5-4 One of the first devices used to record data on a punched card is shown above. The operator had to set the machine and then manually punch the hole. Cards produced by this machine contained round holes. Later card punches produced rectangular holes, which became the industry standard.

The keypunch

As the industry matured, automatic machines called keypunches were developed. A keypunch is a device containing a typewriter-like keyboard and a punching mechanism. Blank cards are placed in the machine. As the operator keys data on the keyboard, holes representing the data are punched into the card (Figure 5-5).

On the first keypunches, a hole was punched in a card when the operator pressed the key on the keyboard. More modern devices contain a small amount of storage where the data keyed on the keyboard is saved until the data for the entire card has been keyed. At that time, the operator depresses a key signaling that the data in storage should be punched in the card.

Figure 5-5 The IBM 029 keypunch is typical of the keypunch machines used to prepare punched cards for processing on computer systems.

Verification of data

When data is transferred by punching from the source document to the punched card, there is the possibility that the keypunch operator can punch the wrong data into the card. This is one of the two major ways in which invalid data enters a computer system.

To ensure the accuracy of the transfer of data from the source document to the punched cards, a process called verification is used. With verification, the cards already punched are placed in a machine called a verifier. This machine resembles a keypunch except that it does not punch holes in the card. Instead, it senses the holes in an already-punched card and compares the value in the card to the values keyed on the keyboard by the verifier operator. Those keypunches with storage can also be used for verification.

If the values in the card are the same as the values keyed by the verifier operator, then it is assumed the value in the card is correct. If the value in the card is not the same as the value keyed by the verifier operator, an error is indicated by the machine. If the card is found to be in error after reviewing the data on the source document, then a new card must be punched.

Although verification is costly because it takes many hours to key the data for comparison to the punched cards, it is essential that valid data enter the computer system. It has been found that the process of verification is more cost-effective than not performing this operation because the cost of correcting errors once they have been read into a computer system is extremely high.

Reading punched cards into main computer storage

To read the data in punched cards into main computer storage, a card reader is used (Figure 5-6). These devices are typically capable of reading 200-1,200 cards per minute into main computer storage.

When the data punched in cards is read into main computer storage in a batch processing mode, the computer operator will place the cards in the read hopper of the card reader. When the program to process the records begins execution, each card input record will be read one at a time and processed by the program. After the cards are read, they are placed in a stacker by the card reader. The operator can then remove the cards from the stacker and store them for future use.

Several techniques are used in card readers to sense the holes in a card. One method senses the holes through the use of metal "brushes," or wires, which drop through the holes in the card and complete an electrical circuit. Other card readers use light beams to read cards. With this method, a row of lights shining on the card stimulates a photoelectrical cell when a hole is sensed in the card, causing the data in the card to be "read."

The holes in the card represent data. When the card is read, this data is changed from the representation in the card to the corresponding representation in main computer storage. Thus, the letter of the alphabet "A" is stored in the punched card as two holes, one in the 12-zone and one is the 1-row (Figure 5-2). When it is read into main computer storage, this representation is converted to an 8-bit representation of the letter "A," as discussed in Chapter 4.

Figure 5-6 The IBM 3504 card reader is typical of card readers used on high-speed computer systems. The cards stacked on the right of the picture have not yet been read. The operator is removing the cards from the stacker where they are placed after they have been read into main computer storage.

The processing cycle — batch processing

The processing cycle using punched cards in a batch processing system is shown in Figure 5-7. The steps include: 1) The source documents are gathered for punching; 2) The data on the source documents is keypunched into the cards; 3) The punched cards are verified; 4) The data in the punched cards is read into main computer storage. A single record stored in a card is read and processed before another record is read; 5) The processing takes place in the processor unit of the computer system; 6) The output record is produced. This sequence of events is the basis for all batch processing systems, regardless of the input media used.

Figure 5-7 The basic processing cycle of input, process, and output is shown for batch processing. The preparation of the input data for this cycle is quite important, as invalid input data will produce unreliable output. Preparation of input data is also expensive, with some experts estimating that 40% of the operations budget in a data processing installation is dedicated to data entry.

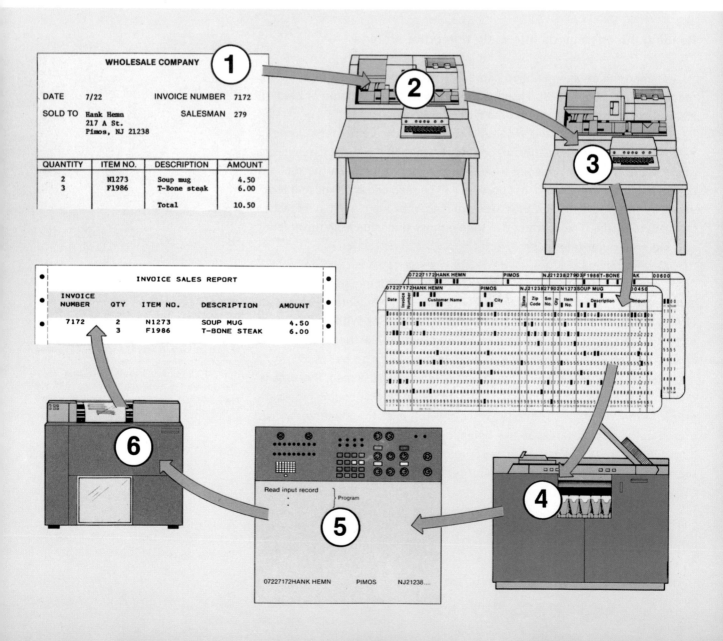

An evaluation of punched cards

Although punched cards have been used for many years as a means for entering data into a computer system, cards have several disadvantages. A significant disadvantage is that reading punched cards into a computer system is relatively slow and, therefore, expensive. Although card readers reading 200–1,200 cards per minute may seem fast, most computer systems have the internal speed capabilities for processing many more than 1,200 card records in a minute. Thus, reading and processing punched cards does not take advantage of the capabilities of a typical computer system.

In addition, cards are bulky, both to handle and to store. For example, a file of name and address cards for 30,000 customers of a company would stand more than 18 feet high.

Since cards have significant disadvantages, their use in recent years as an input media has diminished considerably. In place of punched cards, magnetic media such as magnetic tape and magnetic disk have emerged as the primary means for storing input data.

Magnetic tape data recorder

The first major effort to replace punched cards as the media for input data occurred in 1965 when Mohawk Data Sciences delivered the first keyed data recorder that used magnetic tape instead of punched cards (Figure 5–8).

The data keyed on the keyboard was stored on magnetic tape. Verification of data recorded on the tape was accomplished on the Mohawk machine by reading a record recorded on the tape into a storage unit and then rekeying the data from the source document and comparing the two. In this way, transcription errors could be detected in a manner similar to that used for the verification of punched cards.

Figure 5-8 The Mohawk key-to-tape data recorder marked the first significant departure from punched cards as the input medium. Tape has many advantages over punched cards but was not used extensively until this device was introduced.

The most significant advantage of tape when compared to punched cards is that data can be read into main computer storage at a much faster rate from the tape. This is because the data is stored on the tape with a high "density." Density is the number of characters stored on one inch of tape. The early Mohawk machines stored data at a density of 200 or 800 characters per inch. Thus, the equivalent of 10 punched cards could be stored on one inch of tape. This inch of tape could be read much faster than could the ten cards.

Other advantages of using tape as the input media instead of punched cards include: 1) Tape reels which contain the magnetic tape can be easily transported and stored. Cards are bulky and difficult to store; 2) Magnetic tape is reusable, whereas cards are not. After the input file has been read and processed, the same reel of tape can be used to store another input file; 3) Magnetic tape is cheaper per character stored than cards.

For these reasons, the advent of key-to-tape machines was greeted with a great deal of enthusiasm by the data processing industry. Indeed, between 1965 and the early 1970's, over 10,000 of these new types of data entry devices were installed, in many cases replacing keypunches.

Although the key-to-tape machines were a major breakthrough in data entry, their lifetime was relatively short because of further advances in the field. They were significant, however, because they demonstrated for the first time that magnetic media could be used successfully to replace punched cards as the primary means of data entry in batched processing systems.

Figure 5-9 The IBM 3741 device was the first machine allowing keyed data to be stored on a diskette, or floppy disk. The use of the floppy disk for storing data to be entered in batch systems has increased tremendously since 1972.

Figure 5-10 The diskette, or floppy disk, can be used on data entry devices for storing input data. It is 8" square and flexible. Recently designed floppy disks can store over 1.5 million characters.

Diskette-based data entry devices

Although several machines were developed in the late 1960's that allowed keyed data to be stored directly on magnetic disk in a manner similar to that used for magnetic tape, a significant change in data entry occurred in 1972 when IBM announced the 3741 device. The 3741 allowed keyed data to be stored on a diskette, or floppy disk (Figure 5-9).

The diskette is a flexible piece of Mylar material whose surface is coated with an oxide substance that can store bits of data. The diskette is contained within a protective covering and is about eight inches square (Figure 5-10). When used with the 3741, it is capable of storing approximately 250,000 characters. Diskettes with the capability of storing over 1.5 million characters have been recently developed. The diskette, or floppy disk, can be used over and over again for storing different data.

The diskette-based systems introduced in the early 1970's were generally similar to a keypunch, but stored the data on diskette instead of cards. They were stand-alone systems on which an operator keyed data which was directly stored on the diskette. They contained a display screen so that the operator could see what had been keyed. The systems also provided for verification since the data stored on the diskette could be read back into the device's memory and compared with the data keyed for verification purposes.

The diskette was rapidly accepted as an input medium because it fit easily into the procedures of most punched card installations. It allowed the replacement of punched cards as the input medium with a minimum of changes. When compared to the punched card, the diskette has the following advantages: 1) Unlike the punched card, the diskette is reusable and can reduce the cost of the input media; 2) Changes and corrections can be made easily because data stored on a diskette can be simply and quickly changed; 3) A single diskette can contain almost 2,000 input records; 4) The speed of reading data stored on a diskette is much greater than reading data stored on punched cards; 5) Diskette reading devices are less expensive than punched card readers.

Because of these advantages, the diskette has gained wide acceptance as an input medium. It is rapidly replacing the punched card and card reading devices as a means of entering data into a computer system.

Key-to-disk shared processor systems

One of the most advanced forms of keyboard data entry for batch processing systems is the multiple station, key-to-disk shared processor system. With these systems, a number of keyboard consoles are connected through a minicomputer to a common large disk storage unit. As the data is keyed from the various console stations, the data is stored on the disk under the control of the minicomputer (Figure 5–11).

Thus, each keystation console operator can be given a batch of source documents with data to be recorded. Simultaneously, the operators can be keying various jobs and storing the keyed data on the disk. After the jobs have been completely keyed, the data stored on the disk is normally transferred to magnetic tape for reading into main computer storage of the system which will process the data.

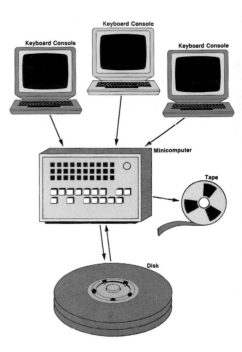

Figure 5–11 With key-to-disk shared processor systems, a series of keyboard console stations is connected to a common minicomputer for control. Data entered at each station is stored on a magnetic disk as temporary storage. After the keying job is complete, the data on the disk is transferred to tape for entering into the computer system.

AMRO BANK

kantorencentrale

Figure 5-12 This Mohawk Data Sciences 2400 System is used to enter banking transactions. Multiple keystations are connected to a minicomputer which controls the input data being entered and edits the data upon entry. The banks using these machines have found them so useful that branches no longer have to be burdened with data preparation and have more time for banking business.

Although there are several variations, the key-to-disk shared processor data entry devices (Figure 5–12) have the following elements in common: 1) A number of keying stations are included with the system. These can range from 2 up to 64 stations. Each station contains a keyboard, a CRT or other visual display system, and the ability to store data on a disk of some type; 2) The keying stations are under the control of some type of processor unit, commonly a minicomputer; 3) The data keyed on the various stations is stored on the disk and, after the keying job is completed, is transferred to magnetic tape for reading into main computer storage.

These key-to-disk systems have several significant advantages over other forms of data entry. First, these systems can greatly improve operator productivity. With each keystation under the control of a computer, the operator need not be concerned with the many tasks involved in machine set up for each new job. Instead, when source documents are received, keying can begin immediately since the required set up is done by the attached minicomputer.

In addition, because of the processing capability of the controlling minicomputer system, a great deal of data editing is possible. Data editing is the checking of input data to ensure that valid data is entered into a computer system. For example, an employee number field can be edited to ensure that it contains only numeric data and no letters of the alphabet. Editing differs from verification in that verification ensures only that the operator keyed the proper data from the source document, while editing can attempt to ensure that the data on the source document is correct. With key-to-disk shared processor systems, the editing is done at the point where the data is initially keyed. This saves time and money and produces accurate input data.

Another significant advantage of key-to-disk shared processor systems is that commonly used data fields can be stored on the disk and be retrieved automatically by the data entry operator. This data can be included in the record being keyed. For example, the data entry operator could key the customer number on the keyboard of the keystation. Based upon the customer number, the minicomputer would retrieve the customer name and address and insert them into the input record being stored on the disk. This capability, of course, cuts down considerably on the number of keystrokes necessary to enter the data into an input record, resulting in increased production. In addition, when this retrieval method is used, fewer fields need to be verified because the data which is stored on the disk and is incorporated into the input record is known to be accurate. With some systems of this type, the verification step in data entry has virtually been eliminated.

Most key-to-disk shared processor systems contain a supervisory console which can be used to enter control programs for jobs to be keyed and which also can be used to obtain operating statistics on each job and each operator. These statistics typically contain the operator identification, a job identification, the operator start and stop time, the number of records keyed, the number of errors, and similar data. The statistics are stored on the disk associated with the system and can be quite valuable in controlling and analyzing each operator's productivity.

The major disadvantage of key-to-disk systems is that they are quite expensive. Therefore, they are normally used only in installations where the volume of input into the computer system is quite high and there is the necessity of preparing the data for batch processing. Although not all large volume data entry installations use key-to-disk shared processor systems, the trend is definitely in this direction. It is anticipated that in the years to come, more companies will be using these devices as a way to at least partially solve their data entry problems.

Local job entry

When using punched cards as the medium for input records, the cards are usually punched in a centralized data entry department. After they are punched, the cards are physically transported to the computer room where they are read on a card reader.

This same procedure can be followed for key-to-tape, key-to-diskette, and key-to-disk systems. Thus, regardless of whether the medium is cards, tape, or disk, the data stored on the medium can be transported to the computer room and read into main computer storage.

Remote job entry

There are, however, several ways in which data can be entered into the computer system for batch processing that does not involve transporting the medium on which data is stored to the computer room.

One of the more frequently encountered methods is called remote job entry. When using remote job entry, an input device such as a card reader or a tape drive is installed in a location remote from the computer system itself. The input devices are connected to the computer system over cables or data communications lines. Conceptually, the data to be processed is read from cards or tape at the remote site the same as if these devices were in the computer room. Thus, when using remote job entry, the power of a large computer system is available at the remote locations. A remote job entry terminal normally also has a printer so that results of the processing can be immediately sent back to the terminal.

In some cases, data sent from a remote job entry terminal will be stored on disk or tape at the computer site for later processing. The important concept to understand, however, is that input devices can be placed at locations far removed from the main computer site; and the data can be read and processed by transmitting the data over cables or communication lines.

TRANSACTION-ORIENTED PROCESSING SYSTEMS

When batch processing is used, the data to be processed on the computer system is recorded as input records on a machine-readable medium and then the input records are processed as a group. An increasingly important means of entering data into a computer system is by means of transaction-oriented processing systems.

With transaction-oriented systems, the data to be processed is not transcribed onto a machine-readable medium prior to processing. Instead, the data is entered directly into main computer storage for immediate processing by the computer program. Thus, each transaction is acted upon as it is entered into the computer system rather than grouping the transactions and processing them in a batch.

Uses for transaction-oriented processing systems

Since data is entered directly into main computer storage from a terminal when transaction-oriented processing systems are used, applications requiring immediate response and action use this mode of data entry.

Applications such as reservations for hotels, automobiles, or airplanes; bank accounts that must contain the current balance as soon as a transaction occurs; order entry systems where the inventory must be updated as soon as items are entered into the inventory or are removed from the inventory; and similar applications all make good use of transaction-oriented data entry.

This form of data entry is not particularly suited to applications such as payroll (checks are not printed as soon as an employee works eight hours); accounts payable (checks are not written as soon as a company buys a product from a vendor); or year-end accounting reports (they use transactions from an entire year). These types of applications are more suited to batch processing.

Computer terminals

The cathode ray tube (CRT) terminal is by far the most popular means of entering data into the computer system in transaction-oriented processing (Figure 5-13). A CRT terminal normally consists of a keyboard and a television-like screen. The keyboard can be arranged in the same format as a standard typewriter; or to facilitate the rapid entering of numeric data, a separate numeric keypad containing only numbers is sometimes provided.

Figure 5-13 This CRT terminal from Hazeltine is typical of terminals used for transaction-oriented processing. The screen contains room for 24 lines of data, each with 80 characters, for a total of 1920 characters. The keyboard is a typewriter keyboard with a numeric pad on the right.

Figure 5-14 Qume manufactures hard copy terminals for applications which require a printed copy of not only the input transaction, but also any output which is sent back to the terminal by the computer program.

Another popular type of terminal creates hard copy as its output instead of displaying the output on a CRT screen (Figure 5–14). Although not as popular as CRT's, the hard copy terminal is used where the output from the computer system received at the terminal must be saved for future reference.

Regardless of the type of terminal used, the method of entering data into the computer system is basically the same. The terminal is connected to the computer system through data communication facilities. A computer program is stored in main computer storage and is active. Communication between the terminal and the program in main computer storage is initiated either by the terminal or by the program. In either case, when there is data to be sent, the terminal operator keys in the data. The data goes directly to main computer storage. It is not stored on an input medium such as punched cards.

Once the data is stored in main computer storage, the program can process the data in a number of ways. It can use the transmitted data to immediately update a file, respond to an inquiry, or otherwise use the data to cause immediate processing. When transaction-oriented processing takes place, the data sent from the terminal is not stored on an input medium; therefore, there is no permanent record of the data entering the computer system. As a result, most systems which utilize this type of processing will store the transaction on tape or disk so that a history of the transactions processed by the computer system will be maintained. If questions or problems arise in the future based upon data entered from a remote terminal, the historical record can be used to investigate what occurred.

Intelligent terminals

Many terminals which communicate directly with a computer in a transaction-oriented processing system do nothing more than pass the keyed data to the computer system and display data transmitted back from the computer system on the CRT screen. These terminals are sometimes referred to as "dumb terminals" because they do not process the data in any way; they merely serve as a form of data entry and a form of output.

As the microprocessor was developed, the concept of incorporating a microprocessor into a computer terminal arose. With a microprocessor, the terminals have the ability to process data without the necessity of sending data to the main computer system. These types of terminals were termed intelligent terminals (Figure 5–15).

Intelligent terminals are normally found at remote sites within the various operating departments in an organization. These departments are usually concerned with order entry, inventory control, and similar applications where accuracy and interaction with the computer system requires an operator who is familiar with the particular application.

The intelligent terminal can aid the operator by prompting the operator to enter the correct data and then performing a detailed edit of the data entered prior to the data ever being sent to the main computer system. In fact, some of the more recent intelligent terminals actually come closer to being minicomputers than terminals. They contain not only the CRT terminal, but also printers, disk devices, and computer storage which allow the terminal to do "offline" processing by itself without being connected to the main computer system. Indeed, the terminals which communicate with the main computer system are tending to become small, sophisticated computers themselves. As more intelligence is placed in these machines, much processing can occur at the site of the terminal prior to sending the data to the large mainframe.

With transaction-oriented processing, there is normally no verify mode on the terminal where the operator would rekey data so that it can be compared to the original keyed data to ensure accuracy. Instead, visual verification is usually performed by the operator by reading the screen after the data has been keyed but before it is sent to the main computer system. In addition, most intelligent terminals have the capability of editing the data entered by the operator in a manner similar to that used for key-to-disk shared processor systems. In this way, intelligent terminals used in transaction-oriented processing systems offer many of the same advantages of key-to-disk shared processor systems used to prepare data for batch processing.

Figure 5-15 This intelligent terminal is used by Hertz to make reservations for car rentals. It can also be used to print the registration form, bill the customer based on mileage, and communicate with the central computer system for other application needs.

The processing cycle — transaction-oriented processing systems

Transaction-oriented processing systems are most useful when the user requires immediate response from a computer system, and the response from the computer system can affect the event which is taking place. This is called real-time processing because it is occurring as the event itself is occurring and is affecting the event.

One type of system which lends itself to transaction-oriented processing is an order entry system. In an order entry system, an order is received from a customer. The company must then process the order so that the material ordered will be shipped, and the customer will be billed. Although batch processing can be used for order entry, transaction-oriented systems provide faster turnaround — thus allowing the customer to receive the goods ordered sooner and allowing billing of the customer to take place with less delay.

A typical system is illustrated in Figure 5–16. The following steps occur: 1) A customer calls an order clerk and orders item number 333, which is a paint sprayer. The customer asks to make sure that the item is on hand. The clerk, sitting before a remote CRT terminal connected to the computer system, displays a "menu" on the screen. A menu specifies a variety of operations which may be performed. The clerk selects the appropriate operation by keying the number of the desired operation. In Figure 5–16, the number "2" would be keyed so that the order can be entered; 2) Information relative to entering order data is next displayed on the CRT screen. The operator would key in the required data. Selected fields which are entered would be edited on intelligent terminals. For example, the zip code could be edited to ensure that numeric data was entered. After the data is entered, it can be sight checked to ensure further accuracy. The data is then sent to the main computer storage of the system; 3) After the data is entered, the computer system will format the screen for entering the part number and quantity. Again, the data will be edited. After the data is entered and sent to the main computer system, the description would be displayed and the price calculated. The system would also check that the item number was in stock and that the customer credit was satisfactory. Since all of this processing would take place in a few seconds, the customer could be informed directly on the telephone that the order will be sent or that the item was out of stock. At the same time, if the ordering criteria is met, a shipping order could be sent to the warehouse remote terminal; and an invoice record could be generated and stored on disk for printing later that evening.

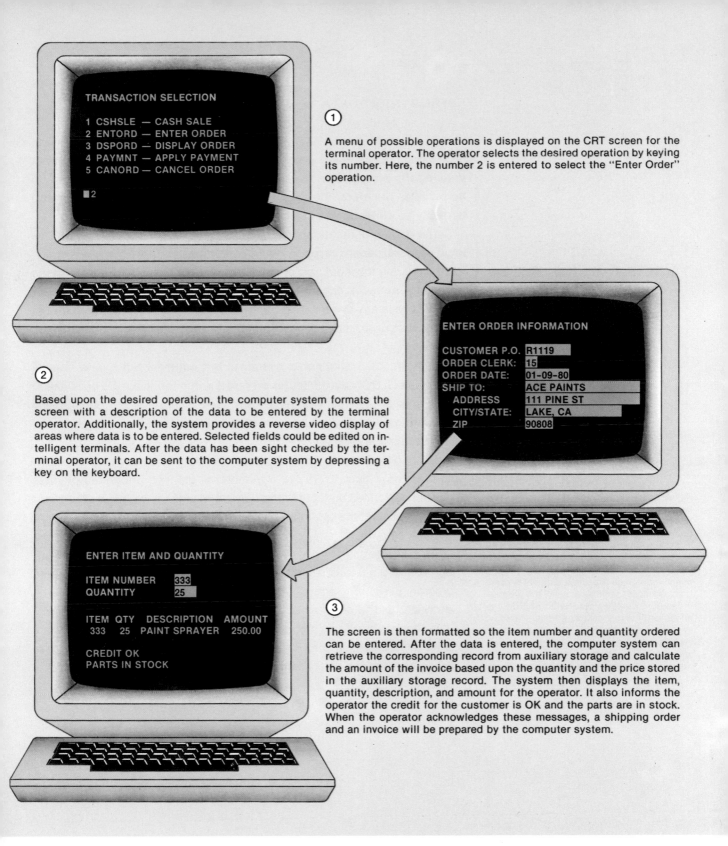

TRANSACTION SELECTION

1 CSHSLE — CASH SALE
2 ENTORD — ENTER ORDER
3 DSPORD — DISPLAY ORDER
4 PAYMNT — APPLY PAYMENT
5 CANORD — CANCEL ORDER

■ 2

① A menu of possible operations is displayed on the CRT screen for the terminal operator. The operator selects the desired operation by keying its number. Here, the number 2 is entered to select the "Enter Order" operation.

ENTER ORDER INFORMATION

CUSTOMER P.O. R1119
ORDER CLERK: 15
ORDER DATE: 01-09-80
SHIP TO: ACE PAINTS
  ADDRESS 111 PINE ST
  CITY/STATE: LAKE, CA
  ZIP 90808

② Based upon the desired operation, the computer system formats the screen with a description of the data to be entered by the terminal operator. Additionally, the system provides a reverse video display of areas where data is to be entered. Selected fields could be edited on intelligent terminals. After the data has been sight checked by the terminal operator, it can be sent to the computer system by depressing a key on the keyboard.

ENTER ITEM AND QUANTITY

ITEM NUMBER 333
QUANTITY 25

ITEM QTY DESCRIPTION AMOUNT
333 25 PAINT SPRAYER 250.00

CREDIT OK
PARTS IN STOCK

③ The screen is then formatted so the item number and quantity ordered can be entered. After the data is entered, the computer system can retrieve the corresponding record from auxiliary storage and calculate the amount of the invoice based upon the quantity and the price stored in the auxiliary storage record. The system then displays the item, quantity, description, and amount for the operator. It also informs the operator the credit for the customer is OK and the parts are in stock. When the operator acknowledges these messages, a shipping order and an invoice will be prepared by the computer system.

Figure 5-16 A transaction-oriented system allows interaction between the operator and computer system for immediate response and feedback.

EDITING INPUT DATA

Regardless of whether data is entered for processing in a batch mode or a transaction-oriented processing mode, the validity of the input data entering the system is critical if the results of computer processing are to be reliable. Therefore, the data entered into a system for processing will normally be edited prior to being used for processing.

The editing of input data can take place at one of several steps in the input process, depending upon the type of processing and the type of equipment preparing the input data. If batch processing is used, the editing of the input data normally occurs as the data is read into the main computer system unless key-to-disk shared processor units are used to prepare the data. In that case, most of the editing will take place on the key-to-disk system.

With transaction-oriented systems, the editing of the data usually takes place on the main computer system if dumb terminals are used and at the terminal if intelligent terminals are used. There are, of course, many combinations which are used in different applications, but generally, editing is done in this way.

Although different applications will have particular criteria for validating input data, there are a number of distinct categories of tests which are performed on input data prior to allowing the data to become part of the processing in a system. Some of these tests are:

Figure 5-17 In the example above, a non-numeric zip code is entered first. The operator is informed that the zip code is not numeric and is requested to re-enter the zip code. When a numeric zip code is entered, the data is accepted. The test for a numeric zip code could be performed by a program in main computer storage if a dumb terminal is used. If an intelligent terminal is used, the program in the minicomputer associated with the terminal would likely do this editing. On some systems, as soon as the non-numeric character (A) was entered, a bell would ring and the keyboard would lock up until the operator backspaced and corrected the error.

1) Tests to ensure numeric or alphabetic data is included in a field (Figure 5–17). For example, a zip code in a field must always be numeric. Therefore, the program performing editing on the input data can check the values in the zip code field to ensure that they are numeric. If they are not numeric, then the data entered is incorrect. If the zip code entered is numeric, there is no assurance that the proper zip code has been entered, but there is assurance that the data entered has the proper format.

2) Tests to ensure the reasonableness of data in a field. A reasonableness check is performed to ensure that the data entered into a system is within normal or accepted boundaries. For example, it may be determined within a company that no employee is authorized to work more than 70 hours in one week. Therefore, if the value in the hours worked field in an input record is greater than 70, the value in the field would be indicated as an error.

3) Range tests to determine if the input data falls within the range of acceptable values. If, for example, a company had departments numbered 03 through 17, then these values are within the range of valid values. Any other values in the department number field of an input record would be in error.

4) Tests for data consistency. In some cases, data entered by itself cannot be found to be invalid. If, however, the data is examined in the context of other data which is entered for the same record, then discrepancies can be found. For example, in an airline reservation system, round trip tickets are commonly purchased. If the terminal operator enters the date on which the passenger is leaving, the editing program has little help in determining whether the date entered is valid. Similarly, if the return date is entered by itself, there is no way to know whether the date is invalid. If, however, the return date is examined in light of the departure date, then errors may be found. For example, if the return date is earlier than the departure date, then it is likely an error has been made in entering the dates (Figure 5-18). Consistency tests can be extremely important in verifying valid input data.

5) Checking for transcription and transposition errors. When the terminal and data entry operators enter data, there is always a possibility that an error will be made in entering the source data. These errors are generally classed as either transcription errors or transposition errors.

Figure 5-18 On the CRT terminal above, the operator has entered the departure date as 08/17/81 and the return date as 08/25/80. Clearly, this is invalid data entering the system (assuming the transaction takes place before 08/17/80); but without testing the data for consistency, the error would not have been found.

A transcription error occurs when an error is made in copying the values from a source document. For example, if the operator keys the customer number 7165 when the proper number is 7765, a transcription error has been made. Errors such as this may occur because the writing on the source document was unclear or the operator may misread the source document. A transposition error happens when two numbers are switched. Such an error has occurred when the number 7765 is entered into the system as 7756. The most common means to detect these types of errors is called a check digit. Through the use of an arithmetic formula, an additional digit is calculated for the number in question. For example, the four digits in the number 7765 would be utilized in a calculation to derive a single digit which is appended to the end of the original number. Thus, the number 7765 could be extended as 77658. The number 8 is the check digit which is appended to the end of the original number. When the entire number is subsequently entered back into the system, the same four numbers used to calculate the check digit (7765) are used in the same formula to again calculate a check digit. If the new check digit matches the one on the number which was read into storage, then the number is assumed valid. If, however, the new check digit in the example were not 8, as would happen if the number entered were 71658 or 77568, then the operator would be notified of an error.

These five examples are but a few of the types of error checking which are applied to input records being entered into a computer system in either a batch processing system or a transaction-oriented processing system. Again, the emphasis is on detecting errors in input records prior to the data entering the system. Once invalid data has been allowed to enter an application system, it is very costly to detect the error and make a correction.

Many times, stories about checks being mistakenly written for $10 million dollars by a computer or about people being billed $250,000.00 for their water bill are a result of input data not being checked closely before it is allowed to enter the application system. There is no reason in a properly designed system for these types of errors to occur.

Data input systems

Batch processing systems are used primarily when large amounts of data are to be prepared and processed. A centralized data entry department is normally used for batch processing systems. This department is designed and organized to prepare large amounts of input data rapidly and efficiently.

Transaction-oriented systems are used when immediate feedback from a computer system is required. The preparation of data for entry into the system is usually on a single record basis which is processed entirely before another record is entered. Although this is much slower than batch processing, it has the distinct advantage in some applications of providing immediate response and feedback.

The choice of the method for processing data, and as a result the way data is entered into a computer system, is largely dependent upon the application involved.

Dedicated and Specialized

Input

Devices

A variety of specialized input devices have been devised to increase the efficiency of entering data into the computer system for certain applications. Some of these devices and their uses are examined on the following pages.

Source Documents That

Can Be Read

By Machine

The process of preparing data for input to a computer system is costly and time-consuming. In an attempt to bypass the data entry step for batch processing, many schemes have been tried. The most successful of these began in the mid-1950's and involved reading data stored on the source document directly into main computer storage without first converting it to a machine-readable medium.

The technology of reading data stored on a source document is called optical character recognition (OCR). There are three basic methods for recording data on a document to be read by OCR devices: 1) Optically readable marks; 2) Bar codes; 3) Optically readable characters, including handwritten characters.

Optical marks on a form consisting of single vertical marks are used to indicate a response to a question or to fill in data. Mark readers are frequently used in test scoring applications and market research applications.

Bar codes are optically read by devices that sense marks or bars that are pre-recorded on tags or merchandise. The width and combination of vertical lines represent data. The Universal Product Code (UPC) is a bar code that is now placed on many consumer products to facilitate check-out at retail stores.

More sophisticated optical character readers scan the shape of a character on a document, compare the character scanned with a predefined shape, and convert the character read into its corresponding bit pattern for storing in main computer storage. OCR-A is the most commonly used font that can be read by OCR machines; but handwritten documents can be read also.

A fourth type of machine-readable data is called Magnetic Ink Character Recognition (MICR). MICR is widely used in the banking industry.

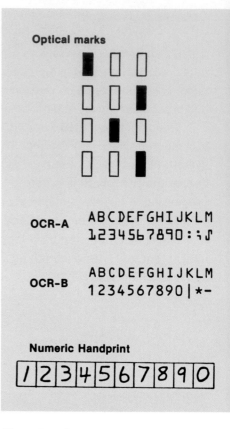

Figure 5-20 The chart above illustrates the most commonly used forms of data that can be read directly from the source document. The optical marks are primarily used for test scoring. Bar codes are used extensively in retail operations. The OCR-A and OCR-B fonts are

Figure 5-19 In the 1950's, the banking industry settled on MICR (Magnetic Ink Character Recognition) as the method for processing checks. The characters are standardized and are used by all banks throughout the U. S. With MICR, human and machine-readable characters are recorded on the bottom of checks. The characters contain a magnetic ink that can be read by MICR devices. The data read can be stored in main computer storage for processing as required.

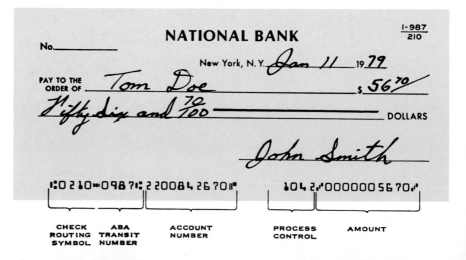

Bar codes

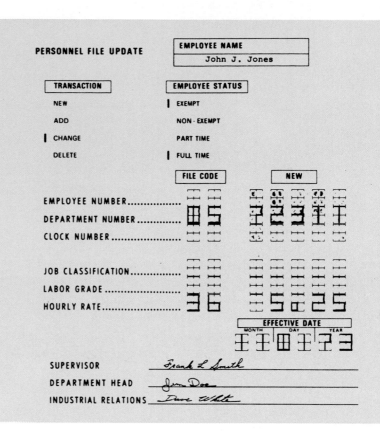

015400 831741

NOPQRSTUVWXYZ
=┤?"$%|&'{}*+,-./■Ⅱ

NOPQRSTUVWXYZ
=+,./<>■

MICR

0 1 2 3 4

5 6 7 8 9

PERSONNEL FILE UPDATE

EMPLOYEE NAME
John J. Jones

TRANSACTION
NEW
ADD
| CHANGE
DELETE

EMPLOYEE STATUS
| EXEMPT
NON - EXEMPT
PART TIME
| FULL TIME

FILE CODE   NEW

EMPLOYEE NUMBER
DEPARTMENT NUMBER 05   7231
CLOCK NUMBER .....

JOB CLASSIFICATION .....
LABOR GRADE .....
HOURLY RATE 36   5625

EFFECTIVE DATE
MONTH DAY YEAR
10 73

SUPERVISOR _Frank L South_
DEPARTMENT HEAD _Jim Doe_
INDUSTRIAL RELATIONS _Dave White_

read by machines which can recognize the characters. The OCR-A font is used in about 75% of the applications using OCR input. On some devices, hand printed data can be read; while MICR is the standard for the banking industry.

Figure 5-21 The Personnel File Update form above allows data to be recorded in the form of machine readable marks and hand printed characters. The hand printed numbers must follow certain size and shape guidelines so they can be scanned by the OCR reader.

Figure 5-22 The subscription renewal form below is typical of forms using the OCR–A font. The OCR–A font has been adopted by the National Retail Merchants Association as the standard for marking merchandise in department stores and other retail outlets.

RUSH RENEW

Your Subscription has run out.

Please rush this card back to us to make sure your copies keep coming without a break in service.
☐ Payment enclosed

1 YEAR FOR $5.00

BX CAL2   L029 ANA 86201 SR600J019

JACK CHALS   DEC 77

152 N E 17TH PL BEW   38109

If you have recently renewed your subscription, please disregard this notice. If a break in service occurs, please allow 6 to 8 weeks for your reinstatement copy to be shipped.
(Add $2 per year postage outside the U.S. its Possessions and Canada.)

The Machines

That

Read

Figure 5-23 The Burroughs B9138 unit (left) is a reader-sorter for magnetic ink character recognition (MICR) documents. This unit reads, endorses, microfilms, and sorts checks in one pass through the system. It is capable of processing 2,600 checks per minute. This or similar devices are used throughout the banking industry.

The devices illustrated on these pages are used to read data directly from the source document rather than requiring the data to be placed on cards, tape, or disk prior to entering a computer system. These optical scanning devices offer both time and money advantages over other data entry methods. The major disadvantage is that the data which is to be read must be specified on the documents in a readable format.

The optical reading of data is an established methodology, dating from about 1955. Improvements have been made since that time to make the reading faster and more accurate. Today, it is claimed by the manufacturers of these devices that more errors are made entering data by data entry operators than by OCR machines reading directly from the source document.

In many cases, the key to justifying optical character reading devices is document volume. As a general rule, if an organization processes 5,000 or more transactions or documents of the same type per day, then OCR devices can be considered as a form of input. Additionally, convenience and speed may be considered.

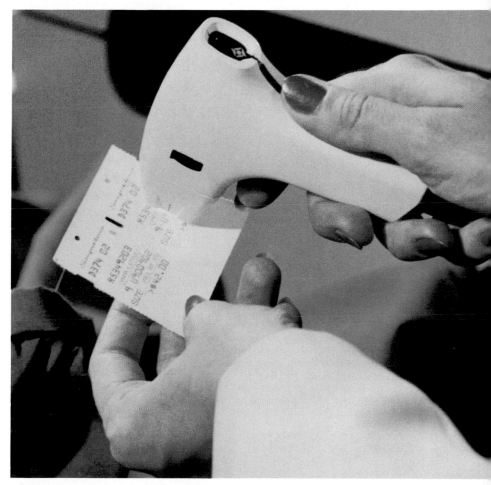

Figure 5-24 The ULTRAPHASE[R] terminal (above) is used to read universal bar codes. The data read, which identifies the product, is stored in the memory of the device. The retailer then enters the quantity to be ordered. The terminal is then connected to a data communications line and the data is sent to a large computer system for processing.

Figure 5-25 The Recognition Equipment Incorporated OCR Wand Reader (above) is being used to read OCR-A font on a typical retail tag. The human-readable characters are scanned by the reading mechanism and are digitized. The resulting digital data is then compared to known digital configurations for characters until a match is found. When a match is found,

the data can then be stored in computer storage or on auxiliary storage for immediate or later processing. Hand-held OCR wand devices are the most widely used OCR data entry systems in use today. They are used in retail outlets and other applications where the reading device must be movable and flexible in its use.

Figure 5-28 Burroughs TD700 terminals are used in a large department store for sales and

Point of

Sale Terminals

The ability to enter data into a computer system at the time and place a transaction with a customer occurs is a major advantage for retail establishments. Point of Sale (POS) terminals allow this to happen.

With POS systems, the terminals serve as the data entry devices to either minicomputers located in the retail establishment or to larger computers located elsewhere. The data entered is used to maintain sales records, update inventory, perform automatic calculations such as sales taxes, verify credit, and other activities critical to the running of the business.

Point of sale terminals are designed to be easy to operate, requiring little technical knowledge.

Figure 5-26 The AmTote division of the General Instrument Corporation was chosen by the State of New Jersey to provide a complete computer system for the nation's first legalized numbers lottery (above). Five hundred terminals are now in operation that dispense and keep track of the distribution of over $1 million in lottery tickets each week.

Figure 5-27 One large nationwide department store chain has installed over 6,000 IBM point of sale terminals that serve both as sales registers and data entry devices (below). These terminals provide the chain with immediate sales and inventory information, saving the company money and producing more timely management information.

inventory control, providing the store with added customer service and convenience.

Point of sale terminals fall into three major categories: general merchandise retail systems, supermarket-oriented systems, and food systems. Although they all perform similar functions, there are a few differences because of the requirements of the different businesses. For example, POS terminals used in retail stores generally have credit authorization capabilities while those used in fast food restaurants do not.

POS terminals are proving a big aid to retail merchants as they attempt to cope with lower profit margins and higher inventory costs. There is little doubt that the terminals are a standard part of the retail industry.

Figure 5-29 The AM International Documentor system (above) is widely used in the food service industry as a point of sale terminal. In addition to performing the traditional cash register function, more than 20 different control reports can be obtained, ranging from the sales volume at any time during the day to the current inventory of food products.

Figure 5-30 As credit cards replace cash, retail store losses from fraud, bad debts, and stolen cards are mounting. More and more stores are using credit authorization systems. To request credit authorization on the Datatrol terminal below, the clerk enters customer identifying information. The system indicates whether credit is authorized or denied.

Figure 5-31 The input station at the left is an IBM 5230 terminal used in a data collection system. The data is being entered under adverse conditions by a worker still operating the forklift. The operator is reporting the removal of an item from inventory as the transaction occurs. Typical of data collection environments, the primary job of the operator is to run a forklift, not to enter data. Therefore, data collection terminals must be simple and quick to operate, so that entering data does not interfere with the main job of the person using the terminal.

Figure 5-32 To assist in control of inventory and the preparation of up-to-date sales reports, Shasta Beverages uses a Mohawk Data Sciences Series 21 System. Keystation operators enter billing and inventory data into the system as the transactions occur. At the end of each day, the data is transmitted to a central computer. The ability to enter data at the site of the transaction allows more accurate data entry than when the data was sent to a data entry department for preparation. The increase in the speed and accuracy of entering the data enables Shasta managers to receive output information faster, allowing a tighter control on sales costs.

Figure 5-33 The IBM 3630 plant communication terminal can be used for data collection in a number of different environments. Here, the OCR wand which can be a part of the terminal is used to read a shipping label typed in OCR font. This data, together with data entered on the keys of the terminal, can be saved on tape or disk or can be sent immediately to a central computer system.

Figure 5-34 Ace Hardware Corporation uses a Mohawk Data Sciences Series 21 System in the warehouse. As the shipments are made, data is entered into the system and stored on disk. At the end of the day, the data is transmitted to their central computer. This allows daily printed reports to be generated for each field office.

Collecting Data

In The

Factory

For many years, the data entry function was confined to a centralized keypunch department and batch processing dominated. Today, however, data entry devices and computer terminals may be found throughout the company, including factory and warehouse locations.

Data collection equipment is also an important part of the factory environment. Data collection includes operations to obtain data in an uncontrolled environment from those people responsible for doing the work being reported on.

In many cases, data collection equipment is found in "hostile" environments, where heat, humidity, and cleanliness cannot be controlled. In addition, the devices are usually operated by people who are not clerically oriented, such as machinists, warehouse workers, or forklift operators. Thus, the terminals must be easy to operate in the environment in which they are found.

Data collection devices range from portable devices carried throughout the factory which allow data to be entered on small tape cartridges to sophisticated terminal systems with multiple input stations that feed data directly into a minicomputer or a large central computer system.

New Frontiers

In Data Entry

As computer technology has become more sophisticated, it has become apparent that devices requiring input data to be keyed, such as keypunches or alphanumeric terminals, cannot adequately serve the input needs of all applications.

For example, the medical profession found it difficult to transfer an X-ray on a piece of film to a computer for analysis by using a keyboard device. For applications such as this, digitizers were developed. A digitizer contains a point-identifying device called a cursor or other reading mechanism which can be passed over the sur-

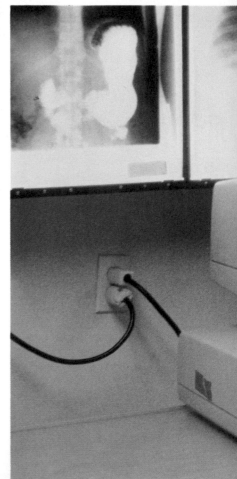

Figure 5-35 The picture above shows a factory inspector reporting on the status of an inspection using the Interstate Electronics Corporation Intelligent Voice Data Entry System. Voice data entry is a technique for using the human voice to enter data directly into a computer system. The heart of the voice terminal is an acoustic pattern classifier that produces a digital code in response to a spoken word. The system is "trained" by an operator who speaks a word to it 8 or 10 times. The electronics in the machine form a 240-bit digital pattern that matches the sound spoken by the operator. Once the system is trained, it will understand the words spoken to it by that particular operator and take the appropriate action when the word is recognized. For example, if the operator spoke the word "bad," the machine could be programmed to add 1 to an accumulator for bad parts; while if the operator spoke the word "good," the machine would add 1 to a good parts accumulator. Some systems have an 800-900 word vocabulary with a word recognition accuracy of about 99%.

face of a drawing or graphic representation of a figure to convert the image to digital data. The digital data can then be displayed on a CRT screen or otherwise be analyzed or processed on the computer system.

Perhaps the most exciting innovation in data entry is direct human-to-computer communication via the spoken word. Electronic voice input terminals permit the direct entry of data into a computer system by human speech. Voice entry is useful when data must be entered by persons who cannot use their hands for keying data or where voice input is faster and more convenient.

Figure 5-36 The technician in the picture below is using a cursor on a Hewlett-Packard digitizer to scan an X-ray of a skull. The digitizer determines the points on the X-ray based upon X–Y coordinates. These coordinates, which can be as many as 1,000 per square inch, are sent to the computer system. From the coordinates obtained, the system is able to reproduce the X-ray on the CRT screen. Digitizers are used not only in health services applications, but in engineering, architectural, and other areas as well.

Figure 5-37 The terminal operator above is using a light pen as input to a computer system. When the light pen is placed on a point on the screen and pressed, it is able to complete a photoelectric circuit which is created by a rapidly moving beam behind the CRT screen. The terminal system is able to determine the X–Y coordinate of the point where the pen was located when the circuit was completed. In this manner, points can be located on the screen and lines drawn between them under program control.

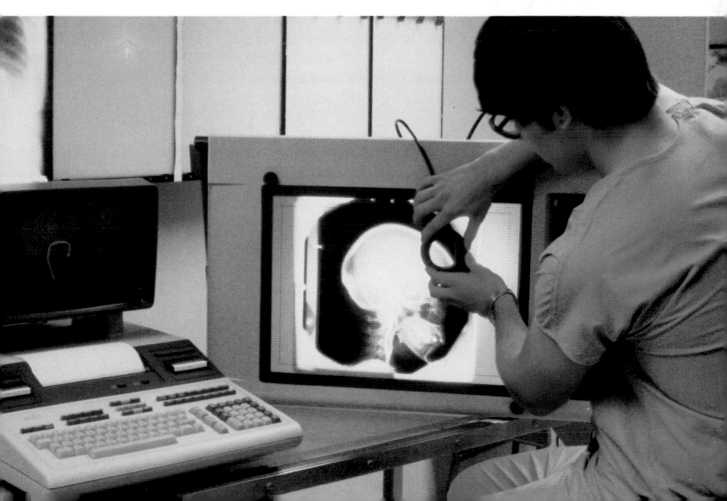

Chapter summary

The following points have been discussed and explained in this chapter.

1. The input step must occur before any data can be processed and any information produced on a computer system.

2. If the data which is fed into the computer is not valid, the information received from the computer system cannot be trustworthy.

3. Two basic systems are used when entering data into a computer system. Transaction-oriented systems require data to be entered directly into main computer storage for immediate processing. In batch processing systems, source documents containing the data are gathered together as a group, or batch. The data is then recorded on an input medium and is processed as a batch of data.

4. It is critical that the data being entered into a computer system for processing is accurate.

5. A punched card is a piece of lightweight cardboard capable of storing data in the form of punched holes recorded in predefined locations.

6. An input record is subdivided into fields.

7. The keypunch is used to punch holes in cards.

8. To ensure the accuracy of the transfer of data from the source documents to punched cards, a process called verification is used. Verifying requires an operator to rekey data and the rekeyed data is compared to the data already punched in cards.

9. A card reader is used to read cards into storage. Card readers typically read 200–1,200 cards per minute. When a card is read, the holes are changed from the representation in the card to the corresponding representation of the data in main computer storage.

10. Since cards have significant disadvantages, they are being replaced by magnetic media such as magnetic tape and magnetic disk.

11. The Mohawk tape data recorder used tape instead of punched cards as the storage medium for input records. It offered the advantages of faster réading, easier handling, a reusable medium, and more economical storage.

12. Floppy disks, or diskettes, were introduced by IBM as a storage medium for input records.

13. For large data entry tasks, key-to-disk shared processor systems are finding increased use. With these systems, a number of keyboard consoles are connected through a minicomputer to a common large disk storage unit. As the data is keyed from the various console stations, the data is stored on the disk under control of the minicomputer.

14. All key-to-disk shared processor systems have the following in common: a number of keying stations are used with the system; the keying stations are under the control of a minicomputer; the data keyed on the various stations is stored on disk and after the keying job is completed, is transferred to tape for entry to the computer system.

15. Key-to-disk shared processor systems offer several advantages: operator productivity is improved; data editing is possible because of the minicomputer; commonly used data fields can be retrieved automatically from the disk by the operator; statistics can be kept for all keying operations.

16. The major disadvantage of key-to-disk shared processor systems is that they are expensive. Therefore, only large volume installations use them.

17. When using local job entry, the medium on which the input data is stored is transported to the computer room for entry to the system. With remote job entry, the device which reads the data is located at a remote site from the computer which will process the data.

18. In a transaction-oriented system, the data to be processed is not transcribed onto a machine-readable medium prior to processing. Instead, the data is entered directly into main computer storage for immediate processing by the computer program.

19. The cathode ray tube (CRT) terminal is the most popular means of entering data in a transaction-oriented system.

20. A CRT terminal includes a television-like screen and a keyboard for entering data.

21. Intelligent terminals include not only the CRT terminal but also a microprocessor and storage which allows the terminal to process data when it is entered without sending it to the main computer system.

22. Data entered into a computer system should be edited to ensure that it is valid data. Some of the tests which can be performed are: numeric and alphabetic tests; reasonableness tests; range tests; consistency tests; transcription and transposition tests.

23. Optical character reading devices are the most successful devices at reading data stored on a source document instead of first placing the data on a machine-readable medium.

24. There are three basic methods of optical character reading: optically readable marks on forms; bar codes; optically readable characters. The OCR–A font is the most widely used readable character font.

25. Point of sale terminals serve as data entry devices to either minicomputers located in the retail establishment or to larger computers located elsewhere.

26. Data collection includes operations to obtain data in an uncontrolled environment from those people responsible for doing the work reported on.

Student Learning Exercises

Review questions

1. What are the consequences if unreliable data is entered into a computer system for processing?

2. What is the difference between batch processing systems and transaction-oriented systems?

3. How do input requirements differ between batch systems and transaction-oriented systems?

4. How is input data prepared using punched cards?

5. Why have more modern installations abandoned the punched card and moved to magnetic media for input?

6. What is a floppy disk, or diskette? What is its significance in data entry?

7. Explain the advantages and disadvantages of key-to-disk shared processor systems.

8. What is the difference between local job entry and remote job entry?

9. Explain the difference between a dumb and an intelligent terminal.

10. What are some typical editing tests which must be performed? Why are they used?

11. What is a check digit? Give an example of its use.

12. What determines whether a batch or transaction-oriented system will be used? Describe some applications which use batch processing. Describe some applications using transaction-oriented processing.

13. What is OCR? What are its advantages? Disadvantages?

14. Where are point of sales terminals used? Why have they become so useful to retailers?

15. What are some of the newer innovations in entering data into a computer system? Describe some applications where they are used.

Controversial issues in data processing

1. Some authorities have suggested that batch processing systems are obsolete and all systems should be transaction-oriented. Others maintain that the only efficient method for processing large volumes of data is batch processing, and that transaction-oriented systems were developed as a marketing scheme by computer manufacturers to sell more computer hardware. Do you think all systems should be transaction-oriented? Be able to defend your position.

2. Voice input is now a reality. By talking into a device, vocal responses can be converted to computer processable data. Assuming that further developments in computer technology will result in microcomputers being as common as television sets in the home, make a list of possible uses of voice input 25 years in the future. Use your imagination!

Research projects

1. Many times punched cards and OCR forms are used as "turnaround" documents. For example, in billing applications a punched card or an OCR document will frequently be enclosed with the bill and will include the statement "PLEASE RETURN WITH PAYMENT." Bring samples of these documents to class and be able to analyze and explain the contents of these documents.

2. Frequent articles appear in newspapers concerning errors which were "caused by the computer." Bring several of these articles to class and discuss "if" and "how" these errors could have been prevented by editing the data prior to processing the data on the computer.

Picture credits

Figure 5-1 Pertec Computer Corp.	Figure 5-23 Burroughs Corp.	Figure 5-31 IBM
Figure 5-6 IBM	Figure 5-24 Bergen Brunswig Corp.	Figure 5-32 Mohawk Data Sciences Corp.
Figure 5-8 Mohawk Data Sciences Corp.	Figure 5-25 Recognition Equipment Corp.	Figure 5-33 IBM
Figure 5-9 IBM		Figure 5-34 Mohawk Data Sciences Corp.
Figure 5-10 IBM	Figure 5-26 General Instrument Corp.	Figure 5-35 Interstate Electronics Corp.
Figure 5-12 Mohawk Data Sciences Corp.	Figure 5-27 IBM	Figure 5-36 Hewlett-Packard
Figure 5-13 Hazeltine Corp.	Figure 5-28 Burroughs Corp.	Figure 5-37 The Atchison, Topeka, and Santa Fe Railway Corp.
Figure 5-14 Qume	Figure 5-29 AM International	
Figure 5-15 RCA	Figure 5-30 Datatrol Incorporated	

Chapter 6
Obtaining Output From The Computer

Objectives

- An awareness of the types of output available from computer systems

- An understanding of the types of printers available, their speeds, and their advantages and disadvantages

- A knowledge of the characteristics of cathode ray tube terminals

- An understanding of the creation and use of detail, summary, and exception reports

- An understanding of the use of CRT terminals in transaction-oriented systems for inquiry and the factors to be considered in developing inquiry systems

Chapter 6

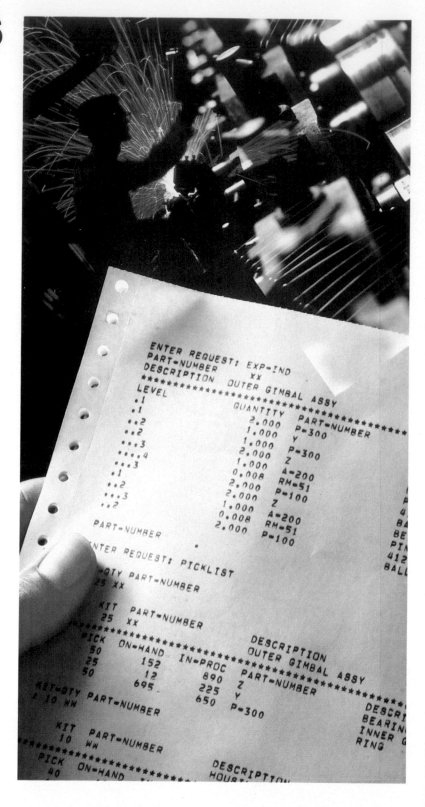

Figure 6-1 The printed report has, since the beginning of computer systems, been the primary means of obtaining output from the computer. Today, however, the printed report is only one of many methods used to obtain information from the computer.

Obtaining Output
From The Computer

"I'm trying to work out ways to program the machine so a sociologist can sit down and talk sociology talk to it and the machine will answer back in sociology talk."[1]

Introduction

The last step in the basic data processing cycle of input, process, and output, is output, which provides the user of the computer with the information that, for most applications, is the primary reason for using the system.

For many years, the primary form of output from computer systems to meet the information needs of computer users has been the printed report (Figure 6-1). Today, however, there are a wide variety of output devices to serve the diverse needs of business and government. In a modern computer environment, computer terminals are used to display information to users, plotters are used to produce complex drawings, microfilm is used to store information which previously would have been printed on reports, and even voice response systems are used to convey information to users in a human voice.

The selection of the type of output to be generated from a computer system and the manner in which the information is to be made available to the user depends upon the needs of the user, the application in which the output is being produced, the hardware and software currently available in an installation, and a number of other factors. In this chapter, some of the types of computer output that can be produced will be explored, together with the advantages and disadvantages of these means of obtaining information from a computer system.

---

1 Aaron Kronenberg in "You Are An Interfacer of Black Boxes," Richard Todd, Harold Ober Associates, 1970.

PRINTED OUTPUT

Since printed reports comprise one of the most widely used forms of computer output, it is important to be aware of the various types of printing devices that are currently available.

In the past, printers were usually large devices intended to print as fast as possible on a computer system. Recently, however, it has been recognized that there is a need for a wide variety of printer systems to meet the diverse needs of computer users. For example, the user of a microcomputer selling for less than $1,000.00 does not need, nor want, a computer printer capable of printing 2,000 lines of print per minute. On the other hand, large scale computer users such as utility companies, which produce millions of lines of print per month, can effectively utilize printers capable of printing many thousands of lines per minute. These diverse needs have resulted in the development of a wide variety of printers for use with computer systems.

Although there are a number of ways printers can be classified, two common classifications are: 1) The method used to place the image on the paper; 2) The speed of the printer. Both factors are important considerations in choosing a printer for a computer system.

Printing characters on the report

Printers accomplish the task of placing characters on a page of paper in one of two ways: 1) Impact printing; 2) Non-impact printing. The selection of the printing method is directly related to the quality of print required, the speed necessary, and the cost factors.

Impact printers

Impact printing devices transfer the image onto paper by some type of printing mechanism striking the paper, ribbon, and character together. Two techniques are commonly used (Figure 6-2). The first technique is front-striking, where a character strikes a ribbon against the paper to form an image in the manner used by typewriters. The second technique utilizes a hammer device in which the ribbon and paper are struck against the character by the hammer to form the image on the paper. Both techniques are widely used in industry today.

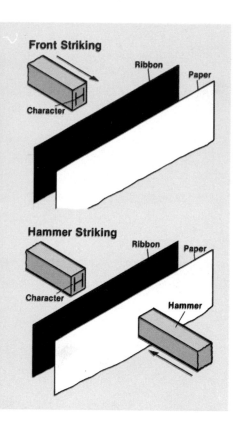

Figure 6-2 Impact printers operate in two ways — front striking and hammer striking. With front striking, the character strikes the ribbon first and then the paper, leaving an impression. Hammers strike the paper which strikes the ribbon and then the character on hammer striking printers.

Impact printers can print either a solid character or a dot matrix character. Dot matrix characters are formed by a series of dots (Figure 6–3). Generally, the quality of the solid character is better than the quality of a dot matrix character, but printers using a dot matrix character are considerably less expensive than solid character printers. Thus, when a printer is purchased, the user must balance price against print quality.

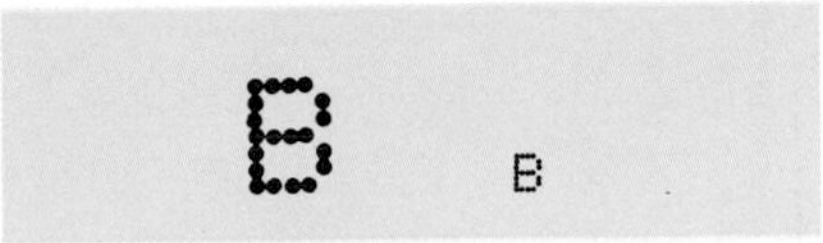

Figure 6-3 The large B on the left illustrates the dots which are used to form a dot matrix character. The character above is formed in an array 7 dots high and 5 dots wide. Depending on the printer, the matrix can be anywhere from 7 X 5 to 9 X 9 dots. The small B on the right is the size that would be printed by the printer.

Non-impact printers

Non-impact printers generally use specially coated or sensitized papers that respond to thermal or electrostatic stimuli to form an image. Some use ink jets or xerography to form an image on plain paper.

Each method used for placing an image on paper has its advantages and disadvantages. Impact printing is relatively noisy because the paper is struck when printing occurs. On the other hand, since the paper is struck, interleaved carbon paper can be used to create multiple copies of pages in a report. Non-impact printers cannot create carbon copies. They are, however, very quiet.

Printer speed classifications

Another common method for classifying printers is speed. Low speed printers print less than 300 lines per minute on a report; high speed printers are capable of printing between 300 and 3,000 lines per minute, while very high speed printers can print in excess of 3,000 lines per minute. A high speed printer printing 3,000 lines per minute will print 396,000 characters per minute or 6,600 characters per second on the report.

The following paragraphs explore the uses of the various speeds of printers.

Figure 6-4 The Dataproducts M–200 Matrix Printer is a low-speed printer that prints 125–300 lines per minute, depending on the number of characters on each line.

Low speed printers

Low speed printers are commonly used with microcomputer or minicomputer systems or in applications where reports are required, but the volume of output data to be produced is relatively low (Figure 6–4). Both impact and non-impact printing techniques are used on low speed printers.

Most low speed printers operate by printing a character at a time in a manner somewhat similar to the operational characteristics of a typewriter. Printers which print a character at a time are called serial printers. These machines typically print from 15 characters per second up to 300 lines per minute (each line can contain up to 132 characters). The cost of low speed printers varies from approximately $500.00 to as high as $10,000.00.

There are numerous factors which influence the speed at which printers operate. Factors such as the number of characters printed per line, and, on some printers, the size of the character printed can all affect the printing speeds.

High speed printers

As the demand for printing information from a computer system increases, the use of high speed printers is required. High speed printers operate in the range of 300–3,000 lines printed per minute.

Most printers in this speed range are impact printers which print a line at a time instead of a character at a time (they are called line printers). The most widely used printers in this range are IBM printers. This is because the IBM 1403 printer was, for a period of fifteen years, by far the dominant printer in the business. Subsequent printers from IBM such as the 3211 printer (Figure 6–5) have retained the popularity of IBM printers. Printers at this speed typically cost from $3,000.00 to over $100,000.00.

Figure 6-5 The IBM 3211 printer is a direct descendent of the IBM 1403 printer, the most popular printer in data processing history. The 1403, which originally sold for about $38,000.00, still costs about $30,000.00 when purchased used even though some of them are 20 years old.

Very high speed printers

For the first twenty years of the existence of computer systems, computer printers did not radically change. Most were impact printers with solid characters whose speed did not exceed 1,000 lines per minute.

More recently, matrix printers and non-impact printers were introduced to satisfy the needs of the growing computer market. With these needs, further research was devoted to the development of different printer technologies. One of the more exciting innovations of the past several years is the development of non-impact printers which can print over 20,000 lines per minute.

Using a process similar to that used for copying machines, Xerox, IBM, and several other companies have developed these very high speed machines (Figure 6-6). They are used in installations which normally print more than one million lines per month. In smaller installations, their cost cannot be justified. Cost of such systems ranges from approximately $150,000.00 to $300,000.00

Figure 6-6 The IBM 3800 Laser Printer is capable of printing up to 20,040 lines per minute using laser and electrophotographic techniques. Here, the operator is making final adjustments to the paper alignment prior to beginning the operation of the machine.

Selecting a printer

The purchaser of a computer system has a sizable choice of printing devices from which to choose. The choice depends upon the amount of printing which must be done, the environment in which the printing is to take place, and the quality which must be obtained on the printed report. With these considerations in mind, the buyer has a large number of options.

DISPLAYED OUTPUT

The printers illustrated on the previous pages are used primarily in batch processing systems, although low speed printers are often found at sites remote from the main computer installation.

With the increased use of remote transaction-oriented processing systems, a need has developed for a device which can serve as both an input and an output terminal. The overwhelming choice for this device is the Cathode Ray Tube (CRT) terminal.

CRT terminals

The CRT terminal, of course, displays data on a television-like screen. The most widely-used CRT device is an alphanumeric terminal, where numeric, alphabetic, and special characters are displayed on the screen. The screens on these devices are similar in size to 9 or 12-inch television screens. The maximum number of lines and characters which can be displayed varies greatly among terminals, although many manufacturers have standardized on a 24-line format with a maximum of 80 characters per line for a total of 1,920 characters on the screen. Nine inch screens with 25 lines and 40 characters per line are used on some microcomputers.

At a minimum, all CRT terminals are capable of displaying letters of the alphabet, numbers, and an assortment of special characters. Some terminals are capable of displaying both upper and lower case letters of the alphabet, which is a desirable feature in word processing applications (Figure 6–7).

Others also offer graphic capabilities, where graphs and drawings can be displayed on the screen (Figure 6–8). These display terminals are useful for management personnel who want to see data displayed in graphical form. As can be seen, some terminals also offer color capabilities.

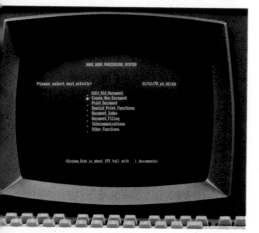

Figure 6-7 The ability to display both upper case and lower case letters of the alphabet as shown on this Wang terminal is useful in word processing applications.

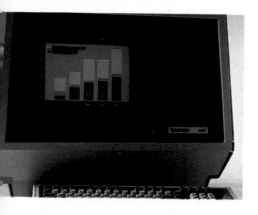

Figure 6-8 The Tektronix terminal above illustrates the types of color graphics which are useful to top-level management for market forecasts and similar activities.

Type of display control

The ability to control the display on the CRT terminal can be an important feature. Three of the more common display controls are: 1) Reverse video; 2) Scrolling; 3) Paging. These display features can be controlled from both the terminal and the computer system which is communicating with the terminal.

Reverse video refers to the process of reversing the normal display light on the CRT. For example, on terminals with reverse video, it is possible to have a dark background with light characters or a light background with dark characters (Figure 6-9). This feature permits the entire screen to be reversed, or single characters, words, or lines can be reversed to highlight areas on the screen. Reverse video is commonly used to format a screen for ease of data entry.

Scrolling refers to the ability to move lines displayed on the screen either up or down. Paging allows an entirely new "page," or screenful, of data to be displayed and changed under terminal control. These capabilities are important when searching a large amount of line data for one particular fact or piece of information.

There are other controls as well which can affect the format of the output displayed on CRT terminals, such as highlighting, underlining, intensity control, and, of course, color. When a terminal is to be used in an application, all of these capabilities must be considered so that the proper terminal is used.

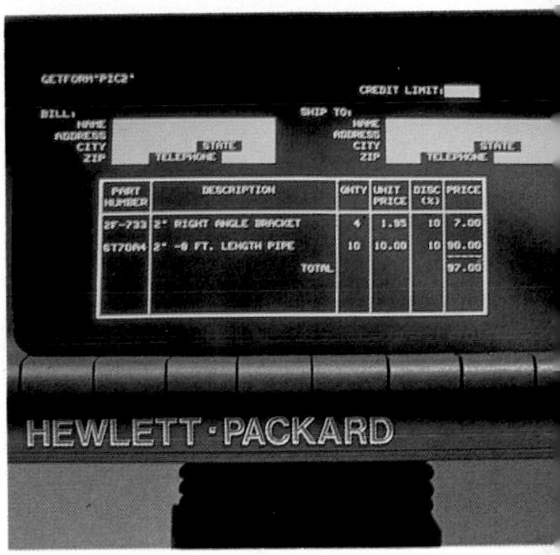

Figure 6-9 The Hewlett-Packard CRT screen above is formatted with reverse video. Reverse video highlights certain information displayed on the screen and also can provide a guide to terminal operators when entering data.

OUTPUT FROM COMPUTER SYSTEMS

It is important to have an understanding of the hardware available for producing output from a computer system; but more specifically, one should also understand the type and form that output can take when produced. In addition, it is important to realize the reasons for producing different types of output information from a computer system. These topics are explored in the following paragraphs.

External vs. internal output

Companies producing output from their computer systems classify the output into two major categories: internal output and external output.

Internal output is that output which is used within the company and which normally is used by individuals in the daily performance of their jobs. For example, an accountant can use information concerning the accounts payable to determine when debts should be paid to take maximum advantage of discounts and yet maintain the cash flow for the maximum benefit of the company.

External output is output which will be used outside the company. Invoices which are sent to other companies or payroll checks which are issued to employees are an example of external output.

Different considerations are used in the design and presentation of the output information depending upon the use of the output. For internal output, the major consideration is that the output is presented so the users of the output can perform their jobs. Generally, there are no restrictions on the format of the output except for its usefulness to the user. Therefore, the needs of the user must be carefully considered when the format in which the output is to be presented is designed.

External output, on the other hand, may have a number of restrictions, based upon company policy, legal requirements, or other reasons. For example, the W–2 form which is prepared for payroll applications must conform to the format and standards of the Internal Revenue Service.

In many cases, external reports are prepared on preprinted forms (Figure 6–10). Preprinted forms contain fixed information which is printed by the paper manufacturer. Although these forms are expensive, they may be required for certain external reports. The high-speed non-impact printers such as the IBM 3800 have the capability of duplicating the preprinted information on plain paper through the use of "overlays." This feature helps keep down the operating costs of these printers.

Thus, systems analysts who design the output from application systems must be aware of the use of the output so that the design will conform to the needs of the user and any restrictions there may be.

Figure 6-10 The W–2 form above is a preprinted form used for external output. The format of the data on this form must conform to the standards established by the Internal Revenue Service.

Presentation of output information

The format in which output information is presented to the user will vary, dependent upon whether the output is from batch processing and is presented on a printer or whether the output is from transaction-oriented processing and is presented on a CRT.

For reports created in batch processing, there are three major presentation formats: 1) Detail printed reports; 2) Summary reports; 3) Exception reports.

Detail printed reports

A detail printed report is one in which each input record is examined to determine if it will be printed on the report. In most cases, a line will be printed on the report for each input record which is read. In some cases, however, only selected input records will be printed. In either case, each input record is examined as the report is produced.

When a line is printed on a detail report, each field in the input record need not be printed, nor do the fields printed on the report need to be in the same sequence as in the input record.

Detail printed reports are usually required by individuals within an organization who need access to the day-to-day operating data which reflects the operating status of the organization. For example, people within the order department should have access to the number of units sold within a store so they can determine when to reorder. The units sold report in Figure 6-11 contains a line for each input record since each input record reflects the sales for an item.

Summary reports

The higher within an organization an individual works, the more summarized the data should normally be. Thus, the manager of a retail store may want to see a report which contains only the total units sold in each department rather than a detailed breakdown of each item (Figure 6-12).

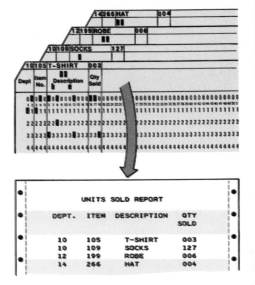

Figure 6-11 The data for the detail printed report above is obtained from each input record which is read, and a line is printed for each input record. If a detail printed report is produced through either selection processing or classification processing (see Chapter 3), then a line may not be printed on the report for each input record, but the report is still a detail printed report.

UNITS SOLD BY DEPT.

DEPT. NO.	UNITS SOLD
10	130
12	006
14	004

Figure 6-12 The summary report above contains the sales for each department. The report can be prepared from the same data which prepared the report in Figure 6-11. The ability to summarize data (Chapter 3) allows the production of summary reports.

Summary reports are more useful for higher-level personnel because their job duties do not require a detailed knowledge of each fact. Indeed, it has been found in many cases that when high-level management is presented with detail printed reports which contain information from each input record, the reports are not used because there is more data than the executive has time to review. When, on the other hand, summary reports are prepared, the executive can review the information. Thus, in some instances the type of report produced can determine whether the executive will use the information for decision-making.

Exception reports

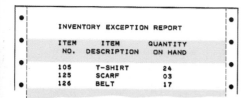

Figure 6-13 The exception report above contains those items with a quantity on hand less than 25. The three items on the report could have been selected from thousands of detail records. Exception reports provide a cost-effective way to present information.

Another method of reporting is the exception report. An exception report contains information which is deemed to be "exceptional," or other than normal. For example, a sales amount below a predefined value, a quantity of parts in inventory below a reorder quantity, or a pay check which contains an excessive amount might be found to be exceptional conditions which should be reported. The report in Figure 6–13 illustrates an exception report containing items in inventory with a quantity on hand less than 25.

Exception reports are normally produced when there is a need to know specific information, either to make decisions or to take specific action. For example, if items must be reordered when the quantity on hand falls below 25 items, then the exception report can be used to determine when items must be reordered. The advantage of exception reports in an application such as this is that they save a great deal of time and money. In a large department store, for example, there may be over 100,000 inventory items. A detail report containing all of these items could be over 2,000 pages in length. To search through the report to determine those items which must be reordered would be a difficult and time-consuming task. With an exception report, however, the items to be reordered, which might number 100–200, could be extracted and placed on a 2–4 page report.

The preparation of unnecessary detailed printed reports can also be expensive in terms of computer time. For example, the preparation of a 2,000 page report could require over an hour of computer time, while a four page report could be prepared in several minutes.

An exception report can be prepared from either detail or summarized data. For example, to prepare the inventory exception report in Figure 6-13, each input record is examined to determine if it should be printed; thus, the exception report is prepared from detail data. Similarly, an exception report can be prepared from summarized data. For example, an exception report could be prepared for a store manager which listed those departments that had sold more than 500 items (Figure 6-12).

Exception reporting is an important technique because it presents the information required at minimum cost and maximum usability.

User considerations for printed reports

The user of the information generated from computer systems is the reason for processing data on a computer. Therefore, it is critical that the information produced be presented in a way which is most beneficial to the user. Toward this end, both the user and the systems analyst who designs the format of the report must be aware of the use of the report and the format which will make the report most useful.

In addition, reports which are to be used outside the company must be designed so that someone completely unfamiliar with the report can read and understand it. For example, bank statements received each month should be clear and concise. Statements which contain unidentified numbers or codes should not be allowed.

Consideration must also be given to reports containing multiple copies. The first two copies are usually quite legible, but on some printers the fourth or fifth copies are difficult to read. Therefore, distribution of the copies must be made so that people who must constantly refer to the information on the report will have good copies. The fourth or fifth copies should normally be used for historical purposes and not as working papers.

Information which is recorded on printed reports can, in some instances, be sensitive data which should not be available to all persons. Thus, report security is a consideration when developing systems which create this type of report. For example, a report containing the profit and loss statement for a company should be closely monitored so that the information does not become available to people who should not see it.

In some companies, this is accomplished by setting up procedures which carefully account for the reports. Further steps for report security include allowing only one approved operator to run the system when these reports are generated; destroying any carbons which are used for the reports; and in some high security applications such as defense work, having a single machine which processes only one highly-sensitive application.

The printed report is one of the most important forms of output from a computer system. With the development of many types of printers for different sized machines, it is assured that the printed report will remain an important form of output for many years to come.

Transaction-oriented output

While the printed report is the principle form of output for batch systems, the display terminal is the primary means of obtaining output from a transaction-oriented system. The CRT terminal is the most widely used display terminal.

The most common approach for obtaining output in a transaction-oriented processing system is the inquiry. An inquiry is a request from the terminal operator to a computer system for information. The information is typically displayed on the CRT screen within a matter of seconds. This approach provides the user with current data and reduces the need for costly reports which could require hours and perhaps days to obtain in a batch processing system.

In today's environment, it is not unusual to find the president of the company, department managers, and secretaries and clerical personnel all having access to computer terminals for inquiry into files to obtain some needed information. The examples in Figure 6–14 illustrate two of the many types of output that can be obtained from inquiries. In the first example, a list of customers whose accounts are over 90 days past due is displayed on the CRT screen.

Example 1

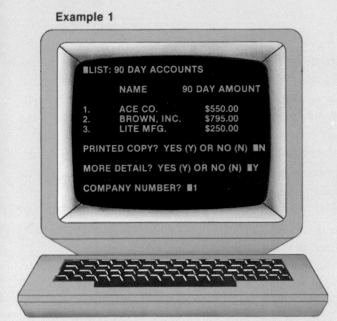

```
■LIST: 90 DAY ACCOUNTS

       NAME          90 DAY AMOUNT

1.     ACE CO.          $550.00
2.     BROWN, INC.      $795.00
3.     LITE MFG.        $250.00

PRINTED COPY? YES (Y) OR NO (N) ■N

MORE DETAIL? YES (Y) OR NO (N) ■Y

COMPANY NUMBER? ■1
```

Example 2

```
ACE COMPANY
423 CEDAR DR.
LONG BEACH, CA  (213) 555-2631
CREDIT RATING:  B
DATE                    AMOUNT
01/02/80                 200.00
02/05/80                 250.00
03/04/80                  50.00
04/19/80                  50.00
PAYMENTS       .00
BALANCE     550.00
PRINTED COPY?  YES (Y)  OR NO (N) ■Y
■END
```

In the second example, a more detailed customer sales history is displayed. These displays are obtained at the request of the user. For example, a credit manager might request the displays illustrated. By reviewing the information obtained, appropriate action could be taken.

In many systems, provision is made for obtaining a printed report of the data displayed on the screen. The printer may be attached to the CRT terminal or may be located in the same vicinity and be communicating directly with the main computer system. To request a printed report of the data displayed on the screen, the operator will normally respond to a question asked by the computer system. This question is sometimes referred to as a prompt, since it prompts the operator to take action.

In the example in Figure 6–14, the screen on the left contains the question PRINTED COPY? after displaying the names of all customers that have accounts 90 days or more past due. The user then enters a "Y" for yes or a "N" for no. If a "Y" is entered, a printed report will be generated from the data on the screen.

Another prompt then appears on the screen to ask if more detailed information is needed. The user again has the opportunity to reply yes or no. If more information is needed, the user enters a "Y" and then enters the number of the company as shown on the screen. This results in a more detailed display appearing on the screen for the customer requested. The display (Example 2) contains the customer's sales history.

Figure 6-14 Inquiries are the primary means of obtaining output information in a transaction-oriented processing system. The two examples above illustrate typical inquiries that could be performed in an accounts receivable application. Example 1 shows the names of those customers who have accounts 90 days or more past due. The last three lines on the screen are called prompts and pose questions to the user which allow additional output to be produced if desired. Through the use of prompts, the user is guided through the steps necessary to obtain a printed copy of the information displayed on the screen and to obtain more detailed information about a customer. Properly designed inquiry systems and displays can greatly simplify the use of the system for the user.

Through properly designed inquiry systems, it is possible for individuals within an organization to display various types of information on the CRT screen that is valuable in providing data for making business decisions. The use of prompts eases the task for the user, a goal in all well-designed computer systems.

Perhaps the greatest advantage of transaction-oriented systems is that the output produced on the terminal is obtained by immediate access to current data and is available to a wide range of users within an organization.

Output considerations in a transaction-oriented system

The output from a transaction-oriented system must be very user oriented. Therefore, a number of factors should be considered in the design of such systems. These factors include: 1) The system should be easy to use; 2) Response time should be brief; 3) Prompts should be used; 4) The user entries should be short and easy to use; 5) All user entries should be acknowledged.

Because transaction-oriented systems are used by a variety of individuals in many areas of the organization, the data displayed should be self-explanatory. Entries made by the terminal user should be short and simple, requiring little skill in typing or data entry.

One of the more critical problems in transaction-oriented systems is response time. Response time is that time required by the computer system to respond to the user after an entry has been made on the terminal. Response time must always be brief. Although five seconds may appear to be a brief period of time, it can seem to be an extremely long time when waiting for a response from the computer system. Although some systems can tolerate longer response times, most systems should respond in a maximum of two seconds, with instantaneous response the ideal.

Even though two seconds may be considered the maximum response time for many systems, some inquiries require more than two seconds of computer processing time to obtain the required information. Therefore, another important factor to be considered in a transaction-oriented system is the desirability of some form of immediate response to the user even though the answer to the inquiry will take longer.

Figure 6-15 In the example above, the inquiry requests the total accounts receivable amount for the company. The processing to acquire this information could require several minutes of computer time. The message "ENTRY RECEIVED" is displayed on the screen immediately so the operator knows the inquiry has been received and is being processed.

For example, if a user enters an inquiry which will require 15 seconds to process, an immediate response should be returned to the user indicating that the inquiry has been received (Figure 6–15). The user is then aware that the Inquiry is being processed and that the output is forthcoming. The answer can then be displayed when the inquiry has been processed. Without this response, the user would have no way of knowing whether the message was received by the computer system.

In summary, displayed output from a transaction-oriented system should be user-oriented, with rapid response times and sufficient prompts to direct the user through all the functions that can be performed for a given application. It is the responsibility of both the user and the systems analyst to develop and design systems which meet these goals.

Output Can

Take Many

Forms

The need for various forms of output from computer systems became apparent as computers were used for many diverse applications. Some of these forms of output which have been developed to meet the needs of computer users are explored on the following pages.

Printers Of

All Types

The diverse needs of computer system users has led to the development of numerous methods for placing images on a sheet of paper. Printers using these methods range from relatively slow, inexpensive units to extremely fast printers costing many thousands of dollars.

The type of printing mechanism used varies, dependent upon the

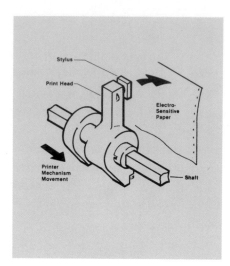

Figure 6-16 The electrographic, non-impact printer utilizes a variety of techniques for printing. Some systems use a specially coated paper that changes color when a voltage is applied to the writing element. Others "burn away" the top layer of the paper to expose the second darker layer, forming the desired image. The advantages of an electrographic printer include relatively low price — $600 to $3,000, and relatively high speed — from 160 to 220 characters per second. The disadvantages include cost of special paper, no multiple copies, and poor print quality with some printers.

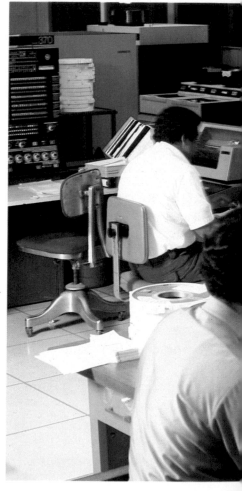

Figure 6-18 Impact matrix printers form each symbol from a pattern of small dots. The print head of a serial dot matrix printer consists of a vertical column of needle-like hammers that move across a page while the hammers are selectively fired against the paper. Some printers have such fine resolution that the letters appear to have been made with shaped characters. Speeds are higher than many shaped character printers, ranging from 30 to 330 characters per second for serial printers, and up to 500 lines per minute with line printers. The prime disadvantage is that print quality may be poor with some large characters, making the report hard to read. Costs range from approximately $2,000 to $9,000.

Figure 6-17 A printing mechanism called the daisy wheel is composed of a set of spokes, or arms, each of which contains an embossed character. The hub rotates to bring the desired character into position, where it is struck by a hammer mechanism. A daisy wheel printer prints from 30 to 55 characters per second. Interchangeable type fonts and high print quality are its principal advantages. Costs for daisy wheel printers range from $3,000 to $7,000.

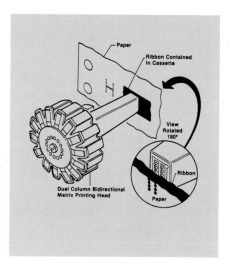

Figure 6-19 Detail printed reports as shown

speed requirements, the need for multiple copies and, of course, the cost of the unit. The examples on these pages illustrate the most widely used printing mechanisms. All, except for the electrographic method, are impact mechanisms, which bring the paper, ribbon, and print character together to form the image.

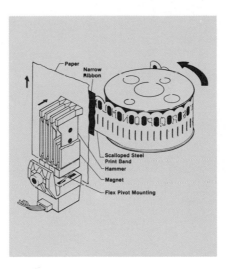

Figure 6-20 One type of widely used impact line printer is the belt or band printer. This type of printer utilizes a horizontally rotating band or belt containing characters. These characters are struck by hammers situated behind the paper and a ribbon, creating the line on the paper. Band printers feature interchangeable type bands for use of different type fonts, have good print quality, high reliability, and can print up to 2000 lines per minute. Cost of such systems ranges from approximately $3,000 to $87,000.

above may generate many thousands of pages.

Figure 6-21 Drum printers feature a cylindrical drum rotating at a constant rate of speed. The drum has a complete set of characters embossed around the circumference for each print position. As the drum rotates, a hammer strikes the required character at each print position. Drums are very reliable, although "wavy" lines are sometimes produced. They do not offer interchangeable fonts. Speeds range from 300 to 3000 lines per minute. Drum printers cost approximately $10,000 to $70,000.

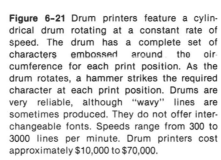

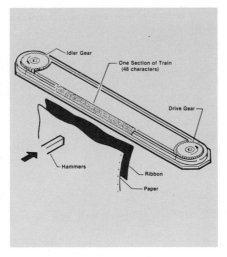

Figure 6-22 The chain, or train, printer contains all of the characters on a chain which rotates at a constant high rate of speed. It also has hammers at each print position. The paper and ribbon are placed between the hammers and the chain. As the chain rotates, the hammer "fires" when the proper character is in the proper print position. The chain printer produces good print quality at up to 3,000 lines per minute. The chain printer was popularized by the IBM 1403 printer. The cost for chain printers ranges from approximately $10,000 to over $100,000.

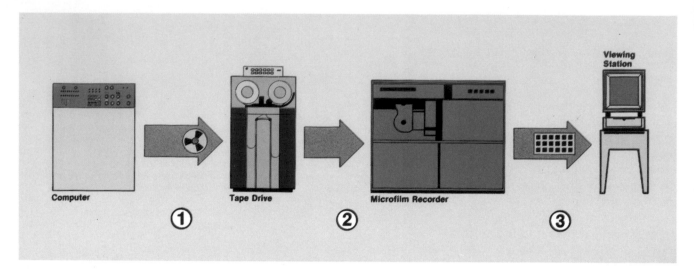

Computer   ①   Tape Drive   ②   Microfilm Recorder   ③   Viewing Station

Figure 6-23 Computer output microfilm requires two basic units — a microfilm recorder and a viewing station. In a typical COM installation, the basic steps in producing output stored on microfilm include: 1) Input to the computer system is processed. The output from the processing is either stored on magnetic tape or is sent directly to the microfilm recorder; 2) The microfilm recorder accepts the data either directly from the computer or from the tape on which the output data is stored. It converts the data to images stored on the film. On some recorders, the film is also developed and is made available for immediate viewing. On other systems, the exposed film must be removed for developing on other equipment; 3) After the film is developed, it can be viewed on a viewer station. In order to find the particular piece of film containing the data to be viewed, some viewers require manual searching while others, using an attached minicomputer, allow computer assisted retrieval (CAR). With CAR, the operator enters identifying information and the system searches pre-defined indexes to retrieve and display the requested information.

Figure 6-24 Output from a computer system is stored on one of several types of film. The two most commonly used forms, microfiche and 16mm roll film, are shown below. A microfiche is a sheet of film approximately 4 inches by 6 inches. Up to 269 data frames, at a reduction rate of 48X, can be stored on a microfiche. 16mm microfilm is commonly housed in cartridges. One hundred feet of film can store up to 2,000 frames. A disadvantage of microfiche is data integrity because a single sheet of film can easily be removed from a file. Data integrity is better with 16mm film.

Figure 6-25 The DatagraphiX AutoCOM II recorder interfaces directly with computer systems.

Figure 6-26 The Kodak IMT-50 terminal can retrieve more than 25,000 8½" x 11" documents from a single 4" x 4" x 1" film magazine. The rotating access file behind the operator allows up to 50 million documents to be stored and retrieved.

Computer Output

Microfilm — Faster

And Smaller Output

Computer output microfilm (COM) is an output technique that is used to record output from a computer system as microscopic images on roll or sheet film. The images stored on COM are the same as reports which would be printed on paper.

The COM recording process reduces characters 24, 42, or 48 times smaller than would be produced from a printer. The information is recorded on sheet film called microfiche or on l6mm, 35mm, or l05mm film.

The data to be recorded on the microfilm can come directly from the computer system (on-line) or from magnetic tape which is pro-

duced by the computer system (off-line). The data is read into a recorder where, in most systems, it is displayed internally on a CRT. As the data is displayed on the CRT, a camera takes a picture of it and places it on the film. The film is then processed, either in the recorder unit or separately.

Microfilm has significant advantages over printed reports for certain applications. Some of these advantages are: 1) Data can be recorded on the film at up to 30,000 lines per minute — much faster than all except the very high speed printers; 2) Costs for recording the data are less. It is estimated that the

cost for printing a 3–part 1,000 page report is $28.03, whereas the cost for the same report on microfilm is $3.60; 3) Less space is required to store microfilm than reports. A microfiche that weighs an ounce can store the equivalent of 10 pounds of computer printout.

To access data stored on microfilm, a variety of readers are available that utilize indexing techniques to provide for ready reference to the data. Some microfilm readers are equipped to perform automatic data lookup, called computer assisted retrieval, under the control of an attached minicomputer.

Graphic

Display Output

Business owners, engineers, scientists, and many others have long used graphs, charts, and diagrams to visually display business concepts and other physical phenomena for analysis and review. It was logical, therefore, to develop machines that could generate these graphic displays from data processed on a computer system.

Although some alphanumeric display terminals can display graphics, the development of high resolution devices has made quality graphics possible on CRT terminals.

These terminals draw lines by connecting small dots on the screen. The screen is electronically composed of many thousands of these dots. Thus, the image displayed is one of continuous lines even though each line is composed of these dots.

Many graphic display terminals have color capabilities and a variety of control features such as a keyboard, light pen, and joy stick. Through the use of these control features, users of the graphic display devices can control the images placed on the screen.

Figure 6-27 The Computervision graphic display device shown above is used by Alfa-Romeo to develop and display body designs for new automobiles. Alfa-Romeo has found the use of these devices allows their engineers to study several different design solutions without tedious revising of drawings and calculations by hand.

Figure 6-28 The terminal illustrated below from Interstate Electronics Corporation is a plasma panel terminal. Plasma terminals generate images from "excited" gases trapped between 2 glass panels. Plasma terminals are lighter and smaller than CRT terminals and are designed to withstand severe shock and vibration.

Figure 6-29 Conrac color monitors are shown in a Honeywell TDC 2000 Process Control System console (opposite). The process control industry, which produces machines to control manufacturing and chemical processing, is a big user of color graphic display devices.

Computer Output

Serves Many Users

Although the printed report, microfilm, and graphic display CRT's are important forms of output, output from computer systems can be presented in other forms.

For applications where hard copy is not required and output can be restricted to a few words or sentences, vocal responses generated from the computer are now possible. Data is processed through special devices which convert digital data to electronically generated words. Thus, computer-

Figure 6-30 Output from computer systems to control a variety of production machinery is widely used in industry. Machines such as lathes, milling machines, and drill presses can all use computer output as control informa-

tion. In the picture above, a computer-controlled polisher is used to polish space telescope lenses to a degree of precision that would be difficult if not impossible to achieve using manual methods.

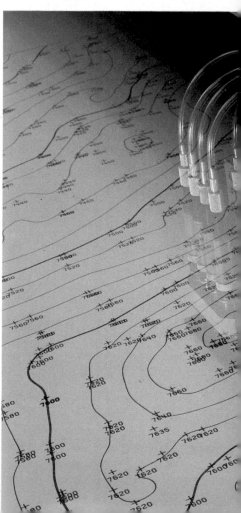

Figure 6-31 Moving at speeds of up to 42 inches per second, the four pens of this

ized voice response to inquiries concerning bank account balances, stock inventories, and even farm commodities prices are being used today.

Other forms of output include specialized printers which produce characters of unusual sizes and shapes, and plotters capable of drawing a variety of complex illustrations. Computerized output is also used to control a variety of machines in production and manufacturing environments.

Calcomp Model 748 flatbed plotter are drawing a detailed contour map. Plotters are used in

Figure 6-32 A special IBM printer developed in Japan (above) permits alphanumeric and

many applications that require hard-copy graphics.

Japanese Katakna characters to be printed in different sizes.

Figure 6-33 This Emhart sewing machine is computer-controlled.

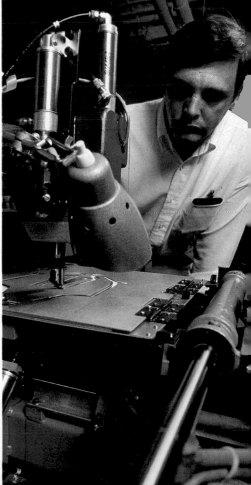

Chapter summary

The following points have been discussed and explained in this chapter.

1. For many years, the primary form of output from computer systems was the printed report.

2. Today, there is a wide variety of output devices, including display terminals, plotters, microfilm, and even voice response systems.

3. The selection of the type of output device depends upon the needs of the user.

4. Two ways in which printers can be classified are the way characters are placed on paper and the printer speed.

5. Printers accomplish the task of placing characters on a page of paper in one of two ways: impact printing and non-impact printing.

6. Impact printers use two basic techniques for printing characters. One method utilizes a front-striking mechanism, and the second technique utilizes a hammer device in which the ribbon and paper are struck against the character to form an image.

7. Impact printers print either solid characters or dot matrix characters.

8. Some non-impact printers utilize a coated or sensitized paper that responds to thermal or electrostatic stimuli to form an image. Others use ink jets or xerography to form an image.

9. Low speed printers print less than 300 lines per minute. High speed printers print from 300 to 3,000 lines per minute, while very high speed printers print in excess of 3,000 lines per minute.

10. The cathode ray tube (CRT) terminal is widely used as an output device in transaction-oriented systems.

11. Many manufacturers have standardized with a 24 line format which has a maximum of 80 characters per line for a total of 1,920 characters on the CRT screen.

12. Some terminals can display both upper and lower case letters of the alphabet as well as a variety of special characters.

13. Many terminals also offer color capabilities.

14. Reverse video refers to the process of reversing the normal display light on the CRT.

15. Scrolling refers to the ability to move lines displayed on the screen up or down.

16. Paging refers to the ability to display an entirely new page on the screen at the operator's request.

17. Output is produced for either external or internal use. External output is output which will be used outside the company.

18. Three major types of reports which can be created are: 1) detail printed reports; 2) summary reports; 3) exception reports.

19. Detail printed reports are usually required by individuals who need access to the day-to-day operating data in an organization.

20. The higher within an organization an individual works, the more summarized the data should be.

21. An exception report contains information which is deemed "exceptional," and is often produced when there is a need to know specific information.

22. Information presented on a report should be presented in a way which is most beneficial to the user.

23. Report security should be considered when developing systems.

24. The most common approach for obtaining output in a transaction-oriented system is the inquiry.

25. In today's environment, it is not unusual to find many individuals in an organization utilizing computer terminals.

26. The output from a transaction-oriented system must be user-oriented.

27. Factors to be considered in the design of a transaction-oriented system include: 1) The system should be easy to use; 2) Response time should be brief; 3) Prompts should be used; 4) The user entries should be short and easy to use; 5) All user entries should be acknowledged.

28. Electrographic non-impact printers print from 160 to 220 characters per second and are relatively inexpensive. Disadvantages include possible poor print quality, cost of special paper, and no multiple copies.

29. The daisy wheel printer prints from 30 to 55 characters per second, produces high print quality, and can feature interchangeable type fonts.

30. The impact matrix printer prints from 30 to 330 characters per second serially, and up to 500 lines per minute with line printers.

31. The belt, or band, printers are highly reliable and can print up to 2,000 lines per minute.

32. The chain, or train, printer can print up to 3,000 lines per minute.

33. Computer Output Microfilm (COM) reduces images up to 48 times smaller than printed reports and stores the images on microfilm. Advantages include reduced size of output and increased speed of output.

34. High resolution graphic output devices can display a variety of complex images on the face of the CRT in several different colors.

35. Plotters can be used to draw complex drawings.

36. Many types of production machines are controlled by the output from computer systems.

Student Learning Exercises

Review questions

1. List two ways in which printers can be classified.

2. Briefly describe the terms "impact printing" and "non-impact printing."

3. What are the speed ranges of: 1) Low speed printers; 2) High speed printers; 3) Very high speed printers?

4. What is meant by a dot matrix printer?

5. A CRT terminal is available with a 24 line, 80 character format. Another terminal has a 25 line, 40 character format. Which terminal would you prefer? Why?

6. What is meant by scrolling? Paging?

7. Briefly explain the terms "detail printed reports," "summary reports," "exception reports."

8. Which type of report will normally be prepared for the president of a company — a detail printed report or a summary report? Why?

9. How is report security maintained in computer installations?

10. What is the most common approach for obtaining output in a transaction-oriented system?

11. List five factors which should be considered in the design of output for transaction-oriented systems.

12. What is meant by a "prompt" when discussing output on CRT's in a transaction-oriented system?

13. List the printer mechanisms commonly used on printers for computer systems. Include the speed ranges for each mechanism.

14. Briefly discuss the advantages of computer output microfilm (COM) as an output media.

Controversial issues in data processing

1. Authorities in business management have pointed out that much of the paperwork generated in a business organization is not used. Some have suggested that very high speed printers which produce 20,000 lines per minute are not needed, and that their use in an organization will further contribute to the paperwork explosion. Should research be continued in developing faster and faster printers?

2. "Automation — The Curse of Modern Society" was the title of a speech given at a recent meeting. In the speech, it was stated that with the ability of the computer to produce output to control machines, skilled drafts- men, machinists, and many other workers will no longer be needed, resulting in mass unemployment. Do you think that the use of computers will lead to unemployment? Be able to defend your position.

Research projects

1. Review the advertisements relating to printers in current data processing periodicals. Prepare a report defining current state of the art in printers relative to speed, type of printing mechanisms used and costs.

2. Bring in samples of external output which have been prepared on the computer for users outside a company. Analyze the output in terms of ease of understanding and ease of reading. If there are any portions of the output which are not meaningful to you as a user, write a letter to the president of the company expressing your concern and requesting an ex- planation. Advise the class of any response which you might receive.

Picture credits

Figure 6–1 National CSS Inc.
Figure 6–4 Dataproducts Corp.
Figure 6–5 MCAUTO
Figure 6–7 Wang Laboratories, Inc.
Figure 6–8 Tektronix, Inc.
Figure 6–9 Hewlett-Packard
Figure 6–16 Dataproducts Corp.
Figure 6–17 Dataproducts Corp.
Figure 6–18 Dataproducts Corp.
Figure 6–19 Lever Brothers Company
Figure 6–20 Dataproducts Corp.
Figure 6–21 Dataproducts Corp.

Figure 6–22 Dataproducts Corp.
Figure 6–24 Eastman Kodak Company
Figure 6–25 DatagraphiX, Inc.
Figure 6–26 Eastman Kodak Company
Figure 6–27 Computervision Corp.
Figure 6–28 Interstate Electronics Corp.
Figure 6–29 Conrac Corp.
Figure 6–30 The Perkin-Elmer Corp.
Figure 6–31 California Computer Products, Inc.
Figure 6–32 IBM
Figure 6–33 Emhart Corp.

Chapter 7
Auxiliary Storage and File Organization

Objectives

- An understanding of the need for auxiliary storage

- An understanding of the storage and access of data stored on magnetic tape

- An understanding of the sequential and random access methods

- An understanding of the file organization methods — sequential, relative or direct, and indexed

- A familiarization with the auxiliary storage devices and media used for both large and small computer systems

Chapter 7

Figure 7-1 The access arms from a Storage Technology disk drive have the ability to move in or out and access data stored at any location on the disk pack.

Auxiliary Storage And File Organization

"The nation's mass storage requirements are 'staggering.' More than 3,000 large business and scientific computer systems have on-line memory capacities exceeding 2 by 10^{10} bits."[1]

Introduction

One of the major requirements in order to utilize computer systems in all areas of application is the ability to store and access data. On small computer systems, the amount of data stored and accessed might not exceed one or two million characters. On larger computer systems, billions of characters of data might be stored and accessed. Large utility companies, for example, may require that all customer records be stored and be accessible for inquiries about payments and billing.

Thus, auxiliary storage (sometimes called secondary storage) is an extremely important part of the data processing installation; for without access to data, processing could not occur.

There are two major considerations when examining the auxiliary storage used with computer systems. The first is the type of media on which the data is stored. On modern computer systems, magnetic tape and magnetic disk are the two primary means of storing data for access by programs executing on the computer system (Figure 7–1).

The second consideration is the manner in which the data is organized and accessed. A proper choice of the organization and access method can enable an application to access and process data with maximum efficiency.

---

1 Editorial, quoting a spokesman from Magnavox Government and Industrial Electronics Co., COMPUTERWORLD, July 30, 1979.

This chapter will examine the media which is used for auxiliary storage on computer systems and the ways data can be organized and accessed for maximum usage.

Magnetic tape

Magnetic tape was first used for storing data in the early 1950's on one of the first Univac computers. The tape was made of flexible metal and was stored on reels. The metal was plated with a thin film of iron, which allowed data to be stored as a series of small magnetized spots. Although the tape provided a compact form of storage, it was extremely heavy and not universally accepted. IBM, in fact, contended at the time that tape was unreliable, untested, and risky; partly, it is said, because their allegations had some elements of truth and partly because the use of magnetic tape threatened the continued use of the 10,000 tons of punched cards IBM sold each year.

Although these early reels of metal tape were capable of storing large amounts of data, it was not until scientists developed a very thin, flexible material called mylar that tape processing gained wide acceptance. This plastic mylar was coated with an iron-oxide which could be magnetized to store data. The oxide-coated mylar tape proved to be successful and was soon universally accepted in the computer industry. Many tape drives were developed to read and write data on the tape (Figure 7–2). In the 1950's and early 1960's, magnetic tape was the primary means for storing large amounts of data, and it is still an important form of auxiliary storage today.

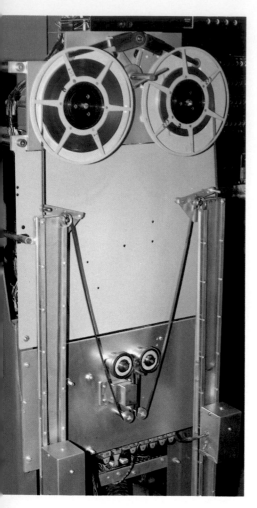

Figure 7-2 One of the first magnetic tape drives developed by IBM is pictured above. This was the first drive to place slack tape in vacuum columns, allowing the tape to be rapidly started and stopped without breaking.

Storing data on magnetic tape

Data is recorded on magnetic tape in the form of magnetic spots that can be read and transferred to main computer storage. The data stored on the tape may include numbers, letters of the alphabet, or special characters. The magnetic spots on the tape are organized into a series of horizontal rows called channels. The presence or absence of magnetic spots representing bits in each of the channels is used to represent a given character on the tape.

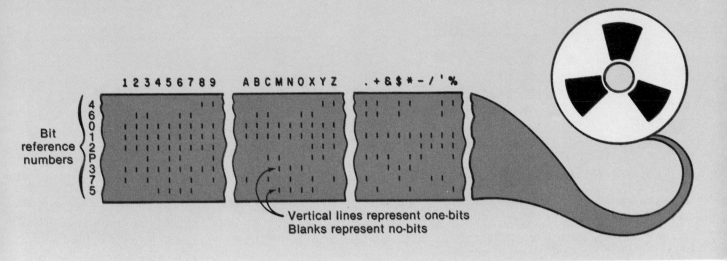

123456789   ABCMNOXYZ   .+&$*-/'%

Bit reference numbers

Vertical lines represent one-bits
Blanks represent no-bits

Although there are several different coding structures used with magnetic tape, one of the most common uses the Extended Binary Coded Decimal Interchange Code (EBCDIC) recorded in 9 channels on the tape. This coding structure divides ½" tape into nine horizontal channels. A combination of bits in a vertical column which consists of the nine horizontal channels are used to represent characters on the tape (Figure 7-3).

Tape density, which is the number of characters or bytes which can be stored on an inch of tape, varies depending upon the tape devices being used. Common densities are 800 bytes per inch (bpi) and 1600 bpi, with some devices capable of reading and writing at a density of 6,250 bpi. This high density is advantageous because a large amount of data can be stored on a reel of tape.

The manner in which tape is stored for processing can vary considerably, from audio tape cassettes such as found on audio tape recorders to large reels of tape. The most commonly found means for storing tape for use on most systems except microcomputers is the 2400 foot reel of ½" tape (Figure 7-4).

Figure 7-3 The most common coding structure found on magnetic tape is EBCDIC stored in nine channels on the tape. Eight channels are used to store the bits representing a character. The ninth channel (marked "P" in the drawing) is a parity channel. It is used to ensure the bits are written correctly to form a character by being either "on" or "off" as required to ensure an odd number of "on" bits for each character. For example, for the letter "A" it is "off" because an A is represented by 3 bits. The parity bit is "on" for the letter "C" because a C is represented by 4 bits and the parity bit must be "on" to ensure an odd number of bits. If an even number of bits are read, then the tape drive indicates an error condition.

Figure 7-4 The 2400 foot reel of ½ inch tape (left) contains an external label which identifies the data stored on the tape. Each time new data is written on the tape, the label will be changed. In addition, internal tape labels are usually magnetically written on the tape itself. Thus, when a program is to read a tape file, it can read the tape label record to ensure the proper tape reel is mounted for processing.

7.3

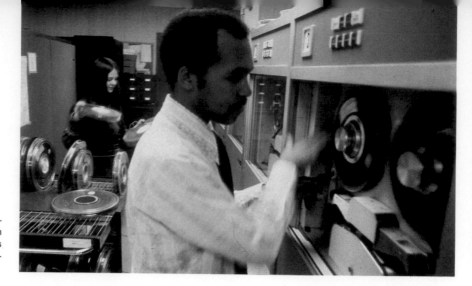

Data is read and written on tape mounted on tape drives (Figure 7-5). The tape is transported over read/write heads from a file reel to a take-up reel. Depending on the density of the data stored on the tape and the speed at which the tape is moved over the read/write heads, data can be transferred from the tape to main computer storage at rates varying from 15,000 to 1,250,000 characters per second. The transfer rate is calculated by multiplying the density times the speed at which the tape is moved. For example, with a density of 1,600 characters per inch and a tape speed of 200 inches per second, the effective transfer rate is 320,000 characters per second.

Format of records stored on tape

When records are stored on tape, they are stored sequentially. Sequential organization means that one record is stored after the other on the tape. Tape records are also read sequentially, one record after another.

Records stored on tape are separated by an interblock gap (Figure 7-6). This gap is used to allow for the starting and stopping of the tape during reading and writing operations. Because of the density of the data stored on the tape, the interblock gap may be longer than the portion of tape used to store the record. Thus, much of the tape recording space is wasted.

To overcome this inefficiency for storing data, blocked records are normally used. Blocking refers to placing two or more individual records, called logical records, into a block to form a physical record (Figure 7-7). Using blocking offers two significant advantages: 1) The tape is used more efficiently, allowing more data to be stored on a reel of tape; 2) Since an entire physical record is read into storage each time data is read from the tape, reading takes place faster because two or more logical records are read each time data is transferred from the tape to main computer storage.

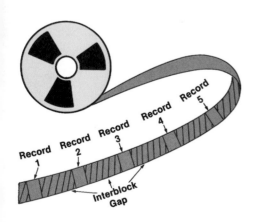

Figure 7-6 Records stored on tape are stored sequentially and are separated by an interblock gap, which allows for the starting and stopping of the tape drive. The interblock gap is typically .6 inch wide.

An increasing number of batch applications and almost all transaction-oriented processing systems require almost immediate access to any record in a file, usually in less than one second. This is not possible with tape because each record must be read one after another. Therefore, the use of magnetic tape for storing active data files has decreased somewhat in recent years.

Tape is very useful, however, in systems where sequential file processing is acceptable or when data which is stored on magnetic disk must be copied for backup purposes. Tape is used in many instances as backup for disk because the data can be easily copied from disk to tape, and the tape can be simply and inexpensively stored until needed.

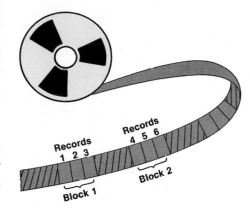

Figure 7-7 Three logical records are stored in a block on the tape shown above. The only restriction on the number of records stored in a single block is the amount of main computer storage that can be used to store the block of records because an entire block of records is brought into main computer storage each time the tape file is read.

Magnetic disk

The early data processing systems were virtually all batch systems which processed data sequentially. For these systems, magnetic tape was adequate. In the mid-1950's, however, it was recognized there was a need for direct access to data stored in files on auxiliary storage. The desire for systems such as airline and hotel reservations mandated that data be stored in such a way to allow it to be retrieved in a very short time. To fulfill this need, magnetic disk storage devices (commonly called direct-access storage devices, or DASD) were developed.

One of the first magnetic disk devices was put into operation by IBM in 1955. This device, called RAMAC (RAndoM ACcess), consisted of fifty fixed disk platters, each approximately two feet in outside diameter (Figure 7-8). These platters rotated on a shaft at a high rate of speed. Access arms containing read/write heads moved up and down, in and out between each disk surface to retrieve data or to store data on the surface of the disk. Totally, the disk device could store five million characters.

Since the introduction of the RAMAC, numerous improvements have been made in the size of disk storage units, the amount of data which can be stored on a disk unit, and the speed at which data can be stored and retrieved.

Figure 7-8 The first magnetic disk unit developed by IBM was called the RAMAC. The unit was extremely large and relatively slow by today's standards, but it was the first direct access storage device available to the industry.

Figure 7-9 In the picture at the right, a computer operator is opening the door of a disk drive prior to removing a disk pack from the drive. The pack which is removed can be stored for later use. A new pack will be mounted on the drive. The ability to remove the disk packs from the drive and replace them with others gives almost unlimited storage. The amount of data which can be processed at one time, however, depends on the number of disk drives which are connected to the processor unit.

Figure 7-10 The disk pack above consists of 11 metal platters. Each surface except the top surface of the top platter and the bottom surface of the bottom platter is coated with a metal oxide. Data is magnetically stored on the coated surfaces.

Modern direct access storage devices

Direct access storage devices have been developed over the years with a number of different configurations and capabilities. The most commonly used devices today consist of a disk drive and a removable disk pack (Figure 7-9). Data can be stored on each disk pack as required.

A disk pack consists of a number of metal platters which are attached to a common hub (Figure 7-10). The platters are typically 14 inches in diameter. Each of the platters is coated with a metal oxide which can be used to record data. Although the amount of data which can be stored on a single disk pack varies, the latest disk packs have eleven metal platters with twenty recording surfaces capable of storing 200 million characters.

Storing data on magnetic disk

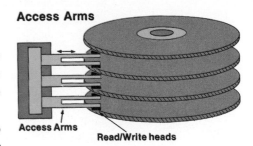

There are a variety of disk storage devices, but most of them have essentially the same operational characteristics. Each single unit consists of a spindle on which the disk pack is mounted. The spindle will rotate the disk pack at a fixed speed, commonly 3,600 revolutions per minute.

In order to write data on the surfaces of the spinning disk pack or to read data stored on the disk pack, the disk drives use either access arms or actuators (Figure 7-11). An access arm or an actuator contains read/write heads for each surface of the disk pack on which data can be magnetically recorded. These read/write heads "float" on a cushion of air and do not actually touch the surface of the disk. The distance between the head and the surface varies from a millionth of an inch to ½ millionth of an inch. When reading data from the disk, the read head senses the magnetic spots on the surface and transfers the data to main computer storage. When writing, the data is transferred from main computer storage and is stored as magnetic spots on the recording surface.

Figure 7-11 The access arms shown above move in and out in order to position the read/write heads over the proper location for reading or writing data on the disk pack. The actuator swings in and out over the disk surfaces to properly position the read/write heads.

Tracks on recording surfaces

The access arm or actuator which is used on a disk drive can be positioned at a number of discrete positions on the recording surface of a disk. Since the disk is rapidly revolving, the heads on the access arm or actuator can reference a circle of data at each discrete position (Figure 7-12). Each of these circular recording positions is called a track. The number of tracks on a recording surface is determined by the capabilities of the disk drive and the recording characteristics of the magnetic oxide placed on the recording surface. This number can range from 200 tracks per recording surface to over 800 tracks.

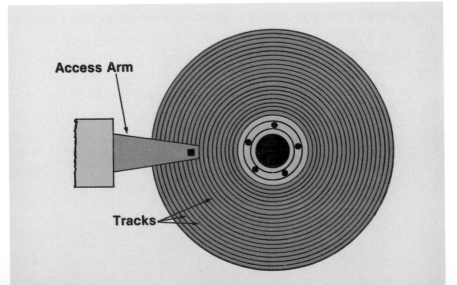

Figure 7-12 The access arm or actuator can be positioned at a number of discrete positions on the disk pack. These positions are called tracks. Since the disk pack spins, the head can read or write from a circle of data at each position of the access arm. The concentric circles shown on the drawing are to illustrate the possible positions of the access arm. The recording surface has no indications of the tracks, such as the grooves found in a phonograph record.

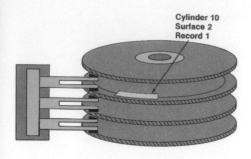

Figure 7-13 With the cylinder concept, the location of a record is determined by the cylinder number, the recording surface number, and the record number. Here, the record is stored on cylinder 10, recording surface 2, and is the first record on that cylinder and surface. Special data stored on each track specifies the beginning of the track so that the first record, second record, third record, and so on, can be identified.

Figure 7-14 The sector method divides each track into a number of sectors. In order to locate data, the particular sector number is specified.

Physical organization of data on magnetic disk

Data is physically organized in one of two ways on a disk pack, depending on the manufacturer and the model of disk drive being used. One means is the cylinder method and the other is the sector method.

The cylinder method uses a cylinder as the basic reference point. On one recording surface, an access arm can reference one track of data (Figure 7-12). A disk pack contains up to 20 recording surfaces. Therefore, there are 20 different tracks, one for each recording surface, that can be referenced by the recording heads on the access arm at each discrete location where the access arm can be positioned. These 20 tracks which can be referenced at one position of the access arm are called a cylinder.

On each track, the data stored can be divided into one or more physical records. Therefore, in order to physically reference a record stored using the cylinder method, a computer program must specify the cylinder number, the recording surface number, and the record number (Figure 7-13).

The sector method for physically organizing data on the disk pack requires that each of the tracks is divided into individual storage areas called sectors. Each sector on the disk pack can hold a specified number of characters and records. Data is referenced using this method by indicating the sector number where the data is stored. The sector concept is illustrated in Figure 7-14.

Whether data is stored using the cylinder method or the sector method is determined by the manufacturer of the disk drive. Many of the latest disk storage units use the sector method. Some manufacturers call this the fixed block architecture.

Accessing data stored on magnetic disk

Because the access arms or the actuator can be positioned at any one of the concentric circular recording positions, or tracks, random access to data stored on the disk is possible. For example, assuming a record in a file is stored near the center of the disk, the access arm or actuator can be rapidly positioned in the proper location to read the required record. This retrieval of data can occur on most disk drives in less than 50 milliseconds (1/20th of a second).

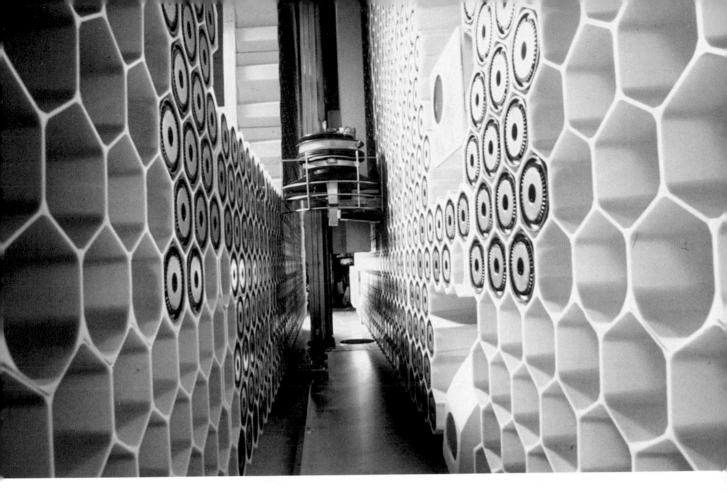

Mass storage devices

In addition to magnetic tape and magnetic disk, other types of devices which offer unique capabilities are available for auxiliary storage. One of these devices is the IBM 3850 mass storage device, which offers on-line access to very large collections of data.

The IBM 3850 uses a cylindrical data cartridge approximately 2 inches in diameter and 4 inches in length to house a 771" long piece of magnetic tape. The tape in each cartridge can store 50 million bytes in a format similar to that found on some IBM disk packs.

The data cartridges are stored in honeycomb-like cells (Figure 7–15). For accessing the data stored in the cartridges, the cartridges are extracted from their cells and the data on the cartridge is transferred to magnetic disk. The time to retrieve a cartridge and place it in the device which reads data is 3 to 8 seconds. After the cartridge is placed in position to be read, the time to locate the first physical position and begin data transfer to the disk is approximately 5 seconds. Thus, mass storage devices are useful only in applications where large volumes of data must be accessed, and the access time is not critical.

Figure 7–15 Up to 472 billion characters can be stored in the IBM 3850 mass storage device. This data is stored on-line to the computer system. Mass storage devices are used when there is a need for the storage of extremely large volumes of data with a relatively slow access time.

Magnetic bubble memory

One of the newest and most promising developments for auxiliary storage is magnetic bubble memory (Figure 7–16). Bubble memory is composed of small magnetic domains (bubbles) formed on a thin single-crystal film of synthetic garnet. These bubbles, only a few ten-thousandths of a centimeter in size, can be moved across the film. The presence or absence of a bubble can be used to indicate whether a bit is "off" or "on."

Since data stored in bubble memory is retained when power to the memory is turned off, it can be used for auxiliary storage. With its potential for storing many millions of bits of data and the very fast speeds of accessing data stored, bubble memory is expected to augment or even replace disk as a form of auxiliary storage in the future.

Figure 7–16 The IBM magnetic bubble lattice device shown above is .00007 square inches. This section can hold 350 bubbles — or bits of information — a density of 5 million bits per square inch.

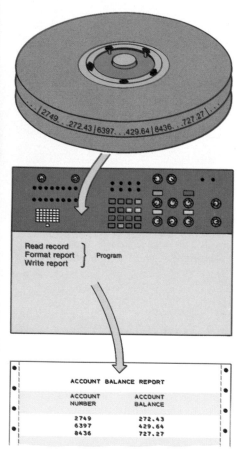

Figure 7–17 In order to create the account balance report above, the records on the disk pack are read in ascending account number sequence. Thus, they are retrieved sequentially because the records are read one after another in a predetermined sequence.

ACCESS TO DATA STORED ON AUXILIARY STORAGE

The most important consideration when determining the type of auxiliary storage which will be used is the type of access which must be provided to the data. There are two ways to access this data: sequential access and random access. Each has its advantages and disadvantages.

Sequential access

Sequential access means that data is retrieved from a file stored on auxiliary storage one record after another in a predetermined sequence (Figure 7–17). In most cases, the data will be accessed in an ascending or descending sequence based upon a key, which is a unique identifying value found in each record. For example, a personnel file could be accessed in ascending sequence by employee number; an inventory file could be accessed in descending sequence by part number; or as illustrated in Figure 7–17, a bank account file could be accessed in sequence by account number.

There is a major limitation when using sequential access — rapid retrieval of records is not possible. This is because the records which are to be retrieved toward the end of the predetermined sequence cannot be retrieved until all of the records preceding them in the sequence have been read into main computer storage. Thus, if there are 1,000 records in a file to be retrieved sequentially, the 900th record to be retrieved cannot be read until the first 899 records have been read.

Since records are read one after another when sequential access is used, sequentially accessed files are used most often in batch processing systems. Sequential access is not normally used in transaction-oriented processing systems because those systems need fast access to data stored on auxiliary storage, and sequential access does not offer fast access.

When data is stored on magnetic tape, sequential access is the only way in which the data can be retrieved. As illustrated, data stored on magnetic disk can also be retrieved sequentially.

Random access

The second method used to retrieve data from auxiliary storage is random access. Random access means that any record stored in a file can be retrieved without reading any other record in the file. Since each record can be accessed without reading another record, random access provides fast retrieval of a record stored on auxiliary storage.

In order to identify what record is to be retrieved, the records which are to be randomly accessed must have some type of identifying field, or key, associated with them. This key can be similar to those used with sequential files, such as employee number, part number, or account number. The records stored in a file to be randomly accessed need not be stored in any particular sequence, since each record is retrieved without reference to the other records stored in the file.

In order to randomly access a record, the key to the record must be known. When the key is known, the record with the corresponding key can be retrieved without examining other records in the file and without concern for the order in which the records are stored in the file. In Figure 7–18, the key to the records stored in the file on disk is the account number. When an inquiry is entered requesting the balance in account number 6397, the program randomly accesses the record for account number 6397 and retrieves the balance. This balance can then be sent back to the terminal. The retrieval of the record for account number 6397 was accomplished without reading other records in the file, as would be required with sequential access (Figure 7–17).

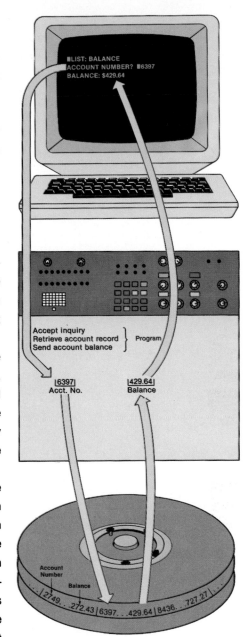

Figure 7-18 The inquiry above requests the balance of account number 6397. The program randomly retrieves the record for account number 6397, which contains the balance. This balance is then sent back to the terminal.

The major advantage of random access, of course, is that any record within a file can be retrieved rapidly from auxiliary storage. This characteristic makes randomly accessed files almost mandatory in transaction-oriented processing systems, because transactions must be handled quickly. Retrieving a record sequentially does not satisfy the time requirement of transaction-oriented systems.

Randomly accessed files must be stored on direct access devices such as magnetic disk. Tape cannot be used because records can only be retrieved sequentially from tape.

The determination of whether sequential or random access is to be used depends upon the needs of the application in which the file is to be used. If rapid retrieval is required, then random access must be chosen.

PROCESSING DATA ON AUXILIARY STORAGE

Regardless of whether the data stored on auxiliary storage is accessed randomly or sequentially, there are two major types of processing which can be performed: 1) data retrieval; 2) file updating.

Data retrieval

Many applications require both the sequential and random access of data stored on auxiliary storage. The application in Figure 7–19 is an example of a program retrieving data both sequentially and randomly.

There are two files required for this application: an invoice file and a customer name file. The invoice file, stored in invoice number sequence on tape, is read sequentially by the program in this batch processing system. Each invoice record, containing the invoice number, the customer number, and the invoice amount, is to be printed on the invoice report.

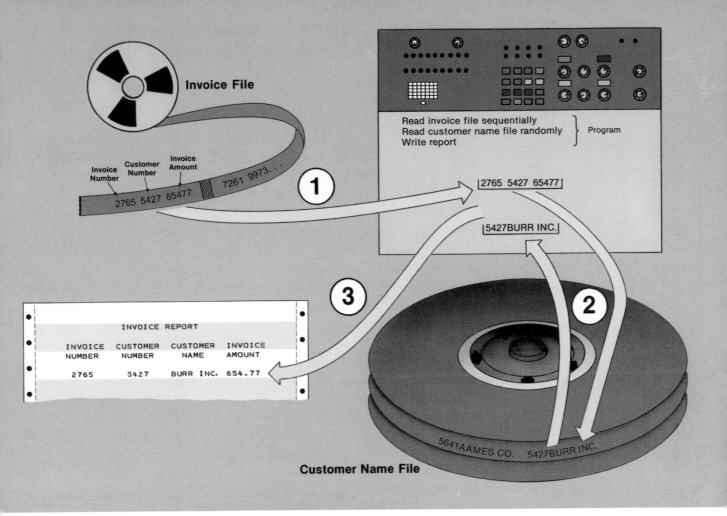

Invoice File

Invoice Number | Customer Number | Invoice Amount

2765 5427 65477 | 7261 9973...

Read invoice file sequentially
Read customer name file randomly } Program
Write report

| 2765 5427 65477 |

| 5427BURR INC. |

① ② ③

Customer Name File

5641AAMES CO.   5427BURR INC.

INVOICE REPORT

INVOICE NUMBER	CUSTOMER NUMBER	CUSTOMER NAME	INVOICE AMOUNT
2765	5427	BURR INC.	654.77

The customer name file, stored on disk, contains the customer number and customer name.

The customer name is also to be included on the report. Since the customer name is not stored in the invoice file, the name will have to be retrieved from the customer name file. Using the customer number from the invoice file as the key, the program randomly retrieves the customer name from the customer name file. The name is then included on the report.

In this example, records in the invoice file are retrieved sequentially in invoice number sequence. Records in the customer name file are retrieved randomly based upon the customer number. Sequential retrieval of the invoice file is used because the report is to be in invoice number sequence. The customer name file is randomly retrieved because the customer numbers in the invoice file are not in any given order. Therefore, the only way in which the customer names can be retrieved, unless the entire customer name file is searched sequentially each time, is randomly.

The ability to retrieve data randomly and sequentially from files stored on auxiliary storage provides a great deal of flexibility in accessing data for computer applications.

Figure 7-19 The invoice report is printed in invoice number sequence using data from both the invoice file and the customer name file. The following steps occur: 1) An invoice record is sequentially retrieved from the invoice file; 2) Using the customer number as the key, a record from the customer name file is randomly retrieved; 3) A line on the invoice report is written.

File updating

The second major type of processing which is performed on data stored on auxiliary storage is updating. Updating is required to keep the data stored in files on auxiliary storage current and up-to-date. In most cases, the updating takes place on master files, which are those files containing data which reflects the current status of a business. For example, a customer master file could contain all of the customers of a company, together with their address and credit status. This customer master file must be kept current.

There are three functions which must be performed when updating files to keep them current: 1) Adding records to a master file; 2) Deleting records from a master file; 3) Changing records currently stored in a master file.

Records are added to a master file when new data is obtained which must be stored in the file to make the file current. For example, if a new customer is acquired, a record would be added to the customer master file to reflect the new customer.

Records are deleted when the record in the master file is obsolete. Thus, if a customer went out of business, the record corresponding to that customer should be removed from the customer master file.

A record is changed in a master file when the data contained within the record becomes obsolete or incorrect. For example, when a customer moves and changes addresses, the record for that customer must be changed to reflect the new address.

The changes, additions, and deletions which are to occur to a master file are usually stored as an input file in batch processing systems; and may be entered a transaction at a time in a transaction-oriented system. Regardless of whether master files are accessed sequentially or randomly, they must be updated with current data; the processing to update the files, however, differs depending upon the access method.

Sequential file updating

When a sequential master file is updated, the transaction file containing the additions, deletions, and changes must be sorted in the same sequence as the master file. The records from the master file and the records from the transaction file are then read and matched. A new master file is created.

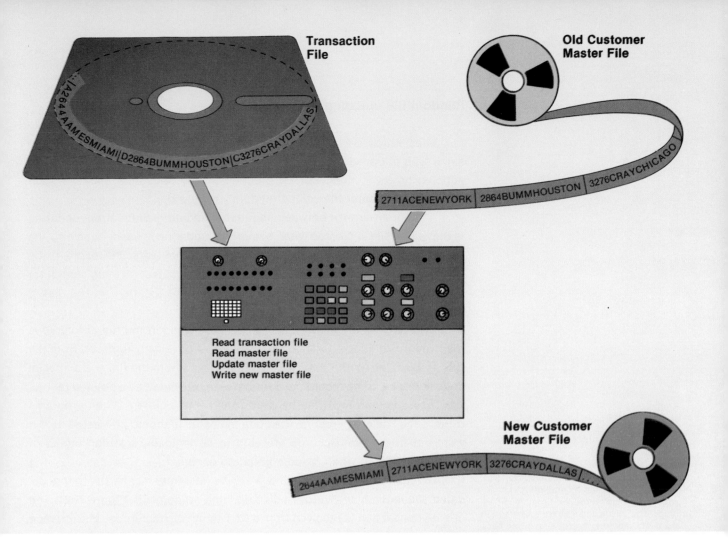

Transaction File

Old Customer Master File

2711ACENEWYORK | 2864BUMMHOUSTON | 3276CRAYCHICAGO

A2644AAMESMIAMI | D2864BUMMHOUSTON | C3276CRAYDALLAS

Read transaction file
Read master file
Update master file
Write new master file

New Customer Master File

2644AAMESMIAMI | 2711ACENEWYORK | 3276CRAYDALLAS . . . .

A typical sequential update is shown in Figure 7-20. The customer master file contains a customer number, the name of the company, and the city in which the company is located. It is stored on the tape in ascending sequence by customer number. The transaction file stored on floppy disk is in customer number sequence also.

Three update records are illustrated in the transaction file. The first is an addition of customer number 2644 (an A in the first position of the record indicates an addition). The next record is to be used to delete customer number 2864 (D in first position). The last record is used to change the city for customer 3276 from Chicago to Dallas (C in position 1).

After the processing is completed, a new master file has been created on another reel of tape. It contains customer number 2644 which was added to the file, customer number 2711 which was unchanged from the old file, and customer number 3276 with the new city, Dallas. Customer number 2864 is not contained on the new customer master file because it was deleted.

Figure 7-20 Sequential file updating involves reading the master file, reading the transaction file, matching the records, and creating a new master file. Here, the new customer master file contains the updated data resulting from the addition, deletion, and change transactions.

Random file updating

Files which are accessed randomly must also be updated with the same type of transactions — additions, deletions, and changes. The transactions, however, need not be grouped in any sequence because each record in the master file will be randomly retrieved.

A major difference between sequential updating and random updating is that a new file is created when sequential updating is used, but a new file is not created when random updating is used. Instead, the record to be changed is retrieved from auxiliary storage, updated in main computer storage, and then is rewritten back into the same location on the disk it occupied before it was changed.

New records to be added to the file are placed in the file at locations reserved for additions. Deleted records are not physically removed from the file. Instead, the record to be deleted is retrieved from the file and a special code is placed in the record indicating it is to be treated as a deleted record. The record is then rewritten back into the same location. When programs retrieve the "deleted" record, the code indicates it should be treated as if it were not in the file. Records are said to be logically deleted instead of physically deleted when random updating occurs.

To illustrate random updating, a similar customer master file to that updated sequentially in Figure 7–20 is updated randomly in Figure 7–21. The update transaction is received from a CRT terminal. Its purpose is to change the city for customer number 3276.

Figure 7–21 The customer master file below is stored on disk and is randomly accessed. To update the file, the record with customer number 3276 is retrieved from auxiliary storage. The city is changed from Chicago to Dallas, and then the record is rewritten back into the same location on the disk.

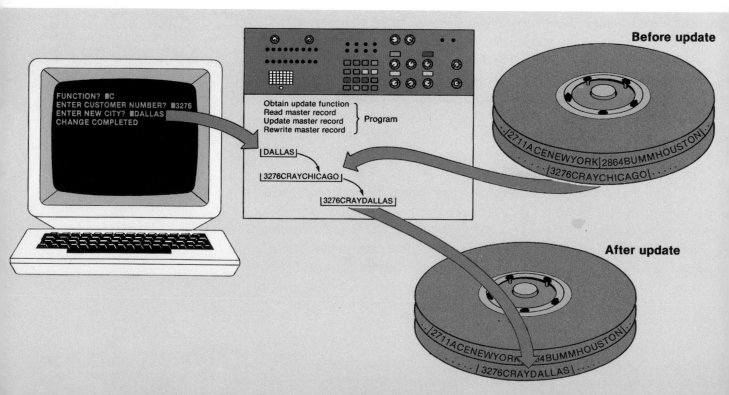

Once the transaction is received by the program in main computer storage, the record in the customer master file is randomly retrieved based upon the customer number. The change to the city from Chicago to Dallas is made in main computer storage. The updated record is then rewritten back into the same location it held prior to being updated. Thus, when a file is randomly updated, a new file is not created; rather, the records are updated and returned to the same location.

Whether the file to be updated is accessed sequentially or randomly, it is important to realize the significance of update processing. Current data in the files stored on auxiliary storage is the key to producing accurate, up-to-date information for users of computer systems. Updating files constitutes a great deal of the processing performed on computer systems and is probably the single most important type of processing which is done.

FILE ORGANIZATION

When data is stored on auxiliary storage, it must be logically organized into files. There are three major file organization methods which are used for storing data on auxiliary storage: 1) Sequential organization; 2) Relative or direct organization; 3) Indexed organization. The following paragraphs discuss these file organizations.

Sequential file organization

As previously illustrated, records which are sequentially organized in a file are stored one after another, normally in a given sequence. The sequence is usually based upon a control field or key in the record (Figure 7–22). Records which are organized sequentially are also retrieved sequentially for processing.

Sequential organization must be used when magnetic tape is the storage medium and can also be used with disk. This means of organization is used most often in batch processing systems where input records can be batched and sorted in the same sequence as the records stored in the file on auxiliary storage. These files are then processed against one another, as shown in the example of sequential updating (Figure 7–20). Since sequential files require sequential accessing, they are not used too often in transaction-oriented systems because of the limitation on rapidly accessing records.

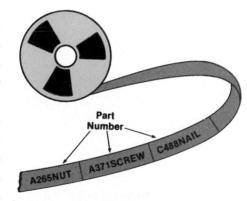

Figure 7–22 The inventory file above contains records stored sequentially. The records are stored in an ascending sequence by part number. Since these records are stored sequentially, they will also be accessed sequentially.

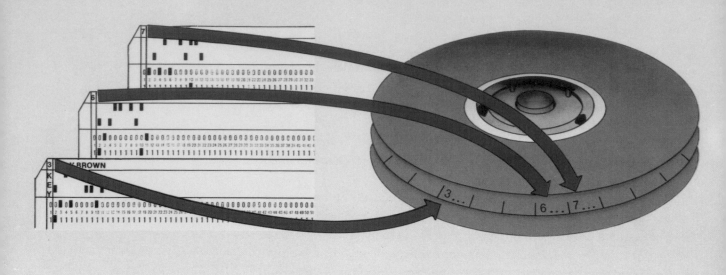

Figure 7-23 In the illustration above, a relative file has been established which has storage locations for ten records. The key in the card records used to load the file is a one digit field with possible values 0-9. Therefore, the key field can be used here to specify the relative location of the records.

Relative or direct file organization

A relative file (sometimes called a direct file) contains records which are stored in relative locations within the file. The location into which a record will be stored is based upon a key value found in the record. For example, a file could be established in which there are ten locations where data could be stored (Figure 7-23). If the key in the record is a one digit value (0-9), then the value in the key would specify the location within the file where the record is stored. For example, the record with the key 3 would be placed in relative location 3; the record with the key 6 would be placed in relative location 6; and the record with key 7 would be placed in relative location 7.

Most uses of relative files are not so simple. For instance, it may be found that the maximum number of records to be stored in a relative file is 100, but the key for the record is a four digit number. In this case, the key of the record could not be used to specify the relative location of the record in the file because the key would specify up to a maximum of 9,999 records. In cases such as these, an arithmetic formula must be used to calculate the relative location in the file where the record will be stored.

One formula which can be used is the division/remainder method. Using this method, a prime number close to the number of records to be stored in the file is chosen. A prime number is a number which is divisible only by itself and one. For example, the number 97 is the closest prime number to 100 without being greater than 100. The key of the record is then divided by the prime number chosen, and the remainder from the division operation is the relative location where the record will be stored (Figure 7-24). For example, if the record key is 3428, the relative location where the record will be stored in the file is location 33.

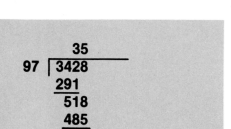

$$
\begin{array}{r}
35 \\
97\overline{)3428} \\
291 \\
\overline{518} \\
485 \\
\overline{33} \text{ Remainder}
\end{array}
$$

Figure 7-24 In the division example above, the key of the record, 3428, is divided by the prime number 97. The remainder from the division operation, 33, is the relative location in the file where the record will be stored.

Once a record is stored in its relative location within a relative file, it can be retrieved either sequentially or randomly. Sequential retrieval can occur by indicating that the record from the first relative location is to be retrieved, followed by the record from the second relative location, and so on. Thus, all of the records stored in the file would be sequentially retrieved based upon their relative location within the file. Note that this does not guarantee that the records will be retrieved in key sequence. For example, the relative location for key 1233 is 69 (1233 ÷ 97 = 12, remainder 69) (Figure 7–25).

The more common access method for relative files, however, is random access. In order to randomly access a record stored in a relative file, the program must first obtain the key of the record to be retrieved. The program then performs the same arithmetic on the key which was performed when the relative location for the record was first determined. Thus, to retrieve the record with a key 3428, the key value would be divided by the prime number 97. The remainder, 33, specifies the relative location of the record in the file. The program would then direct the direct access device on which the file was stored to retrieve relative record 33 in the file.

The random retrieval of a record stored in a relative file, therefore, involves merely a few arithmetic instructions and a single read from the disk. This method allows the fastest access of data stored on the disk of any file organization method.

Although relative file organization allows fast random access to data in the file, it has the potential for wasting a great deal of storage space on the disk. For instance, it may be determined that a maximum of 100 records will be stored in a file. The disk, therefore, is formatted to allow relative record locations for 100 records in the file. The problem arises if the maximum 100 records are not in the file. For example, if a business estimated it would have a maximum of 100 products, the file would be established with 100 locations. When the business begins, however, it may only have 20 or 30 products. Thus, the remainder of the space in the file is wasted. Therefore, in many cases, the systems analyst designing the files must balance the speed of random access on relative files with the potential waste of storage space on the disk.

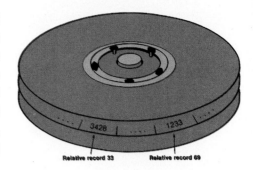

Relative record 33   Relative record 69

Figure 7-25 In the relative file shown above, the record with the key 3428 is stored at relative location 33 while the record with the key 1233 is stored at relative location 69. Thus, records stored in a relative file are not necessarily stored and sequentially retrieved in key sequence.

Indexed file organization

The third major file organization method is indexed file organization. Records are stored in an indexed file in an ascending or descending sequence based upon the key of the record. In this respect, the records stored in the file resemble records stored in a sequential file.

An indexed file, however, also contains an index. An index consists of entries containing the key to the data record stored in the file and also the disk address of the record in the file. This index is usually stored in the file on disk when the file is created and is retrieved from the disk when a record in the file is to be accessed. Using the index, records can be randomly accessed in an indexed file.

For example, a file can consist of inventory records containing the part number, the quantity on hand for the part, and the quantity on order for the part (Figure 7-26). The records in the file illustrated in Figure 7-26 are stored in ascending sequence by part number. The index contains the part number in ascending sequence and also the physical address on the disk where the records are located. In the example, the address is specified by cylinder, surface, and record number. This physical address could also be specified as sector number if records were physically addressed by sector on the device being used.

Figure 7-26 The index in an indexed file contains the record key number and the disk address of the corresponding record. In the example below, the key for the records in the file is the part number. The corresponding disk address specifies where on the disk the record is located.

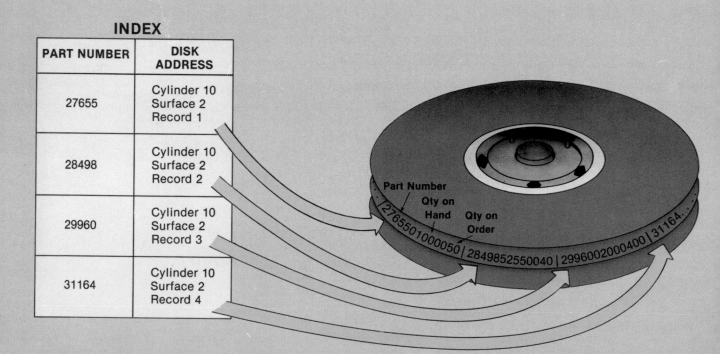

INDEX

PART NUMBER	DISK ADDRESS
27655	Cylinder 10 Surface 2 Record 1
28498	Cylinder 10 Surface 2 Record 2
29960	Cylinder 10 Surface 2 Record 3
31164	Cylinder 10 Surface 2 Record 4

Records can be accessed in an indexed file sequentially or randomly. Sequential access can occur in one of two ways. First, sequential retrieval of records in the file can begin with the first record in the file and continue through the file. Another technique for sequentially retrieving records is to begin the retrieval with a record with a given key. For example, in Figure 7-26 sequential retrieval could begin with the record with key 29960. After the beginning record for the sequential retrieval is located using the index, each subsequent record in the file would be read in the same manner as if retrieval began with the first record in the file.

Random access can also be used with indexed files. To randomly access a record in an indexed file, the index is searched until the key of the record to be retrieved is found. The address of the record found in the index is then used to access the record directly from the file without reading any other records. For example, if an inquiry was received from the stock room asking the number of parts on order for part number 28498, the index would be searched until key 28498 was found (Figure 7-27). The corresponding disk address (cylinder 10, surface 2, record 2) would then be used to read the record directly from the disk into main computer storage.

Even though both relative and indexed files offer sequential and random access, there are several distinct differences. Random retrieval when using relative files is faster than when using indexed files because an index does not have to be searched when using relative files. Instead, the relative record location is calculated and the record is read. Searching the index can be time-consuming for two reasons: 1) The index may be quite long and the search, even at main computer storage speeds, may take some time; 2) Since indexes are often stored on auxiliary storage and are not kept in main computer storage, random retrieval of an indexed file may require that the index is read into main computer storage before it can be searched for the matching record key. Thus, a minimum of two disk reads — one for the index and one for the desired record — may be required. Each time records must be read from the disk, the retrieval operation is slowed.

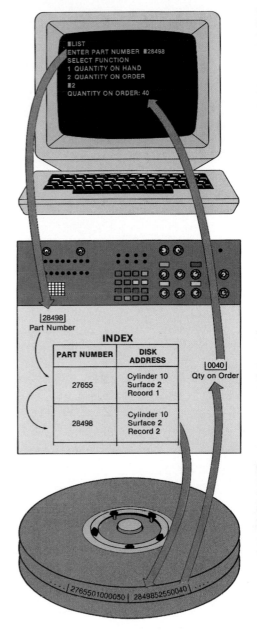

Figure 7-27 To randomly retrieve a record from an indexed file, the key of the record to be retrieved is used to search the file index.

The difference when sequentially retrieving data from an indexed file and a relative file is that the data sequentially retrieved from the indexed file will be in ascending or descending key sequence because the records are stored in the file in this sequence. With relative files, on the other hand, this is not always true (Figure 7-25).

Indexed files offer a compromise between sequential files and relative files. In many applications, they prove to be ideal because they allow both random retrieval and sequential retrieval in key sequence.

DATA MANAGEMENT SYSTEMS

Regardless of whether data is organized as sequential, relative, or indexed files, there is a need for a great deal of programming to organize and access the data stored in the files. For example, when indexed files are used, there is a need to establish the index and store the records when the file is created; a need to retrieve records based upon a key and a search of the index; and a need to add records to the file and modify the index to reflect the addition to the file.

Since this processing must be done for all files regardless of the application, the programming to accomplish these system functions is not normally written by the applications programmer who wishes to use indexed files. Instead, these common data management programs are supplied as a part of the operating system which is obtained with the computer system. The application program, written by the programmer, sends requests for records from the file or sends records to be written in the file to the data management programs (Figure 7-28). The data management programs, in turn, actually cause the files to be accessed or cause records to be written.

In addition to retrieving or writing records, these programs also update indexes if required, update pointers so that the next record is read from sequential files, and translate relative record locations into actual physical addresses on the disk pack.

Data management programs also perform such operations as deblocking or blocking records, writing labels on files for identification purposes, and allocating input/output areas for records which are to be processed from auxiliary storage files.

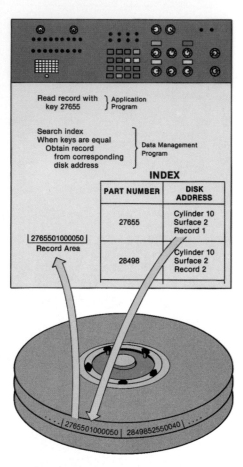

Figure 7-28 In the example above, the applications program requests the record with the key 27655. The read instruction causes control to be passed to the data management program. The data management program searches the index, obtains the disk address of the record, physically retrieves the record and places it in main computer storage. Control is then returned to the application program which can process the record as required.

Data management systems, also referred to as logical input/output control systems (logical IOCS), play an important role in programming because they allow an applications programmer to access data stored on auxiliary storage without the programmer's worrying about all of the detailed physical requirements associated with accessing a record. The programmer, for example, can request that the record with key 3485 be retrieved from an indexed file and the data managment programs will accomplish the task.

These data management programs can be used by all programs which require access to data stored on auxiliary storage. They are not limited to one program.

Auxiliary Storage

For Large and Small

Computer Systems

Both large and small computer systems require auxiliary storage to store data for use by application programs. The following pages illustrate frequently used media and devices for these systems.

The Need

For Large

Auxiliary Storage

As computer systems become larger, there is a corresponding need for larger auxiliary storage units. To serve the medium and large scale users of computer systems, there are a number of auxiliary storage units available. These include: 1) Fixed high-density disks; 2) Removable disk packs; 3) Sealed data modules.

The ability to store increasingly large volumes of data at a relatively low cost per character on direct access devices has become possible during the past decade. As a result, more and more users are utilizing magnetic disk in place of magnetic tape as their primary method for storing active data files.

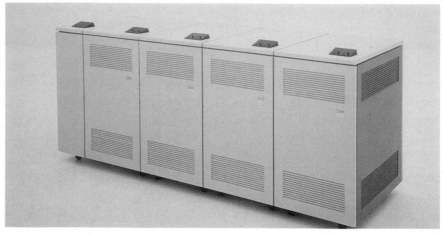

1

Figure 7-29 (1) IBM 3370 direct access storage units use fixed, non-removable disks. Each unit contains a single spindle of six 8-inch disks which is capable of storing 571.3 million bytes of data. Up to 32 units can be attached to an IBM 4331 processor, for a total storage capacity of 18.2 billion characters. The purchase price of $35,000.00 results in an estimated cost of $1.00 for each 16,268 bytes of data — a dramatic decrease from the estimated cost of $1.00 for each 300 bytes of direct access storage in 1964; **(2)** The BASF 1253 disk pack consists of 19 recording surfaces on 11 disks. Each disk is 14 inches in diameter. There are 815 cylinders on the disk pack and it can store 300 million characters.

The pack, which weighs 20 lbs., can be mounted and dismounted on disk drives. Each pack costs $1,100.00; **(3)** The large scale Burroughs B6800 computer system utilizes removable disk packs and the associated drives as the primary direct-access storage; **(4)** The BASF 1370 data module is a disk storage device using the "Winchester" technology. The module contains disk access arms, the read/write heads, and the disks in the sealed cartridge. This data module can store 70 million bytes on the six recording surfaces. The module sells for $1,100.00; **(5)** The IBM 3340 direct access storage facility uses the Winchester modules. These modules are removable in the same manner as disk packs.

5

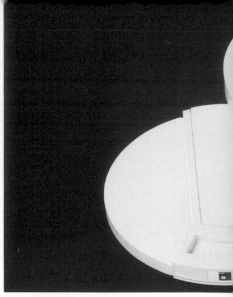

Figure 7-30 The Memorex 8-inch sealed disk unit above can store over 20 million characters with an average access time of 50 milliseconds. It costs less than $3,000.00 and offers more capacity and better reliability than floppy disks.

Figure 7-31 The picture below shows the many types of magnetic media that can be used for small computer systems. These media, manufactured by the 3M Company, include diskettes, tape data cartridges, tape cassettes, magnetic disk cartridges, and magnetic cards.

Figure 7-32 The disk cartridges above from BASF are a form of removable disk storage commonly used in sophisticated word processing systems and minicomputer installations where very large volumes of auxiliary storage are not required, but where it is advan-

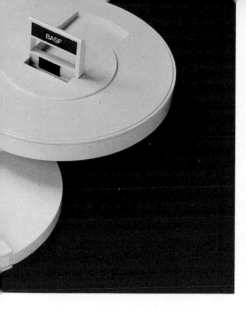

tageous to have removable storage. These units consist of a single disk with data recorded on both the upper and lower surfaces. Storage capacity ranges from 2 million to approximately 20 million characters, with an access time of approximately 75 milliseconds.

Figure 7-33 The Vector Graphics microcomputer (above) uses "mini-floppy" disks as auxiliary storage. Each mini-floppy disk is just over 5 inches in diameter. Mini-floppies are used on microcomputer systems because they offer random access at a low price.

Figure 7-34 The Wang computer system shown below illustrates the use of both floppy disks and disk cartridges for auxiliary storage. In the foreground, the floppy disk unit can be seen resting on top of the CRT terminal. In the background is a drive using a cartridge.

Auxiliary Storage

For Small

Computer Systems

There are a variety of magnetic disk and magnetic tape devices to serve the needs of users who have access to a minicomputer or a microcomputer.

The basic types of magnetic disk systems used with minicomputers and microcomputers are: 1) Floppy disks; 2) Disk cartridges; 3) "Mini" Winchester 8" disk modules.

The improvement in disk technology in the last decade has been amazing; and it is anticipated that disk units capable of storing millions of characters will be available for less than $1,000.00.

These disk devices, together with magnetic tape found on cassettes and cartridges constitute the major forms of auxiliary storage used on small computer systems.

Chapter summary

The following points have been discussed and explained in this chapter.

1. Two major considerations when examining auxiliary storage include an analysis of the media on which the data is to be stored and the manner in which data is organized and accessed.

2. Data is recorded on magnetic tape in the form of magnetic spots that can be read and transferred to main computer storage.

3. Although there are a variety of coding structures used with tape, the most common uses EBCDIC recorded in nine channels on the tape.

4. The term tape density refers to the number of characters that can be stored on one inch of tape. Common densities for tape include 800 bytes per inch, 1,600 bytes per inch, and 6,250 bytes per inch.

5. External labels are normally placed on tape reels for visual identification purposes. Internal tape labels are recorded magnetically on the actual tape, allowing the tapes to be checked to ensure the proper reel is mounted on the tape drive for processing.

6. Data can be transferred from tape to main computer storage at rates varying from 15,000 characters per second to 1,250,000 characters per second. The data transfer rate is calculated by multiplying the density of the tape by the speed at which tape moves past the read/write heads.

7. Records stored on tape are separated by an interblock gap, which is 6 inch wide, to allow for the starting and stopping of the tape during reading and writing operations.

8. Records are normally blocked on tape. Blocking refers to the process of placing two or more logical records on tape to form a physical record.

9. Blocking offers two significant advantages: more efficient use of tape and faster reading and writing speeds.

10. Magnetic tape is often used in systems for backing up magnetic disk files.

11. Magnetic disk packs are comprised of one or more disks. The disks commonly rotate at 3,600 revolutions per minute under read/write heads on a disk drive to read or record data on the surface of the disk.

12. Access arms or actuators position the read/write heads over any one of a number of discrete locations on the disk.

13. A concentric circular recording position on the disk is called a track. The number of tracks on a disk surface can vary from 200 to over 800.

14. Data is physically organized on disk using either the cylinder method or the sector method.

15. The cylinder method uses a cylinder as the basic reference point. A cylinder of data is that data which can be referenced by each discrete positioning of the access arm. To reference a record using the cylinder method, a program must specify the cylinder number, recording surface number, and record number.

16. With the sector method, each track is divided into individual storage areas called sectors. Each sector can hold a specified number of characters and records. Data is referenced by specifying a sector number.

17. Sequential access means that data is retrieved from a file stored on auxiliary storage one record after another in a predetermined sequence.

18. A major limitation of sequential access is that rapid retrieval of any record in the file is not possible.

19. Sequential access is normally used only in batch processing systems.

20. Random access means that any record stored in a file can be retrieved without reading any other record in the file. Random access can only take place on direct access devices.

21. Data to be accessed randomly must be referenced by some control field or key.

22. The major advantage of random access is that any record in a file can be retrieved rapidly.

23. Two major types of processing can be performed on data stored on auxiliary storage: data retrieval and file updating.

24. Three functions are performed when files are updated: additions, deletions, and changes.

25. With sequential file updating, a new master file is created containing the updated data. With random updating, a new file is not created; the updated record is rewritten back into the same location in the file.

26. Data can be stored on auxiliary storage in one of three logical file organizations: sequential, relative, or indexed organization.

27. Records which are sequentially organized are stored one after the other in the auxiliary storage file.

28. In a relative file, records are stored in relative locations within the file. Random access is normally used with relative files.

29. Records stored in an indexed file are stored in an ascending sequence or descending sequence by key. An index is created when the file is built. The index contains the key for the records in the file and the disk address for the records. Data can be accessed sequentially or randomly when indexed files are used.

30. Common data management programs are supplied as a part of the operating system to allow records to be accessed from files.

Student Learning Exercises

Review questions

1. What are the two most common forms of auxiliary storage?

2. What is tape density? What are the common recording densities of magnetic tape?

3. Explain the difference between external and internal tape labels.

4. What is meant by blocking?

5. What is meant by the term "track" in reference to magnetic disk storage?

6. Explain the term "cylinder." How is data referenced using the cylinder method?

7. What is meant by the term "sector"? How is data referenced using the sector method?

8. Explain the operation of a mass storage device. What is its storage capacity?

9. Explain the terms "sequential access" and "random access."

10. What are the advantages of sequential access? Random access?

11. What three functions are performed when records are updated? Give an example of each.

12. Explain how sequential file updating takes place.

13. What occurs when changes take place in records stored on disk when a file is updated randomly?

14. What are the three file organization methods?

15. Explain the differences between relative file organization and indexed file organization.

16. Explain the reasons for and advantages of data management programs.

Controversial issues in data processing

1. All users of computer systems today demand random access to data in a transaction-oriented environment; therefore, magnetic tape is obsolete as a form of auxiliary storage in an up-to-date computer installation. Do you agree or disagree with this statement? Be prepared to defend your position.

2. The costs of semiconductor memory are falling rapidly. In addition, millions of bits of data can be stored on small chips. In a few years, main computer storage in the form of semiconductor memory will be so cheap that auxiliary storage in the form of tape and disk will no longer be required. Write a report attacking or defending this position.

Research projects

1. The traditional auxiliary storage media, magnetic tape and magnetic disk, are being supplemented with new electronic storage methods such as bubble memory. Consult technical trade journals to explore the various new methods which can be used for auxiliary storage. Present a report to the class which identifies these methods, specifies their advantages and disadvantages, and predicts which will be successful in the coming decade and why.

2. Prepare a research report for the class on the latest technology used for auxiliary storage for microcomputer systems. The report should contain the types of auxiliary storage, the amount of data which can be stored, the access times, and the costs. A good source of information may be found in the advertisements in personal computing magazines.

Chapter 8
Data
Communications

Objectives

- A basic knowledge of the components of a modern data communications network

- A knowledge of line speeds and modes of transmission

- A knowledge of line configurations

- An understanding of ways to establish contact when using various line configurations

- An introduction to data communications networks

- A knowledge of computer operations in a data communications environment

Chapter 8

Figure 8-1 This Western Union earth station antenna located in downtown Miami, Florida, is used to transmit data to and receive data from satellites. Communicating data through satellites in orbit above the earth is becoming common for many businesses.

Data Communications

"I see no reason why intelligence may not be transmitted instantaneously by electricity."[1]

Introduction

Communication means the exchange of information. It was recognized in our earliest civilizations, as towns, cities, and nations were formed, that there was a need to communicate over long distances.

Responding to this need, Samuel Morse, in the early 1800's, conceived of the idea of transmitting data in the form of electrical impulses over wire connections between two points. On May 24, 1844, this concept became a reality when Morse tapped out the first telegram from the chambers of the United States Supreme Court to the Baltimore & Ohio Railroad station in Baltimore, Maryland. This first message, which read, "What hath God wrought," traveled only 40 miles on experimental iron wire; but it marked the beginning of a communications system that would revolutionize the world's social and economic life.

Some thirty years later, in 1876, Alexander Graham Bell uttered the words, "Mr. Watson, come here, I want you," into a device, the telephone, which is today a fixture in most parts of the world. The feasibility of transmitting both data and voice over communications lines led to the development of an amazingly complex network of communications systems which allows millions of individuals and companies to be in contact with locations throughout the world.

Today, the ability to communicate has dramatically affected the data processing industry. Combining computer technology with communications technology provides for the processing of data which has been transmitted from remote locations to computer systems over communications lines, through the air, and even through space by satellites located many thousands of miles above the earth (Figure 8–1).

---

1 Samuel Morse, 1832.

Early history of data communications

The ability to remotely communicate with a calculating machine was first demonstrated by Dr. George Stibitz in 1940 at Dartmouth College in Hanover, New Hampshire. Dr. Stibitz explained the use and operating characteristics of a new relay calculator developed by Bell Telephone Laboratories. The unique part of this demonstration was that the calculator was in New York City and the demonstration took place in Hanover, New Hampshire. Stibitz communicated with the calculator by sending data over standard telegraph lines. This was the first time coded data was sent over communication lines to be interpreted and processed by a calculating machine.

As computer technology developed in the 1950's, it became evident that computers and communication facilities could be effectively combined in many application areas. One of the first large-scale commercial applications of the use of computers and data communications was the Sabre airline reservation system. Developed jointly by American Airlines and IBM, the system used approximately 2,000 terminals placed throughout the United States. These terminals were all connected to a central computer by telephone lines. The system became operational in 1962 after six years of development. It was one of the first on-line computerized reservation systems.

Data communications systems of this type required very large main storage capacities, large direct access storage capabilities, and sophisticated programs to properly control the communications system. The technology of the early 1960's had not yet developed to the point where widespread data communications was economically feasible except for the very large user. The seed had been planted, however, and others began to look at the concept of processing data from remote locations.

Data communications today

It is estimated today that over 90 percent of the minicomputers and mainframes sold or leased in the United States have communications capabilities. The data processing and communications industries have become closely integrated, bringing computing power to all parts of the business and commercial world.

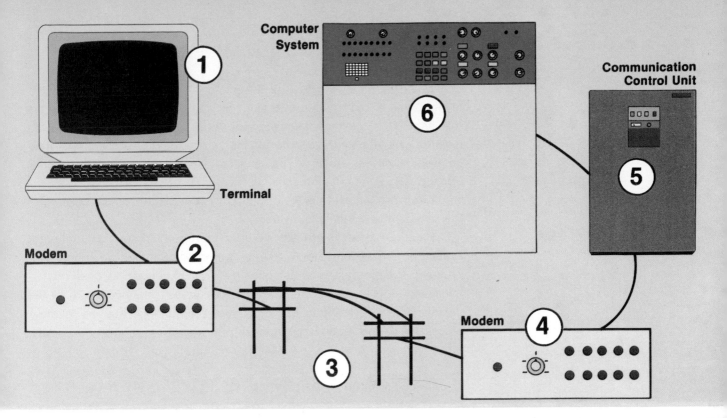

Many configurations are possible when using data communications. A very basic data communication configuration is illustrated in Figure 8-2. This system consists of the following components: 1) A terminal located at a site remote from the computer system with which it communicates; 2) A "modem," which is a device that converts the digital data generated by the terminal to a format (analog) which can be sent over the communication lines; 3) The communication channels over which the data is sent. These channels can be telephone lines, coaxial cables, microwave systems, satellite systems, or fiber optics channels; 4) A modem at the other end of the line which converts the data back to a digital format for processing on the computer system; 5) A communications control unit that monitors the communication lines and controls the data which is sent over the lines; 6) The computer system, which contains the programs necessary to cause the data communications to occur and the main computer storage where the data is stored.

A message to be sent from the terminal to the computer system is processed in the following manner. The terminal operator would enter the data to be sent to the computer system. When the operator indicates the data should be transmitted, it is electronically sent to the modem, which is physically located in close proximity to the terminal. The modem changes the data from digital data (data stored as discrete binary bits) to analog data (data stored as waveforms or frequencies). The data is then sent from the modem down the communication line.

Figure 8-2 The basic configuration for a data communications system is illustrated above. To perform an inquiry using this configuration, the terminal operator would send the inquiry over the network to the computer system. When the response to the inquiry is ready, the computer system would send the answer back to the terminal over the same communication network.

When the data arrives at its destination, it is again sent through the modem, which converts it from analog form back to digital form. The data is then sent to the communications control unit, which checks it for any possible errors and, if necessary, converts the data to the proper code for storing in main computer storage. The data is then placed in main computer storage, where it can be processed.

When data is sent from the computer system to the terminal, essentially the same steps are used in reverse.

The entire process of transmitting data from a terminal to a computer system or from a computer system to a terminal is under the control of a program. The program must establish the line connection between the terminal and the computer system and perform other tasks necessary for the communication of data to or from remote terminals. Thus, as in other processing performed on a computer system, a program controls the activity.

COMPONENTS OF A DATA COMMUNICATIONS SYSTEM

As noted, there are a number of components which comprise the data communications system. The following paragraphs examine these components in more detail.

Terminals

The many and varied types of terminals which can be used in data communications systems have been explored in previous chapters. For inquiry systems, the most widely used terminal is the CRT terminal, although hard copy terminals are also used extensively.

Terminals in a data communications network are not limited to CRT's or hard copy machines. Indeed, other computer systems can act as terminals in a network (Figure 8–3). Computer systems which act as terminals in a data communications network can process data "locally" on the system and can also communicate with the "host" computer system when required.

For example, the Univac 90/25 shown in Figure 8–3 contains a card reader and printer. Therefore, batch processing using cards as input and the printer as output can be performed on the system. At certain periods during the day or night, the computer system can indicate to a larger host machine that it is ready to send data. Once a line connection is made, the Univac 90/25 can transmit data which is stored in its main computer storage or it can transmit data read from punched cards. In return, the computer system receiving the data from the Univac 90/25 can send data back which will be printed on the printer.

Thus, a computer system which acts as a terminal in a data communications network can also serve as a stand-alone computer.

Figure 8-3 The Univac 90/25 computer system above can be used both as a stand-alone computer system and a terminal in a data communications network.

Modems

With many communications lines, such as telephone lines, a terminal cannot be directly connected to the lines because telephone lines were designed to carry voice signals. These voice signals are described in electronic terminology as analog signals and represent a full range of frequencies or tones. On the other hand, data being transmitted from a computer is represented by the presence or absence of an electrical impulse (representing a bit "on" or a bit "off"). This is called digital data representation.

To allow digital data to be transmitted over telephone lines, most systems require the digital impulses to be converted to analog impulses. This task is accomplished by a modem (Figure 8-4). A modem (derived from "modulate-demodulate") is an electrical device which accepts a digital signal and converts it to an analog signal, or can accept an analog signal and convert it to a digital signal. A modem is required at both the sending and receiving end of the line to convert the signals.

Some channels are capable of transmitting digital signals. These systems do not require modems.

Figure 8-4 The modems above, made by Universal Data Systems, Inc., are used to convert analog signals to digital signals and vice versa. The different models shown are used for different types and speeds of communication lines.

Acoustic couplers

Most modems are directly connected to the terminals and the computer systems. This means that the terminals must remain in one area. In some applications, it is necessary that the terminal move from place to place. For example, an engineer or mathematician may want to take a CRT terminal home to tie into a nation-wide data communications network; or a salesman on the road may wish to transmit sales orders or inquire into a data base to find parts availability from many different locations (Figure 8-5).

To provide portability of terminals, a special type of modem called an acoustic coupler is used. When using an acoustic coupler, a standard telephone headset is placed into the acoustic coupler, which is attached to the terminal device (Figure 8-6). The acoustic coupler converts the digital signals generated by the terminal into a series of audible tones which are picked up by the mouthpiece of the headset in the same manner as if one were speaking into the telephone. These analog signals are then transmitted over standard telephone lines to the computer system. On the receiving end, of course, a modem will convert the analog signal into digital signals for use by the computer system.

Figure 8-5 The salesman in the picture above is using a numeric keyboard terminal and a special acoustic coupler to make an inquiry into the computer system. The answer he receives will be in the form of voice output from the computer system.

Figure 8-6 The General Electric terminal at the right is connected to a computer system through the use of an acoustic coupler. The telephone headset in the coupler sends the analog signals to the modem located at the computer site.

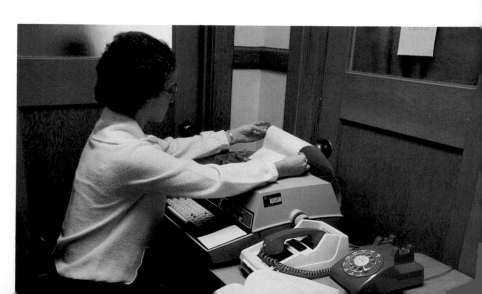

Data communication channels

Data is transmitted from a terminal to a computer system or from the computer system to a terminal over communication channels. These channels, which are also termed communication lines or data links, include the following types: 1) Standard telephone lines; 2) Coaxial cables; 3) Microwave transmission; 4) Satellite communications; 5) Fiber optics. The following sections discuss these various communication channels.

Telephone lines

Standard telephone lines are widely used as communication channels. Telephone lines are particularly useful to the user of data communications because the complex network of lines that has already been established permits data to be transmitted to very nearly any location in the world.

Coaxial cables

Coaxial cables are high-quality communication lines that have been laid under the ground or under the ocean. The electrical characteristics of the coaxial cable are such that data can be transmitted at a much higher rate than with standard telephone lines. A coaxial cable under the Atlantic Ocean has provided an important means for intercontinental telephone communications for many years. These cables are also heavily used for data communications.

Microwave transmission

Microwave systems transmit signals through open space much like radio signals. They provide a much faster transmission rate than is possible with either telephone lines or coaxial cables. Microwave systems transmit data on a line of sight path, and are characterized by antennas positioned on tops of buildings, mountain tops, or high towers. Long distance microwave channels consist of a series of relay stations spaced approximately 30 miles apart. Two stations must be within sight of one another. For transmitting long distances, signals are amplified and retransmitted from station to station.

Communication satellites

Quickly gaining importance as a means for data communications are communication satellite systems. Positioned in space approximately 22,000 miles above the earth are a number of communication satellites. These satellites serve as relay stations for the transmission of signals generated from the earth.

Satellite communication is ideal for long distance communication. Earth stations consisting of ground antennas beam signals to the satellite (Figure 8–7). The satellite amplifies and retransmits the signals to another earth station which can be located many thousands of miles away. Transmission by satellite allows large amounts of data to be sent long distances at rapid speeds. Its use has increased dramatically in recent years.

Fiber optics

Fiber optics is a relatively new technology that may serve to replace conventional wire and cable in thousands of communication systems.

This technology is based upon the ability of smooth hair-thin strands of transparent material to conduct light with high efficiency. The major advantage of fiber optics over wire cables includes substantial weight and size savings and increased speed of transmission. A one and one-half pound fiber optic cable can transmit the same amount of data as thirty pounds of copper wire. A standard coaxial cable can carry up to 5,400 different voice channels, while a single fiber optic cable can carry up to 50,000 channels.

Although fiber optics has not yet been used on a large scale, it promises to dramatically increase data communication capabilities once it becomes widely installed.

Figure 8–7 The 16-foot diameter antenna located on top of a 40-story building in Portland, Oregon, is part of a communication link between the First National Bank Center in Portland and the Western Bancorp Data Processing Co. in Los Angeles. Banking and account data is transmitted from this antenna to a satellite which then retransmits it to a similar station in Los Angeles. Satellite communication systems such as this one owned by the American Satellite Company offer increased reliability over land-based communication systems.

Figure 8-8 The photo at the right shows a fiberguide cable which is used to transmit sound over a beam of light. The cable, protected with steel wires embedded in its sheath, contains 12 ribbons, each encapsulating 12 glass fibers, or light guides.

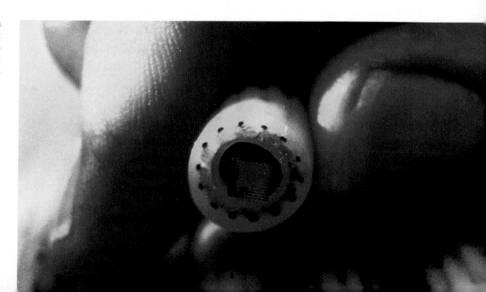

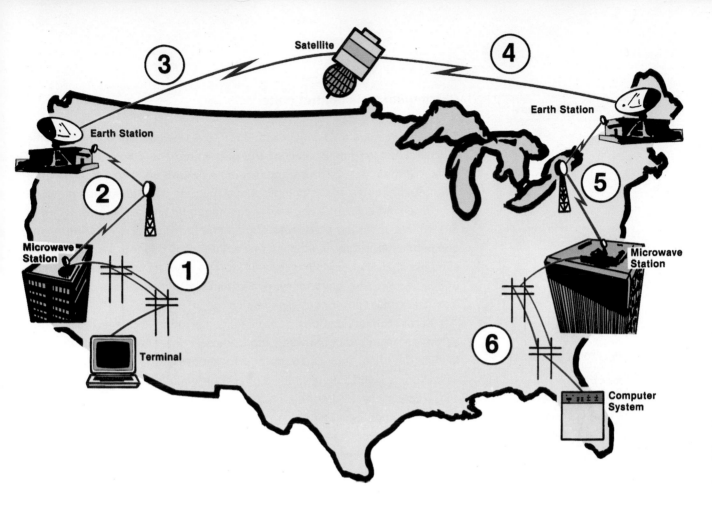

Transmitting data over communication channels

When transmitting data over long distances, there is the possibility that a number of different types of communication channels could be called into use.

The illustration in Figure 8-9 demonstrates that data could be transmitted as follows: 1) At the terminal location, an entry is made into a terminal. The data is sent over telephone lines from the terminal to a microwave station; 2) The data is then sent by microwave signals from the microwave station to the earth station; 3) At the earth station, the data is converted to the appropriate form and is sent to the satellite; 4) The satellite relays the data to the earth station on the other side of the country; 5) The data received from the satellite is sent from the earth station to a microwave station; 6) The data is finally transmitted over telephone lines to the computer system. When data is sent from the computer system, the transmission would take place in a similar manner but in the opposite direction.

Not all data communication networks are as involved as the one just illustrated. The potential for this type of network exists, however, if it is required to satisfy the data communication requirements of an organization.

Figure 8-9 A data communication network using different types of communication channels is shown above. The ability to use different methods based upon the distance to be covered and the amount of data to be sent gives great flexibility to communication network designers.

Communications control units

A communications control unit interfaces between the modem and the computer system at the end of the line where the computer system is located (Figure 8–10). The communications control unit provides a path for data transfer between the computer and the data communication network.

When data is sent along a communication line, it is sent in the form of bits which, together, constitute a character of data. One function of the communications control unit is to assemble these bits into a character and send the character to main computer storage. The communications control unit appears to the computer system as just another peripheral device, such as a card reader or a floppy disk reader.

Some communications control units perform functions beyond just acting as an interface between the computer system and the data communication lines. They can perform error recovery when a signal is lost or when "noise" which distorts the signal is detected on a line. They interpret and process control information which is sent down the line, such as a character which indicates the end of the message. They can also interface with many communication lines and control each one so that the computer system need not perform these functions.

Front-end processors

The most sophisticated communications control units, sometimes called front-end processors, can be programmed by the user. These units, which are actually minicomputers designed specifically for the task of front-end processor, can be programmed to edit input records for valid data, control the network and allow only authorized users to have access to the computer system, and a host of similar activities.

The advantage of a front-end processor is that the tasks accomplished by the front-end processor do not have to be performed by the main computer system. This allows the main computer system to concentrate on processing application programs and producing useful output. It has been found with large data communication networks that up to 30 percent of the processing time for a computer system can be spent in monitoring the communication lines and performing the same functions which can be performed by a front-end processor. Thus, in large systems, the use of a programmable front-end processor can increase significantly the amount of processing which can be accomplished by the main computer system.

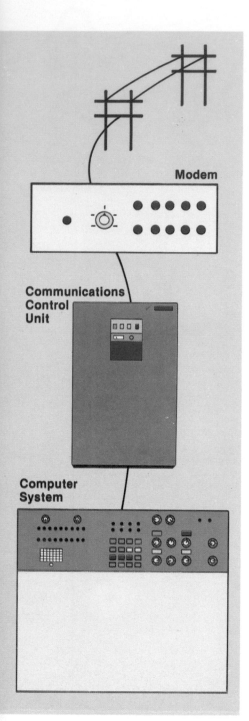

Figure 8-10 The communications control unit is the interface between the data communication lines and the computer system. Programmable communications control units are called front-end processors.

Computer systems in data communication environments

The final element of a data communication network to consider is the computer system. It is the function of any data communication network, of course, to place data in the computer system for processing or to transmit processed data from the computer system to users located at a site remote from the computer. The computer system, therefore, is the hub of the data communication network.

Any data communications which takes place with a computer system will be under the control of a program stored in main computer storage. It is this program which processes data received over the network and sends messages back to the terminals in the network. If a programmable front-end processor is not used, the program also has the responsibility for controlling the network, establishing contact with the terminals, and processing any line errors which may occur.

Computer systems used as the "host" computer in data communication networks can vary considerably in terms of size and capabilities. In large networks, with many lines and terminals requiring large amounts of applications processing, big mainframe computer systems are normally used (Figure 8–11).

Figure 8-11 The large-scale computer systems pictured below are used by CompuServe, Inc. to provide data processing services to many users linked to the system through a large data communication network.

These machines require large main computer storage (typically several million positions), sophisticated systems and applications programs, and a multitude of communications equipment.

Where smaller data communications networks are found, smaller host computers can be used (Figure 8-12). In many cases, these smaller computer systems do nothing but process data communications applications for a limited number of users. Many special purpose computer systems which are used for a single application have communications capabilities.

It is important to realize that the host computer system, regardless of size, contains programs to control the communications occurring on the network and to process the data to provide the information requested by users of the network.

SPEED AND DATA TRAFFIC

Two major considerations when designing a data communications network are the speed at which data must be transmitted and the amount of data, or traffic, which must be handled on the network. Using these considerations, the network designer must determine the speed of the lines which are to be used, the mode in which data is to be transmitted, and the type of line. These subjects are discussed in the following paragraphs.

Line speed

Line speeds are measured by counting the number of bits which can be sent over the line in one second. Different grades of channels provide a variety of speeds in which data can be transmitted over the channel. The grades of channels are commonly classified as follows: 1) Low speed, or narrow band; 2) Medium speed, or voice band; 3) High speed, or broadband.

Low speed channels have a bit transmission rate of 40 to 300 bits per second (bps). Included in this category are telegraph communications lines. These channels are normally used for low-speed teletypewriter communications and for other low-speed devices which can use low-speed lines.

Medium speed lines operate at rates varying from 300 bits per second to 9,600 bits per second. This speed range is accomodated by lines which are used for ordinary voice communications (hence the term "voice grade" to describe these lines). The most commonly used medium speed lines are telephone lines.

Specific data transmission speeds are normally provided. Common speeds include 600 bits per second, 1,000 bits per second, 2,400 bits per second, 4,800 bits per second, and 9,600 bits per second. At the higher speeds, the lines must be specially "conditioned" by the addition of electronic components which minimize interference on the line and ensure that the data is sent on the line without error.

High-speed communications channels, commonly called broadband or wideband, permit transmission rates in excess of 9,600 bits per second. Speeds normally available include 19,200 bps, 40,800 bps, 50,000 bps, and 230,000 bps. High speed channels require microwave, fiber optics, or satellite transmission. They are normally used for computer-to-computer communication since computers usually send data to each other faster than terminals send data to computers.

When considering the speed at which data is to be sent, the designer will usually determine the speed at which the terminals can operate. Based upon these speeds, the speed of the lines will be determined.

Mode of transmission

Two modes of transmission are used when transmitting data over communication lines. These modes are called asynchronous transmission and synchronous transmission.

When asynchronous transmission is used, one character at a time is transmitted or received. Each character, which is composed of 7 or 8 bits (depending upon the code used for character definition), is identified by a start bit or a stop bit. Thus, the character "A" transmitted in asynchronous mode would be preceded by a start bit and would be followed by a stop bit (Figure 8–13). The next character down the line would also be preceded by a start bit and followed by a stop bit.

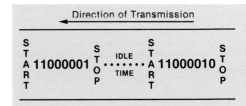

Figure 8–13 In the example above, asynchronous transmission is used to transmit the letters "A" and "B." The start bit notifies the modem that a character is being sent. The bits for the character follow the start bit. After all the bits for the character have been transmitted, the stop bit indicates the end of the character. A start bit can immediately follow the stop bit or there can be idle time following the stop bit, depending on the terminal sending the data.

8.13

Asynchronous transmission is normally used for transmission at speeds under 2,000 bits per second. The start and stop bits, of course, add overhead to the data transmitted because an 8–bit character would require 10 bits on the line for transmission.

Asynchronous transmission is many times used when the terminals in the data communications systems enter data a character at a time. For example, a "dumb" CRT terminal might not contain any storage. Therefore, each time the terminal operator depresses a key on the keyboard, a character is sent down the line to the computer system. Since most persons do not type more than 300–400 characters per minute, the per second rate is about 5–7 characters per second, which translates into approximately 50–70 bits per second when using 8–bit characters. This rate is quite slow when compared to the line capabilities of 600–2,000 bits per second. Therefore, voice grade lines with asynchronous transmission are quite acceptable for applications of this type.

For applications where faster transmission is required, such as when data stored on a magnetic tape is transmitted to a computer system over a data communications channel, synchronous transmission is used (Figure 8–14). Synchronous transmission allows characters to be sent down the line as a group without start-stop bits. Each character is identified by the 7 or 8 bits comprising the character. The beginning of one character and the end of the character is determined by a timing mechanism within a modem. Once transmission is begun, the timing mechanism samples the communication channel at specified intervals to obtain the bit. When it has sampled the required number of bits, the character is sent to the communications control unit.

Synchronous transmission is normally used where transmission rates exceed 2,000 bits per second. It can be used on both voice grade lines and broadband lines.

The mode of transmission used depends upon the type of terminals used in the data communications network and the speed at which the data must be transmitted. Depending upon the mode chosen, the type of line and the appropriate modem are used.

Type of transmission lines

There are three types of transmission lines which can be used: 1) Simplex lines; 2) Half-duplex lines; 3) Full-duplex lines.

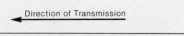

Direction of Transmission

11000001110000101 1000011··

Figure 8–14 Synchronous transmission allows data to be sent as a group over a data communication channel. At specified time intervals, the line is sampled by the modem and the bit is detected. The accumulated bits are then sent to the communications control unit. Since the data is sent without start-stop bits and without idle time between each character, much faster speeds are achieved with synchronous transmission. The biggest disadvantage with synchronous transmission is that on occasion, because of line interference, the modem and the line get out of synchronization. When this occurs, much of the data which is sent is lost and must be retransmitted.

A simplex channel allows data to be transmitted in one direction only. For example, if a simplex channel were used, an input terminal could only send; it could never receive (Figure 8–15). In a modern data communications environment, simplex channels are normally not used because even if data is only sent from a terminal, there is usually an acknowledgement made to the sending terminal.

On a half-duplex channel, it is possible to transmit in either direction. The transmission, however, can occur in only one direction at a time (Figure 8–16). This type of transmission is typically found in transaction-oriented systems where the terminal operator would enter data and then receive a response from the computer system. In this case, the data entered by the terminal operator would be going one direction on the line and the computer system could not communicate with the terminal when the data was being entered. When the computer system responds to the terminal, the operator cannot enter data. When half-duplex lines are used, the transmission flow in one direction must be stopped each time the direction of transmission is reversed. The time to accomplish this is called "turnaround time" and is typically 50 to 250 milliseconds (thousandths of a second).

Data can be transmitted in both directions at the same time on full duplex communication channels (Figure 8–17). A major advantage of full duplex communication channels is that turnaround time is not required. Therefore, if there are high-speed communications occurring between two computer systems, they do not have to wait for turnaround. Although the time may seem insignificant, if five messages were sent from computer A to computer B, and five messages were sent back from computer B to computer A, a total of nine turnarounds will be required if half-duplex lines were used. This could amount to almost 2½ seconds. When 9,600 bits are sent in one second, the time lost for turnaround could have been used to send 24,000 bits, or 3,000 characters, on a full-duplex line.

Full duplex lines are normally used when high-speed transmission is taking place, typically between two computer systems.

Character coding when using data communications

As noted in Chapter 4 when discussing internal data representation, each character is represented by a combination of bits (some of the bits "on" and some of the bits "off") according to a predetermined code. Data is transmitted on a data communications channel as a series of bits, with each character represented by the same method as in main computer storage.

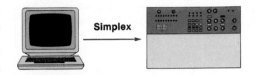

Figure 8-15 A simplex channel allows data to be transmitted in one direction only. Although the arrow above illustrates a terminal to computer direction, the one-way communication could take place from the computer to the terminal.

Figure 8-16 A half-duplex line allows data to be sent in both directions, but it cannot be sent in both directions at the same time.

Figure 8-17 A full-duplex line allows data to be sent in both directions at the same time. A major advantage of full duplex lines is that no turnaround time is required to reverse directions of transmission.

CHARACTER	BIT REPRESENTATION
0	0 1 1 0 0 0 0
1	0 1 1 0 0 0 1
2	0 1 1 0 0 1 0
3	0 1 1 0 0 1 1
4	0 1 1 0 1 0 0
5	0 1 1 0 1 0 1
6	0 1 1 0 1 1 0
7	0 1 1 0 1 1 1
8	0 1 1 1 0 0 0
9	0 1 1 1 0 0 1
A	1 0 0 0 0 0 1
B	1 0 0 0 0 1 0
C	1 0 0 0 0 1 1
D	1 0 0 0 1 0 0
E	1 0 0 0 1 0 1
F	1 0 0 0 1 1 0
G	1 0 0 0 1 1 1
H	1 0 0 1 0 0 0
I	1 0 0 1 0 0 1
J	1 0 0 1 0 1 0
K	1 0 0 1 0 1 1
L	1 0 0 1 1 0 0
M	1 0 0 1 1 0 1
N	1 0 0 1 1 1 0
O	1 0 0 1 1 1 1
P	1 0 1 0 0 0 0
Q	1 0 1 0 0 0 1
R	1 0 1 0 0 1 0
S	1 0 1 0 0 1 1
T	1 0 1 0 1 0 0
U	1 0 1 0 1 0 1
V	1 0 1 0 1 1 0
W	1 0 1 0 1 1 1
X	1 0 1 1 0 0 0
Y	1 0 1 1 0 0 1
Z	1 0 1 1 0 1 0

Figure 8-18 The ASCII code uses seven bits to represent numbers and letters of the alphabet. ASCII code is widely used for data communication systems. In addition, some computer systems use ASCII as the code for data representation in main computer storage.

There are two primary codes used for data transmitted along a data communication channel. The first is the Extended Binary Coded Decimal Interchange Code (EBCDIC) which was illustrated in Chapter 4. The second is the American Standard Code for Information Interchange (ASCII). This code was developed by the International Standards Organization and is published by the American National Standards Institute.

ASCII utilizes seven bits to represent numbers, letters of the alphabet, and special characters (Figure 8–18). It is used more often than EBCDIC because it is treated somewhat as a standard in the data communications industry.

When ASCII is used for communications and the computer system uses EBCDIC, the ASCII bits must be translated to the EBCDIC representation of characters. This translation takes place either in the communications control unit prior to placing the data in main computer storage, or it takes place under program control after the data has been placed in main computer storage. Almost all terminals utilize the ASCII code, so the translation problem is not found at the terminal end of the line.

LINE CONFIGURATIONS

Regardless of the type of communication channel, the speed at which data is transmitted, the mode of transmission, or the coding used for the characters on the channel, the terminals and computer systems must be arranged in some type of line configuration. There are two major line configurations: 1) Point-to-point lines; 2) Multidrop or multipoint lines.

Point-to-point lines

A direct line between a terminal and a computer system in a data communications network is called point-to-point. In a point-to-point line, each terminal transmits data to and receives data from a computer system by means of an individual line that links the terminal directly to the computer system (Figure 8–19). No other terminals are on the line.

This type of line between the terminal and the computer system might be used when the computer system and the terminal will be communicating with each other on an almost continuous basis and fast response time is required. In many cases, point-to-point lines are used when a computer system acts as a terminal to a larger computer system.

Point-to-point lines are expensive because only one terminal can use a line into the computer system. This means that two modems and a "port" in the communications control unit are used for only one terminal.

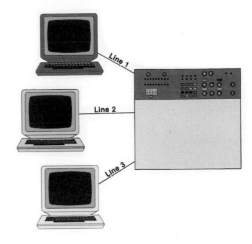

Figure 8-19 When a point-to-point line is used, the terminal is connected directly to the computer system. Only one terminal is used for each line into the computer system.

Multidrop or multipoint lines

A multidrop or multipoint line has more than one terminal on a single line connected to a computer system (Figure 8–20). When a multidrop line is used, only one terminal at a time can transmit to the computer system. More than one terminal on the line, however, can receive data at the same time.

A multidrop line decreases line costs considerably because the line is used by many terminals. This line configuration is normally found in inquiry systems with multiple CRT terminals because each terminal uses the line for only a short period of time.

For example, an operator could use a CRT terminal to enter an inquiry. While the data is being transmitted to the computer system, other terminals on the line would not be able to send data. The time required for the data to be transmitted to the computer system, however, would likely be less than one second. As soon as the inquiry is received by the computer system, a second terminal could send an inquiry. Thus, it would appear to the terminal operator as if there were no other terminals on the line, even though there may be many terminals using the same line.

The number of terminals to be placed on one line is a decision made by the designer of the network based upon the amount of traffic which will be found on the line. For example, one hundred or more terminals could be contained on a single line, provided each of them was only going to be sending short messages, such as inquiries; and each terminal was going to use the communication lines only a few hours per day.

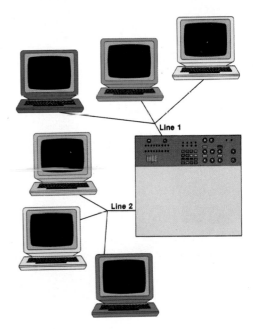

Figure 8-20 A multidrop line has more than one terminal on a single line. In the example above, there are three terminals on line 1 and three terminals on line 2. On each line, only one terminal at a time can transmit to the computer system. However, more than one terminal on a line can receive data from the computer system at the same time.

On the other hand, if longer messages were required and the terminals were to be used almost continuously, the number of terminals on one line would have to be smaller.

An analysis of the characteristics of the data communications network is required in order to determine the type of line between the terminals and the computer system, and the number of terminals which will be contained on a multidrop line if such line is to be used.

ESTABLISHING THE CONTACT FOR DATA TRANSMISSION

The method for establishing contact between a terminal and a computer system or between a computer system and a terminal depends upon whether a point-to-point line is used or a multidrop line is used. These methods are discussed in the following paragraphs.

Establishing point-to-point contact

When point-to-point lines are used, one terminal is placed on one line to the computer system. A point-to-point line may be one of two types: 1) Leased line; 2) Switched line.

A leased line is a permanent circuit used to connect a terminal with a computer system. With a leased line, the terminal is always attached to the computer system via the line.

A switched line is so-called because it is established through the regular voice telephone network rather than being a direct connection as found with a leased line. Each time a terminal communicates with a computer system over a switched line, it can be using different circuits because the circuit will be selected by the telephone company switching devices.

On a switched line, the terminal establishes contact with the computer system by dialing the telephone number of the computer system. The modem for the line at the computer site is assigned a telephone number just as if it were a regular telephone. When its number is dialed by the terminal operator, either using a dial on the terminal or automatically, the modem "answers" the call and establishes the line connection (Figure 8–21). The modem also informs the terminal, through the use of a control character sent down the line, that it is ready to receive data. The terminal can then begin sending data to the computer system.

Figure 8–21 The Teletype® terminals shown above contain a Touch-Tone® dialing system. To establish contact between the terminal and the computer system, the terminal user would dial the telephone number of the computer system. Once contact is made, the terminal and the computer can carry on a "conversation" in the same manner as two people talking on the telephone.

The computer system can initiate contact with the terminal by appropriate computer commands which "dial" the number of the terminal. The terminal modem then responds in the same manner as when the computer system modem is dialed.

Contact between a terminal and a computer system linked by leased lines in a point-to-point line configuration is normally done by merely entering a control character or flipping a switch on the terminal or by the computer system addressing a message to the appropriate line. Since the terminal is always connected to the computer system via the leased line, the electronics of the system are established so that the computer system "listens" for a request from the terminal to send data for a period of time (usually much less than a second), and then the line is changed so that the terminal "listens" for a request from the computer system to send data. In this way, merely touching a key can initiate the contact between the computer system and the terminal.

Establishing multidrop line contact

A leased line is almost always used for multidrop line configurations. Contact is established by one of two methods: 1) Polling; 2) Addressing, or selection.

Polling is performed by the computer system and the associated communications control unit. It is used to establish contact when the terminal has data to send to the computer system. When polling is used, the computer system and the communications control unit ask each terminal on the multidrop line if it has some data to send to the computer. The question is asked by special control characters which are transmitted to the terminal. If a terminal does not have data to send when it is asked, the next terminal on the line will be asked if it has data to send.

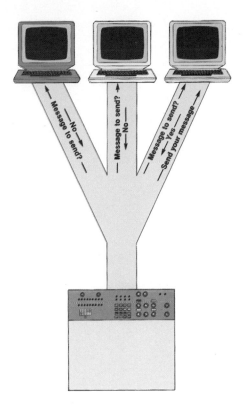

Figure 8-22 When terminals on a multidrop line are polled, the computer system or communications control unit "asks" the terminal if it has a message to send. If it does not, the terminal "answers" no. If it does, the terminal "answers" yes and the computer directs the terminal to send its message.

The sequence in which terminals are polled is specified by a predefined list. This list is developed based upon the expected traffic from each terminal on the line. For example, assume there are three terminals on a line. The first terminal is located in the order office of the company and is in almost constant use. The second terminal, located in the shipping and receiving department, transmits and receives for a total of about 3 hours per day. The third terminal is located in the company president's office and is used about ½ hour per day.

Since the terminal in the order department is used for 8 hours almost continuously, it should be polled much more than the terminal in the president's office. Therefore, the polling list may look like this: order office, shipping and receiving, order office, shipping and receiving, order office, president, order office. As can be seen, the order office is polled four times, the shipping and receiving department is polled twice, and the president's office is polled once. After the list had been polled, the system would start again at the beginning of the list. The time normally required to make one pass of the list, assuming all negative responses, would be less than 500 milliseconds.

Once a terminal sends a response that it has data to send, it gains control of the line and the polling does not continue until after the terminal has sent its message. Thus, the danger exists that once a terminal gains control of the line, it can keep control of the line for a long time. To overcome this condition, some systems include a programmed "timeout" which allows the terminal to control the line for a specified period of time and then breaks the connection so that other terminals on the line are not excluded from using the line.

Addressing

In order for the computer system to send data to a terminal in a multidrop configuration, a technique called addressing (or selection) is used. The computer system addresses the particular terminal on the line and sends the message to that terminal. For example, if the message to be sent from the computer system were to be displayed on terminal B on line 1, then the appropriate control characters would precede the message on the line to identify terminal B, line 1. Terminal B would then receive the message.

Since the computer system can address any terminal on the line, a message can be sent to more than one terminal on the line at the same time. Thus, the message can be preceded by control characters which specify the message is to be sent to terminal B, terminal D, and terminal J on line 1.

Polling and addressing are widely used in most data communication systems to establish contact between computer systems and terminals.

DATA COMMUNICATIONS NETWORKS

The various elements of data communications which have been discussed thus far must be organized into a system, or network, in order to solve the problems for which they are used. Although a network can be defined as any system composed of one or more computers and terminals, most networks are composed of multiple terminals, and possibly multiple computers, to enable the network to function most efficiently and productively.

Although many combinations can be used, network design is usually categorized as one of two types: 1) Star network; 2) Ring network.

Star networks

A star network contains a central computer system and one or more terminals connected to the computer system, forming a "star." A "pure" star structure consists of only point-to-point lines between the terminals and the computer system (Figure 8–23).

A star network, however, can be modified to include some point-to-point lines and some multidrop lines. In Figure 8–24, the star network utilizes both point-to-point and multidrop lines.

Figure 8-23 In a "pure" star network, each terminal is connected point-to-point to the central computer system.

Figure 8-24 A "modified" star network contains both point-to-point lines and multidrop lines.

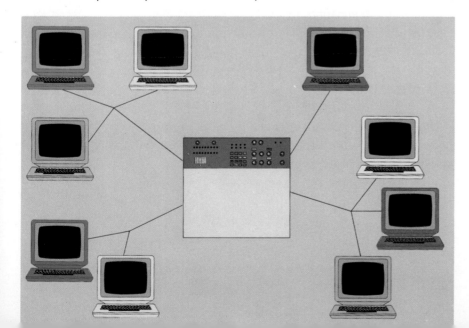

A star network configuration with both point-to-point and multidrop lines would be used when the central computer system contains all of the data required to process the input from the terminals, and some terminals have more traffic than others. For example, the one terminal in Figure 8–24 that is on a point-to-point line might be used constantly throughout the day. The terminals on the multidrop lines would likely be used less frequently, so they do not require a point-to-point line.

It is important to note that in a star network, the computer system is "centralized." All of the terminals communicate with one computer system, which will contain the programs necessary to control the network and the data which will be used for processing requests by the terminals.

Ring networks

A ring network does not utilize a centralized computer system. Rather, a series of computer systems communicate with one another (Figure 8–25). A ring network can be useful when all of the processing is not done at a central site, but rather processing is accomplished at "local" sites. For example, a computer system could be located in three departments: the accounting department, the personnel department, and the shipping and receiving department. The computers in each of these departments could perform the processing required for each of the departments. On occasion, however, the computer in the shipping and receiving department, for example, could communicate with the computer in the accounting department to update certain files and data stored on the accounting department computer system.

Ring networks, at this point in time, have not been extensively implemented for data communications systems which are used for long distance communication. Instead, they are normally used for more local communications within a single building or plant.

Multiplexers

Additional electronic equipment can be added to a data communications network to give it added capabilities and more efficient transmission of data.

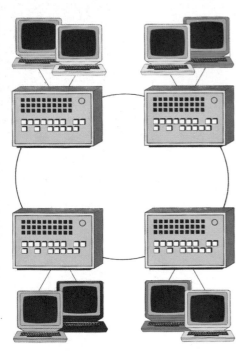

Figure 8-25 In a ring network, computer systems are connected to one another as shown above. Typically, minicomputers are used in ring networks.

In order to make more efficient use of a line or channel, a multiplexer can be used. A multiplexer is an electronic device which can effectively divide a channel capable of a certain speed into multiple channels of a slower speed. For example, assume that a channel between a remote terminal and a computer system was capable of transmitting 9,600 bits per second. Assume further that this speed was much greater than could effectively be used by the terminal. A multiplexer will allow that channel to be divided, or multiplexed, into a number of channels of slower speed. Thus, the 9,600 bps channel could be divided into four 2,400 bps channels (Figure 8-26). Multiple terminals could then be connected to the multiplexer and each would have a line which was compatible to its speed requirements.

A multiplexer is transparent to the network because it does not affect the manner or speed in which data is transmitted. It merely subdivides an existing channel into slower channels to provide more economic use of the channel.

Concentrators

In some networks, remote concentrators are used. A concentrator is normally a minicomputer located at the terminal side of a long distance line (Figure 8-27). It functions as a data communications unit and is usually programmable. Its main benefit is to reduce line costs by accepting information from many terminals over slow speed lines and transmitting the data to the main computer system over a high-speed line.

Generally, the capacity of the high-speed line from the concentrator to the host computer system is less than the total capacity of all the lines feeding into the concentrator. Therefore, the possibility exists that the terminals can temporarily generate more data than the concentrator can transmit. When this occurs, the concentrator will store the data received from the terminals on auxiliary storage. When the line to the host computer is no longer busy, the data will be retrieved from auxiliary storage and transmitted to the host computer system.

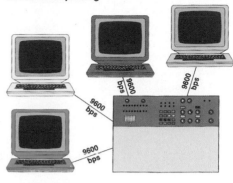

Before Multiplexing

After Multiplexing

Multiplexer

9600 bps

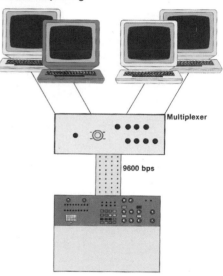

Figure 8-26 Multiplexing allows a single communications channel to be subdivided into slower channels.

Figure 8-27 The concentrator, which is usually a minicomputer, is connected to the computer system over a single line.

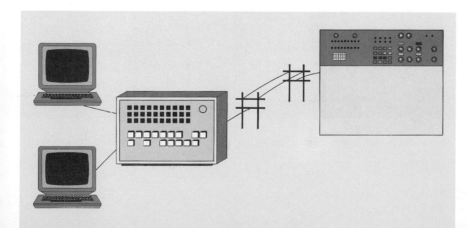

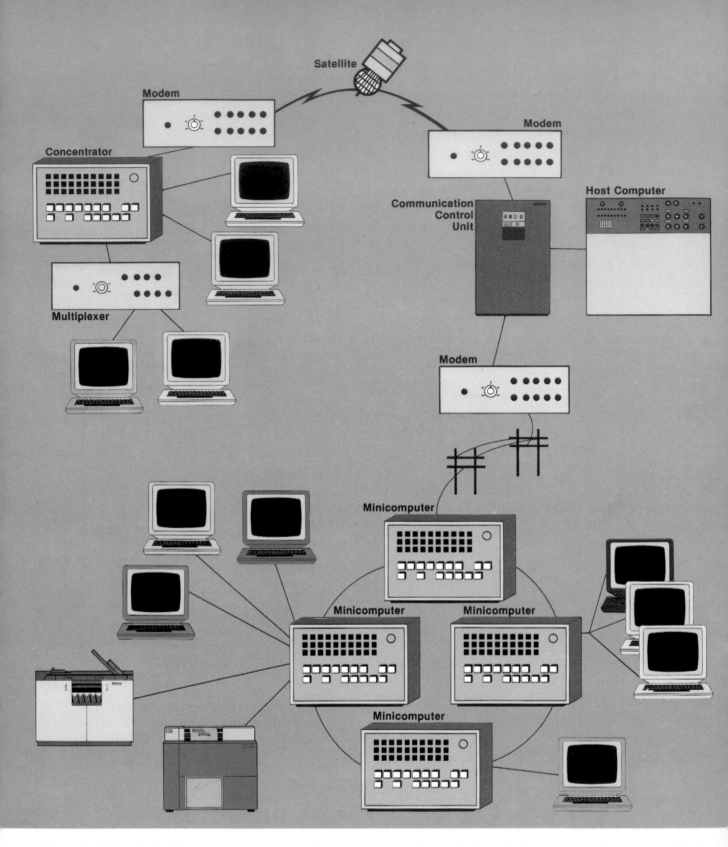

Figure 8-28 The "typical" network shown above illustrates many of the potential solutions to network design problems.

A sample network

The design of a network is almost completely application dependent. The configuration used can vary considerably, depending upon such factors as the number of computer systems in the network, the number of terminals required, the speed needed for responses to terminals, the distances over which data is to be transmitted, and a multitude of other considerations. At the risk of generalization, however, a "typical" sophisticated data communications network is illustrated in Figure 8–28.

The network shown in Figure 8–28 utilizes both the star configuration and the ring configuration. In addition, it contains both point-to-point and multidrop line types. Concentrators and multiplexers are included to illustrate how they can be integrated into a data communications network.

COMPUTER OPERATION AND DATA COMMUNICATIONS

The host computer system in a data communications network contains the program to control the network and the application programs to process the data transmitted to it. Most host computer systems, however, are concerned with more processing than just the data communications network. For example, at the same time applications are being processed for the data communications systems, the computer system may be running batch processing jobs, compiling programs, and controlling another communications network.

A computer system is able to process multiple applications in the same time frame through the use of multiprogramming. Multiprogramming is the concurrent execution of two or more computer programs on one computer system. The computer system is controlled in a multiprogramming environment by a monitor, or supervisor, program which schedules and monitors the activities of the computer system. The manner in which this is accomplished is explained in the following paragraphs.

Interrupts

Multiple programs can be stored in main computer storage and can process data in the same time frame through the use of multiprogramming. In order to understand multiprogramming, it is useful to examine the concept of an interrupt.

When a program issues an input/output command, such as read a disk record, the program is placed in a "wait state" while the disk is accessed and the data is placed in main computer storage.

The transfer of data to or from an input/output or auxiliary storage device is monitored by a channel, which is an electronic device associated with the computer system that controls the physical transfer of data between the input/output device and main computer storage. While the program is in a wait state, awaiting the completion of the transfer of data between an input/output device and main computer storage, it does no further processing. Thus, the computer system is idle while data is transferred. This time may seem insignificant, since data can be accessed and transferred to main computer storage from a disk in less than 50 milliseconds. However, a computer system which can execute one million instructions in a second can execute 50,000 instructions in the 50 milliseconds required to transfer a record from disk to main computer storage.

When the transfer of data from the disk to main computer storage is complete, the channel generates an interrupt, which indicates to the central processing unit that the transfer has been completed. The program which requested the data can then be given control to process the data.

The interrupt, therefore, is important in that it indicates to the computer system when an input/output operation has been completed.

Multiprogramming

Multiprogramming is possible because of the time required to perform input/output operations and the ability of the interrupt to indicate when an input/output operation is complete.

The example in Figure 8–29 illustrates a simplified use of multiprogramming. Main computer storage is logically divided into three areas, or regions. One is used for the supervisor program, which controls and schedules the resources of the computer system. The supervisor program is normally a part of the operating system supplied with the computer.

Two regions are used for the application programs in this example. In region 1, a data communications program is stored and is executing. In region 2, a market forecast program is stored.

The following steps take place: 1) The region 1 program issues a read command to read data from the remote terminal. Control is passed through the data management programs to the supervisor program. The supervisor issues the actual physical command to obtain data from the terminal.

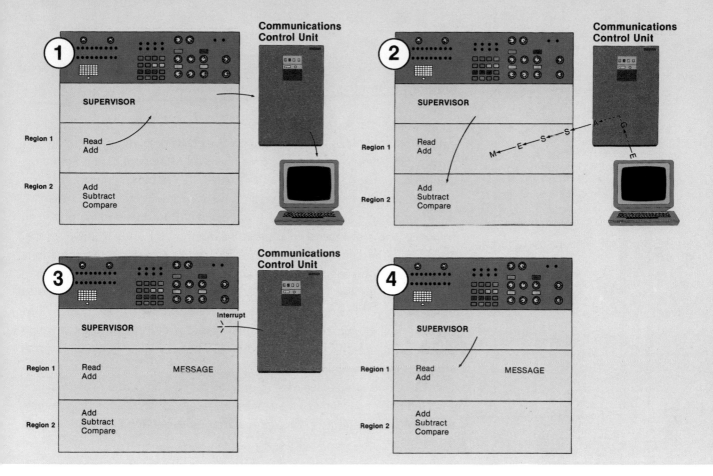

2) When the command from the supervisor is executed, the communications control unit is directed to transfer data obtained from the terminal to main computer storage. In systems without multiprogramming, the computer system would be in a wait state while this data transfer occurred. With multiprogramming, however, the supervisor will pass control to the market forecast program in region 2. This program will execute its instructions during the time required to transfer data from the terminal, through the communications control unit, and into main computer storage.

3) When all of the message has been transferred from the terminal to main computer storage over the communications line, the channel to which the data communications unit is attached will send an interrupt to the supervisor program. The supervisor will interpret the interrupt and determine that it was caused by the completion of the transfer of data from the terminal to main computer storage.

4) Since the data transfer is complete, the program in region 1 will again be given control so that it can process the message acquired from the terminal. The execution of the program in region 2 will be suspended until the program in region 1 again issues an input/output command. At that time, it will regain control during the time required to transfer data from the terminal to main computer storage.

Figure 8-29 The example above illustrates multiprogramming on a computer system controlling a data communications network.

Multiprogramming and data communications

Through the use of multiprogramming, the programs which control the data communications networks and process data received from remote terminals can execute in the same time frame as other application programs. Data communications programs are usually "I/O bound," meaning that a great deal of the time they are being run on a computer system is spent in input/output operations. This is true because data communications lines transmit data slowly when compared to the transfer rates of disk or tape. Therefore, other programs can be executing while the data communications program waits for the transfer of data to or from remote terminals.

When a front-end processor is used, even more time is available to other programs. The front-end processor will perform many of the activities such as polling, addressing, and other line control functions which would otherwise have to be accomplished by the data communications program stored in main computer storage.

Thus, through the use of multiprogramming, a computer system can be used not only to accomplish the processing required for data communications, but also to execute the programs required for other applications.

IMPLICATIONS OF DATA COMMUNICATIONS

The ability to communicate data over long distances through the use of data communications has presented problems to the data processing industry which did not exist previously. Among these are regulation of carriers and control over access to data.

Regulation of carriers

Data communications lines are made available by common carriers. A common carrier is a company or organization which contracts with state or federal governments to carry the property of others at regulated charges. Common carriers are regulated by government agencies.

There are approximately 3,000 communications common carriers in the United States. The dominant domestic carriers are American Telephone and Telegraph (AT&T) and Western Union. A number of specialized common carriers have been formed to provide specific types of data transmission and data communications facilities.

Until the Carterfone decision by the Federal Communications Commission in 1969, only AT&T modems could be used on any data communications systems which used the AT&T telephone system. The Carterfone decision said that modems and equipment from others as well could be used on AT&T telephone systems. Since that time, the ability to configure networks according to the needs of an organization has been increased considerably.

The industry and government face the responsibility in the coming years to develop regulations and policies which will allow efficient and reasonable use of data communications for all potential users in the data processing community.

Control over access to data

Since terminals can use common telephone lines for access to data, there is a potential for "tapping" lines to gain unauthorized access to data stored on the auxiliary storage of large computer systems. This activity has taken place in the past and poses a considerable challenge to the industry as a whole.

Equally important to many persons is the ability to access, over long distances, data which may be incriminating to some people. For example, police departments have access to a number of data banks, such as the National Crime Information Center data bank supported by the Federal Bureau of Investigation, over data communications lines (Figure 8–30). Although it has been found that such information can be helpful in tracking down and arresting criminals, it has also been found on occasion that abuses of the system have led to mistakes and the invasion of the privacy of citizens. Without data communications, this type of activity would not be possible. The ability to communicate data has led to these problems.

Conclusion

Communicating data over long distances from computer systems to users located at a remote site has afforded the opportunity to produce more and better information faster and with more reliability. It has also created an environment in which abuses can take place, sometimes at the extreme risk of life and property. In the years to come, the data processing and communications industries must shoulder the responsibility to produce policies which are socially and morally acceptable.

Figure 8–30 The police officer in the picture above is retrieving a report sent over a data communications network.

Beaming Data

Around the World

The satellite communications systems currently in use in the world have over 235 earth stations in more than 90 countries. The Intelsat system satellites alone provide more than 625 satellite pathways.

All types of communications can occur simultaneously over these satellite systems — telephone, telegraph, television, data, and facsimile. More than 85% of the system traffic is used for telephone service.

In the future, systems will be established which can transmit over one million bits per second for data communications systems. It has been predicted that satellite communications will become the most important communications method in the world.

Figure 8-31 The Intelsat IV-A satellite above has a capacity of 6,000 separate circuits plus two television channels. The satellite, which weighs 3,340 pounds at launch, is built by Hughes Aircraft and is launched on an Atlas Centaur rocket.

Figure 8-32 The Elam, West Virginia earth station at the left is the U.S. hub for satellite communications in the Atlantic Ocean region. Through its two antennas, Elam handles a larger volume of traffic than any other earth station in the world. Elam provides direct lines of communication between the U.S. and over 40 countries in North and Latin America, Europe, Africa, and the Middle East. The two disk-shaped antennas stand taller than a 10-story building. It was through the use of this station that over a billion people on six continents were able to view live the Apollo–Soyuz space mission.

Figure 8-33 The Intelsat V satellite (below) has a 51.1 foot "wingspan." It has an average of 12,000 circuits plus two television channels. Some of these satellites will be launched with the NASA space shuttle flights.

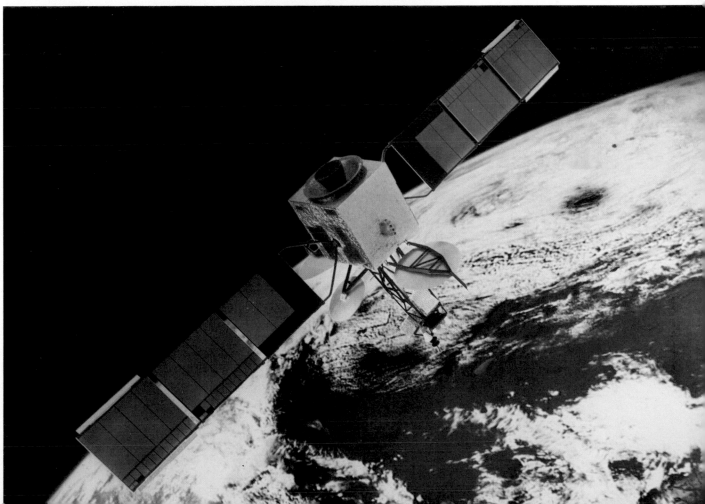

Chapter summary

The following points have been discussed and explained in this chapter.

1. It is estimated today that over 90 percent of the minicomputers and mainframes sold or leased have communications capabilities.

2. A basic data communication configuration consists of: 1) A terminal; 2) A modem to convert digital data generated by the terminal to an analog form which can be sent over communications lines; 3) A communications channel such as telephone lines; 4) A modem at the receiving end of a communications line to convert the analog signal received back to a digital signal; 5) A communications control unit that monitors the communications lines and controls the data which is sent over the lines; 6) The computer system which processes the data.

3. To provide for the portability of terminals, a special type of modem called an acoustic coupler is used.

4. Common types of communications channels include standard telephone lines, coaxial cables, microwave transmission, satellite communications, and fiber optics.

5. The communications control unit interfaces between the modem and the computer system at the end of the line where the computer system is located. Its purpose is to provide a path for data transfer between the computer system and the data communications network.

6. Sophisticated communications control units are called front-end processors. They control the network, relieving the main computer of these tasks. This allows the main computer system to concentrate on processing application programs and producing useful output.

7. The grades of communication channels are: 1) Low-speed, or narrow band; 2) Medium-speed, or voice band; 3) High-speed, or broadband.

8. Low-speed channels have a bit transmission rate of 40 to 300 bits per second. Medium-speed lines operate at rates varying from 300 bits per second to 9,600 bits per second. High-speed communications channels transmit data at rates in excess of 9,600 bits per second. Speeds available vary from 19,200 bits per second to 230,000 bits per second.

9. Two modes of transmission are used when transmitting data over communications lines. These modes are called asynchronous transmission and synchronous transmission. When asynchronous transmission is used, one character at a time is transmitted. Each character is preceded by a start bit and is followed by a stop bit. Synchronous transmission allows characters to be sent down the line as a group without start-stop bits. The

beginning of a character and the end of a character is determined by a timing mechanism. Synchronous transmission is used for fast transmission.

10. Three types of transmission lines include: 1) Simplex lines; 2) Half-duplex lines; 3) Full-duplex lines. A simplex channel allows data to be transmitted in one direction only. A half-duplex channel allows data to be sent in both directions, but not at the same time. A full-duplex channel allows data to be sent in both directions at the same time.

11. ASCII is a code commonly used in data communications.

12. A direct line between a terminal and a computer system in a data communications network is called point-to-point. In a point-to-point line, each terminal transmits data to and receives data from a computer system by means of an individual line that links the terminal directly to the computer system.

13. A multidrop or multipoint line has more than one terminal on a single line. On a multidrop line, only one terminal at a time can transmit to the computer, but more than one terminal can receive data.

14. A leased line is a permanent circuit used to connect a terminal with a computer system. A switched line is one that makes contact through established voice telephone lines and networks by dialing.

15. Contact is established on a multidrop line by polling and addressing. With polling, the computer system and the communications control unit ask each terminal on the multidrop line if it has data to send. In order for the computer system to send data to the terminal in a multidrop line, addressing is used. With this technique, the computer system addresses the particular terminal on the line that is to receive the data.

16. A star network contains a central computer system and one or more terminals connected to the computer system. In a ring network, a series of computer systems communicate with one another. A ring network is useful when all of the processing is not done at a central site.

17. A multiplexer is an electronic device which can divide a channel capable of a certain speed into multiple channels of a slower speed.

18. A concentrator is normally a minicomputer located at the terminal side of a communications line that can accept information from many terminals over slow-speed lines and transmit the data to the main computer over a high-speed line.

19. A computer system is able to process multiple applications in the same time frame through the use of multiprogramming. Multiprogramming is the concurrent execution of two or more programs on one computer.

20. An interrupt indicates that an input/output operation is done.

21. Most data communications programs are executed on a computer system which uses multiprogramming.

Student Learning Exercises

Review questions

1. What are the basic components of a data communications system?

2. What is the purpose of a modem?

3. What is an acoustic coupler?

4. List the five basic types of communications channels.

5. What is the purpose of a communications control unit?

6. How does a front-end processor differ from a communications control unit?

7. List the various grades of channels and their speeds.

8. Explain the difference between asynchronous and synchronous transmission. What are the uses for each of them?

9. Explain the terms simplex lines, half-duplex lines, and full-duplex lines.

10. What is ASCII? When is it used?

11. Describe the differences between point-to-point and multidrop lines.

12. What is a leased line? A switched line?

13. Explain the use of polling and addressing.

14. What is a star network? A ring network?

15. What is the function of a multiplexer? A concentrator?

16. Define multiprogramming.

17. Illustrate through the use of a diagram the operations that occur on a computer system using multiprogramming when a message is transmitted from a terminal to the computer system.

18. Describe some of the issues facing the data processing and data communications industries in the years to come.

Controversial issues in data processing

1. As a student or an employee of a company, you learn how to use a computer terminal to access a computer over communication lines. Even though you are not authorized to do so, you use the terminal and computer for your personal use. Have you committed a crime by "stealing" computer time? Defend your position.

2. Giant "data banks," using large auxiliary storage devices, now provide governmental agencies with the ability to store vast amounts of information about the citizens of this country. With the ability to establish data communications networks throughout the country having access to this data, a serious threat to our privacy exists, according to some authorities. Does the entire concept of data communications pose a threat to our privacy? What controls should be established to prevent unauthorized access to information stored in a computer system?

Research projects

1. Many retail stores now use computer terminals and data communications facilities for such applications as credit checking, check verification, and point of sale terminals. Contact the manager of a retail establishment and determine what use they make of data communications facilities. Prepare a report for the class on your findings.

2. Multi-national corporations have a need to transmit data from one country to another using data communications facilities. Often the types of communications lines, communications codes, and terminals are not compatible. Prepare a research report on the problems facing the data processing and data communications industries with the increased demand for world-wide data communications facilities.

Picture credits

Figure 8-1   Western Union Corp.
Figure 8-3   Sperry Univac
Figure 8-4   Universal Data Systems, Inc.
Figure 8-5   Lever Brothers Company
Figure 8-6   General Electric Company
Figure 8-7   American Satellite Company
Figure 8-8   Bell Laboratories

Figure 8-11   CompuServe, Inc.
Figure 8-12   Digital Equipment Corp.
Figure 8-21   Western Union Corp.
Figure 8-30   General Electric Company
Figure 8-31   Communications Satellite Corp.
Figure 8-32   Communications Satellite Corp.
Figure 8-33   Communications Satellite Corp.

Chapter 9
Data Base and Distributed Data Processing

Objectives

- An understanding of the interrelationships of data within an organization

- A knowledge of the reasons for a data base

- A basic knowledge of the components of a data base and how data is stored and accessed in a data base

- An understanding of the concepts of distributed data processing

- An understanding of the need for distributing data bases and a basic knowledge of the methods used

Chapter 9

Figure 9-1 When using distributed data processing, the computing power is placed where it is required, such as the warehouse shown here.

Data Base and Distributed Data Processing

"Sooner or later, data base management systems will be on all computers."[1]

Introduction

The ability to store large amounts of data on auxiliary storage and the ability to communicate with terminals and computers over long distances gives users of computers many varied options concerning the way they will process data and produce information from the computer system.

The key to successfully using this computing power is to analyze the needs of the company or organization; and then organize both the data and the computing power in such a way that it reflects the structure of the company.

One method of organizing the data so that it corresponds to the needs and structure of a company is the data base. A data base is a collection of data which can be used by more than one application. The computing power of a company can be organized to reflect the structure of a company through the use of distributed processing, where computers are placed in locations throughout the company to be used by those departments requiring computing power (Figure 9–1).

This chapter will examine the use of data bases and distributed processing and the way in which they can maximize the results obtained from the use of computer systems.

DATA BASE CONCEPTS

When data is stored in sequential, relative, or indexed files, each record in the file contains limited data about a single entity. For example, a company could have four files used for four different applications.

---

1 Aaron Zornes, from a speech given at the Mini/Micro Computer Conference and Exposition, September 26, 1979.

These files might be: 1) A customer master file; 2) An invoice master file; 3) An inventory master file; 4) A parts usage file (Figure 9–2).

The customer master file could contain the customer number, customer name, customer address, and customer credit code. This data in the file is used to produce a customer listing, as well as other reports.

The invoice master file contains the customer number, customer name, part number ordered, quantity of parts ordered, and the unit price for the part. The data in this file is used to produce an invoice listing and also the invoices which are sent to the customers.

The inventory master file contains the part number, part description, unit price, the vendor from whom the part is purchased, the quantity on hand, and the quantity on order. This file is used to produce an inventory listing, as well as other reports.

The parts usage file is used to produce the parts usage analysis report. It contains the part number, the part description, the vendor name, the customer name, and the quantity ordered by the customer.

Although each file is used for a different purpose, the data within each file is interrelated. For example, the customer information is required for both the invoice processing and the parts status processing. The information in the inventory master file is used for both the invoicing operation and the parts usage analysis report.

The point is that the data used within an organization is usually related. In order to produce the information required to manage and run a business, the data stored in files on auxiliary storage must be organized and coordinated to reflect this relationship.

In the past, this task has been accomplished by the applications programmers and the systems analysts. They had to sort files in the proper order, create new files, and otherwise manipulate the data so that the required information could be produced.

In many cases, this coordination and manipulation took place on an as-needed basis. New files were created as the need arose without coordination that reflected the total information needs of the company. This uncoordinated manipulation of data in files for each application created several major problems.

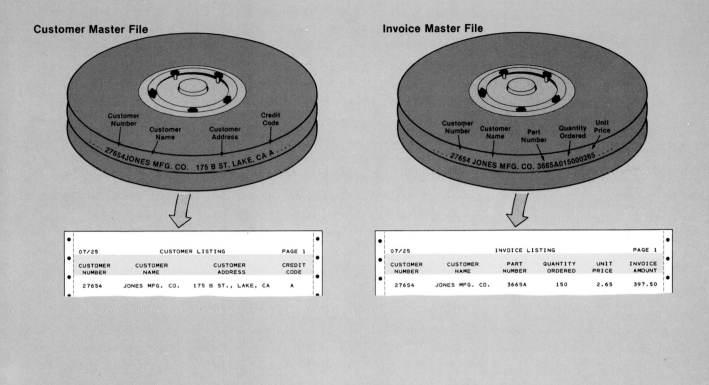

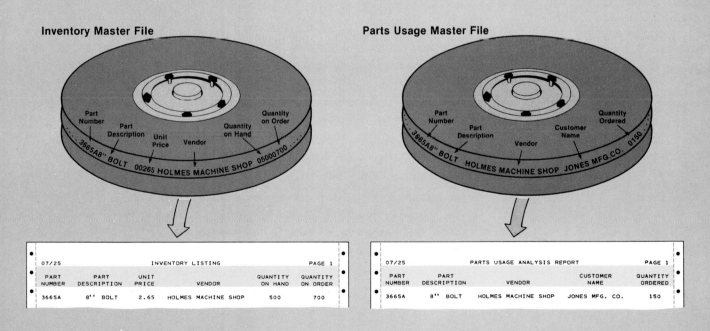

Figure 9-2 The data required to fulfill the processing needs of an organization exhibits, in most cases, many interrelationships.

First, there is a great deal of data redundancy; that is, the same data is stored in more than one file. For example, the parts usage file contains some of the same data that is in the customer master file. The consequences of redundant data are that data management in an organization is a difficult and error-prone activity. The major problem concerns updating the data. Since the data is redundant and is stored in multiple files, separate programs must be written to update each file. Thus, an update program must be written to update the customer file; another update program must be written to update the invoice master file; a third update program must be written to update the inventory master file; and a fourth update program must be written to update the parts usage master file.

Coordination of the update process is required so that all files containing the data to be updated are in fact updated. For example, when a customer purchases a part from the company, the invoice file must be updated to reflect the purchase; the inventory file must be updated to show a reduction in quantity on hand; and the parts usage file must be updated to show the sale. If one file is updated while another is not (unfortunately a common occurrence in some organizations), then the various reports generated from the data will not correspond to one another and management may be making decisions based upon obsolete or inaccurate information.

Redundancy of data is also quite costly, since the duplicated data requires space on auxiliary storage, which costs money. Therefore, one of the major problems in a company using individual files is data redundancy.

A second major problem is the inevitable changes which must be made to records stored in a file on auxiliary storage. For example, assume in the inventory master record that space was allocated for the name of a single vendor which supplied the part. Assume further that a second vendor, which supplied the same part, was acquired by the company. The name of the second vendor would have to be added to the inventory record.

Not only would the file have to be reorganized, but every program which referenced the file would have to be changed. This is because the format of the record in the file is defined within the program.

Thus, programs using single files are dependent upon the format of the files; if the files are changed, the programs have to be changed. This maintenance to change programs to react to changes in data is a major problem in most data processing organizations.

A third major problem associated with files stored on auxiliary storage is changes introduced with new hardware and software. As advances in disk technology are introduced, faster and more abundant storage is offered by computer manufacturers. In order to take advantage of these faster and less costly devices, files must be transferred from the old devices to the new devices. In many cases, changing from one device to another also means that the programs processing the files have to be changed. Thus, hundreds or even thousands of programs may have to be changed each time a new type of disk device is purchased.

Therefore, dependence upon the type of physical device and organization of data presents problems for data processing installations.

Data base

To combat the problems of data redundancy, program dependence on data, and data dependence on computer hardware, the concept of data base was introduced in the late 1960's. A data base may be defined as a collection of interrelated data stored together with a minimum of redundancy to serve multiple applications, with the data stored so that it is independent of the programs which use it and is independent of the type of hardware on which it is stored.

When a data base is organized and stored on auxiliary storage, application programs can reference data in the data base independent of how the data is stored and organized. For example, an inventory program that must reference inventory data to determine how many parts are in stock can do so, while an accounting application can reference the same inventory data to determine the price of the part. Both of these references can take place without the program knowing the way the data is stored and organized.

A data base is created, accessed, and updated by a data base management system. The data base management system consists of a series of programs written by a computer manufacturer or by software vendors. It generally provides five major features: 1) Establishment of data relationships within the data base; 2) Data independence; 3) Comprehensive data security; 4) Recovery capabilities; 5) Query language capability.

To illustrate how these features interact with one another, the following paragraphs will discuss the building and use of a data base.

Building a data base

A data base is built only after considerable investigation has been done to determine the information needs of an organization and the data which should be placed in the data base. This investigation is performed by the data base administrator, which is a person (or department) that has responsibility for managing the data within a company or organization.

The data base administrator (commonly called the DBA) must determine not only what data should be in the data base, but also what relationships exist between the data. For example, it may be determined that data concerning a part in inventory should be included in the data base. From the inventory management group, it is found that the part number, part description, quantity on hand, and quantity on order are required.

The accounting group needs the part number, the part description, and the price of the part so that invoices can be prepared. Other groups within the organization would be polled to determine similar requirements.

After gathering the data requirements, the data base administrator must design the manner in which the data is to be organized and accessed. There are two major data base organizations which are in use today: hierarchical data bases and network data bases.

Hierarchical data base

A hierarchical data base (sometimes called a tree structure) is composed of a hierarchy of elements (Figure 9-3). An element is a data record which contains application-oriented data. The data base establishes a fixed relationship between the elements in the hierarchy. Data is retrieved from the hierarchical data base by the data base management system by moving along the "paths" of the hierarchy according to requests from the application program.

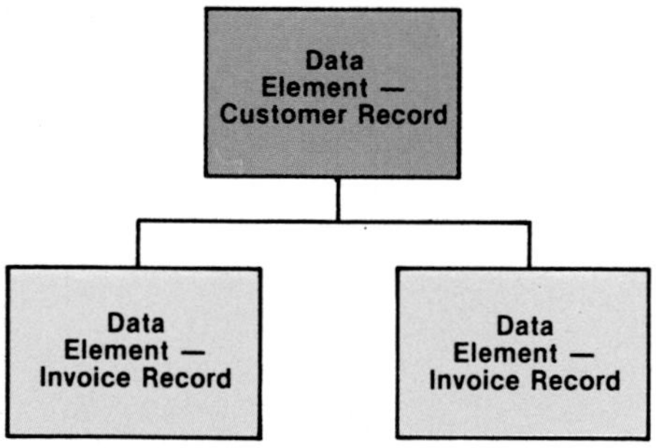

Network data base

Another format of a data base which provides a different type of access to the data is the network data base. In a network data base, individual files are established for each major element of data. These elements are linked together through the use of pointers in the records which point to other records in other files. These pointers are nothing more than disk addresses where the records in a file are stored.

Figure 9-3 The diagram above illustrates the relationship of the data elements within a hierarchical data base. The customer record is a root element because it has elements below it in the hierarchy. To retrieve data, the program could request all of the invoices for a given customer. The data base management system, following the paths in the hierarchy, would retrieve the data and return it to the program.

To establish a network data base, the data base administrator first defines a data base schema. This schema identifies the relationships between the data which is to be stored in the data base. For example, it would indicate that a record in the customer file must point to a record in the invoice file.

The data base administrator uses a special language which is associated with the data management system to actually specify these relationships and build the data base on direct access devices. The language, commonly called a data definition language, allows the data base administrator to specify all the files and records which are to be stored in the data base and to indicate the relationships among the records.

The example in Figure 9-4 illustrates a very simplified version of a network data base. The customer file contains customer information, including the customer number, customer name, customer address, and credit rating. It also includes pointers, which are established by the data base management system, that point to records in the invoice file. These pointers will point to each invoice in the invoice file for the given customer.

The invoice records contain the invoice number, the date of the invoice, and pointers. The pointers in the invoice file point to an item file, which contains each item for the invoices; and they also point back to the customer file. The item file record contains the quantity ordered and the part number ordered. It also contains pointers which link the record to records in the inventory file; and also with records in the invoice file.

Figure 9-4 In a network data base, separate files are created. Each record contains application data and also pointers. These pointers are used to point to records in the same or different files that are related.

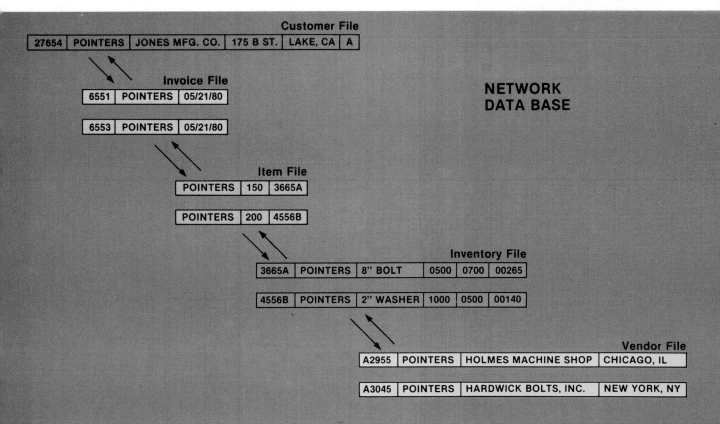

The inventory file contains records with the part number, description, quantity on hand, quantity on order, and price. The inventory file also contains pointers to the vendor file, which identifies the vendors from which the parts are purchased; and pointers which point back to the item file.

Accessing the data base

Once the data base is established, the data within it must be accessed by programs to retrieve or update the data. The applications programmer, together with the data base administrator, must first define a subschema of the data base for use with the program. A subschema is that portion of a data base required by a program.

For example, to create the customer listing report (Figure 9-2), the program needs access to only the customer file portion of the data base. Therefore, the subschema for that program would specify only the customer file. To create the parts usage report (Figure 9-2), on the other hand, the program needs access to the customer file, the item file, the inventory file, and the vendor file. Thus, the subschema for the program which prints the parts usage analysis report would specify these required files.

To illustrate the sequence of events when accessing a data base, assume a line is to be printed on the parts usage report. The program would request from the inventory file the part number and part description. It would also specify that it needed the vendor name from the vendor file, the quantity ordered from the item file, and the customer name from the customer file.

Using the pointers, the data base management system would step through the data base acquiring the data requested by the program. For example, a pointer in the inventory file record points to the vendor. The inventory record also contains a pointer to the item file, from which the quantity ordered can be retrieved. This type of stepping through the data base takes place under control of the data base management system. Therefore, the data is essentially program independent, since all the program does is request the data. It is up to the data base management system to retrieve the data.

When a data base management system is used, it interfaces between the problem program and the data management programs discussed in Chapter 7 (Figure 9-5).

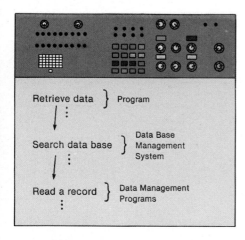

Figure 9-5 When a data base management system is used, it interfaces between the applications program and the data management programs. The data base management system is used to logically search the data base and request specific I/O functions from the data management programs.

Comparison — data base vs. flat files

Single files are sometimes called flat files, since they exhibit no relationships to other files. In comparing the flat files in Figure 9-2 to the data base in Figure 9-4, there are several significant differences. First, the redundant data in the flat files has been eliminated in the data base. For example, the customer name which appeared in three different files in Figure 9-2 appears in just the customer file in the data base. The part description, which appeared in both the inventory master file and the parts usage master file in Figure 9-2, appears in only the inventory file in the data base.

The update processing which would be required for the data in the four files in Figure 9-2 has been simplified considerably. For example, if the unit price for a part is changed, it would have to be changed in both the invoice master file and the inventory master file in Figure 9-2. In the data base, the unit price need only be changed in the inventory file. Similarly, if the vendor for a given part changed, two files would be updated in Figure 9-2. In the data base, only a pointer would have to be changed.

The ability to retrieve data is also enhanced with the data base. For example, if a report was required which listed all of the vendors and the parts which they supplied, the inventory master file would have to be sorted and another file created in Figure 9-2. Through the use of the appropriate subschema, the data could be retrieved directly from the data base.

Thus, the use of a data base can offer significant advantages over the use of flat files, both in terms of cost and in terms of ease of access and manipulation.

Query languages

Most data base management systems provide a query language, as well as the organization and access of the data in the data base. A query language is a very high-level language which allows users to specify their information requirements (Figure 9-6). Using the request from the user in the query language, the data base management system will search the data base, acquire the data requested, perform any calculations required, and return the information to the user.

A query language can be a very useful tool because it allows users to request and receive information from the computer system without requiring programmers in the data processing department to write a specific program to satisfy the needs of the user. Although not widely used now, it has been forecast that query languages will become very important in the future.

Figure 9-6 The example of a query language above shows the ease with which information can be retrieved from a data base by users of the system.

Data base usage

Data base management systems are found on large computers, minicomputers, and even some microcomputers. The systems on large machines may have more features than those on smaller machines because of the larger storage capabilities, but some of the data base management systems found on smaller machines are extremely powerful tools in the management and processing of data.

Advantages of data base systems

The major reason for developing data bases was to reduce data redundancy, allow the data to be referenced by multiple applications without the programs being data dependent, and to allow the data to be stored and accessed independently of the type of auxiliary storage being used. These goals have been reached with most available data base systems.

There have been several other advantages gained as well. In many data processing applications, data in files or a data base should not be available to all persons. For example, only authorized personnel should have access to employee salary data. With single file processing, this security was often difficult to maintain and enforce. When data bases are used, the access to all data contained in the data base can be controlled at a central point by the data base management system. Therefore, security of the data stored in a data base is increased significantly over the security of data not stored in a data base.

In addition, since the data is organized and controlled by a single set of programs (the DBMS), access to all data is increased. This has important consequences in transaction-oriented systems, since these systems require data to be on-line to the computer system. Indeed, it can be said that the increased use of transaction-oriented systems has gone hand-in-hand with the increased use of data bases.

Disadvantages of data base systems

Although there are significant advantages of data base systems, there is one major disadvantage: the development and control of a data base is a difficult and complex task. The ability to first define the data that should be in the data base and then establish logical relationships between the data is a skill which presents significant challenges to data base administrators.

DISTRIBUTED DATA PROCESSING

In the late 1950's and early 1960's, computer systems could be found scattered throughout a company. Whenever a department required a computer, it was placed in that department under control of that department. This decentralized approach gave way to a centralized approach in the middle and late 1960's, where large computer systems in centralized data processing departments were used for most of a company's data processing needs. The centralized approach was justified on two grounds: economies of scale and better control.

With large, centralized computer systems and more sophisticated hardware and software came timesharing. Timesharing allows a user at a remote terminal to interact with the computer system in such a way that it appears to the user that no one else is using the system. Timesharing in the late 1960's and early-to-middle 1970's was extensively used, both in-house and from timesharing vendors.

The development of the minicomputer and more sophisticated data communications techniques, however, required a rethinking of the centralized approach. It was found that large, centralized computers were becoming overloaded with work and were, in some cases, unable to perform the processing required. In addition, the centralized data processing department was not able to respond to the needs of the user with sufficient dispatch to satisfy the requirements of the organization.

To combat this problem, data communications capabilities were used to develop networks of a large centralized computer system and many smaller minicomputers which were located in the area where the processing was required. This concept is called distributed data processing (Figure 9-7).

Figure 9-7 The picture below illustrates a basic concept of distributed data processing — place the computer in the area where it is to be used and use it for only the applications in that area.

Distributed processing makes use of the various types of networks explained in Chapter 8. The exact network configuration will vary considerably, based upon the needs of the organization. A common feature of distributed processing, however, is the use of minicomputers or even larger computers in the divisions or departments where they are required. These machines can perform local processing such as handling local inquiries and producing reports required by department management.

In addition, these machines communicate with other machines within the organization. They may communicate with other minicomputers and/or with a large centralized computer system. Theoretically, at least, distributed processing systems offer the best of both decentralized and centralized types of organization because individual tasks are performed wherever needed or wherever they can be handled most efficiently. This allows computer systems to be tailored to the needs of the company.

In many distributed systems, there are more smaller systems used and less reliance on a large, centralized computer system. This approach has the following advantages: 1) There is more system reliability because the large computer system does not have to be running in order for the network to run; 2) There are less communication costs because the minicomputers handle a larger percentage of the work and do not have to communicate with the central computer system as often; 3) Employee productivity is improved because they can receive information rapidly as opposed to perhaps waiting for a large computer system to respond to their requests for information; 4) There is more timely information, since the data is entered into the computer system and updated on the computer system at a local site, rather than a remote site.

Distributed data bases

When distributed processing is used, the processing power is distributed according to need. A requirement for processing, however, is that data is available. Therefore, not only must the computing power be distributed, the data must be also. Several approaches are used when distributing the data.

In some systems, all of the data is kept at the central computer system, and the remote computer systems must request data from the central computer (Figure 9–8). Although this approach allows centralized control over all data, it many times is inefficient and costly, because communication lines must be used constantly to make the required data available to the remote computer systems.

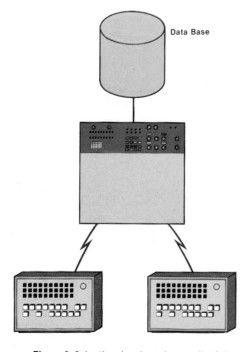

Data Base

Figure 9–8 In the drawing above, all of the data required for the network is stored in a data base at the central computer site. The remote systems must access the data over the data communication lines.

A second approach can be termed a shared technique. Most of the data required will be contained in the data base on the large central computer system. Parts of this data base, however, will be duplicated in the data bases located at the remote sites (Figure 9–9). The duplicated data at the remote sites is data required for the particular applications processed at the remote computer system. This technique allows faster and less costly access to the data at the remote site. It does, however, present difficulties when updating the data, because both sets of data must be updated in order to ensure compatibility and accuracy.

A third way allows each remote site to have its own data base containing that data required for its operation (Figure 9–10). This data is not duplicated at the central site. The major difficulty with this arrangement is that data located on one computer at a remote site may be required by another computer at another site. Therefore, with this configuration, the remote computer systems must normally be able to communicate with both the central computer system and with each other. This capability can introduce complexities in software control which are not found with the other two methods.

Regardless of the method used, there is a requirement for data base systems which are able to organize and access the data. Most data base management systems available from software vendors are capable of allowing these three methods, or combinations thereof, to be implemented.

Thus, distributed data processing involves not only the distribution of computing power to locations where that power is required, it also requires an organized and well-coordinated distribution of the data which is required for processing.

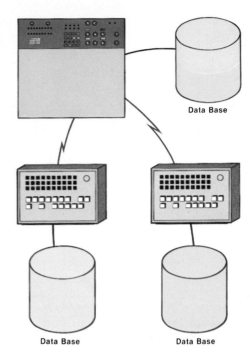

Data Base

Data Base   **Data Base**

Figure 9–9 In the example above, most of the data is contained at the central computer site, but parts of the data base are duplicated and stored for use at the remote sites.

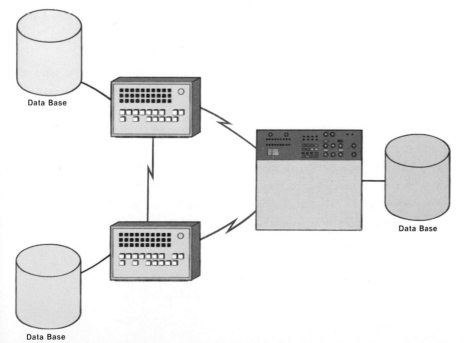

Data Base

Data Base

Data Base

Figure 9–10 In this example, each remote site, as well as the central, has its own data base. The data is not duplicated at the central computer site. When this arrangement is used, the remote computer systems will normally communicate not only with the central system but with each other as well.

Chapter summary

The following points have been discussed and explained in this chapter.

1. It has been predicted that sooner or later, data base management systems will be on all computers.

2. The key to successfully using computing power is to analyze the needs of the company and then organize both the data and the computing power in such a way that it reflects the structure of the company.

3. The computing power of a company can be organized to reflect the structure of the company through the use of distributed processing.

4. Data used within an organization is usually related.

5. In order to produce the information required to manage and run a business, the data stored in files on auxiliary storage must be organized and coordinated to reflect the relationships of data in an organization.

6. In the past, new files were created by programmers and analysts on an as-needed basis.

7. Without proper coordination and organization, there is a great deal of data redundancy, which is the same data stored in more than one file.

8. When data redundancy is found, a major problem occurs with updating, because multiple files must be changed whenever a single piece of data must be updated. If one file is updated while another is not, then the various reports generated from the data will not correspond to one another and management may be making decisions based on obsolete or inaccurate information.

9. Redundancy of data is quite costly.

10. Programs using single files are dependent upon the format of the files. If the files are changed, then the programs have to be changed. This can create major maintenance problems in an installation.

11. When single files are used, the programs are related to the type of device on which the data is stored. When the type of device is changed, programs may have to be changed also.

12. A data base may be defined as a collection of interrelated data stored together with a minimum of redundancy to serve multiple applications, with the data stored so that it is independent of the programs which use it and is independent of the type of hardware on which it is stored.

13. Application programs can reference data in a data base independent of how the data is stored and organized.

14. A data base is created, accessed, and updated by a data base management system, which consists of a series of programs written by a computer manufacturer or software vendor.

15. A data base provides the following features: a) Establishment of data relationships within the data base; b) Data independence; c) Comprehensive data security; d) Recovery capabilities; e) Query language capabilities.

16. A data base is built only after considerable investigation has been done to determine the information needs of an organization and the data which should be placed in the data base.

17. The data base administrator must determine not only what data should be in a data base, but also what relationships exist between the data.

18. A hierarchical data base is composed of a hierarchy of elements, or records.

19. In a network data base, individual files are established for each major element of data. These elements are linked together through the use of pointers in the records which point to other records in other files.

20. The data base administrator uses a special language called data definition language to establish the schema and to load the data base.

21. A subschema is that portion of a data base required by a program.

22. When a data base management system is used, it interfaces between the problem program and the data management programs.

23. A query language is a very high-level language which allows users to specify their information requirements.

24. Data base management systems are found on large computers, minicomputers, and even some microcomputers.

25. Security of data stored in a data base is increased significantly over the security of data not stored in a data base.

26. Timesharing allows a user at a remote terminal to interact with the computer system in such a way that it appears to the user that no one else is using the system.

27. A common feature of distributed processing is the use of minicomputers or larger computers with communications capabilities located in the divisions or departments where they are required.

28. When distributed processing is used, both the computing power and the data must be distributed.

29. There are three general approaches to distributing data: a) All data is contained at the central computer site; b) Most of the data is stored at the central computer site but some of it is duplicated and stored at the remote site; c) Each remote site has its own data base.

Student Learning Exercises

Review questions

1. What is the key to successfully using computing power?

2. Is data in a company related? In what ways? Give several examples.

3. How should data be organized and coordinated within an organization?

4. What is data redundancy?

5. What problems does data redundancy present?

6. State the definition of a data base. What problems is a data base designed to overcome?

7. What is a data base management system? What features does a data base management system provide?

8. What preliminary steps must be performed by the data base administrator prior to building a data base?

9. Describe a hierarchical data base. Give an example.

10. What is a network data base? Determine the data and illustrate the relationships of data in a network data base for a personnel application.

11. What is a schema? A subschema?

12. What is a query language? Why would people want to use a query language?

13. Why is data security important? Why can a data base management system provide better security than single file organization?

14. Give the definition of timesharing.

15. What is distributed data processing? What are its advantages? Its disadvantages?

16. What are the three general approaches to distributed data? What are the advantages and disadvantages of each?

Controversial issues in data processing

1. Some authorities see distributed data processing as a fad which is being pushed by computer manufacturers. They claim that by distributing computers throughout a company, overall control of the data processing effort within an organization will be lost. Others argue that placing the computing power in the locations where it is required will reduce costs and allow the people who need information from the computer system to generate that information without depending upon a large data processing department. Which viewpoint do you support? Do you think there are compromises which can be made to give the best of both worlds?

2. One of the major problems when implementing a data base system is determining what data should be stored in the data base and the interrelationships between the data stored in the data base. Some people feel that this problem is so complex that a complete data base for company-wide data is impossible to construct. Others point out that if a company will take the time and effort to analyze their data requirements, then this type of data base is possible. Do you think this task is too difficult to accomplish? Support your answer with concrete examples.

Research projects

1. Cincom Systems, Inc. (TOTAL), IBM (IMS), AG Software (Adabas), and Hewlett-Packard (IMAGE) are four of the largest vendors of data base systems. Prepare a report on one or more of these data base systems and present it to the class.

2. Data processing magazines, newspapers, and periodicals contain many articles on distributed processing and how it can be and is used. Research these articles and prepare a report for presentation to the class concerning how distributed processing is used in three different systems.

Picture credits

Figure 9–1 Data General Corporation
Figure 9–7 Mohawk Data Sciences Corporation

Chapter 10
Systems Analysis and Design

Objectives

- An understanding of the structure of the data processing department and its function within the organization

- An understanding of the five phases utilized in a system project

- A familiarity with the tools used in systems analysis and design, including data flow diagrams and systems flowcharts

- A knowledge of the major business systems applications

Chapter 10

Figure 10-1 Many different types of storage media may be used in the design of systems to be implemented on the computer.

Systems Analysis and Design

**"The corporations which will excel in the 1980's will be
those that manage information as a major resource."[1]**

Introduction

Although the computer hardware, file organization methods, data
bases, and communications facilities of modern computer systems are an
important part of the data processing environment, these hardware devices
and processing methods must all interact in the form of a system to
produce useful output (Figure 10-1).

In any business organization, there are many systems. There are accounting systems, billing systems, inventory control systems, and many
others. With the application of the computer to business problems, the
need to precisely define the system to process data becomes very significant, because without a properly designed system, the most sophisticated
hardware is virtually worthless.

Any system is made up of a series of procedures. Procedures are a
series of logical steps by which all repetitive actions are initiated, performed,
controlled, or completed. Thus, a system is composed of a network of
related procedures designed to perform a specified task.

It is the purpose of this chapter to examine the relationship of the data
processing department, which designs systems, with the remainder of the
company which uses these systems; and to explore many of the techniques
used to assure that systems are properly and efficiently designed and
implemented in a business organization.

---

1 John Diebold, as quoted in INFOSYSTEMS, October, 1979

The computer in the business organization

Forty years ago, there were no computers used for business applications. There were, however, very large corporations operating profitably. A question commonly posed, therefore, is if companies in the past have been able to operate effectively without the use of computers, why have computers become such an indispensable tool of both small and large business organizations today.

Most authorities cite three primary reasons for the widespread use of computer systems in the business organization: 1) The computer in a properly designed business system can reduce the costs of doing business; 2) The computer can assist in producing more timely and more accurate management information useful in directing and controlling the business; 3) The use of a computer can result in improved customer service, leading to increased revenues.

With these benefits accruing from the use of the computer, the effect on a company can be significant. The most evident effect is on the users of the computer system who interact daily with the systems. With properly designed systems, these people find their jobs easier to do, and they are more productive.

Management also is impacted significantly by the use of computers. With the increased availability of information, management personnel are in a position to make more intelligent and more timely decisions concerning the running of the business.

Customers also notice benefits from computer usage — faster availability of products and better service.

The use of computer systems does, however, place a burden on the company using them. The management of the data and information used and produced by a computer system requires close control and constant monitoring. Indeed, the data used in computer applications has become one of the major assets of a corporation. Without the data, many companies today could not function. Therefore, the design of systems, the writing of programs, and the control of the corporation data is a major activity in many companies.

Most companies using computer systems have a data processing department whose function is to design and implement application systems on the computer. The members of this department have a large responsibility because the success of the corporation could be riding on the ability of these people to develop and implement systems which are responsive to the needs of the corporation.

The organization of the data processing department

Most systems are designed by members of the data processing department within a company. The people who design the systems are called systems analysts.

Systems analysts are responsible for designing and developing systems which will be implemented on the company's computer. When designing a system, analysts work with management and others within the organization in an attempt to assure that the output from the system will meet the needs of the company.

In addition to systems analysts, two other groups of people in the data processing department play a major role in implementing systems on the computer. The groups are the programming staff and the operations staff.

Programmers are responsible for writing the instructions for the computer system which will cause the data to be processed as specified in the system. Programmers work closely with systems analysts on new projects to ensure that the programs are written in accordance with the design of the system.

Operations personnel are responsible for carrying out the day-to-day processing tasks that must be performed on the computer once a system becomes operational. Employees in this group are responsible for preparing the input data in a batch processing environment, operating the computer, and controlling and disbursing the output.

Systems analysts, programmers, and operations personnel normally work under the control of a data processing manager (sometimes called the director of data processing). The director of data processing is responsible for the overall administration and control of the data processing department.

The organizational structure of a company or departments within a company is often illustrated by an organizational chart. The organizational chart for a typical data processing department is illustrated in Figure 10-2.

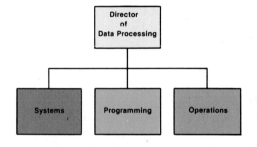

Figure 10-2 Most data processing departments consist of three groups — systems, programming, and operations — all reporting to the director of data processing.

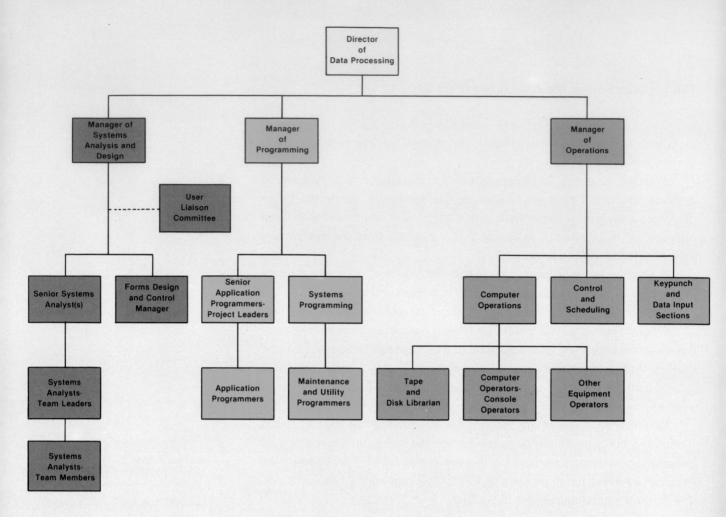

Job classifications in data processing

A detailed organizational chart of a large data processing department is shown in Figure 10-3. There are many categories of personnel who are required in a data processing department.

Within all organizations, however, there is a great variation in the structure and job duties of personnel in data processing departments. Large organizations will frequently have managers in each of the areas of systems analysis, programming, and operations. In addition, each project will many times have a manager.

In smaller organizations, there may be a merger of job duties. For example, individuals may be assigned the combined duties of both systems analysis and programming (these people are commonly called programmer/analysts). Programmer/analysts are responsible for both systems design and programming. Very small departments may even combine the jobs of programming and systems analysis with operations responsibilities.

The data processing department and the company structure

In the middle and late 1950's, most business applications being processed on a computer were of an accounting nature. The director of data processing, therefore, normally reported to a member of top management concerned with the financial aspects of the business, such as the controller or the vice-president of finance.

In the 1960's, with the widespread use of the computer in many areas of business, there was a movement away from strict control of data processing activities by the financial management of the company. Today, in many organizations, the position of director of data processing has become a top management position on the vice-presidential level. This position is often called the vice-president of information systems (Figure 10–4).

As the organizational structure of the data processing department has changed, so too has the function of the data processing department. Today, it is no longer considered the group that prepares some of the financial reports and the payroll. Instead, it is viewed as the group that provides a service function for sales, manufacturing, personnel, engineering, and other departments of the company.

As a profession, data processing has risen in status in most organizations. Some observers are predicting that the next generation of corporate presidents will emerge from the ranks of data processing professionals.

Figure 10-4 In many organizations, the director of data processing is now a top-level management position on the vice-presidential level.

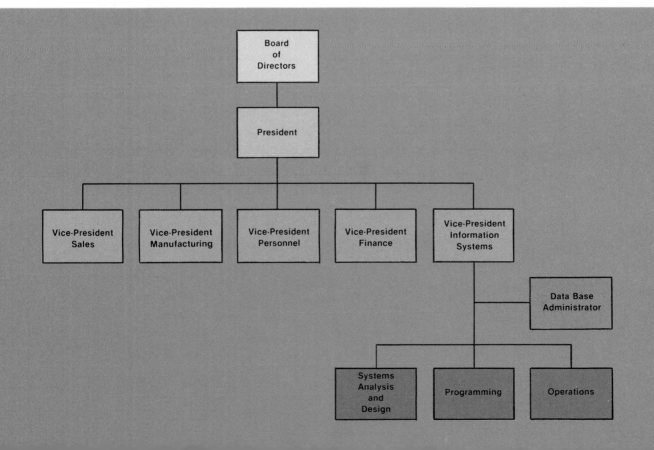

The data base administrator

With the widespread use of data base systems, a position called data base administrator has been developed in many organizations. Because information has come to be recognized as a valuable resource, a data base administrator is assigned as the "guardian" of that data. The data base administrator is responsible for developing and maintaining the data base, controlling the updating of the data base, and even controlling who has access to the data within the business organization (Figure 10–5).

On an organizational chart, the data base administrator is frequently illustrated as serving in an advisory or staff position to the vice-president of information systems (Figure 10–4).

Figure 10-5 The data base administrator above is responsible for creating, updating, and controlling access to the data base. Much of the interaction between the data base administrator and the data base itself is accomplished on CRT terminals.

Job duties in distributed processing systems

As the industry has shifted from batch processing systems to transaction-oriented systems and distributed processing, the organizational structure of many data processing departments has also changed. In the past, most systems analysts, programmers, and operations personnel worked in a centralized department supporting the main computer system.

Today, in a distributed processing environment, some companies are organizing their data processing departments to provide direct systems and programming support at the level where the computing power is located (Figure 10–6). In this approach, each department in a company that is supported by a small computer system in a distributed network would have its own staff of programmer/analysts and operators employed by and working for the supervisor of that department. For example, the payroll department could employ a programmer/analyst, the billing department could employ a programmer/analyst and an operator, and so on.

Some authorities feel that a computer specialist employed at the local level will result in more effective utilization of computing power in a distributed processing environment.

Figure 10-6 The use of small computer systems such as the IBM System/38 at the right in distributed processing networks has forced a change in the organization of the data processing department.

INTRODUCTION TO SYSTEMS ANALYSIS AND DESIGN

Regardless of the type of data processing organization that may exist within a company, the job duties of the systems analyst or programmer/analyst remain the same — to analyze, design, and implement systems using the computer.

The process of reviewing current systems and procedures, such as an order entry system which is done manually, and converting such a system to one in which the data is processed on the computer is called systems analysis and design.

In the past, many manual or obsolete computer systems were converted to run on the newest types of computers simply because the new computer was available. Today, however, the systems analysis and design function has become more scientific in its approach. A specific methodology exists for analyzing, evaluating, designing, and implementing new systems.

The primary task of the systems analyst is to develop new systems for implementation on a computer. Although the types of new systems implemented can vary tremendously, typically new systems are derived for the following reasons: 1) Conversion of a manual system to one running on the computer; 2) Conversion of a batch system to a transaction-oriented system; 3) Conversion of a system using separate files to a system using a data base; 4) Integrating several currently existing systems to one larger system using a data base.

The specific techniques used in systems analysis and design are discussed on the following pages.

Conducting a system project

The process to develop a system for implementation on a computer follows a well-defined, scientific problem-solving approach which can be broken down into a series of specific phases. These phases are:

Phase 1 — Initiation of the system project and the preliminary investigation

Phase 2 — Detailed system investigation and analysis

Phase 3 — System design

Phase 4 — System development

Phase 5 — System implementation and evaluation

PHASE 1 — Initiation of the system project and the preliminary investigation

Within most organizations, once the benefits of computer systems become known, the requests for new system projects will exceed the capacity of the systems department to implement the new systems. Inquiries such as "can we have more month-end reports for sales analysis," and "we would like to have on-line inquiry into our accounts receivable data base" are typical of the projects which must be given consideration by the systems group.

Regardless of the source of the request for systems service, the manager of the systems department is faced with the task of evaluating each request for assistance. Some will be rejected and others, which appear to offer benefit to the company, will be given a priority for investigation.

The preliminary investigation

Prior to making a full-scale commitment to design and implement a system on the computer, a preliminary investigation is normally undertaken. The purpose of the preliminary investigation is to determine if a problem or request for assistance which has come to the attention of the systems department warrants further investigation and analysis.

The primary method of conducting the preliminary investigation is through the personal interview. The interviews are conducted with managerial and supervisory personnel. These people should have sufficient knowledge of the problem to provide the analyst with some insight as to whether further investigation and a commitment of resources in terms of people and money is necessary and desirable.

One of the most important aspects of the preliminary investigation is to uncover the true nature of the problem. Often the stated problem and the "real" problem are not the same. For example, a request for on-line inquiry into an accounts receivable data base may not indicate the real problem in the accounting department. Instead, it may be that the information required for bad debt collection is not available in the accounts receivable data base. It is the purpose of the preliminary investigation to determine the real source of the problem.

The outcome of the preliminary investigation should be a report to management indicating the nature of the problem (Figure 10–7). Included should be a recommendation concerning the need for further action if deemed desirable.

MEMORANDUM

```
DATE:          March 1
TO:            Management Review Committee
FROM:          George Lacey, Manager, Systems
SUBJECT:       Finding of Preliminary Investigation of Order Entry System
```

Introduction

A preliminary investigation of the wholesale auto parts order entry system was conducted by the systems department at the request of accounting department supervisor, Lavelle Stinson. The findings of the preliminary investigation are presented in this report.

Objectives of the Preliminary Investigation

The preliminary investigation was conducted to investigate several major complaints concerning the wholesale ordering system. The accounting department has been receiving numerous complaints that orders sent in the mail and given over the telephone have not been shipped promptly. In addition, customers have complained that they have not been notified of parts out of stock for many days after orders have been given to the company. The objective of this preliminary investigation was to determine if the problems actually exist in the form stated, and if so, recommend a course of action.

Finding of the Preliminary Investigation

It is the conclusion of the systems department that the problems as specified do, in fact, exist. With the increased growth of the company during the past several years, the volume of orders for wholesale auto parts has tripled. Orders are currently processed manually by available personnel in the accounting department. The volume is such that many orders are not forwarded to the shipping department for three to four days after receipt. Some customers are cancelling orders because of the delay. It does not appear that any minor revisions in the existing system will provide long-range benefits.

Recommendations

As a result of the preliminary investigation, the systems department recommends that a detailed systems investigation of the order entry system take place. It appears that there is a need to design a new system. It is estimated that one analyst assigned for one month could carry out the investigation recommended, at an estimated cost of $3,000.00.

It is expected at the conclusion of the detailed systems investigation that the analyst will have defined the problem in sufficient depth to be able to offer a specific solution to the order entry problem so that our company may provide the service required by our customers.

George Lacey

Figure 10-7 The outcome of the preliminary investigation should be a report recommending either that no further action should be taken or that a detailed system investigation and analysis should be performed.

PHASE 2 — Detailed system investigation and analysis

After the preliminary investigation, management will either authorize continued study of the proposed system project or will direct that no further action be taken. If management authorizes further study of the problem, a detailed investigation and analysis is undertaken.

This phase of the system study is divided into two parts: 1) A detailed investigation in which the emphasis is on WHAT is taking place in the current system; 2) An analysis of what is taking place with an emphasis on WHY the procedures found are occurring.

Detailed system investigation

The basic fact-gathering techniques used during the detailed system investigation are: 1) The interview; 2) Questionnaires; 3) Gathering the current system documentation and operating forms; 4) Personal observation of current procedures.

During this fact-gathering phase of the system study, the analyst must develop a critical and questioning approach to each of the procedures within the system to determine what is actually taking place. Far too often in many organizations, operations are being performed not because they are efficient or effective, but because "they have always been done this way."

Specific steps undertaken at this time to gather the facts include: 1) Review the organizational chart of the structure of the company to determine who are the workers, supervisors, and management personnel associated with the system under study; 2) Conduct interviews with selected personnel to determine what is actually taking place in the current system, rather than what is supposed to take place according to the written rules of the company; 3) Obtain actual copies of operating documents; 4) Document and record all of the data flow within the currently existing system and the actual procedures which are followed.

Documentation of the facts

Prior to analyzing the facts to determine why certain procedures are followed and what can be done to improve them, the facts as found must be documented. Although a number of methods exist to document what takes place within a system, one of the more effective is the data flow diagram, as illustrated in Figure 10–8.

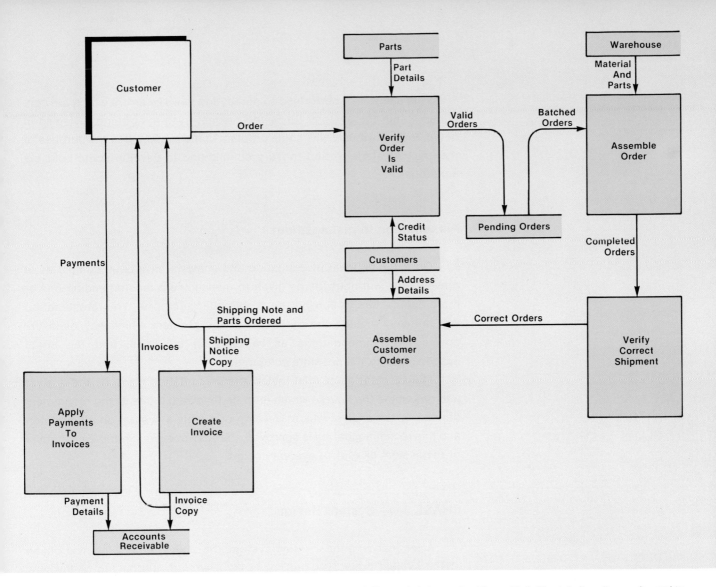

The data flow diagram above illustrates graphically the flow of data and the procedures used for an auto parts order entry system. By detailing the processing occurring in the present system in this manner, the analyst can examine each of the steps involved to determine exactly what happens in the present system.

Figure 10-8 The data flow diagram is used to graphically illustrate the flow of data through a system. The shaded square is used to illustrate input to the system. The vertical rectangles show procedural steps. The open-ended boxes illustrate data which must be available to the particular procedure.

Analysis of present system

Once the system has been documented, the analyst must review it. Each of the procedures should be analyzed as follows: 1) Who performs each of the procedures within the system; 2) What procedures are followed; 3) Where are the operations being performed; 4) When is a procedure performed; 5) How is the procedure performed. Within each of these questions, the analyst must ask WHY are things done this way.

This analysis is performed to detect any flaws or errors which are contained within the system. Since the present system is being reviewed in detail, there obviously was some problem in the system. It is the purpose of the analysis stage to find those problems and to develop some possible solutions.

Presentation to management

Once the detailed investigation and analysis have been completed, a presentation will normally be given to management recommending one or more approaches to solving the problem (Figure 10–9). This presentation will normally include the definition of the problem which has been uncovered, recommendations as to possible solutions, and the costs associated with the possible solutions.

Management must then review the presentation made by the analyst and determine the course which is to be followed. If one of the recommendations by the analyst was to develop or modify a system on a computer, and this recommendation is approved, the analyst moves into the next stage of the system project — system design.

PHASE 3 — System Design

After analyzing the existing system, the analyst enters the next phase of the system project — the phase involved with the design of the new system. System design is a creative act of devising in part, or in full, new methods and procedures for processing data.

The system design phase of a systems project requires the analyst to perform the following activities: 1) Design the system output; 2) Design the system input; 3) Design the files, data base, and processing methods; 4) Present the system design to management and users for approval.

Designing the system output

During the detailed system investigation and analysis, the analyst should have gained a thorough understanding of the type of output that is being produced in the existing system. Therefore, during the system design phase, the analyst must review the current output to determine if the output being produced is meeting the needs of the users and management.

MEMORANDUM

DATE: April 1
TO: Management Review Committee
FROM: George Lacey, Manager, Systems
SUBJECT: Detailed Investigation and Analysis of Order Entry System

Introduction

A detailed systems investigation and analysis of the order entry system was conducted as a result of approval given by the management review committee on March 1. The findings of the investigation are presented below.

Objectives of Detailed Investigation and Analysis

The study was conducted to investigate two major complaints of the wholesale auto parts order entry system. Complaints have been received that orders were not being shipped promptly, and customers were not notified of out of stock conditions for many days after sending in orders. The objective of this study was to determine where the problems existed and to develop alternative solutions.

Findings of the detailed investigation and analysis

The following problems appear to exist within the order entry system:

1. Three clerks in the accounting department open orders received in the mail and handle all telephone calls relative to orders for wholesale auto parts. The volume of orders is so great during the first three days of the week that orders received are not being forwarded to the shipping department for several days.

2. There is no available means to determine if a part is in stock until the orders are sent to the shipping department. If an item is not in stock, the order is returned to the order department, where the customer is notified. Often there is a 5-7 days' delay in notifying customers of an out-of-stock condition.

Alternative solutions

There are several alternative solutions to improve the order entry system:

1. Revise the manual order entry system. Hire more order entry clerks. Assign specific job duties to accounting personnel. Provide daily inventory reports to order entry clerks to remedy out-of-stock problems. This is only a temporary solution if the company continues to grow.

2. Place the order entry system on the computer. Computer terminals would be installed in the accounting department for order entry clerks. As orders are received, they would be entered into the computer. Orders could be immediately edited for proper part numbers, and checks could be made to determine if stock is available. Estimated costs 1) Systems analysis and design - $17,500; 2) Programming and implementation - $25,000; 3) Training, new forms, and maintenance - $5,000; 4) Computers costs 1 year - $12,000.

The systems department recommends alternative 2 as offering the most effective solution to the order entry problem.

George Lacey

Figure 10-9 The report for the detailed investigation and analysis should contain the results of the investigation and alternative solutions to the problem, together with costs to implement the solutions.

Specific steps to be undertaken during this phase include: 1) Define the output requirements for the new system; 2) Review the types of output media that might be useful; 3) Define the specific contents of the output that is to be produced; 4) Consider the methods for the disposition and handling of the output.

Defining the output requirements

In defining the output requirements of a new system, the analyst is concerned with what information is needed by the users of the new system. It is not the responsibility of the systems analyst to tell the user what type of output they are going to receive. Instead, the analyst, in conjunction with the user, must define the informational needs of the user of the system and then provide guidance to the user so that the system which is designed will produce this information.

Figure 10-10 The printer above from Trilog is capable of printing color graphics. This ability allows color graphics which are displayed on a CRT screen to be reproduced on paper when hard-copy is required for an application.

Determining the type of output media

During the design of the system output, the analyst must be aware that the printed report is not the only form of output available from a computer system, and that consideration should be given to other output media if appropriate. The various forms of output include not only the printed report but also computer output microfilm, CRT terminals, plotters, audio response units, and even color reports (Figure 10-10). Each of the various forms of output should be considered if such output will contribute to a more effective system.

Designing the printed report

To determine the format and specific content of each report for the new system, the analyst must consult with those who will be using the new system. The parties must decide on the specific content of each report, including report and column headings; the fields to be printed on the report; totals to be printed; and the number of copies of the report.

The exact format of a printed report is commonly illustrated on a printer spacing chart (Figure 10-11). The programmer uses the printer spacing chart when coding the program to ensure that the program will produce the output in exactly the required format.

PRINTER SPACING CHART

```
XX/XX/XX                    INVENTORY REPORT                              PAGE XØX
                          WHOLESALE AUTO SUPPLY

  ITEM              DESCRIPTION            UNIT PRICE   QTY ON HAND   QTY ON ORDER   AVAILABLE
 XXXXXX     XXXXXXXXXXXXXXXXXXXXXXX          XXX.XX       X,XXX         X,XXX         X,XXX
 XXXXXX     XXXXXXXXXXXXXXXXXXXXX            XXX.XX       X,XXX         X,XXX         X,XXX
```

Designing terminal oriented output

In addition to designing the output for the printed report, the analyst must also design any output that is going to be displayed on CRT terminals. When using terminal output, the analyst must be aware of the number of characters which can be displayed horizontally across the screen, the number of vertical lines that can be displayed, the number of colors available, whether reverse video is possible, and other characteristics of the terminal that might influence output design.

The actual design of the terminal output is normally shown on a form similar to the printer spacing chart (Figure 10-12).

Figure 10-11 The printer spacing chart is used to design the format of a printed report. The numbers at the top of the chart indicate the print positions on a page. X's are placed in the columns where data is to be printed. The words and punctuation are written on the printer spacing chart in the same way as they will appear on the report.

Figure 10-12 The analyst must also design the format of the data that is to be displayed on the screen. It is, therefore, necessary to be aware of the terminal capabilities; that is, the number of characters that can be displayed horizontally, and the number of lines that can be displayed vertically.

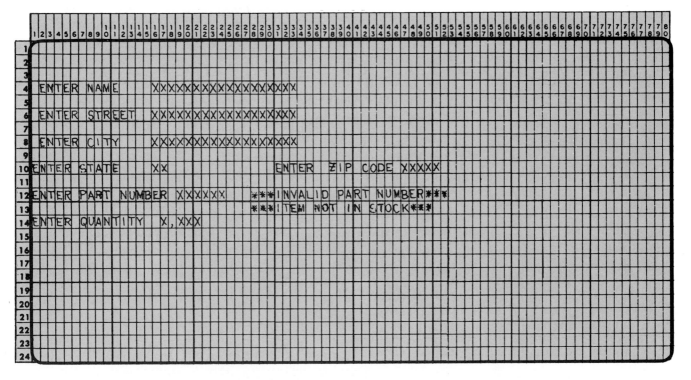

The design of the output from a system is critical to the successful implementation of a data processing system because it is the output which provides the information to the users and is the basis for the justification of most computerized systems. The analyst, therefore, must spend considerable time and effort in determining what information must be produced from the system, the format in which it will be presented, and the methods to be used to place the output in the hands of the users.

Design of system input

Once it is determined what the output of a system will be, it then must be determined what data is necessary to generate the required output. As an additional consideration, the analyst must also define the method of data entry into the computer system.

The method of entry into the computer system will depend to a large extent on whether batch processing or transaction-oriented processing is to be used. Typical questions which must be answered, depending upon the type of processing to be performed, include: 1) What media, if any, is to be used for storing input records; 2) How is the data to enter the system; 3) Can the data be captured at its source; 4) What is the volume of input; 5) How often is it necessary to input the data; 6) What editing and safeguards must be provided to ensure valid input data; 7) If transaction-oriented processing is used, what response time is required to the input terminals; 8) For transaction-oriented systems, is hard-copy required, or will CRT terminals be satisfactory.

The analyst must also be concerned with the design of the format of the input to the computer system. In a batch processing system, this will include the design of the input records and possibly a redesign of some of the source documents used for the system.

Numerous factors must be considered when designing input records for batch systems. These factors include: 1) The length of the record; 2) The length of each field in the record and the type of field (alphanumeric or numeric); 3) The type of codes which might be incorporated into a field, such as the value "A" to indicate that a transaction record is to be added to a master file or the value "C" to indicate the transaction record is to change the master file.

The screen design and the procedures for entering data in a transaction-oriented system must be specified at this point in the system design. It is important that the analyst design these procedures with the terminal operator in mind, because the easier and more natural it is to enter data into the terminal from a source document, the less likely there will be errors made when the data is entered. The reliability of input data is one of the major concerns in a system on the computer. The analyst, therefore, must develop procedures which are less likely to cause errors when used for entering data into the computer system.

Design of system files and data base

The analyst must also, during the system design phase of the system project, determine the data which must be stored on auxiliary storage for use by the system. As a first step, the analyst will develop a data dictionary.

A data dictionary contains the following: 1) A list of the various data elements required for the system; 2) The attributes of the data, such as the length of the field; 3) The points in the system where the data is required; 4) The type of access required for the data (random or sequential); 5) The amount of activity which can be expected for the data; 6) The amount of data which must be stored for the system.

If the organization has a data base administrator, the analyst will work with the data base administrator to determine what data may already be in a data base, what data will have to be added to a data base, whether the data base will support the activity and access speed requirements of the new system, and what other problems must be considered to solve the data requirements for the new system.

If a data base administrator is not available, then the analyst will have to answer the above questions as well as design either the files or data base consisting of files to solve the data requirements. In either event, the design of the data base and files, based upon elements which have been discussed in previous chapters, is critical to the successful implementation of a new system.

Design of system processing

After the input data, the output information, and the data to be stored in files or a data base have been determined and designed, the analyst must determine how the system will operate in order to produce the information required of the system.

There are several "tools" which can be used to accomplish the design of the processing within the system. The data flow diagram (shown previously in Figure 10-8) can be used to show the logical flow of data through the system. Another tool which is commonly used to illustrate the processing within the system is the system flowchart.

The system flowchart is particularly useful to show not only the logical flow of data but also the physical components such as disk drives, magnetic tape, and so on which will be used in the system.

Upon completion, the system flowchart should show all of the computer runs and their relationships, identify each file and/or data base, identify each report and each terminal site used in the system, indicate the number of programs to be written, and provide management with a means of reviewing the overall plans for the system.

Special symbols are commonly used for the system flowchart. These symbols are illustrated in Figure 10-13.

Figure 10-13 These system flowcharting symbols are used to graphically illustrate the procedural steps and the physical components of a system. The symbols representing the physical devices are drawn on the flowchart where they are used.

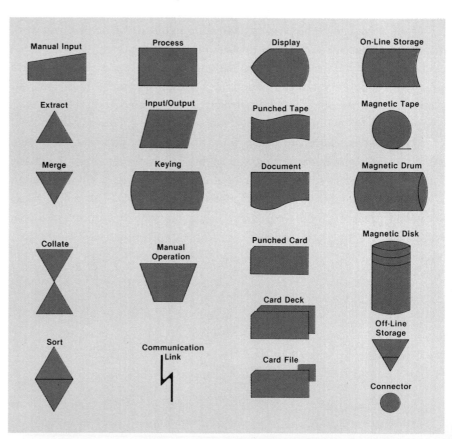

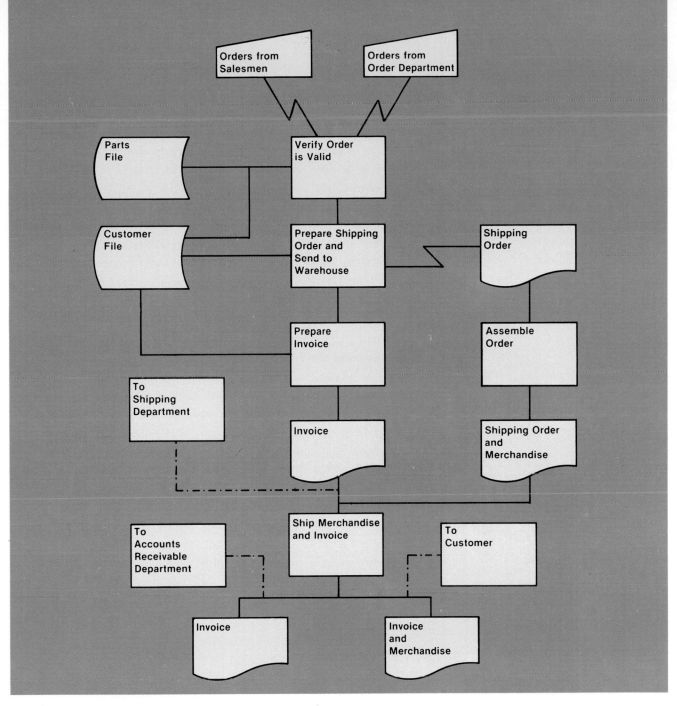

A system flowchart for an order entry system is shown in Figure 10-14. Through the use of the flowchart symbols and the attached lines, the procedural flow through the system is illustrated.

The design of the system processing must continue until all processes have been defined and documented. During the design of the processing, the analyst should be in constant contact with the users of the system to ensure that the system will accomplish what the user wants and that the procedures are compatible with the way the users conduct their work.

Figure 10-14 The system flowchart illustrates the actual steps which will occur in the system and the devices which will be used. This flowchart must be reviewed by the users of the system to ensure the system will perform in the manner required.

Design of system controls

An important aspect of the design phase of the system project is the establishment of a comprehensive set of system controls. System controls are defined as a plan to ensure that only valid data is accepted and processed, completely and accurately.

Adequate controls must be established for two basic reasons: 1) To ensure the accuracy of the processing and the accuracy of the information generated from the system; 2) To prevent computer-related fraud.

There are four basic types of controls that must be considered by the systems analyst. These controls are: 1) Source document control; 2) Input control; 3) Processing control; 4) Output control.

Source document control

There are many sources of input data in a business organization, such as sales orders, time cards, production statistics, etc. If management information is to be generated from this input, it is essential that all source documents are accounted for when the data is prepared for processing on the computer. Therefore, controlling the reliability of the computer system should begin at the starting point — with source documents and the data which is entered from the source documents.

Source document controls include the serial numbering of input documents such as invoices and paychecks, document registers in which each input document is recorded and time stamped as it is received, and batch totaling and balancing to some predetermined totals to assure the accuracy of processing.

Input controls

Input controls are established to assure the complete and accurate conversion of data from the source documents to a machine-processable form. As discussed in Chapter 5, key verification is an important form of input control. With a transaction-oriented processing system, the editing of data as it enters the system is a form of input control.

Processing controls

Processing controls refer to procedures that are incorporated into computer programs within the system to assure the complete and accurate processing of the data throughout the system.

Two types of processing controls are group controls and individual record checking. Group controls refer to those procedures used in batch processing systems in which groups of data which have been processed are balanced to some manual totals to assure the accuracy of processing. For example, the totals for the invoices processed for the day could be balanced against manual totals taken for the same group of invoices. If the totals do not agree, the error must be found before processing proceeds.

Individual record checking includes editing the fields in an input record for numeric data, blank fields, reasonable values, and other potential errors which may occur. These types of checks are performed in a batch system when the data is read into the computer system. In a transaction-oriented system, the editing can be performed at the terminal if an intelligent terminal is used or on the computer as the data is entered if a dumb terminal is used.

Audit trail

Another important form of control is the audit trail. An audit trail is designed to enable any input record or process executed on the computer system to be traced back to the original source data. When data is stored electronically on devices such as magnetic disk without careful consideration as to controls, it may be possible to alter the data without leaving a visible track to what caused the alterations to occur. Auditing is designed to make sure this does not happen.

Computer auditing is quickly becoming a specialized accounting function. It can be an extremely difficult task, especially with transaction-oriented processing systems. Such controls as recording each transaction received from a terminal on tape or disk are usually built into transaction-oriented systems so that all transactions can be traced back to the terminal from which they were entered.

Backup considerations

In virtually every data processing system which is developed, the possibility exists that errors may occur which accidentally alter or destroy data stored on auxiliary storage in data bases and files. This may occur because of natural disasters, such as fire, flood, or power outages; or it may occur through improper processing of the data.

It is essential, therefore, to provide a means to ensure that any lost data can be recovered. The most common method used is backup files. A backup file is merely a copy of a file, typically stored on magnetic tape. If for some reason the file or data base is destroyed or becomes unusable, the backup file can be used to recreate the file or data base.

Backup becomes extremely critical in transaction-oriented systems because updates to a data base or master file can occur at any time. Therefore, most systems will provide for creating a backup file on a regular basis (sometimes every hour) and saving the transactions which occur to the file after the backup file is made. If the data base is rendered unusable, the data base can be recreated from the backup file and then the transactions which have been saved can be processed against the data base to bring the data base back to the status it had when it was destroyed.

Another consideration in transaction-oriented systems is the ability to restart the system if it goes down. For example, if a transaction has been sent to a computer system and has partially updated a data base when power is lost, it is necessary to both restore the data base and let the user know that the transaction was not processed. Various techniques are used to solve this type of problem, including backup files and messages sent to terminals asking them to resend those transactions which were not processed.

Since some on-line systems perform critical functions, such as controlling space flights or monitoring patients in a hospital, there may also be consideration given to having a backup computer system. This system could normally be used for other processing but when the system controlling the on-line application goes down, the backup computer system automatically takes over the processing. Although this type of arrangement is not common, it should be considered in those systems which perform critical applications.

System design approval

The final step in the system design phase of the system project is the presentation to management and the users of the system (Figure 10-15). Although great efforts may have been expended in designing the new system, it is management's responsibility to give final authorization to enter the next phase of the system project — system development.

Three levels of management are normally involved in this approval — data processing management, user department management, and corporate management. The data processing management must concur that the system is feasible and can be implemented as designed. The user department management must approve the design as being responsive to their needs. Corporate management must weigh the costs of implementing the system versus the potential savings or increased availability of data.

Approval at all levels is extremely important because once the system enters the development and implementation phases, large sums of money may be involved, and the affected user departments must begin to prepare for the new computer system.

Figure 10-15 A presentation made to management and the users of a computer system is an important step in the system design process. In order to make the presentation as clear as possible, the analyst should use visual aids such as overhead transparencies, slides, video tape, and any other medium which will aid management and users in understanding the system.

10.23

PHASE 4 — System Development

Once the system design phase of the project has been completed and the design has been approved by management at all levels, the project enters the system development phase.

The major tasks common to all system projects during the system development phase are: 1) Establish a project development and implementation plan; 2) Develop detailed programming specifications; 3) Program and test the system; 4) Prepare final documentation of the system.

Establish a project plan

One of the first steps in the system development phase is to develop a detailed schedule of each of the activities that is to be performed. These time schedules should include a week by week estimate of the time to be spent in each of the major tasks in the system development. Unless a realistic schedule is developed and followed, it is unlikely the project will be implemented on time. The most widely used method to document the schedule is the bar or Gantt chart (Figure 10-16).

Develop detailed programming specifications

One of the more important steps in the system development phase involves the development of detailed programming specifications by the systems analyst.

Figure 10-16 The bar or Gantt Chart is commonly used to graphically illustrate schedule deadlines and milestones. This Gantt Chart contains the schedule for the steps used in the system development phase of the system project.

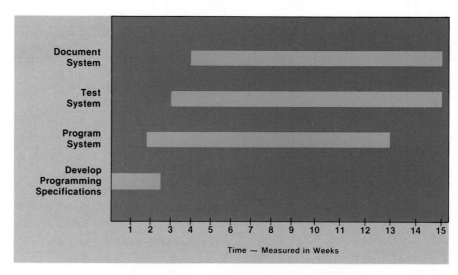

These programming specifications should include: 1) A brief description of the system; 2) A systems flowchart; 3) A data flow diagram; 4) The format of the input, output, and files to be created and processed; 5) The format and content of any data base to be used by the program (subschema); 6) A detailed description of the processing that is to take place in the program.

The communication of the detailed specifications is one of the most vital steps in the entire process of systems analysis and design. Without clearly documented program specifications, the programmer will be unable to design and write a program which will fulfill the requirements of the system. It is critical that the programmer understand the data to be processed and the procedures which must be implemented within the program. The only way for this to happen is for the analyst to provide sufficient documentation which clearly specifies what should take place in the program.

Programming the system

The process of producing a set of instructions for the computer from the detailed specifications that have been prepared by the systems analyst is the job of the computer programmer. This process involves: 1) Reviewing the program specifications; 2) Designing the program; 3) Coding the program; 4) Testing the program; 5) Documenting the program.

The first step in writing a program is to review the program specifications received from the systems analyst. The programmer must be absolutely sure that there are no questions or misunderstandings about what the program is to accomplish. Without a thorough understanding of the processing to be accomplished and the data to be processed, it is not possible to develop a program which will perform properly.

Program design entails the development of the structure of the program and then the development of the logic to solve the problem presented by the program. For many years, program flowcharts were used to assist programmers in the development of the logic for a program. These flowcharts are similar to system flowcharts but contain the detailed steps required for the solution to a problem. Today, with new approaches to problem solving, a methodology called structured design is commonly used.

After the program is designed, the programmer must code the program in a programming language. There are a variety of programming languages available to the programmer. The dominant language for medium and large-scale business applications is COBOL. When using COBOL, the programmer writes instructions using English-like statements.

After the program has been written by the programmer, it must be tested to ensure that it processes data properly and produces the required output. The first step usually involves removing any errors from the program caused by the improper use of the programming language. These errors are normally identified by the compiler which translates the program from source code to machine language. They are called to the attention of the programmer by messages called diagnostics.

After these errors have been removed from the program, it is tested by actually executing on the computer system. Specially prepared test data is used to ensure that the program will process all data correctly under all circumstances.

The preparation of the test data and the testing of the program is a vital part of the system development process. Far too often programs are placed in production that are not fully tested, resulting in erroneous output being produced and sent to the user.

After the programs in the system have been tested individually (commonly called unit tests), the entire system of programs must be tested as a whole. This process is called system testing. System testing includes not only further testing of the programs in the system, but also tests the procedures which have been established for users to interact with the system. Such things as screen layout in transaction-oriented systems, the prompts which aid when entering data on a terminal, distribution of reports produced from the system, and a number of other elements of the system are tested during the system test. In this way, the system should be completely "debugged" when it is implemented in production.

A continuing part of both the system and program development is the documentation which must be developed. This documentation should include documentation for the programs that have been developed, documentation for operations personnel (Figure 10-17), and documentation for the users of the system. It is quite important that the documentation prepared for a system be accurate and adequate. If it is not, then the users of the system will be seriously affected.

CONSOLE RUN FORM

PROGRAM NAME	PROGRAM NUMBER	ANALYST	PROGRAMMER
PAYROLL EDIT	PAYRL04	MARD; COSWELL	KOHLER

SYSTEM	FREQUENCY	DEADLINE	DATE
PAYROLL	WEEKLY	WEDNESDAY, 8 A.M.	6/5/76

RUN DESCRIPTION:
Using the time cards, additions, terminations, and changes as input, this program performs all the editing functions of the payroll system to ensure valid data entering the payroll system.

INPUT/OUTPUT INSTRUCTIONS

DEVICE TYPE	UNIT	USE	FILE DESCRIPTION	SOURCE	DISPOSITION	RETENTION PERIOD
Cards	00C	I	Additions, Changes, Terminations, Time Cards	Staging Area	File Storage	6 Months
Printer	00E	O	Exception Report		Control Desk	
Tape	182	O	PYRLT03-Edited Transactions	Scratch	To PAYRL05	1 Day

PRINTER INSTRUCTIONS

FORM	NO. OF PARTS	VERTICAL SPACING	CARRIAGE CONTROL TAPE	EST SIZE	SPECIAL INSTRUCTIONS
Standard	1	6/inch	Standard	2 Pages	Return To Control Immediately

RESTART INSTRUCTIONS:
Restart From Beginning

MESSAGES:
None

SPECIAL INSTRUCTIONS:
None

Figure 10-17 The console run form shown above is typical of the type of documentation required for operations personnel. It specifies all the information required for the computer operator to run the program.

PHASE 5 — Implementation and Evaluation

After testing has been completed and the documentation prepared, the system is ready to be implemented on the computer and run in a production environment. Assuming that the testing and documentation have been properly completed, the implementation should be a relatively smooth transition from the old system to the new system.

Converting to the new system

Conversion refers to the process of making the change from the old system to the new system. The difficulty of conversion is directly dependent upon the complexity of the system being implemented. Two commonly used methods are direct conversion and parallel conversion.

Direct conversion

With direct conversion, at a given date the old system ceases to be operational and the new system is placed into use. To those unfamiliar with converting large systems, this may seem the most logical approach. Direct conversion, however, is in most cases risky, in spite of the great care which may have been taken in designing the system. In most complex systems, it is unlikely that the results for all processing will be exactly as planned because of the hundreds of variables that are found. Direct conversion, therefore, should be performed only with simple systems where, if an error occurs, it will not create an undue hardship within a company.

Parallel conversion

In many systems, it is desirable to provide for further testing of the system prior to implementation. An approach called parallel conversion is commonly used to provide this additional testing.

Parallel conversion consists of processing data in both the old and new systems simultaneously and comparing the results. If the output from both systems is identical, it indicates that the new system is functioning in the proper manner. The disadvantage of parallel conversion is, of course, that a complete duplication of effort is required in that both the old system and the new system must be run concurrently.

Post implementation evaluation

Regardless of the method of implementation used, it is important to conduct a formal post implementation evaluation of the system. This evaluation should consist of a careful analysis to determine if the system is, in fact, performing as it was designed to do; if operating costs are as anticipated; and if any modifications are necessary to make the system operate effectively.

After the system has become operational and a post implementation evaluation has been conducted, the analyst should prepare a final report to management reviewing the history of the project, the actual costs associated with the project, and the benefits of the project.

System maintenance

An ongoing process after the system has been implemented is system maintenance. Maintenance consists of two major activities: 1) Changes to correct errors in the system; 2) Changes to give the system additional capabilities or to conform with government or company regulations.

On occasion, systems will be implemented which appear to function correctly only to find at a later time, sometimes a year or two later, that the system malfunctions when certain conditions occur. For example, a transaction-oriented system may function normally unless two certain terminals each enter the same inquiry at the same time. When this occurs, one of the terminals does not receive an answer. This condition may be one that the programmers and systems analysts did not test for in the system test, and it may not have occurred until six months after the system was implemented. When it does occur, however, the system must be changed to correct the error.

Changes must also be made when additional capabilities are requested and approved or when government or company regulations require change. For example, a new government report required for payroll deductions would require a change to the existing system to produce the new report.

Maintenance activities require a great deal of the time of many programmers and analysts. Systems which are well documented and contain well designed programs are much easier to maintain than those which do not follow good documentation and coding standards.

MAJOR APPLICATIONS FOR BUSINESS SYSTEMS

The computer has found virtually unlimited applications in modern business, from basic accounting functions to controlling the design and manufacture of products. Through the years, however, six standard systems involved with the accounting applications within a business have been widely implemented. These systems are: 1) Order entry; 2) Inventory control; 3) Accounts receivable; 4) Accounts payable; 5) General ledger; 6) Payroll.

Traditionally, these six accounting systems have been among the first systems implemented on a computer. Most accounting systems have precisely defined procedures and are labor intensive, making them ideally suited for implementation on the computer. Some of the characteristics of these systems are explained below and on the following pages.

Order entry

All businesses which are involved with the sale of merchandise of any kind must have an order entry system. Order entry systems define the procedures to process an order when it is received by a company. Orders can be received either in the mail, over the telephone, or from sales people.

Regardless of the source, the orders must contain some form of customer identification, such as customer number or customer name; the products ordered; and the quantity ordered. This data must be processed so that the merchandise ordered can be shipped promptly to the customer and so that the customer can be promptly billed.

In a transaction-oriented system, orders are entered into the computer system through terminals. When the order is entered, the system will retrieve customer information, such as customer address and customer credit status. When the quantity and type of product ordered is entered, the system should check the inventory to be sure the product is available. If it is not, the operator is notified and the product is placed on backorder. The price for the product will also be retrieved by the system. Once the entire order has been entered, the system will generate an invoice and any other documents that are required for shipping the order to the customer.

Order entry systems are often tied into both the inventory system and the accounts receivable system because both of those systems are affected by orders received from customers. Many times a data base will be established which contains files for these three systems. An order entry system is quite important for most companies.

Inventory control

Closely related to the order entry system is the inventory control system. Companies involved in the sale of merchandise must have merchandise on hand to sell. This merchandise on hand to sell is called the inventory of the company. As orders are received from customers, merchandise is removed from the inventory and shipped to the customer. This, of course, reduces the amount of merchandise available for sale. When the inventory reaches a certain level, merchandise must be purchased or manufactured by the company to refill its inventory.

The basic purpose of an inventory control system is to maintain inventory at a proper level to meet customer requirements, while at the same time ensuring that the company has a minimum investment in the inventory.

Most inventory control systems require at least one file of inventory data. The records in this file normally contain the item number, item description, quantity on hand, quantity on order, quantity reserved for use, unit cost, unit price, and minimum allowable inventory levels. These records are updated as merchandise is sold and as merchandise is placed into inventory.

Information obtained from an inventory control system may consist of stock status reports (Figure 10–18); inventory exception reports; analysis reports depicting which items have a high turnover and which items remain in inventory for a long period of time; periodic sales reports; and any other information which management deems necessary in controlling the company's inventory.

Inventory systems have been found to be one of the most cost-effective systems placed on computers because unmanaged inventories can be very expensive for companies.

Figure 10-18 The inventory stock status report below, produced by the FACTS system from the GRI Computer Corporation, contains much of the information necessary to manage an inventory. Reports such as this can help significantly in reducing inventory costs and providing better service to customers.

DAVIS ELECTRONICS   I N V E N T O R Y   S T O C K   S T A T U S   8/01   PAGE   1

----ITEM---	ITEM DESCRIPTION	CAT	MIN	U/M	LEAD	BEG QTY	QTY REC	QTY SOLD	QTY ADJ	ON HAND	ON ORDER	AVAIL	RESVED	UNIT PRICE	UNIT COST	TOTAL COST
1							0	0	0	DELETED		0	00	.00	.00	.00
10102	LIQUIFRAM, HYPALON					0	600	106	0	494	0	494	.01	.00	.99	489.06
10104	HEAD, PLEX			EA		0	211	0	0	211	0	211	.02	.00	6.00	1266.00
10123	FOOT VALVE STRAINER	0250	2500	EA		0	684	0	0	684	2500	3184	.05	.00	.54	369.36
10125	SPACER	0100	2500	EA		0	2048	770	0	1278	0	1278	1.00	10.75	.96	1226.88
10170	DATA PLATE	0500	2500	EA		0	2750	0	0	2750	0	2750	.01	.00	.15	412.50
10175	POTENTIOMETER	0600	2500	EA	6-12	0	2500	0	0	2500	0	2500	.01	.00	2.25	5625.00
10181	PILOT LIGHT	0500	2500	EA	6	0	3600	0	0	3600	5000-	1400-	.35	.00	.60	2160.00
10182	WIRE TERMINAL			EA		1000	0	0	0	0	0	0	.42	.00	.00	.00
10183	WIRE TERMINAL			EA		1000	0	0	0	0	0	0	.21	.00	.00	.00
10193	WIRE TERMINAL	1000		EA	4	0	4000	2000	0	2000	0	2000	1.00	.00	.02	40.00
10194	SOLDER			FT		1000	0	0	0	0	0	0	.00	.00	.00	.00
10232	HOUSING	0500		EA	4	0	391	0	0	391	2000	2391	.00	10.00	3.40	1329.40
10277	SOLENOID	0400		EA	14	0	200	0	0	200	0	200	.01	.00	17.73	3546.00
10339	HELICAL COMPRESS SPR	0600	2500	EA	4-6	0	2135	0	0	2135	0	2135	.01	.00	.44	939.40
10340	SCREW	1000		EA	1	0	6700	0	0	6700	0	6700	1.00	.00	.02	134.00
10349	TRANSFORMER			EA		1000	0	0	0	0	0	0	.21	.00	.00	.00
10477	PUMP BOX			EA	2	0	1500	0	0	1500	0	1500	.02	.00	.48	720.00
10488-06	WIRE, 18 BLACK 6"			IN		1000	0	0	0	0	0	0	.21	.00	.00	.00
10488-56	WIRE, GREEN 6"	0400		FT	2	0	2400	0	0	2400	0	2400	.02	.00	.02	48.00
10488-96	WIRE, 18 WHITE 6"			IN		1000	0	0	0	0	0	0	.21	.00	.00	.00
10439-56	WIRE, 22 GREEN 6"			IN		1000	0	0	0	0	0	0	.21	.00	.00	.00
10492	VALVE SEAT	0150		EA	4	0	1930	0	0	1930	0	1930	.01	.00	.75	1447.50
10596	VARISTOR			EA		100	0	1043	0	1043	0	1043-	.21	3.00	.00	.00-
10663	TRANSFORMER ASSEMBLY			EA		0	0	45	0	45-	0	45-	.00	6.00	.00	.00-
2						0	0	0	0	DELETED		0		.00	.00	.00
COMPANY TOTAL						7100		3964		27635		27185		29.75		19753.10
							31649		0		500-			5.28	34.35	

```
  DAVIS ELECTRONICS                  D E T A I L   A G E D   T R I A L   B A L A N C E              6/01          PAGE    1

ACCOUNT        NAME                    TOTAL  ---------================  A G E I N G  -----------------------  DESCRIPTION
          TO    DATE    REFERENCE      DUE          CURRENT     OVER 30    OVER 60     OVER 90    OVER 120

   E110 ELCO WEBSTER CORP.
          72   6/07    050003        5,000.00      5,000.00                                                   SPACER
          72   6/07    050003       10,270.00     10,270.00                                                   VARISTOR
          72   6/07    050003          763.50        763.50                                                   SALES TAX
          72   6/07    050003            2.13          2.13                                                   FREIGHT
                       ACCOUNT TOTAL 16,035.63     16,035.63                                                             0

   F110 FAR ASSOCIATES
          72   6/07    050008           90.00         90.00                                                   SPACER
          72   6/07    050008            4.50          4.50                                                   SALES TAX
                       ACCOUNT TOTAL    94.50         94.50
```

Accounts receivable

Accounts receivable is the accounting term used to describe the money owed by customers of a company for merchandise which has been sold or for services which have been rendered on a charge basis. It has been estimated that approximately 90 percent of business in the United States is done on a credit basis; therefore, accounts receivable systems are an important part of most business organizations.

Any well-designed accounts receivable system must provide for the prompt billing of customers; an accurate accounting of merchandise or services purchased; payments received and balance due; and the immediate notification to management of slow paying or delinquent accounts.

The basic procedures in an accounts receivable system are: 1) Establish customer accounts with appropriate credit limits; 2) Maintain a record of all purchases and payments; 3) Prepare billing statements for customers when payments are due; 4) Provide for the prompt recording of payments made by the customer; 5) Prepare ageing reports for the accounts; that is, reports which list all the accounts, indicating which accounts are current and which accounts are past due (Figure 10-19); 6) Provide for followup of delinquent accounts.

Figure 10-19 The aged trial balance report above is an accounts receivable report which indicates which accounts are current and which accounts are past due.

Accounts payable

Accounts payable refers to the amount of money a company owes to other companies in the payment of its bills for merchandise or services rendered. The two major functions of an accounts payable system are: 1) Payment of bills; 2) Assignment of charges to various departments of the company (called the chart of accounts) for the bills which have been paid.

```
DAVIS STATIONARY SUPPLY                    ACCOUNTS PAYABLE CHECK REGISTER            6/01              PAGE  1

VENDOR       -----INVOICE-----PURCHASE    DUE              DISCOUNT                          CHECK      CHECK
NUMBER    TC NUMBER      DATE REFERENCE    DATE    GROSS    LOST -*-       NET                DATE       NUMBER

000001 AMCO ENGINEERING CO.
       51 12345673      12/09             12/09   100.00   10.00 *      100.00  -INVOICE-
                            CHECK  TOTAL          100.00     .00       100.00               6/01        5473
000080 ODEC INC.
       51 34567890      12/09             12/10  5,000.00   50.00 *    5,000.00  -INVOICE-
                            CHECK  TOTAL        5,000.00     .00      5,000.00               6/01        5479

REPCO
       51 123456        05/28  12345      02/25   123.00    2.46       120.54  -INVOICE-
       51 12345677      01/23             12/12   123.45    2.47       120.99  -INVOICE-
       51 12345677      01/23             12/12     .00                       -INVOICE-
       51 1234566       05/28             02/25   123.00    2.46       120.54  -INVOICE-
       51 5555          05/10  99         06/10   100.00    2.00        90.00  -INVOICE-
                            CHECK  TOTAL                                                     6/01        5480
        DAVIS STATIONARY SUPPLY       TOTALS    5,232.45             5,318.99
                                                           4.47

                            DISCOUNTS TAKEN      4.47
                            DISCOUNTS LOST      60.00
```

Figure 10-20 The accounts payable check register lists the vendors to whom checks were paid, invoice identification, the amount of the check, discounts, the check date, and the check number.

Bills must usually be paid promptly in any business to take advantage of discounts which are often provided if the bills are paid within certain time limits, and to maintain good credit ratings. In addition, management must know how much was spent, what departments within the company made the expenditure, to whom it was paid, and for what purpose.

In accounts payable systems, checks are normally written based upon invoices or bills which are received by the company. After the bills are verified as being accurate, management makes the decision concerning when the bill should be paid. As a general rule, bills will be paid in time to take advantage of discounts offered, but there are occasions when a bill will not be paid for a period of time based upon other considerations. The accounts payable system should provide the information to management which it requires to make these decisions.

The output from an accounts payable system commonly includes the checks made payable to the vendors; an accounts payable check register listing the vendors paid, the check numbers of the checks written, the check date, the check amount, and any discounts which have been taken or lost (Figure 10-20); a chart of accounts report which indicates which departments spent the money; and an accounts payable aged trial balance report which lists the money still owed by the company, the dates on which the payments are due, and to whom the money is owed.

General ledger

All companies must have a complete historical record of all financial transactions. This data originates from customer orders on credit, cash sales, accounts receivable, accounts payable, inventory, and payroll. The general ledger of a company provides this record.

The basic elements of a general ledger system involve posting all financial transactions to a data base. From this data, the company can extract two important accounting reports: the profit and loss statement (sometimes called the income statement) and the balance sheet.

As the name implies, the profit and loss statement reports on income, expenses, and profits or losses. The balance sheet reports on all assets (such as cash on hand, accounts receivable, inventory, and so on) and liabilities (amounts due and payable, etc.). The balance sheet reveals the worth of the business.

The general ledger is compiled from data acquired from many of the other accounting systems. In many cases, an accounting data base is established so that the general ledger system can extract the required data from the data base to prepare the general ledger reports.

Payroll

Historically, one of the first applications which has been placed on the computer is the payroll system. The primary objective of a payroll system is the prompt and accurate payment of employees for services rendered; accurate reporting to the employees, employer, and government agencies of money paid to employees; and accurate computation and reporting of deductions for state and federal taxes, social security taxes, and other required and voluntary deductions.

Payroll systems vary greatly with the size and type of company. With most systems, however, the actual paychecks, a payroll register, and a deduction register are produced. More sophisticated systems have programs which will produce labor distribution reports, cost analysis reports, and a number of other payroll analysis reports. An accurate and efficient payroll system is a requirement to keep employees happy and government agencies adequately informed of payroll transactions.

Other business application systems

Many other types of business application systems utilize the processing capabilities of the computer. Each of these systems must be responsive to the needs of the user and be cost-effective for the company when they are installed. The systems analysts in the data processing department have a large responsibility to ensure that systems are satisfactory to all parties when they are implemented on the computer system.

Chapter summary

The following points have been discussed and explained in this chapter.

1. Any system consists of a series of related procedures designed to perform a specific task.

2. Three reasons for the widespread use of computer systems are: 1) The computer can reduce the cost of doing business; 2) The computer can assist in producing more timely and more accurate management information; 3) The use of a computer can result in improved customer service.

3. The people who design systems are called systems analysts.

4. Most data processing departments consist of three groups: systems, programming, and operations.

5. The data base administrator is responsible for developing and maintaining the data base, controlling the updating of the data base, and even controlling who has access to data within the business organization.

6. New systems are commonly derived for the following reasons: 1) Conversion of a manual system to one running on the computer; 2) Conversion of a batch system to a transaction-oriented system; 3) Conversion of a system using separate files into a system using a data base; 4) Integrating several currently existing systems into one larger system using a data base.

7. The phases of a system project are: 1) Preliminary investigation; 2) Detailed system investigation and analysis; 3) System design; 4) System development; 5) System implementation and evaluation.

8. The purpose of the preliminary investigation is to determine if a problem or request for assistance warrants further investigation.

9. The outcome of the preliminary investigation is a report to management indicating the true nature of the problem and suggesting further action if desirable.

10. The detailed system investigation and analysis is divided into two parts: 1) What is taking place in the current system; 2) Why are the procedures found occurring.

11. The basic fact gathering techniques used are the interview, questionnaires, current documentation, and personal observation.

12. A data flow diagram is used to graphically illustrate the flow of data through the current system.

13. After the detailed investigation and analysis, a presentation should be given to management recommending possible solutions and the costs and benefits for the solutions.

14. In the system design phase, the analyst must design the system output, the system input, the system files and data bases, and the processing methods to be used.

15. When designing the system output, the analyst must define the output requirements of the system, review the types of output media that might be useful, define the specific contents of the output that is to be produced, and consider the methods for the disposition and handling of the output.

16. Questions to be answered when designing the system input include: What media is to be used for storing input records? How is the data to enter the system? Can the data be captured at its source? What is the volume of input? How often is it necessary to input the data? What editing and safeguards must be provided to ensure valid input data? What response time is required for transaction-oriented systems? Is hard copy required for transaction-oriented systems?

17. When designing the system files and data base, the analyst should develop a data dictionary which contains: 1) A list of the various data elements required for the system; 2) The attributes of the data, such as the length of each field; 3) The points in the system where the data is required; 4) The type of access required for the data (sequential or random); 5) The amount of activity which can be expected for the data; 6) The amount of data which must be stored for the system.

18. The system flowchart is used to show the logical and physical flow of data through a system.

19. When designing a system, the analyst must establish source document controls, input controls, output controls, and processing controls.

20. An audit trail enables any input record or process executed on the computer system to be traced back to the original source data.

21. It is essential to ensure that any lost data in a system can be recovered. The most common method to accomplish this is backup files.

22. After the design has been completed, it must be approved by three levels of management — data processing management, user department management, and corporate management.

23. In the system development phase, there are four tasks to be done: 1) Establish a project development and implementation plan; 2) Develop detailed programming specifications; 3) Program and test the system; 4) Prepare final documentation of the system.

24. After the system has been developed, it must be implemented and maintained.

25. Six of the major systems which are commonly implemented on computers are: 1) Order entry; 2) Inventory control; 3) Accounts receivable; 4) Accounts payable; 5) General ledger; 6) Payroll.

Student Learning Exercises

Review questions

1. Define the terms, "system" and "procedure."

2. List the three major reasons for the use of computer systems.

3. Draw an organizational chart of the major groups in the data processing department of a typical company.

4. What does a data base administrator do? To whom does the d.b.a. report?

5. What are the reasons a data processing system is developed?

6. List the phases which are followed when undertaking a system project.

7. What use is a data flow diagram?

8. What is the outcome of the preliminary investigation?

9. Briefly summarize the activities which take place during the detailed system investigation and analysis phase.

10. What tasks must be performed in the system design phase?

11. What must be considered when designing the system output?

12. What questions must be answered when designing the system input?

13. What is a data dictionary? What is contained in a data dictionary?

14. When and for what purpose is a system flowchart used?

15. What is an audit trail? Why is it necessary?

16. Discuss briefly the backup requirements of a transaction-oriented system.

17. What four tasks must be done in the system development phase? Briefly discuss these tasks.

18. List six major systems which are commonly implemented on computers and describe each system.

Controversial issues in data processing

1. Very large systems with many terminals and computers at remote locations may take 3–5 years to design and implement. Some people argue that undertaking such projects is a futile task because by the time the system is implemented, computer technology and the needs of the company have changed to such an extent that the system is virtually worthless. Would you approve any system project that would take 3–5 years to design and implement at a cost of several million dollars, knowing of the rapid changes in technology and anticipating considerable growth of your company? What would be your alternatives?

2. It is the responsibility of systems analysts and programmers to design and implement systems that can best serve the needs of the company. The types of output generated from a system should be determined by these data processing specialists, not by users, many of whom are psychologically resistant to change! Do you agree or disagree with this statement?

Research projects

1. New system design methodologies are constantly being investigated in an attempt to improve the system design process. Research the new developments in system design techniques and prepare a report summarizing your findings.

2. A major problem facing systems analysts is documenting and defining the system so that it is readily understandable by programmers who must implement the system. An area of study called requirements analysis has been developed to deal with this problem. Prepare a research paper on the latest techniques of requirements analysis.

Picture credits

Figure 10-1 Eastman Kodak Company
Figure 10-5 IBM
Figure 10-6 IBM
Figure 10-10 Trilog, Inc.

Figure 10-15 Tymshare, Inc.
Figure 10-18 GRI Computer Corp.
Figure 10-19 GRI Computer Corp.
Figure 10-20 GRI Computer Corp.

Chapter 11
Program Design and Flowcharting

Objectives

- An understanding of the reasons for the review of program specifications

- An understanding of the flowchart as a program design tool

- A knowledge of the three control structures found in structured programming

- A knowledge of structured design

- An introduction to egoless progamming and structured walkthroughs

- An understanding of the logic required to solve seven problems commonly found in business applications programming

Chapter 11

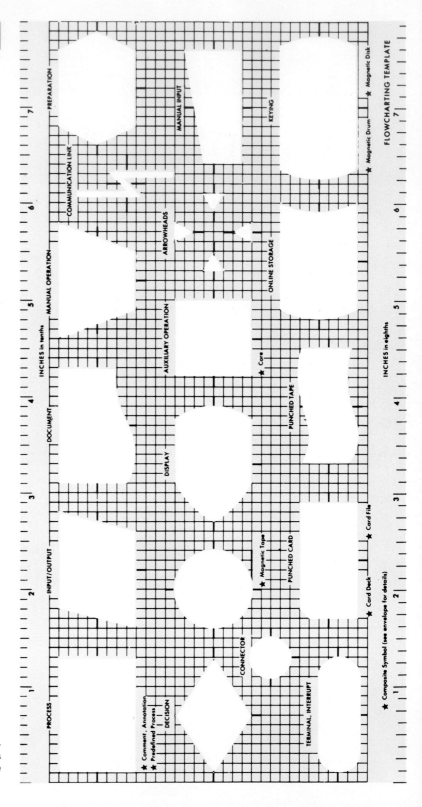

Figure 11-1 A template containing the standardized symbols used for drawing flowcharts is a commonly used aid when designing the logic for a program.

Program Design and Flowcharting

"Computer programming as a practical human activity is some 25 years old, a short time for intellectual development. Yet computer programming has already posed the greatest intellectual challenge that mankind has faced in pure logic and complexity."[1]

Introduction

As noted by Harlan Mills (above), the task of programming a computer has posed some difficult challenges to those charged with this responsibility. Complex programs may require hundreds and even thousands of individual instructions to accomplish a given task. Because of this complexity and the number of variables which can occur with even the simplest of programs, it is important that the programmer approach writing a program in a systematic, disciplined manner. Toward this end, a program development cycle has been established. It consists of: 1) Review of program specifications; 2) Program design; 3) Program coding; 4) Program testing; 5) Program documentation.

The purpose of this chapter is to examine the first two elements of the program development cycle — review of program specifications and program design.

What is a program?

Before analyzing the program development cycle in detail, it is useful to examine the nature of a computer program. A program can be defined as a series of instructions which directs the computer to perform a sequence of tasks that produce a desired output.

---

1 Harlan D. Mills, "The New Math of Computer Programming," COMMUNICATIONS OF THE ACM, Vol. 18, No. 1, January, 1975.

To execute a computer program, it must be loaded into main computer storage as a series of machine language instructions. The electronics of the computer system interpret the instructions found in the program and carry out the processing directed by the program.

Although the instructions which are actually executed on the computer system must be in machine language, the programmer who writes the program does not normally write in machine language. Instead, the programmer uses a source language which will then be translated into machine language for actual execution on the computer.

The source language, regardless of which one is used, has program statements which fall into six major categories: 1) Statements to define files and records which are to be processed by the program; 2) Statements to define other data within the program, such as total accumulators, headings which will appear on a report, and other data required to produce the proper output from the program; 3) Statements which move data from one location in main computer storage to another location; 4) Statements which cause arithmetic operations to occur, such as adding two values stored in main computer storage, multiplying two values, and so on; 5) Statements which compare two values stored in main computer storage and determine whether one value is less than, equal to, or greater than another value; 6) Statements which cause data to be read into main computer storage from input or auxiliary storage devices; and statements which cause data to be written from main computer storage to output devices or auxiliary storage devices.

Thus, some instructions define data, others operate on that data, and still others bring data into main computer storage and write data from main computer storage. It is the task of combining these six types of instructions into a combination which will process data correctly and produce the proper output that is the function of a computer programmer.

REVIEW OF PROGRAM SPECIFICATIONS

The first step in the program development cycle is a review of the system and program specifications and documentation provided by the systems analyst for the program to be written. These specifications normally contain record and screen layouts, printer spacing charts, flowcharts, and a written narrative which provides a detailed description of the processing that is to occur.

It is extremely important that the programmer thoroughly understand all of the various aspects of the problem to be solved. These aspects include the output to be produced, the input that is available to produce the output, and the processing that must occur to produce the output. In addition, the programmer must have a detailed knowledge of the various fields, records, and files which are utilized in the system.

It is the programmer's responsibility to directly implement the procedures defined by the systems analyst. Changes such as changing the format of a report because the programmer thinks it will improve the system should not be made at the programmer's discretion. If there are any questions, the programmer should discuss them with the systems analyst.

At the end of the review of the system and program specifications, the programmer should completely understand what processing is to be performed, what data is to be processed, and how the output is to be derived from the data available to the program.

PROGRAM DESIGN

After the system and programming specifications have been carefully reviewed and all questions have been answered by the systems analyst, the programmer begins the next phase of the program development cycle — designing the structure and logic of the program.

The design phase of the program development cycle is one of the most important; for if a program is properly designed, it will be easily implemented in code in the selected programming language. At the end of the design phase, the structure and logic of the program should be detailed in such a fashion that the resulting program code from the design will be efficient, will always produce correct output (reliable), will work under all conditions (robust), and will be easily modified (maintainable).

Early design methodologies

When the stored program concept proved to be a reality in the late 1940's, it soon became apparent that the task of writing instructions for a computer could be extremely complex, involving thousands of individual instructions. A programmer could not begin writing a program by immediately writing the first instruction, followed by the second instruction, and so on until the last instruction had been written. Some method was required to plan the program before coding began.

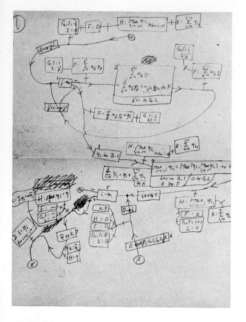

Figure 11-2 This "flowchart" by John von Neumann was used for the solution of a problem involving game theory.

SYMBOL	REPRESENTS
	Processing A group of program instructions which perform a processing function of the program.
	Input/output Any function of an input/output device (making information available for processing, recording processing information, tape positioning, etc.).
	Decision The decision function used to document points in the program where a branch to alternate paths is possible based upon variable conditions.
	Predefined process A group of operations not detailed in the particular set of flowcharts.
	Terminal The beginning, end, or a point of interruption in a program.
	Connector An entry from, or an exit to, another part of the program flowchart.
	Offpage connector A connector used instead of the connector symbol to designate entry to or exit from a page.
	Preparation An instruction or group of instructions which changes the program.

Figure 11-3 The ANSI flowchart symbols are commonly used throughout the industry to sketch the logic of a program.

To provide a means of expressing the logic which would lead to a solution of a problem and to show the interrelationships of instructions within a program, symbols which graphically represented the solution to the problem were used. Utilizing these symbols, which is called flowcharting, was first done by John von Neumann (Figure 11-2).

For the many years following von Neumann's early work, flowcharting the solution of a problem prior to writing the code for the program has been the primary means of program design. So important is its use that the American National Standards Institute (ANSI) published a set of flowcharting standards. These standards specified specially-shaped symbols that should be used to represent the various operations that can be performed on a computer (Figure 11-3).

Flowcharting as a program design tool

When designing a program using the flowchart as the basic design tool, the programmer normally begins by defining the precise sequence in which each operation is to be performed. The programmer must think through the individual steps in the solution to the problem, including the input to be read, the calculations to be performed, the comparing operations or decisions to be made, the alternative actions to be taken based upon the results of the comparisons, and the output to be produced. Each of these individual steps is illustrated by means of one of the flowcharting symbols, which provide a graphic representation of the steps that are to occur in the program.

The value of a flowchart is that it graphically represents the steps in the solution of a problem together with the essential details and their relationships. In flowcharts, symbols and words support one another. By placing a brief description within the symbol, the sequence of operations which is to be performed is apparent.

A representative flowchart is illustrated in Figure 11-4. Each step which is to be performed in the program is specified within one of the flowcharting symbols. By following the flowchart, the processing which is to occur within the program can be seen.

Figure 11-4 The flowchart on the opposite page illustrates the use of the standardized flowcharting symbols to graphically display the logic required to solve a problem.

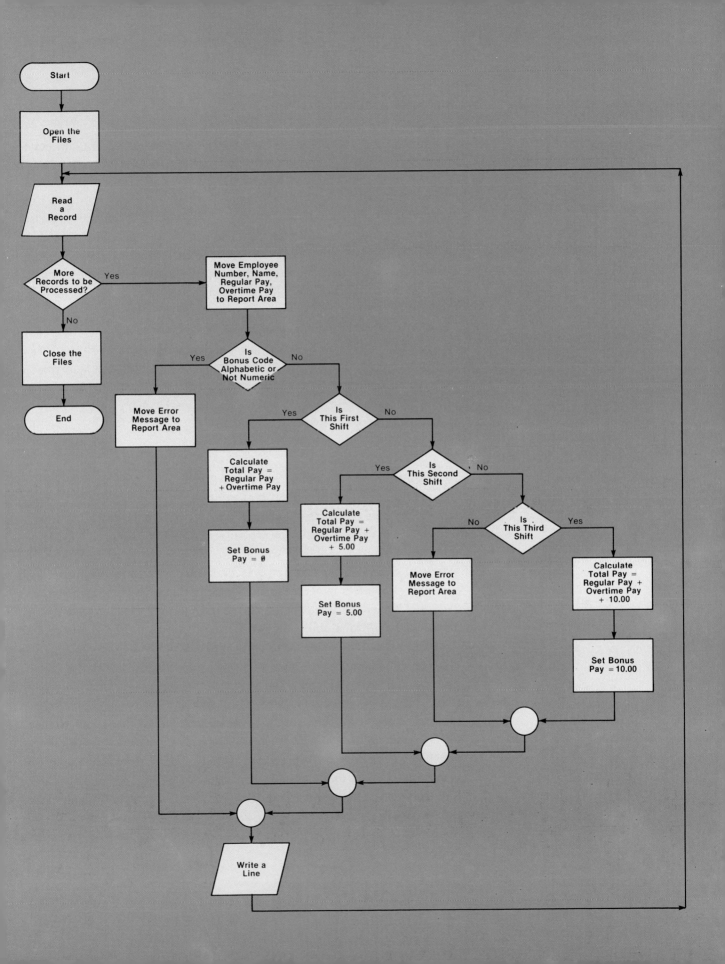

Problems with flowchart designs

Although the flowchart is a valuable tool when designing and documenting the logic used within a program, it was found that programmers using the flowchart to design programs applied their own set of rules to the development of the logic of the program. There was little scientific basis on which to base the logic of the program. Therefore, the programmer began the design of the program by recording the individual steps which appeared to be necessary, coping with each new combination of conditions as they were encountered or discovered. Thus, the programmer was not, in fact, aware of the overall design of the program until the flowchart was actually completed.

This method of program design led to programs which were not really designed, but rather were more or less patched together to work. There was neither an organized structure to the program nor a methodology to approach the program design. Programmers could pass control to various parts of the program whenever necessary, leading to programs which were difficult to read, understand, and modify.

Development of structured programming

As the data processing industry began to mature in the 1960's, it was recognized that there was a great need to develop a design methodology that would result in programs which were reliable and easy to modify and maintain. Considerable research was undertaken by mathematicians and computer scientists aimed at changing the writing of a program from an "art" to a "science." It was necessary to change programming from an undisciplined, individualized expression of one's ideas for the solution of a logical problem to a disciplined approach using scientific techniques.

The first major breakthrough occurred in the mid-1960's, when research by computer scientists indicated that a technique called structured programming could help attain these goals. The earliest beginning of structured programming theory can be traced to a paper presented by two mathematicians, Corrado Bohm and Guiseppe Jacopini, at the 1964 International Colloquium on Algebraic Linguistics and Automata Theory in Israel. Their paper proved that a few basic control structures could be used to express any programming logic, no matter how complex. These basic control structures are: 1) Sequence; 2) If-Then-Else; 3) Do While.

Structured programming is defined as a method of programming that uses these three control structures to form highly structured units of code that are easily read and, therefore, easily maintained. The following paragraphs contain an explanation of these three control structures.

Sequence

When using the sequence control structure, one event occurs immediately after another. In Figure 11-5, the rectangular boxes represent a particular event that is to take place. For example, an event could be a computer instruction to move data from one location in main computer storage to another location. Each event takes place in the exact sequence specified, one event followed by another.

If-Then-Else

The second control structure is termed the If-Then-Else structure (Figure 11-6). This structure is used for conditional statements. The "If" portion of the structure tests a given condition. For example, the number of hours worked might be tested to determine if the employee worked overtime. The "Then" portion of the statement is executed if the condition tested is true. For example, if the person did work overtime, the "Then" portion of the statement would be executed.

The "Else" portion of the statement is executed when the condition tested is not true. For example, if the employee did not work overtime, then the Else portion of the statement would be executed.

Do While

The third logical structure, the Do While structure, is used to allow program looping. Looping means that one or more events are to occur so long as a given condition remains true. In Figure 11-7, the condition is tested. If the condition is true, event 1 will take place. The same condition is again tested. If it is still true, then event 1 will occur again. This looping will continue until the condition being tested is not true. At that time, the control will exit from the loop and subsequent processing will occur. In most cases, some processing in event 1 will change the condition so that it becomes not true and the looping is terminated.

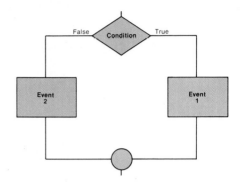

Figure 11-5 In the sequence control structure, one event occurs immediately after another.

Figure 11-6 The If-Then-Else structure is used for conditional statements. If the condition is true, event 1 takes place. If the condition is false, event 2 occurs.

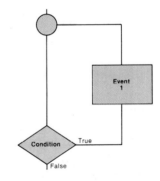

Figure 11-7 The Do While structure is used to control looping. If the condition is true, event 1 will be performed. The condition is then tested again. If it is still true, then event 1 will again be performed. This looping will continue until the condition is false when it is tested. When this occurs, control will exit from the loop.

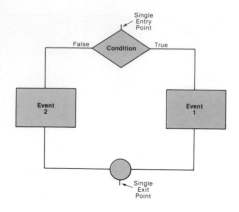

Figure 11-8 All three control structures used with structured programming have one entry point and one exit point. With this feature, it is easy to follow the logic in a program.

These three control structures, the Sequence, the If-Then-Else, and the Do While, can be used to solve any programming logic problem. They form the basis for a scientific approach to computer programming.

An important concept which is incorporated into structured programming is that there is but one entry point and one exit point in each of the three control structures. For example, when the If-Then-Else structure is used, control enters the structure at the point where the condition is tested (Figure 11-8). When the condition is tested, one event will be executed if the condition is true and one event will be executed if the condition is false. Regardless of the result of the test, however, the structure is exited at a common point.

This feature substantially improves the understanding of a program because, when reading the program, the programmer can be assured that whatever happens within the If-Then-Else structure, control will always exit at the common point. Prior to the use of structured programming, many programmers would pass control to other parts of a program without following the single entry-single exit rule. This practice led to programs which were extremely difficult to read and, therefore, to modify.

Expressing logic using pseudocode

Flowcharting is used to graphically illustrate the logic which is to be implemented in a program to solve a problem. One of the requirements of flowcharting is to draw the graphic symbols required. It has been found that this requirement can be time-consuming and not conducive to complete program design because if an error is made when drawing the flowchart, many times the entire flowchart must be redrawn.

As an alternative to flowcharting, some authorities in program design advocate the use of pseudocode when designing the logic for a program. Pseudocode is nothing more than the logical steps to be taken in the solution of a problem written in English statements (Figure 11-9). The advantage of pseudocode is that a great deal of time need not be spent in drawing symbols and determining how to arrange the symbols on a sheet of paper while at the same time attempting to determine the program logic. The major disadvantage is that a graphic representation, which many people find useful when examining program logic, is not available with pseudocode.

```
DO WHILE more records
    Move name and address
              to output area
    IF state = California
        Move local message
                  to output area
    ELSE
        Move remote message
                  to output area
    ENDIF
    Write a line
    Read a record
ENDDO
```

Figure 11-9 Pseudocode is used to express logic in English statements. Although pseudocode is easier to use than flowcharts, some programmers prefer flowcharts because of the graphical representation of the logic in a flowchart.

Structured design

Structured programming was a significant improvement in terms of specifying and structuring the logic for solving a problem on a computer, but a serious problem still remained in the design of large computer programs. The problem was that the programs were so large that it was virtually impossible to design the logic for the entire program with any kind of continuity and vision. In a word, the programs were just too complex to be well-designed. Indeed, it is a tribute to programmers that these complex programs ever worked properly on computer systems.

One of the early programming methods used to simplify programs was the subroutine. A subroutine is a series of computer instructions which, together, accomplish a given task. The subroutine can be "called" by other portions of the program to accomplish the task. For example, a subroutine could be written to take the square root of a number (Figure 11-10). When the square root of a number is required, the program can pass control to the subroutine which determines the square root. The subroutine will take the square root of the number and pass it back to the portion of the program which called it.

Although subroutines helped simplify programs, there was still a need to develop a methodology which would allow the overall structure of a program to be designed and which also would allow the program to be broken down into a series of small pieces for which the logic could easily be developed; and, subsequently could be easily understood by those who must read and understand the program.

Recognizing this need in the late 1960's, Larry Constantine, then employed by IBM, began to examine currently existing programs in an attempt to determine those attributes of the program which made the program easy to read and understand and those attributes which contributed to making a program difficult to read and understand.

As a result of this investigation and similar work by others, an article entitled "Structured Design," written by Wayne Stevens, Glenford Myers, and Larry Constantine was published in the IBM Systems Journal in 1974. This article described a design methodology called structured design, which resulted in a program consisting of many small portions of code called modules. A module, which is similar to a subroutine, performs one given task within the program.

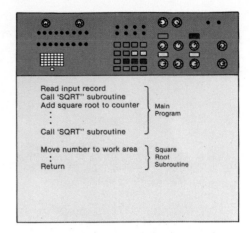

Figure 11-10 In the example above, a square root subroutine is used in the program. The square root subroutine is called from two different parts of the main program. Thus, the programmer can use the subroutine from anywhere in the main program. Many subroutines perform tasks which are needed for more than one program. These subroutines, once written, can be stored on disk or tape to be included in programs when necessary.

The structured design methodology presented a technique whereby a large program could be decomposed into small modules, each of which performed a particular function in the program. The major benefit of this technique is that each of the modules is logically fairly simple, particularly when compared to the logic required for a very large program. By combining the processing of each of these small modules into a complete program, the program accomplishes the desired result.

There are several variations of methods for deriving the structure of a program. One of the most widely taught methods uses the IPO Chart as the primary design tool (Figure 11–11). The basic steps using this technique are: 1) The output, input, and major processing tasks for the first module in the program are defined. The output from the first module is the output which is to be produced from the program. The input to the module consists of the files and elements from a data base which are going to be used by the program.

Figure 11-11 The IPO Chart is used to specify the output, input, and major processing tasks required in a program. Each of the major processing tasks is examined to determine if the task should be performed in a separate module. Through this repeating process, the structure of a program is determined and is illustrated by a hierarchy chart.

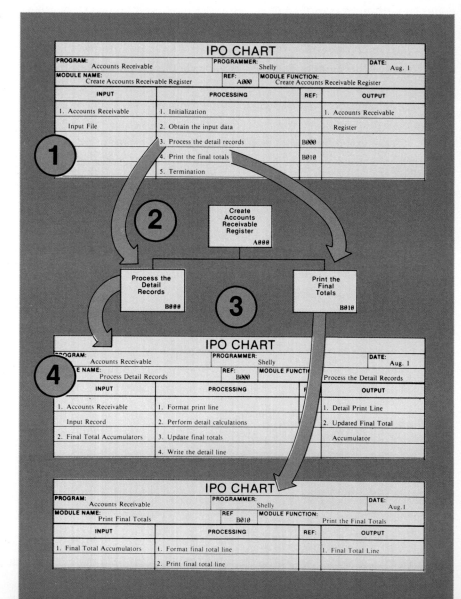

The major processing tasks are obtained by asking the question, "What tasks must be accomplished to obtain the given output from the given input?"

2) Once these tasks for the highest level module are determined, the program designer must ask if any of the tasks appears to be either lengthy or complex; that is, is any one of the tasks going to require a significant number of programming statements to accomplish or does the task appear to require some complex logic. If either of these cases is true, then the task will appear in a separate module. It will not be accomplished in the module being analyzed. In the example in Figure 11-11, the tasks, Process the detail records and Print the final totals, are to be accomplished in separate modules.

3) When the decomposition of the module is complete, a hierarchy chart is drawn to show the relationship of each of the modules within the program.

4) An IPO Chart is used to specify the output, input, and major processing tasks to be accomplished for each of the new modules which has been made a part of the program.

This process continues until all of the program has been decomposed into small, manageable modules. The logic for each module is then designed. The logic can be designed using either flowcharts or pseudocode, but pseudocode is an easier-to-use method (Figure 11-12).

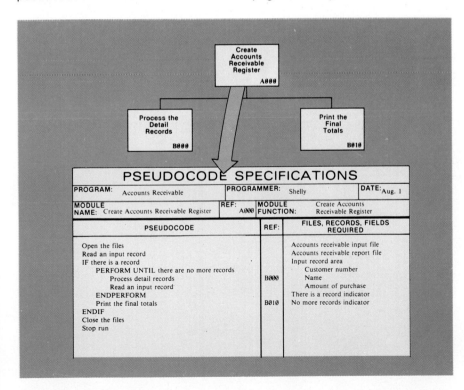

Figure 11-12 After the structure of the program has been determined, the logic for each module in the program is designed. The pseudocode in this example illustrates the logic for the module whose function is to create an accounts receivable register. The pseudocode specifications form can be used for recording the pseudocode.

The logic for each program module is developed independently. Since each module accomplishes a specific task within the program, combining the modules will accomplish the function of the program.

Most programs which are written are not as small as the previous program. The hierarchy chart for a more complex program is shown in Figure 11–13.

Other design methodologies

At about the same time structured design was developed and distributed throughout the industry, several other design techniques were developed. The two other major methodologies are the Jackson methodology (named after Michael Jackson, its originator), and the Warnier methodology (named after Jean-Dominique Warnier). These two design methodologies are based upon the data which is to be processed, under the theory that if the structure of the program mirrors the data which it processes, then the program will be easy to design and easy to read and understand.

Figure 11-13 The hierarchy chart below illustrates the structure of a medium-sized program. Each module in the program accomplishes a specific task. Together, they accomplish the processing required of the program.

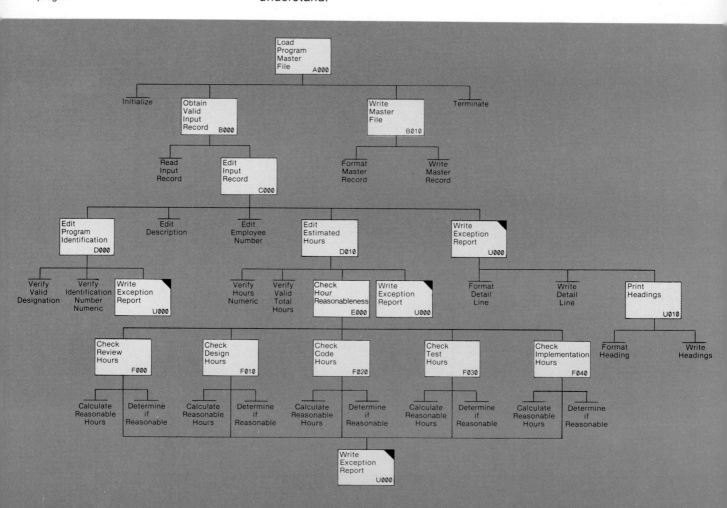

All three design methodologies — structured design, the Jackson methodology, and the Warnier methodology — have their strengths and weaknesses; but all three have contributed significantly to the process of designing programs.

Egoless programming and structured walkthroughs

For many years, program design and program coding was thought by programmers to be an individual activity. Indeed, many programmers were protective of their programs, not allowing anyone to see their program design or program coding while they were performing these activities.

Recognizing that this attitude was not one to foster well-designed and well-coded programs, Dr. Gerald Weinberg of Ethnotech, Inc., wrote a book in 1971 entitled The Psychology of Computer Programming. In his classic book, Weinberg criticized this attitude and proposed in its place an attitude he called "egoless programming." When egoless programming is practiced, the individual views his or her program not as an extension of themselves, but rather as a product which should be examined to make it better. As a result of Weinberg's work, as well as others, the concept of program reviews and structured walkthroughs emerged.

A structured walkthrough is an organized review of a program by other programmers. As a programmer designs and writes a program, it is important to approach the task with the idea that it will be done properly the first time, without any errors. On occasion, however, the programmer will inadvertently make an error in the program design or program coding. The intent of the walkthrough is to find any errors which have been made in the program — either errors in the use of a programming language or errors in the design of a program.

In order for a walkthrough to be successful, it is important that the programmer adopt the attitude that a discovery of errors is welcome, since the program will be a valued asset to the company only when it contains no errors. The discovery of an error in a walkthrough is not an indictment of the individual programmer. Indeed, Weinberg states "we do know through our experiences with egoless programming that there is no particular reason why your friend cannot also be your sternest critic."[2] The review of program design is an important step in the development of a program, and should be a part of each programming project.

---

2 Gerald M. Weinberg, THE PSYCHOLOGY OF COMPUTER PROGRAMMING, Van Nostrand Reinhold Company, 1971.

COMMON DESIGN PROBLEMS

When defining the logic of a program or a program module, there are a number of common logic problems that occur in business applications. These basic problems involve the logic to perform the following types of processing: 1) Basic input/output operations; 2) Basic calculating, counting records, and accumulating totals; 3) Basic comparing operations; 4) Processing different record types; 5) Table searching; 6) Control break processing; 7) Merging two files.

Each of these types of logic problems can be implemented using one or more of the three basic control structures — Sequence, If-Then-Else, or Do While. The flowcharts on the following pages illustrate the logic to solve each of these problems. These flowcharts contain the basic logic necessary for the solution to the problems. They do not contain such language-dependent requirements as moving fields from an input area to an output area or printing headings on the report. The intent of these structured flowcharts is to illustrate the overall approach taken to solve these basic problems using the three structured programming control structures.

Figure 11-14 The flowchart below shows the logic for basic input/output operations using sequential files. The arrows within the loop would not be drawn by the programmer. They are used in this and subsequent illustrations merely to point out the control structures being used.

Basic input/output operations

The flowchart in Figure 11-14 illustrates the basic logic to read a series of input records containing an employee number, employee name, and employee job title, and prepare a printed report listing these fields.

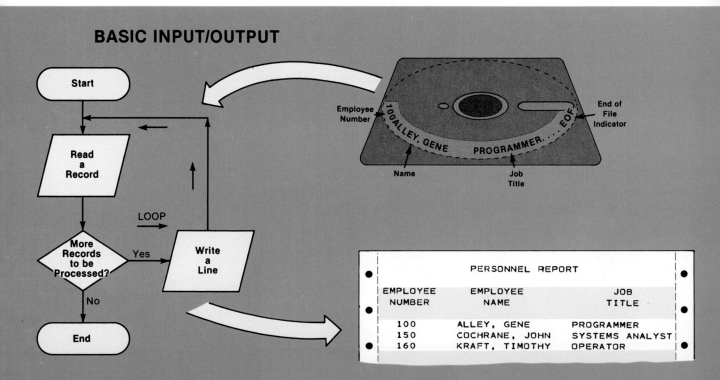

The input file in the example is stored on floppy disk. With all sequential input files, regardless of the medium on which they are stored, there must be some type of end-of-file indicator, which indicates the end of the data in the file. This is accomplished by placing special end-of-file characters after the last data record in the file. In the example, the entry EOF is used to illustrate this end-of-file marker.

The basic logic structure to implement this application is the Do While structure, which controls program looping. In the logic shown, a read statement reads an input record. A test is then made to determine if the end-of-file indicator has been read. If it has not, there are more records to be processed. If there is a record to be processed, it is used to provide the data for writing a line on the report.

The read statement is again executed and the test for more records is performed. If there is a record to be processed, a line is written on the report and the read statement is again performed. This processing will continue until the end-of-file indicator is read, at which time the program is ended.

The Do While structure implements this loop, allowing all of the input records to be read and the report written.

Counters, accumulators, and printing final totals

A variety of calculations can be performed on a computer system, including adding, subtracting, multiplying, and dividing. When calculations are involved in the processing of data, there is often a need to accumulate totals and print these totals after all of the input records have been processed. These totals are called final totals.

In addition, it is many times desirable to count the number of input records that have been read and processed. For example, in a payroll application, it may be desirable to count the number of records processed and to accumulate a final total of the pay for all employees. This information may be necessary to maintain control over the number and amount of paychecks which are issued.

To illustrate the concept of counting the number of input records processed and accumulating a final total, a payroll application will be designed. In this example, a report of gross pay is to be prepared. The input records contain the employee number, employee name, hours worked, and pay rate. The report will contain these fields plus the gross pay for the employee, which is calculated by multiplying the hours worked times the pay rate. After all records have been processed, the total number of employees and the total payroll amount is to be printed.

COUNTERS, ACCUMULATORS, AND PRINTING FINAL TOTALS

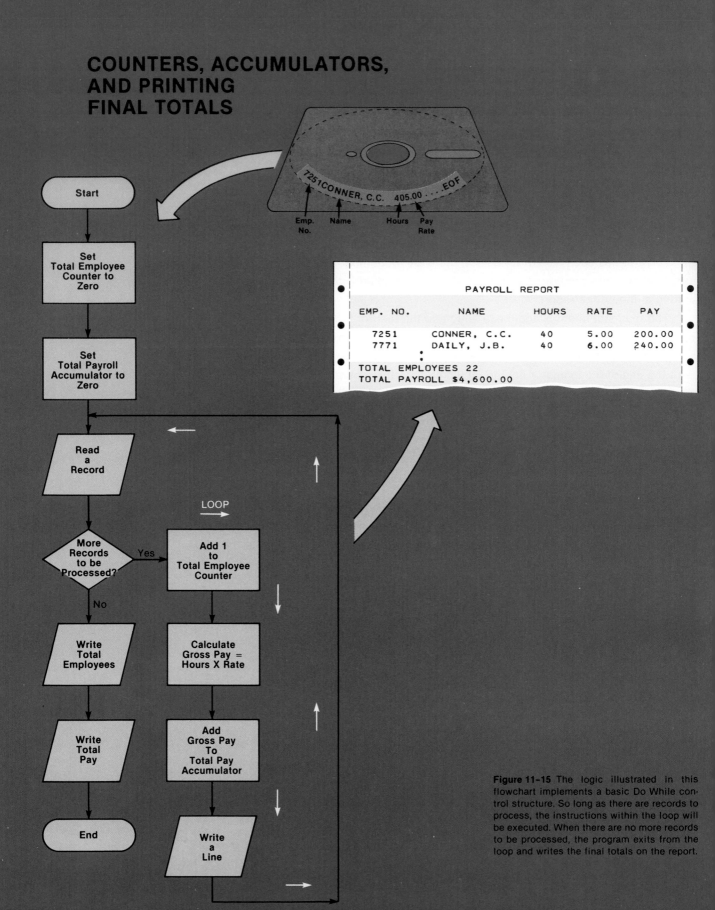

Figure 11-15 The logic illustrated in this flowchart implements a basic Do While control structure. So long as there are records to process, the instructions within the loop will be executed. When there are no more records to be processed, the program exits from the loop and writes the final totals on the report.

The logic to produce the report is illustrated by the flowchart in Figure 11–15. The basic structure to implement the required logic consists of the Sequence and the Do While control structures. The major difference between this program and the previous program is the increased number of individual operations that must be performed.

To count the number of records processed and accumulate the totals to be printed after all records have been processed, it is necessary to reserve areas of main computer storage for these totals. In addition, these areas must be set to zero as one of the first steps in the program logic so that the totals will be accumulated properly (Figure 11–16).

When a record is read and there is a record to be processed, the value "1" is added to the total employee counter, which is used to count the number of records read and processed. The gross pay is calculated by multiplying the hours times the pay rate. This value is then added to the value in the total pay accumulator. For the first record, the value in the total pay accumulator will be zero, since it was set to zero at the start of the program. Subsequent records will increase the value in the accumulator, which will contain the total gross pay for all employees. This processing will continue as long as there are records to be processed.

When the end-of-file indicator is read, the program exits from the Do While loop. Upon exit from the loop, the total number of employees is written on the report and then the total gross pay is written. The program then terminates.

It is important to note that although this program accomplishes considerably more processing than the program illustrated in Figure 11–14, the basic structure of the program is the same; that is, a loop is entered when there are more records to process. This looping continues until all of the input records have been read and processed. At that time, the program exits from the loop. This ability to loop is an important characteristic of computer programs because a single set of instructions can be written to process an unlimited number of input records in exactly the same way.

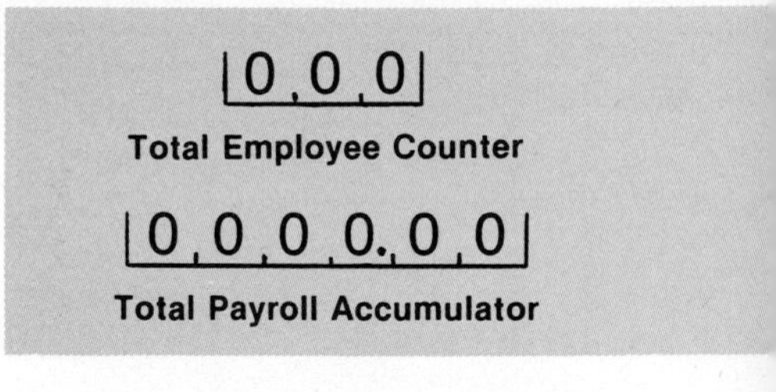

| 0 , 0 , 0 |

Total Employee Counter

| 0 , 0 , 0 , 0 , 0 |

Total Payroll Accumulator

Figure 11-16 The total employee counter field and the total payroll accumulator field must be set to zero prior to processing any input records.

Basic comparing

Another important characteristic of programs is their ability to compare the values stored in two fields and perform alternative operations based upon whether the value in one field is less than, equal to, or greater than the value in the other field. Comparing is implemented using the If-Then-Else control structure.

In order to illustrate the If-Then-Else control structure, an application which produces a sales report is illustrated in Figure 11–17. The input to the program is an input record containing the salesperson number, the salesperson name, and the sales amount. The report contains the salesperson number, the salesperson name, the sales amount, and the commission amount. The commission is calculated as follows: If the sales are greater than $500.00, then the commission is equal to the sales amount times 7%; while if the sales are equal to or less than $500.00, then the commission amount is equal to the sales amount times 5%. After all input records have been processed, the total of commissions paid to all sales people is to be printed.

The first step in the logic of the program is to set the total commissions accumulator to zero. A record is then read. If there is a record to process, the loop is entered. The first step in the loop is to determine if the sales are greater than $500.00. This is done by comparing the sales amount in the input record to a constant value of $500.00 which would be defined by the program and be stored in main computer storage.

If the sales amount is greater than $500.00, then the commission is calculated by multiplying the sales amount by 7%. If the sales amount is not greater than $500.00, the commission is calculated by multiplying the sales amount by 5%.

After the commission is calculated, it is added to the total commission accumulator and a line is printed on the report. The loop is then repeated so long as there are records to process.

It is important to note that there is a single entry into the comparison which determines the commission percentage. In addition, there is one exit point after the commission is calculated. Thus, regardless of whether the commission percentage is 5% or 7%, the If-Then-Else structure exits at a common exit point. Applying the concept of a single entry point and a single exit point greatly improves and simplifies the logic for programs and results in programs that are substantially easier to read, modify, and maintain.

After all records have been processed, the total commission for all employees is printed and processing is terminated.

BASIC COMPARING

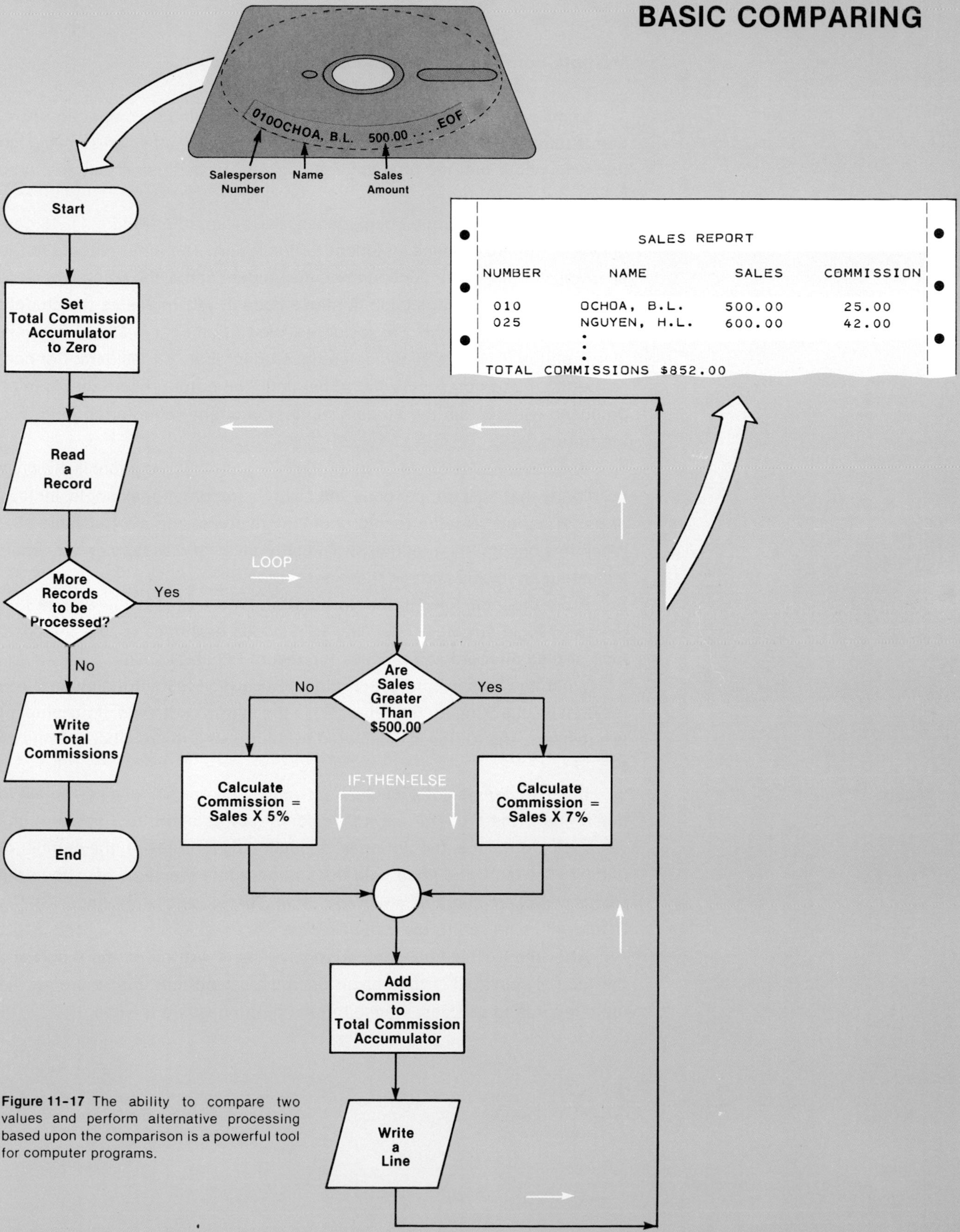

Figure 11-17 The ability to compare two values and perform alternative processing based upon the comparison is a powerful tool for computer programs.

Multiple comparisons — use of record codes

In many programs, there will be more than a single comparing operation required within the logic of a program. It is important when such design problems occur that the program logic be approached using only the three basic control structures.

To illustrate multiple comparisons, the example in Figure 11–18 contains the logic to produce a student tuition report. The input records to the program contain the student number, the student name, the number of units being taken, and a status code. A status code of "R" indicates the student is a resident of the state. For residents, the tuition cost is $25.00 per unit.

A status code of "N" indicates the student is a non-resident. For non-residents, the tuition cost is $50.00 per unit. The output record that is to be produced will contain the student number, student name, total units, and the tuition.

Whenever codes are to be recorded in an input record, there is always a possibility that an improper code will be in the record. For example, instead of an "R" or an "N," the record could, by mistake, contain the value "S." When this occurs, the program should print an error message on the report indicating an invalid code in the input record.

From the logic used in the flowchart in Figure 11–18, it is evident that the basic logic structure is similar to previous examples in that the basic loop of read a record and process the record is established.

When the loop is entered, the first comparison tests if the student is a resident by checking for the value "R" in the status code field. If the student is a resident, the tuition is calculated by multiplying the number of units by $25.00.

If the student is not a resident, a comparison operation is performed to determine if the student is a non-resident (status code field contains the value "N"). If it does, the tuition is calculated by multiplying the number of units by $50.00. If the code field does not contain the value "N," then the status code field contains an invalid value. Therefore, the message "Status Unknown" is moved to the output report.

After the If-Then-Else comparisons, a line is written on the report and the loop is repeated. These basic operations continue until there are no more records to process, at which time the processing is ended.

Figure 11–18 The flowchart on the opposite page illustrates the use of multiple comparison operations to prepare a school tuition report.

COMPARING — RECORD CODES

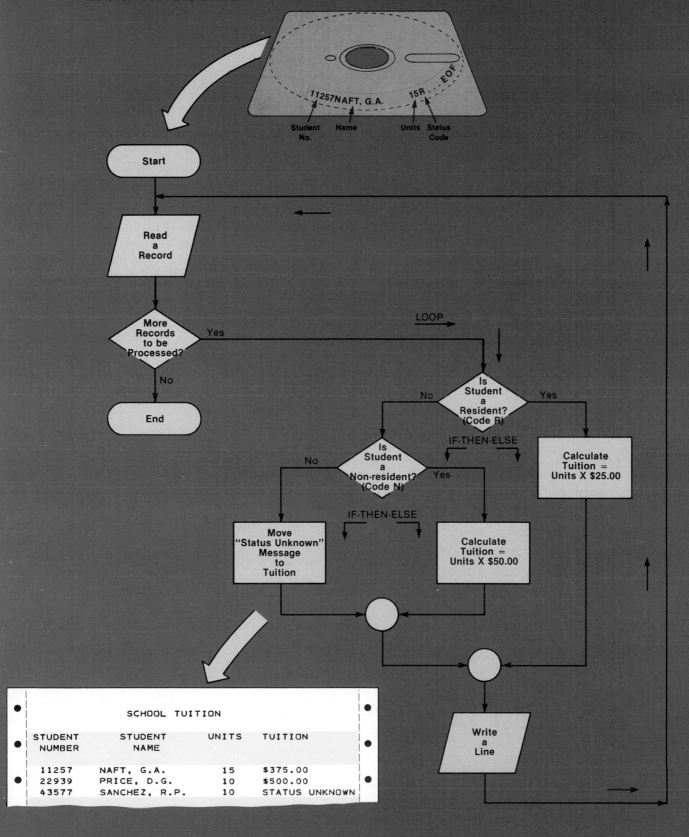

Student No. Name Units Status Code

11257NAFT, G.A. 15R · · · EOF

Start

Read a Record

More Records to be Processed? Yes → LOOP →

No

End

Is Student a Resident? (Code R)

No ← | → Yes

IF-THEN-ELSE

Calculate Tuition = Units X $25.00

Is Student a Non-resident? (Code N)

No | Yes

IF-THEN-ELSE

Move "Status Unknown" Message to Tuition

Calculate Tuition = Units X $50.00

Write a Line

SCHOOL TUITION

STUDENT NUMBER	STUDENT NAME	UNITS	TUITION
11257	NAFT, G.A.	15	$375.00
22939	PRICE, D.G.	10	$500.00
43577	SANCHEZ, R.P.	10	STATUS UNKNOWN

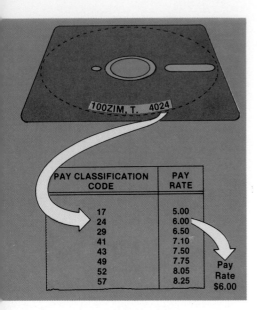

Figure 11-19 The table above contains the pay classification code and the related pay rate (together called a table element). In order to extract the pay rate, the table is searched element by element until a pay code in the table is found to be equal to the pay code in the input record. When this occurs, the corresponding pay rate can be used for processing.

SUBSCRIPT	PAY CLASSIFICATION CODE	PAY RATE
(1)	17	5.00
(2)	24	6.00
(3)	29	6.50
(4)	41	7.10
(5)	43	7.50
(6)	49	7.75
(7)	52	8.05
(8)	57	8.25

Figure 11-20 Each element in the table is identified by a subscript. A subscript is a field containing a value referencing an item in the table. The value in the subscript field can be varied so different elements can be referenced.

Searching a table

In some business applications, data is stored in the form of a table and is accessed as required during the processing of the input records. For example, assume a company has 20 different pay classifications for 2,000 employees. Rather than storing the pay rates in the individual payroll record for each employee, a pay classification code would instead be stored in the record. A table would then be created that contained the pay classification codes and the related pay rates (Figure 11-19). When the pay rate is required for processing the payroll, the pay classification code could be used as the basis for extracting the pay rate from the table.

For example, if a pay classification code of 24 is contained in the input record, the table could be searched until pay classification code 24 is found. The corresponding pay rate could then be extracted from the table.

The benefit of a table, as used in this example, is the ease with which changes can be made to the employee pay rates. For example, if there was a cost of living pay increase for all employees, only the twenty entries in the table would have to be changed, rather than the entries in each of the 2,000 payroll records.

To reference the various elements within a table, a subscript is commonly used. A subscript is a field which contains a value referencing a particular element within a table. For example, the value 1 in the subscript field would reference the first element in the table; the value 2 in the subscript field would reference the second element in the table; and so on (Figure 11-20).

The logic for a table search and for creating a payroll report is shown in Figure 11-21. In this example, the input records contain the employee number, employee name, the hours worked, and the pay classification code. The payroll report contains the employee number, employee name, hours worked, the pay rate, and the gross pay (hours X pay rate). The pay rate is to be extracted from the table.

After a record is read and it is determined that there are records to be processed, the main loop is entered. The first step is to set a subscript field to the value 1. This is done to initialize the subscript for the table search. A loop is then entered where the pay code in the input record is compared to the first element in the table. The first element is identified by the value 1 in the subscript field. The condition to exit from the loop is one of the following: Either the pay code in the input record is equal to the pay code in the table or the value in the subscript is greater than the number of entries in the table (that is, the value in the subscript is greater than 20 in this example).

SEARCHING A TABLE

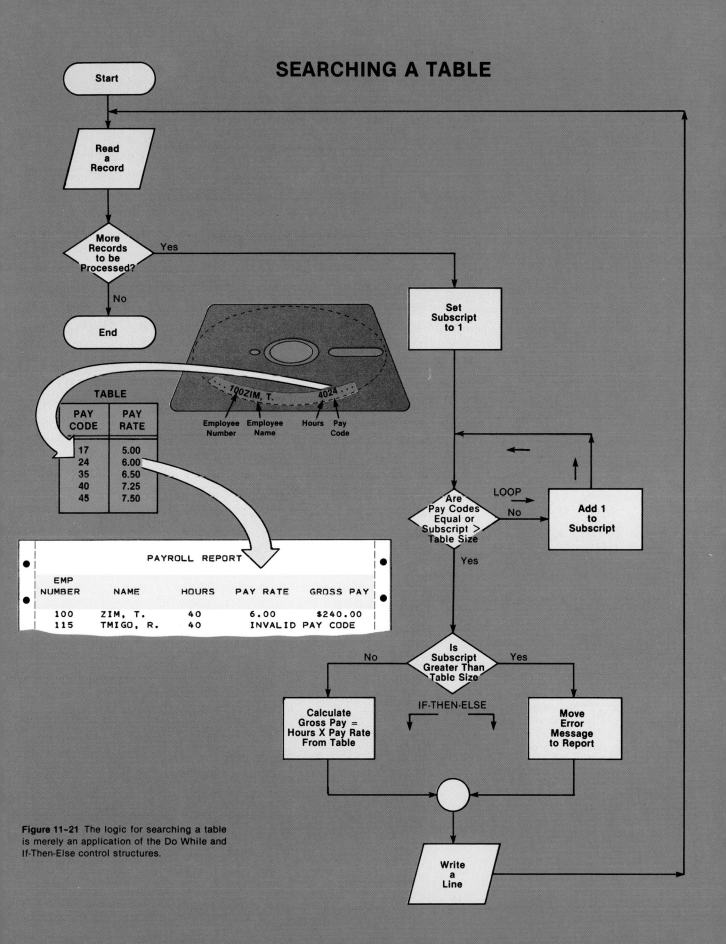

Figure 11-21 The logic for searching a table is merely an application of the Do While and If-Then-Else control structures.

If neither of these conditions is true, then the loop will be entered. The only instruction within the loop is to add the value 1 to the subscript. The conditional statement is then analyzed again. On the second "pass," the pay code in the input record will be compared to the second element in the table because the subscript will contain the value 2. The condition tested again is whether the pay code in the input record is equal to the pay code in the table or whether the value in the subscript is greater than 20. If neither of these conditions is true, the loop will again be entered and the value in the subscript will be incremented by 1.

This looping will continue until either the pay code in the input record is equal to a pay code in the table or the value in the subscript is greater than 20. When one of these conditions is true, an exit from the loop will occur and the next conditional statement will check if the subscript is greater than the table size (20). If it is, it means that the pay code in the input record was not found in the table; that is, the pay code in the input record is in error. When this occurs, an error message is moved to the report.

If the subscript is not greater than the table size, it means that a pay code was found in the table which was equal to the pay code in the input record. Using the pay rate from the table associated with the pay code, the gross pay is calculated.

A line is then written on the report and the main loop is then repeated, reading an input record and checking to determine if there is a record to process. When all of the input records have been read and processed, the program is ended.

The logic required to perform a table search is widely used in programming for both business and scientific applications. It is important that the programmer understand this logic, for it is an important programming technique.

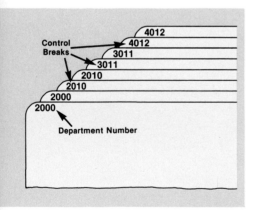

Figure 11-22 A control break occurs when data in a control field changes from that found in the field in the previous record. In the example above, a control break occurs when the department number changes.

Control breaks

Often when input records are being processed, it is required to print totals based upon conditions encountered during the processing of the records. For example, when preparing an inventory report, it may be required to print totals indicating the amount of inventory contained within each department of a company. In applications such as this, these totals are printed when a control break occurs.

A control break occurs when the data in a given field in an input record changes from the value found in the same field in the previous record (Figure 11-22).

In order to illustrate control break processing and the logic required to implement control break processing, an application creating an inventory report will be examined. The input records contain the department number, item number, item description, the quantity on hand, and the unit cost.

The format of the report is shown in Figure 11-23. It contains each of the fields from the input record plus the inventory value, which is calculated by multiplying the quantity on hand by the unit cost. In addition, when there is a control break, that is, when the department number changes, the total inventory value for the given department is printed. After all of the input records have been processed, a final total of all items in the inventory is printed.

Figure 11-23 When the department number changes (a control break occurs), the total inventory value for the department is printed. After all records have been processed, the total inventory value for all departments is printed.

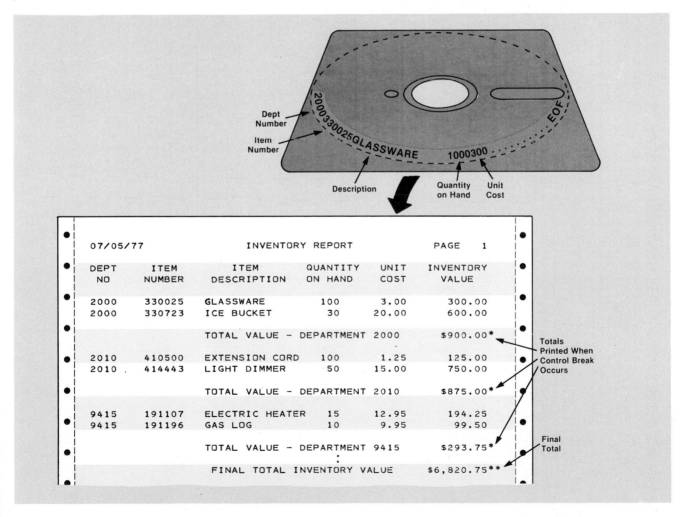

CONTROL BREAKS

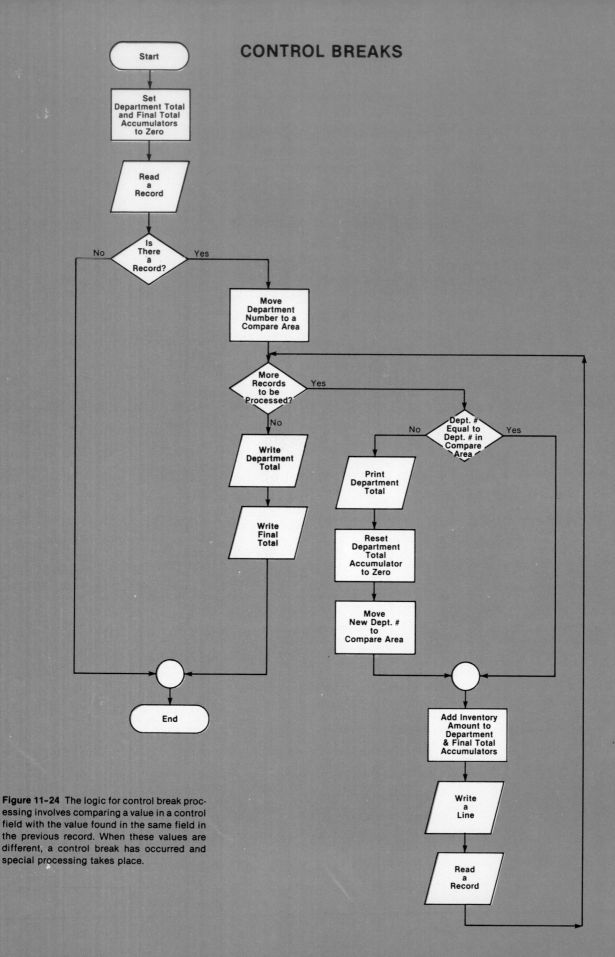

Figure 11-24 The logic for control break processing involves comparing a value in a control field with the value found in the same field in the previous record. When these values are different, a control break has occurred and special processing takes place.

The basic logic required for control break processing involves reading the input records, comparing the value in the control field with the value found in the previous record, printing control break totals if the values are different, and printing the detail information for the record just read.

The flowchart in Figure 11–24 illustrates the logic to produce the inventory report. The first step is to set the department total accumulator and the final total accumulator to zero. The first record is then read. This read operation, which is performed only one time, is called a prime read because it reads the first record only. This approach is used many times when the Do While loop of structured programming is used.

After the first read operation, a test is performed to determine if in fact a record was read. If for some reason there are no records in the input file, the program will be terminated.

If a record was read, the department number in the first input record is moved to a department number compare area (Figure 11–25). This operation is necessary so that as subsequent records are read, the department number in the records can be compared to the department number from the first record. When a change in department occurs, the control break processing must take place.

The Do While loop is then entered to process the file of records. The first step in the loop is to compare the department number in the record to be processed with the department number in the compare area. With the first record, they will be equal. Therefore, the inventory amount is added to the department and final total accumulators, the detail line is written on the report, and another record is read.

The read statement at the end of the Do While loop will either read another input record to be processed or will read the end-of-file indicator. If the end-of-file indicator is read, the loop will be terminated. If another input record is read, the department number in the record just read is compared to the department number in the compare area. If they are equal, the same detail processing just described will occur.

If they are not equal, a control break has occurred. The first step is to print the department total, which is contained in the department total accumulator. The value in the department total accumulator is then reset to zero, so that the values for the next department may be accumulated. The new department number is then moved to the department compare area so that subsequent records will be compared to the new department number.

After the control break processing has been executed, the input record with the new department number will be processed just as if a control break had not happened.

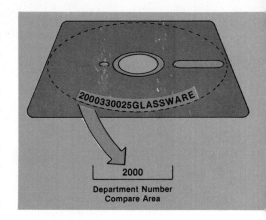

Figure 11-25 The department number from the first record read must be moved to the department number compare area. The department number stored in the compare area will be compared to the department number in each subsequent record which is read. When the department number in the record is different from the department number in the compare area, a control break has occurred. As part of the processing of the control break, the new department number will be moved to the compare area.

After all of the input records have been read and processed, the Do While loop is exited. At that time, the department total for the last department must be printed and then the final total is printed. After the final total has been printed, the program is terminated.

Many business applications require control break processing of some kind. Therefore, it is important to understand the control break logic.

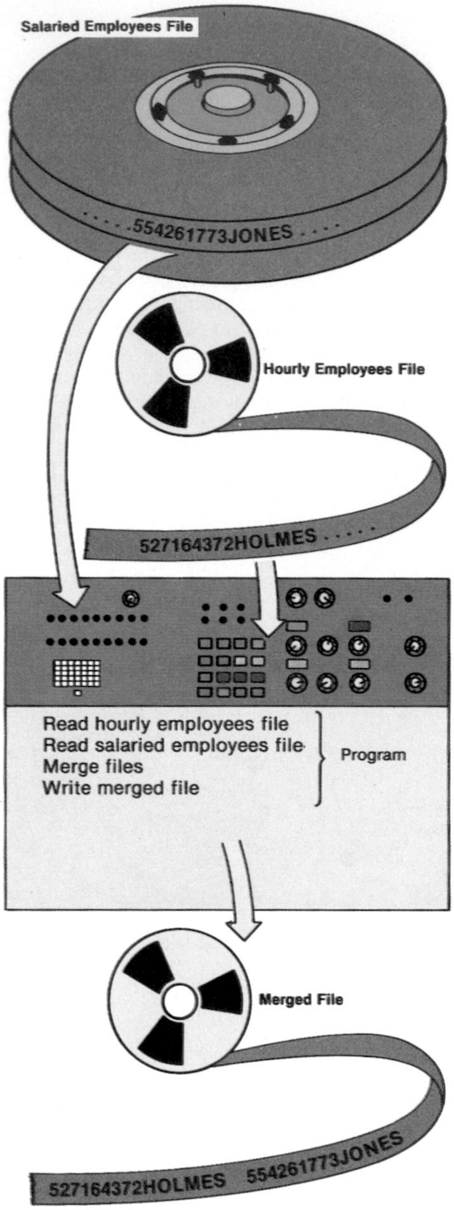

Merging two files

In some applications, it is necessary to merge two or more files into a single file. Merging is the process in which two or more files are combined into one file. For example, two sequential files, one containing the salaried personnel in social security number sequence and the other containing hourly employees in social security number sequence, can be merged into a single file (Figure 11-26). The merging takes place based upon the social security number, since both files are in an ascending sequence by social security number.

Each record in the two files to be merged contains the social security number and the employee name. The merged output file records will contain the same data.

The logic required to merge the two files is shown in Figure 11-27. To begin, a record from the hourly employees file is read and a record from the salaried employees file is read. If there is a record from both files, a Do While loop is entered. The If statement in the loop asks if the social security number in the record from the hourly employees file is less than the social security number in the record from the salaried employees file. If it is, then the record from the hourly employees file will be written on the new merged file. If, however, the salaried employee social security number is less than the hourly employee social security number, the record from the salaried employee file will be written on the new merged file.

After the record is placed on the new file, a record must be read from whichever file the record was obtained. Thus, if the record on the new file came from the hourly employees file, a new record will be read from that file; while, if the record came from the salaried employees file, a record must be read from that file. The loop is then repeated.

It should be noted in this application that the files should never contain records with equal social security numbers because each social security number is unique. Therefore, this condition is not tested for in this logic.

Figure 11-26 When merging takes place, the records from two or more input files are combined and written on one output file.

MERGING TWO FILES

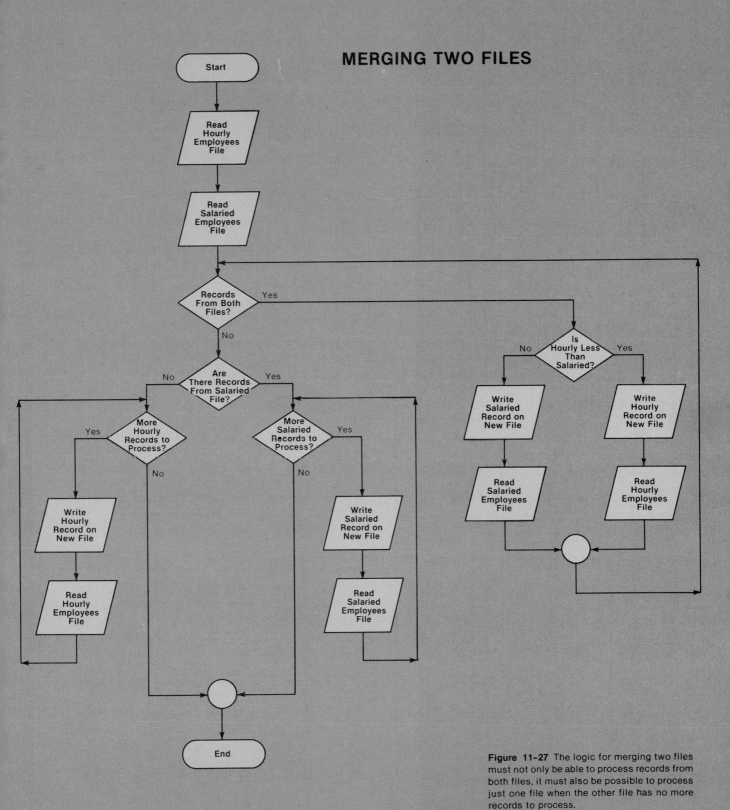

Figure 11-27 The logic for merging two files must not only be able to process records from both files, it must also be possible to process just one file when the other file has no more records to process.

So long as there are records from both files to read and process, the looping will continue. When reading records from two files, one file will reach end-of-file before the other. When end-of-file is reached for either file, the loop is exited and a conditional statement asks if there are records from the salaried file. If there are, it means that the hourly file has no more records. Therefore, a Do While loop is entered which writes the current salaried employee record and then reads another record from the salaried file. This loop will continue until there are no more records from the salaried file. When this occurs, there are no more records left in either input file, so the program is terminated.

If, after one of the files is found to be at end-of-file there are no records in the salaried file, it means there are records in the hourly employees file. A Do While loop is, therefore, entered to write the current record from the hourly employees file and then read a record from the file. This looping will continue until there are no more records in the hourly employees file, at which time the program will be terminated.

This merging logic, or variations on this logic, is used in many business applications where two or more sequential files are input to a program. Thus, this logic should be understood, as it is commonly found in business application programs.

DECISION TABLES

In some applications, there can be a number of conditions which may occur within the program. In some cases, it is difficult to keep all of the conditions and the processing which is to occur as a result of these conditions in mind. Decision tables can be used to help clarify the actions which must be taken under certain conditions within the program.

A decision table is a graphical representation of the logical decisions that must be made concerning certain conditions which can occur within a program. In a decision table, both the conditions which must be tested and the actions which will be taken are graphically represented (Figure 11–28). The conditions which may occur are placed in the upper left-hand portion of the decision table (called the condition stub). The actions to be taken based upon the conditions are specified in the lower left-hand portion of the table (called the action stub).

		1	2	3	4	5	6	7	8
CONDITIONS	Account Current	Y	Y	Y	Y	N	N	N	N
	Purchase Within Credit Limit	Y	N	Y	N	Y	N	Y	N
	Payment Received Last 25 Days	Y	Y	N	N	Y	Y	N	N
ACTIONS	Unconditionally Approved	X							
	Approve, Subject to Credit Office			X					
	Deny, Subject to Credit Office		X		X	X	X	X	
	Send to Credit Office		X	X	X	X	X	X	
	Unconditionally Deny								X

Figure 11-28 A decision table is a graphical representation of the logical decisions which must be made concerning certain conditions which can occur within a program. It consists of the condition stub (upper left), condition entry (upper right), action stub (lower left), and action entry (lower right).

The upper right portion of the table is called the condition entry part of the table. It is in this area that the different combinations of conditions which can occur are specified. In the example in Figure 11-28, the conditions pertain to an order entry system. The programmer has three criteria on which to base the approval of credit — account current, purchase within credit limit, and payment received in last 25 days. The condition entry part of the decision table is used to indicate the various combinations of these three conditions that can occur.

There are five actions which can possibly be taken — unconditionally approved; approve, subject to credit office; deny, subject to credit office; send to credit office; and unconditionally deny. The actions to be taken are indicated in the lower right portion of the table, which is called the action entry area.

The numbers across the top of the table are called the rules, and identify the vertical columns. Each vertical column gives the combination of conditions that can occur and the corresponding actions which should be taken. For example, Rule 1 says if the account is current (Y), the purchase is within the credit limit (Y), and a payment has been received within the last 25 days (Y), then the credit should be unconditionally approved. Rule 2 says that if the account is current (Y), the purchase is not within the credit limit (N), and payment has been received within the last 25 days (Y), then credit is denied, subject to review by the credit office. In Rule 2, two actions are taken — the credit is denied and the credit request is sent to the credit office for review. The other rules are read in a similar fashion.

Decision tables can be useful to systems analysts when they document the program specifications because decision tables can many times be more clear than a narrative. In addition, they are useful to programmers when a combination of conditions must be checked to ensure that the proper processing will be included in the program.

Chapter summary

The following points have been discussed and explained in this chapter.

1. Computer programming has posed the greatest intellectual challenge mankind has faced in pure logic and complexity.

2. The program development cycle consists of: a) Review of program specifications; b) Program design; c) Program coding; d) Program testing; e) Program documentation.

3. A program can be defined as a series of instructions which directs the computer to perform a sequence of tasks that produces a desired output.

4. Program statements fall into six major categories: a) Statements to define files and records; b) Statements to define other data; c) Statements which move data; d) Arithmetic statements; e) Comparison statements; f) Input/output statements.

5. At the end of the program specifications review, the programmer should completely understand what processing is to be performed, what data is to be processed, and how the output is to be derived from the data available to the program.

6. The earliest program design methodologies used the flowchart as the design tool. Flowcharting symbols were standardized by the American National Standards Institute.

7. When designing a program using the flowchart, the programmer begins by defining the precise sequence in which each operation is to be performed.

8. The value of a flowchart is that it graphically represents the steps in the solution of a problem.

9. The use of a flowchart alone did not produce well-designed programs because there was no scientific basis on which to base the logic of the program.

10. Structured programming is defined as a method of programming that uses three control structures: a) Sequence; b) If-Then-Else; c) Do While. These three structures are used to produce highly structured units of code that are easily read and, therefore, easily maintained.

11. The sequence structure specifies that one event is to occur immediately after another.

12. The If-Then-Else structure is used for conditional statements. The "If" portion of the structure tests a given condition. If the condition is true, the "Then" portion of the structure is executed. If the condition is not true, the "Else" portion of the structure is executed.

13. The Do While structure is used to allow program looping. Looping means that one or more events are to occur so long as a given condition remains true.

14. There is but one entry point and one exit point in each of the three control structures.

15. Pseudocode is an expression of the logical steps to be taken in the solution of a problem written in English statements.

16. The advantage of pseudocode is that a great deal of time need not be spent in drawing symbols and determining how to arrange symbols on a sheet of paper, while at the same time attempting to determine the program logic. The disadvantage is that a graphic representation is not available with pseudocode.

17. A subroutine is a series of computer instructions which, together, accomplish a given task. A subroutine can be stored in a library on tape or disk and can be included in a program when required.

18. Using a design methodology called structured design results in a program consisting of many small portions of code called modules. Each module performs one task within the program.

19. The major benefit of structured design is that each of the modules is logically fairly simple, leading to a program which is easier to design and easier to read and understand when maintenance must be performed.

20. The most widely taught method for deriving the structure of a program uses the IPO Chart as the primary design tool.

21. The IPO Chart is used to specify the output, input, and major processing tasks required in a program. Each of the major processing tasks is examined to determine if the task should be performed in a separate module. Through this repeating process, the structure of a program is determined and is illustrated by a hierarchy chart.

22. When egoless programming is practiced, a program is viewed as a product which should be examined to make the product better.

23. A structured walkthrough is an organized review of a program by other programmers with the intent of finding any errors which have been made in the program.

24. Seven common design problems are: a) Basic input/output operations; b) Basic calculating, counting records, and accumulating totals; c) Basic comparing operations; d) Processing different record types; e) Table searching; f) Control break processing; g) Merging two files.

25. A decision table is a graphical representation of the logical decisions that must be made concerning certain conditions which can occur within a program.

Student Learning Exercises

Review questions

1. What are the steps in the program development cycle?

2. Define the term "computer program." Name the six major categories of program statements.

3. What is the function of the program specifications review? What should the result of this review be?

4. What is a flowchart? How is it used when designing a program?

5. Why are flowcharts alone not sufficient to design a large computer program?

6. What is structured programming? Draw the three control structures used in structured programming.

7. What is pseudocode? What are the advantages and disadvantages of pseudocode?

8. Explain the significance of structured design. Outline the basic methodology to develop the structure of a program.

9. What is the use of an IPO Chart? Pseudocode Specifications?

10. What is egoless programming? Why must it be practiced when program walkthroughs are conducted?

11. Draw a flowchart illustrating the logic for a basic input/output program.

12. Draw a flowchart which illustrates the logic used for table searching.

13. Draw a flowchart which shows the logic used when control break processing is to occur.

14. What are seven common design problems found in business applications programming? Give an example of each.

15. What is a decision table? Devise a logical problem, state the problem in narrative form, and then draw a decision table illustrating the solution to the problem stated.

Controversial issues in data processing

1. Some programmers feel that it really is not necessary to spend a great deal of time designing a program. They think that the program should be coded as quickly as possible and then they can test the program to find any errors which occur. They are backed up in many cases by their department management, who feel that a programmer is really "working" when coding a program, not when designing a program. Do you feel that this approach will develop good programs? Defend your position.

2. A number of studies have been conducted to determine the type of people who are programmers. These studies tend to indicate that programmers prefer to work alone and do not seek active social interaction with their peers when they are working. In order to successfully implement egoless programming and structured walkthroughs, however, there must be a great deal of interaction among the programmers reviewing programs. Do you think that programmers prefer to work alone because they do not believe in egoless programming? Or, do you think programmers are just naturally "loners"? What can be done to encourage programmers to participate in walkthroughs and program reviews? Should a different type of person be hired for programming jobs?

Research projects

1. Different design methodologies, ranging from none at all to structured design, are used in computer installations. Contact some large and small installations in your area and find out the way in which they design their computer programs. Prepare a report on your findings for the class.

2. Obtain a copy of The Psychology of Computer Programming by Gerald M. Weinberg, published by Van Nostrand Reinhold Company. Pick a chapter in the book and prepare a report on the chapter to be given orally in class. Include the major points that Weinberg makes, the anecdotes that he uses to explain his points, and the reasons Weinberg feels as he does.

Chapter 12
Programming Languages — Coding and Testing Programs

Objectives

- A familiarization with the seven most widely used programming languages: Assembler Language, FORTRAN, COBOL, PL/I, RPG, BASIC, and Pascal

- An understanding of compilers and interpreters

- An introduction to program testing procedures

- An understanding of the role of program documentation

- An understanding of the role and use of operating systems

Chapter 12

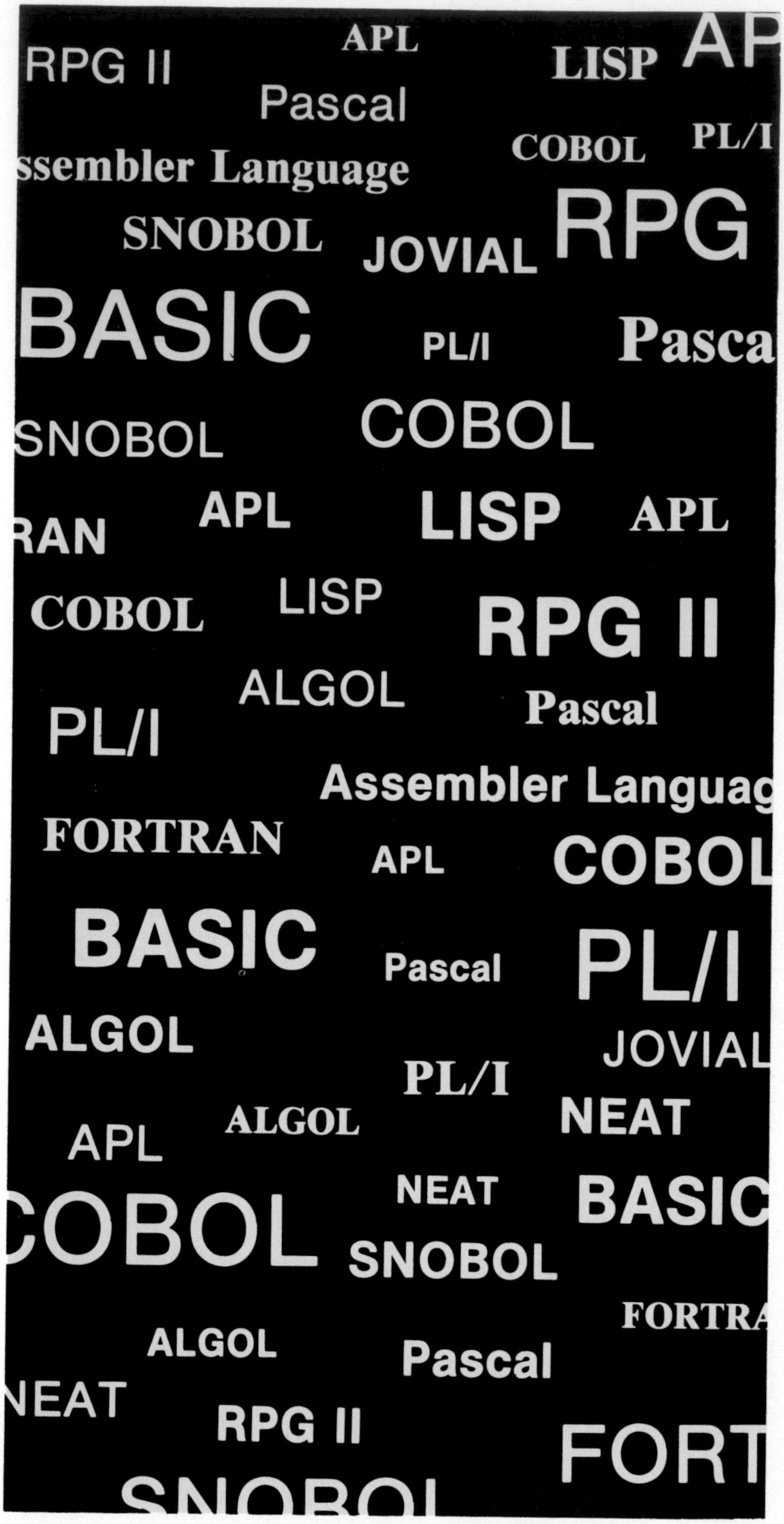

Figure 12-1 More than 200 programming languages have been developed during the past 30 years for use in all application areas.

Programming Languages — Coding and Testing Programs

"There is a world of difference between a correct program and a good program."[1]

Introduction

As discussed in Chapter 11, the writing of a program is accomplished as a series of steps called the program development cycle. The steps in the program development cycle are:

1. Review the system and program specifications.
2. Design the program.
3. Code the program.
4. Test the program.
5. Document the program.

The material in Chapter 11 covered the first two steps in the program development cycle. This chapter will cover coding the program, testing the program, and documenting the program.

Before discussing the detailed steps, however, it is useful to review languages which are available to the programmer when coding the program. Therefore, the major programming languages are also investigated in this chapter.

MAJOR PROGRAMMING LANGUAGES

Although it has been documented that there are over 200 different programming languages which have been developed during the past 30 years, the major programming languages in use today are: 1) Assembler Language; 2) FORTRAN; 3) COBOL; 4) PL/I; 5) RPG; 6) BASIC; 7) Pascal. These programming languages are widely used in industry, government, and education (Figure 12–1).

---

1 Weinberg, Wright, Kaufman, Goetz, HIGH LEVEL COBOL PROGRAMMING, Winthrop Publishers, 1977.

Assembler language

The programming for the first stored-program computer systems was performed in machine language, which is a language directly "understood" by the computer's electronic circuitry. Since machine language programming was a very difficult and burdensome task, programming languages were developed to facilitate the coding process.

The first programming languages were symbolic programming languages, commonly called assembler languages. These languages use symbolic notation to represent the machine language instructions. Symbolic programming languages are closely related to machine language and the internal architecture of the computer system on which they are used. They are called low-level languages since they are so closely related to the machines. Nearly all computer systems have an assembler language available for use.

An assembler language program consists of a series of individual statements or instructions which direct the computer to carry out the processing that is to occur. An assembler language statement consists of three parts: 1) A label; 2) An operation code; 3) One or more operands.

The label is a name which is used to identify and reference an instruction in the program. The operation code is a symbolic notation which specifies the particular operation to be performed, such as move, add, subtract, and so on (Figure 12–2). The operand represents the register or the location in storage where the data to be processed is located. An example of assembler language instructions is shown in Figure 12–3.

All assembler languages for all computers are not the same. This is because the language is directly related to the internal architecture of the computer, and assembler languages are not designed to be machine-independent. Thus, the format of the instruction and the exact instructions available will vary from machine to machine.

A segment of an assembler language program written for an IBM System/370 computer system is illustrated in Figure 12–4. Programs are normally written on specially designed coding forms, since many languages require entries such as the labels, operation codes, and operands to be recorded in predetermined columns so that the translator programs used to translate the code from symbolic to machine language can locate the various portions of the instruction.

INSTRUCTION	SYMBOLIC OPERATION CODE	MACHINE LANGUAGE OPERATION CODE
Add Decimal	AP	FA
Compare Decimal	CP	F9
Divide Decimal	DP	FD
Edit	ED	DE
Multiply Decimal	MP	FC
Subtract Decimal	SP	FB
Zero and Add	ZAP	F8
Branch and Link	BALR	05
Branch on Count	BCTR	06
Convert to Binary	CVB	4F
Convert to Decimal	CVD	4E
Insert Character	IC	43
Move	MVC	D2
OR	OR	16
Pack	PACK	F2
Store Character	STC	42
Start I/O	SIO	9C
Test Channel	TCH	9F
Test I/O	TIO	9D

Figure 12-2 Many individual operation codes comprise the instruction set of an assembler language. Some languages have over 100 individual instructions that can be used when writing a program.

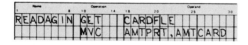

Figure 12-3 The two assembler language instructions above cause an input record to be read (GET), and a field to be moved (MVC). The GET statement is called a "macro." From this single statement, a series of machine language instructions will be generated. Most assembler languages provide a limited number of macros to handle complex operations such as input/output processing. The MVC operation code generates a single machine language instruction to move data from one area to another.

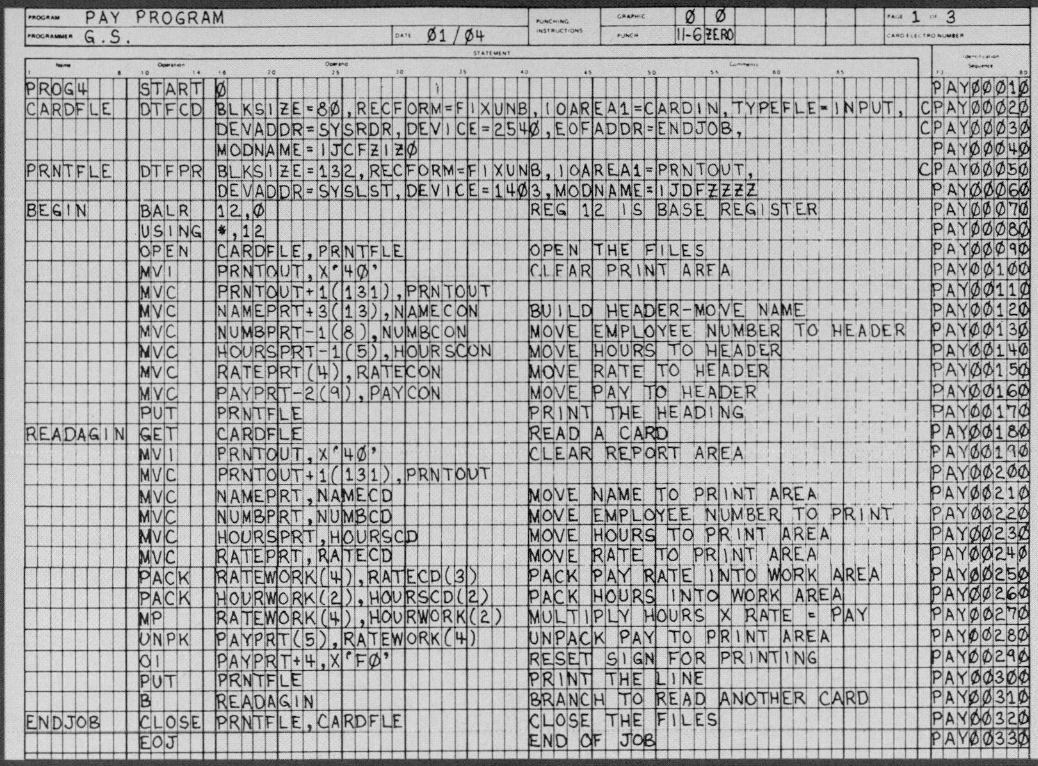

```
PROGRAM  PAY PROGRAM                              GRAPHIC  0  0        PAGE 1 OF 3
PROGRAMMER  G.S.              DATE 01/04  PUNCH  11-6 ZERO

PROG4    START  0                                                          PAY00010
CARDFLE  DTFCD  BLKSIZE=80,RECFORM=FIXUNB,IOAREA1=CARDIN,TYPEFLE=INPUT,   CPAY00020
                DEVADDR=SYSRDR,DEVICE=2540,EOFADDR=ENDJOB,                CPAY00030
                MODNAME=IJCFZIZ0                                           PAY00040
PRNTFLE  DTFPR  BLKSIZE=132,RECFORM=FIXUNB,IOAREA1=PRNTOUT,              CPAY00050
                DEVADDR=SYSLST,DEVICE=1403,MODNAME=IJDFZZZZ                PAY00060
BEGIN    BALR   12,0                    REG 12 IS BASE REGISTER            PAY00070
         USING  *,12                                                       PAY00080
         OPEN   CARDFLE,PRNTFLE         OPEN THE FILES                     PAY00090
         MVI    PRNTOUT,X'40'           CLEAR PRINT AREA                   PAY00100
         MVC    PRNTOUT+1(131),PRNTOUT                                     PAY00110
         MVC    NAMEPRT+3(13),NAMECON   BUILD HEADER-MOVE NAME             PAY00120
         MVC    NUMBPRT-1(8),NUMBCON    MOVE EMPLOYEE NUMBER TO HEADER     PAY00130
         MVC    HOURSPRT-1(5),HOURSCON  MOVE HOURS TO HEADER               PAY00140
         MVC    RATEPRT(4),RATECON      MOVE RATE TO HEADER                PAY00150
         MVC    PAYPRT-2(9),PAYCON      MOVE PAY TO HEADER                 PAY00160
         PUT    PRNTFLE                 PRINT THE HEADING                  PAY00170
READAGIN GET    CARDFLE                 READ A CARD                        PAY00180
         MVI    PRNTOUT,X'40'           CLEAR REPORT AREA                  PAY00190
         MVC    PRNTOUT+1(131),PRNTOUT                                     PAY00200
         MVC    NAMEPRT,NAMECD          MOVE NAME TO PRINT AREA            PAY00210
         MVC    NUMBPRT,NUMBCD          MOVE EMPLOYEE NUMBER TO PRINT      PAY00220
         MVC    HOURSPRT,HOURSCD        MOVE HOURS TO PRINT AREA           PAY00230
         MVC    RATEPRT,RATECD          MOVE RATE TO PRINT AREA            PAY00240
         PACK   RATEWORK(4),RATECD(3)   PACK PAY RATE INTO WORK AREA       PAY00250
         PACK   HOURWORK(2),HOURSCD(2)  PACK HOURS INTO WORK AREA          PAY00260
         MP     RATEWORK(4),HOURWORK(2) MULTIPLY HOURS X RATE = PAY        PAY00270
         UNPK   PAYPRT(5),RATEWORK(4)   UNPACK PAY TO PRINT AREA           PAY00280
         OI     PAYPRT+4,X'F0'          RESET SIGN FOR PRINTING            PAY00290
         PUT    PRNTFLE                 PRINT THE LINE                     PAY00300
         B      READAGIN                BRANCH TO READ ANOTHER CARD        PAY00310
ENDJOB   CLOSE  PRNTFLE,CARDFLE         CLOSE THE FILES                    PAY00320
         EOJ                            END OF JOB                         PAY00330
```

Advantages and disadvantages of assembler language

The principal advantage of assembler language is that a program can be written which is very efficient in terms of execution time and main storage usage. This is because nearly every instruction is written on a one-for-one basis with machine language, allowing the programmer to code the program using only those instructions absolutely needed to process the data. In addition, because all the instructions of a computer are available to the assembler language programmer, the programmer can readily manipulate individual records, fields within records, characters within fields, and even bits within bytes.

There are several significant disadvantages of assembler language. First, since assembler language reflects the architecture of the machine it is used on, there is little compatibility between different assembler languages, meaning that a program coded in assembler language for one machine will not run on machines from a different or even, sometimes, the same manufacturer.

Additionally, an assembler language programmer will normally have to write a larger number of statements to solve a given problem than will a programmer using a high-level language. Also, because assembler language statements are almost one-for-one with the computer's machine language, assembler language programs are often more difficult to write, read, and maintain than programs written in high-level languages.

Figure 12-4 The assembler language program above is for the IBM System/370 computer system. The program consists of a series of individual steps leading to the solution of the problem. The English-language statements down the center of the coding sheets are comments that serve to document the program.

SYMBOL	MEANING
+	Addition
–	Subtraction
*	Multiplication
/	Division
**	Exponentiation

Figure 12-5 The FORTRAN arithmetic operators are used in statements to specify the calculations that are to occur.

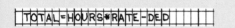

Figure 12-6 The FORTRAN statement above will cause the data in the field referenced by the variable name HOURS to be multiplied by the data in the RATE field. The value in the DED field is subtracted from the multiplication result and the final answer is stored in the TOTAL field. This type of notation in a programming language greatly simplified writing instructions of a mathematical nature.

FORTRAN

A programming language in which the program statements are not closely related to the internal characteristics of the computer is called a high-level programming language. As a general rule, one statement in a high-level programming language will develop a number of machine language instructions. This is in contrast to assembler languages, where one statement normally generates one machine language instruction. High-level programming languages were developed to make programming easier and less error-prone.

One of the earliest high-level programming languages was FORTRAN (FORmula TRANslation). FORTRAN, developed by IBM and released in 1957, was originally designed as a programming language to be used by scientists, engineers, and mathematicians. The language is noted for its ability to express mathematical expressions and equations easily.

When using FORTRAN, a programmer expresses mathematical operations through the use of arithmetic operators which are combined to form the expression (Figure 12-5).

To form the expression, a variable name which identifies the field where the result of the operation is to be stored is written on the left side of an equal sign; and the arithmetic operation to be performed is written on the right of the equal sign (Figure 12-6). After the expression is evaluated, the answer is placed in the location in storage identified by the variable name on the left.

Although FORTRAN was originally developed by IBM and was not intended to be a universal language, by the early 1960's virtually all manufacturers of computer systems had either delivered or were committed to producing some version of FORTRAN.

In May, 1962, a committee was established to develop a standard for FORTRAN which would specify those features of the language that should be available for all machines. In 1966, after nearly four years of development, FORTRAN standards were published through the auspices of the American Standards Association (now known as the American National Standards Institute or ANSI). The American Standards Association was the authority for establishing industrial standards in the United States. Thus, FORTRAN has the distinction of being the first programming language that was standardized.

A FORTRAN program is illustrated in Figure 12-7. The program is written on a special coding form that is designed to identify the columns where entries must be made.

| | PROGRAM | ECONOMIC ORDER QUANTITY | | PUNCHING INSTRUCTIONS | GRAPHIC | Ø Ø | |
| PROGRAMMER | G. S. | | DATE 01/04 | | PUNCH | II-6 ZERO | |

```
C     THIS PROGRAM CALCULATES ECONOMIC ORDER-QUANTITY
C
  100 FORMAT('1',8X,'REPORT OF ECONOMIC ORDER QUANTITY')
  200 FORMAT(I3,F4.2,F4.3,F6.0)
  300 FORMAT(1X,I3,5X,I6,F5.2,5X,F5.3,5X,I6)

    1 READ(1,200)NUMBER,SCOST,CCOST,REQ
      IF(NUMBER-999)2,3,3
    2 EOQ=SQRT(2.0*(REQ*SCOST)/CCOST)
      IEOQ=EOQ
      IREQ=REQ
      WRITE(3,300)NUMBER,IREQ,SCOST,CCOST,IEOQ
      GO TO 1
    3 STOP
      END
```

Advantages and disadvantages of FORTRAN

A significant advantage of FORTRAN is the easy expression of complex mathematical calculations through the use of arithmetic operators. In addition, because FORTRAN is a high-level language, the programmer can concentrate on the solution to the problem rather than the internal characteristics of the computer, as is necessary when programming in assembler language.

The primary disadvantage of FORTRAN and many other high-level languages is that they do not have the versatility or capabilities of an assembler language in manipulating records, individual characters, or bits within a byte.

In addition, FORTRAN has several disadvantages when used as a business programming language. It has limited file processing capabilities, limited ability to define and effectively process alphabetic data, and limited ability to control the format of the printed report (such as printing commas, decimal points, and other punctuation). For these reasons, FORTRAN is not widely used for business applications programming. It is very widely used, however, in scientific applications and is a very effective language when solving the problems for which it was designed.

Figure 12-7 The FORTRAN program above illustrates calculating an economic order quantity. Note in the calculation statement the entry SQRT. SQRT is one of many functions that are a part of the FORTRAN language. This entry causes the square root of the expression to be taken. Other functions available with FORTRAN can perform such tasks as determining the sin, cosine, or tangent of an angle; finding the cube root of a number; and finding the largest number in a list of many numbers.

COBOL

One of the most widely used programming languages for business applications is COBOL (COmmon Business Oriented Language). COBOL was developed by a group of computer users and manufacturers and was released in 1960 as a high-level business-oriented programming language.

One of the stated objectives was that the language was to be machine-independent, meaning that a program written in COBOL should be able to be run on a variety of computer systems from a variety of manufacturers with little or no change. COBOL was also designed to be written in English-like form and to be self-documenting.

Nearly every manufacturer of medium and large-scale computer systems has undertaken the implementation of COBOL. The success of COBOL can be credited to two major factors. First, there was a definite need for a business-oriented high-level programming language, as it was recognized that programming in a low-level language was difficult and error-prone; and FORTRAN was not entirely suited for business applications.

Secondly, there was strong pressure from the federal government for the establishment of a common language for business. Recognizing the need for a programming language that could be used on a variety of computer systems, the federal government in the early 1960's specified that if a company wanted to sell or lease computer systems to the federal government, it had to have COBOL software available unless it could demonstrate that COBOL was not needed for the particular class of problems to be solved. Since the federal government was the single largest user of computers, manufacturers quickly recognized the value of developing this software.

After going through a number of revisions, COBOL was officially approved as a United States standard in 1968. Subsequent revisions of the language led to the 1974 ANSI Standard COBOL, which is currently in use on most computer systems.

Writing instructions in COBOL

COBOL was designed to enable statements to be written in English-like form. Every effort was made to create formats for statements which could be easily written and understood. COBOL statements are composed of "verbs" to cause such functions as input/output, comparing, and calculations to be performed. Typical verbs in COBOL are: READ, WRITE, IF, ADD, SUBTRACT, MULTIPLY, DIVIDE, and MOVE. These verbs are utilized in COBOL sentences to express the operation to be performed.

SEQUENCE			A	B	COBOL STATEMENT													IDENTIFICATION	
(PAGE) 1 3	(SERIAL) 4 6	CONT. 7	8	12		16	20	24	28	32	36	40	44	48	52	56	60 64 68	72	76 80
Ø1Ø	Ø1Ø			MULTIPLY LOAN-AMOUNT-INPUT BY INTEREST-RATE-CONSTANT GIVING															SUBLIST
Ø1Ø	Ø2Ø				INTEREST-AMOUNT-WORK ROUNDED.														SUBLIST
Ø1Ø	Ø3Ø			MOVE INTEREST-AMOUNT-WORK TO INTEREST-AMOUNT-REPORT.															SUBLIST
Ø1Ø	Ø4Ø			ADD LOAN-AMOUNT-INPUT, INTEREST-AMOUNT-WORK GIVING															SUBLIST
Ø1Ø	Ø5Ø				TOTAL-AMOUNT-WORK.														SUBLIST
Ø1Ø	Ø6Ø			MOVE TOTAL-AMOUNT-WORK TO TOTAL-AMOUNT-REPORT.															SUBLIST
Ø1Ø	Ø7Ø			MOVE NO-OF-PAYMENTS-INPUT TO NO-OF-PAYMENTS-REPORT.															SUBLIST
Ø1Ø	Ø8Ø			DIVIDE TOTAL-AMOUNT-WORK BY NO-OF-PAYMENTS-INPUT GIVING															SUBLIST
Ø1Ø	Ø9Ø				MONTHLY-PAYMENT-REPORT ROUNDED.														SUBLIST
Ø1Ø	1ØØ			WRITE LOAN-REPORT-LINE															SUBLIST
Ø1Ø	11Ø				AFTER PROPER-SPACING.														SUBLIST
Ø1Ø	12Ø			MOVE SPACE-ONE-LINE TO PROPER-SPACING.															SUBLIST
Ø1Ø	13Ø			READ LOAN-INPUT-FILE															SUBLIST
Ø1Ø	14Ø				AT END														SUBLIST
Ø1Ø	15Ø					MOVE 'NO' TO ARE-THERE-MORE-RECORDS.													SUBLIST

A portion of a COBOL program is illustrated in Figure 12-8. From these statements, it can be seen that COBOL is a substantial improvement in terms of reading the program over the programming in machine language which was required a few years prior to the release of COBOL.

Figure 12-8 The COBOL program consists of a series of English-like statements. COBOL was designed to be easy to read and, when properly written, should be easy to maintain.

Structure of a COBOL program

One of the characteristics of COBOL is the formal structure that must be followed when coding a program. Every COBOL program is divided into four divisions. These divisions are: 1) The Identification Division; 2) The Environment Division; 3) The Data Division; 4) The Procedure Division.

The Identification Division is used to document the program. It contains information identifying the author of the program, where the program was written, the date the program was written, and related information.

The Environment Division is used to specify the type of computer on which the program will be translated and executed. In addition, this division also contains statements which associate assigned files with the input/output devices to be used for the files. In theory, this is the only division which must be changed when a COBOL program is to be run on different computer systems.

The Data Division is used to describe the files, records, and fields which will be processed by the program. COBOL was one of the first programming languages where the data was described separately from the instructions which actually process the data. This feature is important because it enables a program to be more easily changed and modified after it has been written.

The Procedure Division contains the instructions which are to be executed by the computer system. The instructions in the Procedure Division implement the logic which was developed in the program design phase to solve a particular problem. A COBOL program is illustrated on the following pages.

COBOL Coding Form

SYSTEM		PUNCHING INSTRUCTIONS		PAGE 1 OF 6
PROGRAM	SUBSCRIPTION LIST REPORT	GRAPHIC	0 0 2 Z 1 1	
PROGRAMMER	SHELLY / CASHMAN DATE DEC 9	PUNCH	11-6 ZERO TWO 0-9 12-9 ONE	

Sheet 1

SEQUENCE (PAGE) (SERIAL)	CONT.	A	B	COBOL STATEMENT	IDENTIFICATION
001010		IDENTIFICATION DIVISION.			SUBLIST
001020					SUBLIST
001030		PROGRAM-ID.	SUBLIST.		SUBLIST
001040		AUTHOR.	SHELLY AND CASHMAN.		SUBLIST
001050		INSTALLATION.	ANAHEIM.		SUBLIST
001060		DATE-WRITTEN.	12/09/76.		SUBLIST
001070		DATE-COMPILED.	05/26/77.		SUBLIST
001080		SECURITY.	UNCLASSIFIED.		SUBLIST
001090					SUBLIST
001100		**			SUBLIST
001110		*		*	SUBLIST
001120		*	THIS PROGRAM PRODUCES A LISTING OF PERSONS ON A MAGAZINE	*	SUBLIST
001130		*	SUBSCRIPTION LIST.	*	SUBLIST
001140		*		*	SUBLIST
001150		**			SUBLIST
001160					SUBLIST
001170					SUBLIST
001180					SUBLIST
001190		ENVIRONMENT DIVISION.			SUBLIST
001200					SUBLIST

Sheet 2

SEQUENCE (PAGE) (SERIAL)	CONT.	A	B	COBOL STATEMENT	IDENTIFICATION
002010		CONFIGURATION SECTION.			SUBLIST
002020					SUBLIST
002030		SOURCE-COMPUTER.	IBM-370.		SUBLIST
002040		OBJECT-COMPUTER.	IBM-370.		SUBLIST
002050					SUBLIST
002060		INPUT-OUTPUT SECTION.			SUBLIST
002070					SUBLIST
002080		FILE-CONTROL.			SUBLIST
002090			SELECT SUBSCRIPTION-INPUT-FILE		SUBLIST
002100			ASSIGN TO SYS007-UR-2540R-S.		SUBLIST
002110			SELECT SUBSCRIPTION-REPORT-FILE		SUBLIST
002120			ASSIGN TO SYS013-UR-1403-S.		SUBLIST
002130			EJECT		SUBLIST
002140		DATA DIVISION.			SUBLIST
002150					SUBLIST
002160		FILE SECTION.			SUBLIST
002170					SUBLIST
002180		FD	SUBSCRIPTION-INPUT-FILE		SUBLIST
002190			RECORD CONTAINS 80 CHARACTERS		SUBLIST
002200			LABEL RECORDS ARE OMITTED		SUBLIST

Sheet 3

SEQUENCE (PAGE) (SERIAL)	CONT.	A	B	COBOL STATEMENT	IDENTIFICATION
003010			DATA RECORD IS SUBSCRIPTION-INPUT-RECORD.		SUBLIST
003020		01	SUBSCRIPTION-INPUT-RECORD.		SUBLIST
003030			05 NAME-INPUT	PICTURE X(25).	SUBLIST
003040			05 ADDRESS-INPUT	PICTURE X(25).	SUBLIST
003050			05 CITY-STATE-INPUT	PICTURE X(20).	SUBLIST
003060			05 EXPIRATION-DATE-INPUT	PICTURE X(8).	SUBLIST
003070			05 FILLER	PICTURE XX.	SUBLIST
003080					SUBLIST
003090		FD	SUBSCRIPTION-REPORT-FILE		SUBLIST
003100			RECORD CONTAINS 133 CHARACTERS		SUBLIST
003110			LABEL RECORDS ARE OMITTED		SUBLIST
003120			DATA RECORD IS SUBSCRIPTION-REPORT-LINE.		SUBLIST
003130		01	SUBSCRIPTION-REPORT-LINE.		SUBLIST
003140			05 CARRIAGE-CONTROL	PICTURE X.	SUBLIST
003150			05 EXPIRATION-DATE-REPORT	PICTURE X(8).	SUBLIST
003160			05 FILLER	PICTURE X(5).	SUBLIST
003170			05 NAME-REPORT	PICTURE X(25).	SUBLIST
003180			05 FILLER	PICTURE X(5).	SUBLIST
003190			05 ADDRESS-REPORT	PICTURE X(25).	SUBLIST
003200			05 FILLER	PICTURE X(5).	SUBLIST

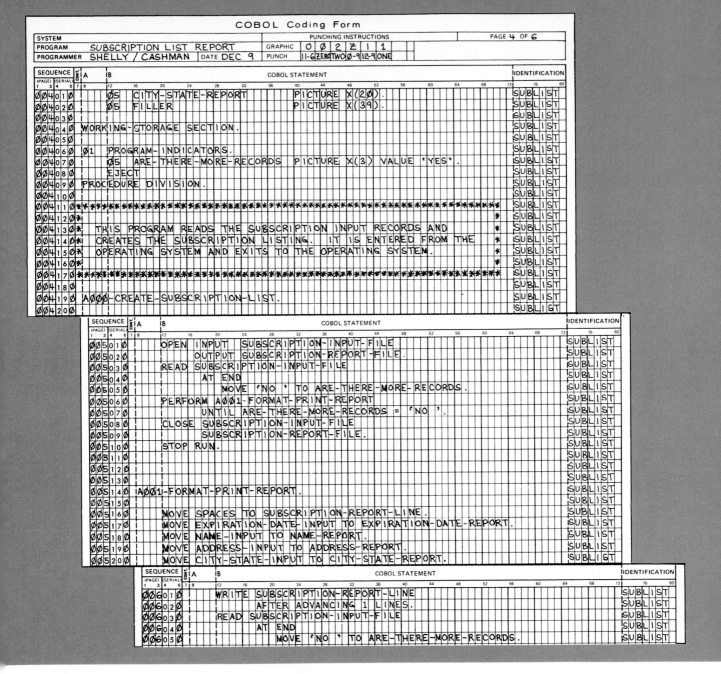

COBOL Coding Form

SYSTEM			PUNCHING INSTRUCTIONS			PAGE 4 OF 6
PROGRAM	SUBSCRIPTION LIST REPORT		GRAPHIC	O Ø 2 Z 1 1		
PROGRAMMER	SHELLY / CASHMAN DATE DEC 9		PUNCH	11-G ZERO TWO Ø-9 12-9 ONE		

SEQUENCE (PAGE) (SERIAL)		A	B	COBOL STATEMENT	IDENTIFICATION
004010			Ø5 CITY-STATE-REPORT	PICTURE X(2Ø).	SUBLIST
004020			Ø5 FILLER	PICTURE X(39).	SUBLIST
004030					SUBLIST
004040		WORKING-STORAGE SECTION.			SUBLIST
004050					SUBLIST
004060		Ø1 PROGRAM-INDICATORS.			SUBLIST
004070			Ø5 ARE-THERE-MORE-RECORDS PICTURE X(3) VALUE 'YES'.		SUBLIST
004080			EJECT		SUBLIST
004090		PROCEDURE DIVISION.			SUBLIST
004100					SUBLIST
004110		***			SUBLIST
004120		*		*	SUBLIST
004130		* THIS PROGRAM READS THE SUBSCRIPTION INPUT RECORDS AND		*	SUBLIST
004140		* CREATES THE SUBSCRIPTION LISTING. IT IS ENTERED FROM THE		*	SUBLIST
004150		* OPERATING SYSTEM AND EXITS TO THE OPERATING SYSTEM.		*	SUBLIST
004160		*		*	SUBLIST
004170		***			SUBLIST
004180					SUBLIST
004190		AØØØ-CREATE-SUBSCRIPTION-LIST.			SUBLIST
004200					SUBLIST

SEQUENCE (PAGE) (SERIAL)		A	B	COBOL STATEMENT	IDENTIFICATION
005010			OPEN INPUT SUBSCRIPTION-INPUT-FILE		SUBLIST
005020			OUTPUT SUBSCRIPTION-REPORT-FILE.		SUBLIST
005030			READ SUBSCRIPTION-INPUT-FILE		SUBLIST
005040			AT END		SUBLIST
005050			MOVE 'NO ' TO ARE-THERE-MORE-RECORDS.		SUBLIST
005060			PERFORM AØØ1-FORMAT-PRINT-REPORT		SUBLIST
005070			UNTIL ARE-THERE-MORE-RECORDS = 'NO '.		SUBLIST
005080			CLOSE SUBSCRIPTION-INPUT-FILE		SUBLIST
005090			SUBSCRIPTION-REPORT-FILE.		SUBLIST
005100			STOP RUN.		SUBLIST
005110					SUBLIST
005120					SUBLIST
005130					SUBLIST
005140		AØØ1-FORMAT-PRINT-REPORT.			SUBLIST
005150					SUBLIST
005160			MOVE SPACES TO SUBSCRIPTION-REPORT-LINE.		SUBLIST
005170			MOVE EXPIRATION-DATE-INPUT TO EXPIRATION-DATE-REPORT.		SUBLIST
005180			MOVE NAME-INPUT TO NAME-REPORT.		SUBLIST
005190			MOVE ADDRESS-INPUT TO ADDRESS-REPORT.		SUBLIST
005200			MOVE CITY-STATE-INPUT TO CITY-STATE-REPORT.		SUBLIST

SEQUENCE (PAGE) (SERIAL)		A	B	COBOL STATEMENT	IDENTIFICATION
006010			WRITE SUBSCRIPTION-REPORT-LINE		SUBLIST
006020			AFTER ADVANCING 1 LINES.		SUBLIST
006030			READ SUBSCRIPTION-INPUT-FILE		SUBLIST
006040			AT END		SUBLIST
006050			MOVE 'NO ' TO ARE-THERE-MORE-RECORDS.		SUBLIST

Advantages and disadvantages of COBOL

COBOL as a business language has several important advantages. One of the most important is that COBOL is designed to be machine-independent. A program written in COBOL should be able to be run on any computer system that supports the COBOL language, regardless of manufacturer. Although this ideal has never truly been realized because of frequent additions to the language by some manufacturers, COBOL has been widely implemented in a common form on many computers.

Figure 12-9 COBOL programs consist of four divisions. Some consider the "wordiness" of COBOL a disadvantage; however, COBOL was not designed to be a concise language. It was designed to be easily written, read, and understood.

12.9

In addition, COBOL has strong file handling capabilities and is capable of supporting sequential, indexed, and relative files. COBOL is also relatively easy to write and, if properly written, can be easily understood by other programmers.

Since COBOL contains many features and elements, the translator program which translates a COBOL source program into machine language is usually a large program. This means it requires a large amount of main computer storage in which to operate. This is a potential disadvantage because smaller computer systems with a limited amount of main computer storage may not be able to implement COBOL.

Some observers consider the "wordiness" of COBOL a disadvantage, for more coding is required to produce a given result than is required, for example, with FORTRAN, which is noted for its concise notation.

COBOL is also less than an ideal language for coding when using structured programming because some of the structures which make structured programming easier and more understandable are not available in COBOL. By making a few adjustments, however, COBOL can be successfully used for structured programming.

It is important to recognize, notwithstanding the disadvantages, that many hundreds of thousands of programs have been written in COBOL during the past twenty years. It is apparent, therefore, that because of its widespread use, COBOL will remain an important language for many years to come.

PL/I

In the late 1950's, computer applications and computer classifications were clearly divided among the scientific community and the business community. Scientific users needed fast computational capability with limited input/output operations. Business users, on the other hand, needed decimal arithmetic, the ability to process alphabetic data, and fast input/output devices. As computers became more widely used in all application areas, there was a merging of the needs of the scientific and business user. In hardware, this was typified by the IBM System/360 computer system which was designed for both business and scientific use.

There was also a need for more commonality between programming languages. Responding to this need, IBM began the development of a new programming language in the early 1960's. Their purpose was "to recommend a successor language for currently available FORTRAN's . . . while still remaining a useful tool to the engineer."

```
                                    PL/I
                  GENERAL PURPOSE CARD PUNCHING FORM

System    NAME AND ADDRESS LIST        Punching Instructions        Sheet 1 of 2
Program   LIST PROGRAM          Graphic  O  Ø  Z  2
Programmer SHELLY          Date Ø2/12   Punch  II-6ØI40-9 TWO

PGM1:    PROCEDURE OPTIONS (MAIN);                              LIST0010
         DECLARE   CARDIN FILE RECORD                           LIST0020
                   INPUT SEQUENTIAL                             LIST0030
                   ENVIRONMENT (MEDIUM (SYS004,2540)            LIST0040
                   F(80) CONSECUTIVE);                          LIST0050
                                                               LIST0060
         DECLARE   1   NAME_CARD,                               LIST0070
                   3     NAME_IN         CHARACTER (25),        LIST0080
                   3     ADDRESS_IN      CHARACTER (25),        LIST0090
                   3     CITY_IN         CHARACTER (25),        LIST0100
                   3     FILL1_IN        CHARACTER (5);         LIST0110
                                                               LIST0120
         DECLARE   PRINT FILE RECORD                            LIST0130
                   OUTPUT SEQUENTIAL                            LIST0140
                   ENVIRONMENT (MEDIUM (SYS005,1403)            LIST0150
                   F(121) CTLASA CONSECUTIVE);                  LIST0160
                                                               LIST0170
         DECLARE   1   PRINT_OUT,                               LIST0180
                   3     CTL_CHAR      CHARACTER (1) INITIAL (' '),  LIST0190
                   3     NAME_OUT      CHARACTER (25),          LIST0200
                   3     FILL1_OUT     CHARACTER (5) INITIAL (' '),  LIST0210
                   3     ADDRESS_OUT   CHARACTER (25),          LIST0220
                   3     FILL2_OUT     CHARACTER (5) INITIAL (' '),  LIST0230
                   3     CITY_OUT      CHARACTER (25),          LIST0240
                   3     FILL3_OUT     CHARACTER (35) INITIAL (' '); LIST0250
                                                               LIST0260
```

Sheet 2 of 2

```
         DECLARE   1   PROGRAM_INDICATORS,
                   3     YES           BIT(1)  INIT('1'B),
                   3     NO            BIT(1)  INIT('Ø'B'),
                   3     MORE_RECORDS  BIT(1);

         ON ENDFILE (CARDIN)

             MORE_RECORDS = NO;

         OPEN FILE (CARDIN)
              FILE (PRINT);
         MORE_RECORDS=YES;
         READ FILE (CARDIN) INTO (NAME_CARD);

         DO WHILE (MORE_RECORDS);
             NAME_OUT = NAME_IN;
             ADDRESS_OUT = ADDRESS_IN;
             CITY_OUT = CITY_IN;
             WRITE FILE (PRINT) FROM PRINT_OUT;
             READ FILE (CARDIN) INTO (NAME_CARD);
         END;
         CLOSE FILE (CARDIN), FILE (PRINT);
         END PGM1;
```

The design objectives were that the language should: 1) Be useful in a wide variety of application areas including engineering, business, and systems programming; 2) Be designed in such a way that the programmer could use virtually all of the power of a computer without resorting to assembler language; 3) Be designed in such a way that any programmer could easily use the elements of the language at his own skill level; 4) Be able to be written in free form with no prescribed columns for recording statements, which would assist in terminal operations; 5) Contain default options which provide for the language to select specifications required by the program if they are not explicitly specified by the programmer.

Figure 12-10 PL/I programs combine some features of COBOL and some features of FORTRAN. It has the necessary structures for structured programming.

The language that was developed from these design specifications was called PL/I. PL/I was released in 1966. The designers of the language used some of the computational concepts previously incorporated into FORTRAN and some of the file processing capabilities of COBOL. Thus, a PL/I program has some characteristics of FORTRAN and some characteristics of COBOL (Figure 12–10).

Advantages and disadvantages of PL/I

· The strongest characteristic of PL/I is its breadth and detail. With the wide capabilities of PL/I, it is feasible to write applications and systems programs in any area without resorting to a lower-level programming language like assembler language. This characteristic may also be considered one of its weaknesses, however, because it is difficult to master all of the components of the language.

PL/I is quite a good language for structured programming because it contains all of the structures required. Because it is good for structured programming, PL/I finds some use in the computer community, but it has never achieved the success and widespread use anticipated by IBM.

RPG

RPG, or Report Program Generator, was first widely implemented in the middle and late 1960's when small-scale computer systems became readily available to a substantial number of users. Developed originally by IBM, RPG has become a "defacto" standard in the industry and is widely implemented on many different computers from different manufacturers.

RPG was originally developed to allow reports to be easily generated. To write a program in RPG, the programmer fills out a series of forms with the required entries in predetermined columns. The basic forms are called the File Description Specifications, Input Specifications, Calculation Specifications, and Output Specifications.

The entries on the forms are used to develop a program using fixed program logic which is part of the programming language itself. When the source program is translated from the entries on the forms to an object program, this fixed logic is used to generate the sequence in which data will be processed. The intent, of course, is to free the programmer from the necessity of designing the logic required for processing the data. A sample RPG program is shown in Figure 12–11.

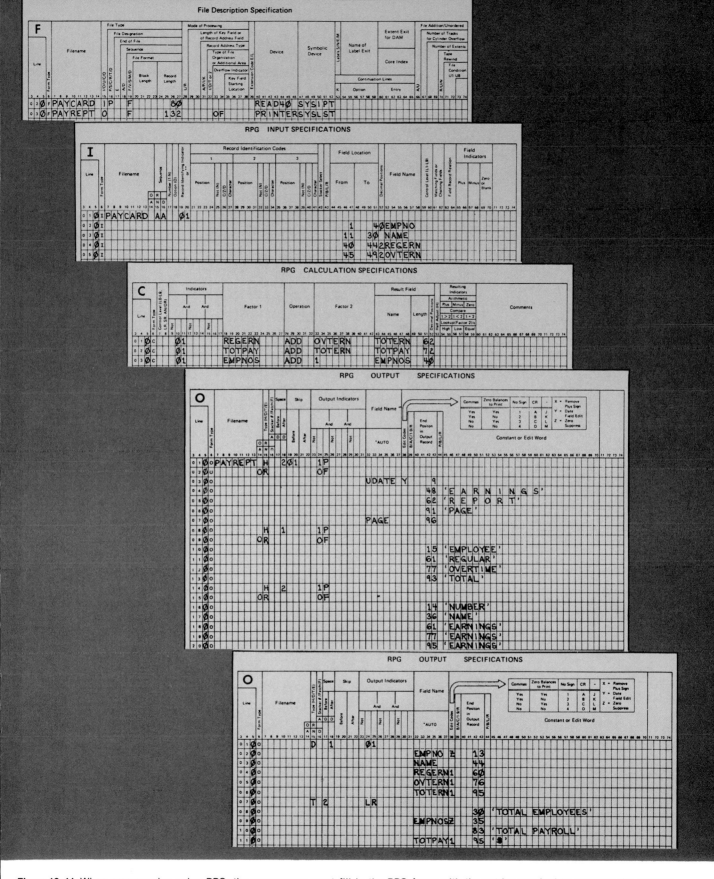

Figure 12-11 When programming using RPG, the programmer must fill in the RPG forms with the entries required to generate the program.

Since the original announcement of RPG in the early 1960's, a number of enhancements have been added to the original language, including file processing capabilities for tape, disk, and data bases. In the early 1970's, RPG II was announced by IBM for the IBM System/3 computer system. RPG II has become a widely used language for machines from a number of manufacturers. RPG III was announced in 1979 for use with the IBM System/38 computer system. Its main enhancement was the use of the language to process data stored in a data base.

Advantages and disadvantages of RPG

The principal advantage of RPG is the ability to generate routine business reports quickly and easily. In addition, the language can be relatively easily learned.

Because of the fixed logic, however, programming problems which do not readily fit into the fixed logic can be difficult to program. As with most programming languages, the evolution of RPG has been that of changing from a rather limited language designed to produce reports to one with added capabilities which require the skills of a sophisticated programmer. Today, RPG II programmers are developing complex programs far beyond the capabilities originally intended when RPG was introduced.

BASIC

BASIC, which stands for Beginner's All-Purpose Symbolic Instruction Code, is a programming language that was developed at Dartmouth College in 1965 for use in an academic environment by students. Under the direction of Dr. John Kemeny and Dr. Thomas Kurtz, BASIC was first implemented on a General Electric 225 computer system in an interactive timesharing environment. An interactive language allows the programmer to communicate directly with the computer system when programming and, in turn, the computer communicates directly back to the programmer. This interaction between the programmer and the computer system occurs through computer terminals such as the CRT terminals.

BASIC became widely used in timesharing environments in colleges and universities in the late 1960's. With the introduction of microcomputers in the mid-1970's, BASIC received a great impetus because these systems use BASIC as the primary language (Figure 12–12).

```
10   LET P = 469
20   LET R = 0.09
30   FOR Y = 1 TO 10 STEP 1
40   LET P = P*(1+P)
50   PRINT Y,P
60   NEXT Y
70   END
```

Figure 12-12 BASIC, originally developed to be utilized in an academic environment, is now widely used on personal computers and small business computer systems as well.

Today, BASIC is used by thousands of students receiving training in computer programming using microcomputer systems. In addition, with extensions to the language, including file handling capabilities, BASIC is widely used with many small business-oriented computer systems.

Advantages and disadvantages of BASIC

The primary advantage of BASIC is its ease of use. Part of the ease of use, of course, is because of its somewhat limited capabilities. In recent years, however, with extensions to the language, BASIC has become a more powerful language.

The extensions have, though, been primarily implemented by individual manufacturers of small computer systems. Therefore, there are many incompatibilities between BASIC compilers and interpreters at this time; thus, a BASIC program written for one computer will not necessarily run on another computer.

Most versions of BASIC do not have the structures required for structured programming. Some authorities, therefore, do not recommend the use of BASIC because modern programming techniques cannot be readily used.

Pascal

Pascal is one of the newer programming languages which has gained wide acceptance. Unlike many other languages, Pascal is not an abbreviation but rather was named after the mathematician Blaise Pascal (1623-1662), who developed one of the earliest calculating machines.

Pascal was one of the first major programming languages developed after the concept of structured programming was introduced. The Pascal language was originally specified by Niklaus Wirth, a computer scientist at the Institut fur Informatik, Zurich, Switzerland, in 1968. The first Pascal compiler became operational in 1971.

Pascal provides for data names of any length, a multitude of data types and structures, and a number of control structures such as If-Then-Else and While-Do which make it very easy to implement the concepts and principles of structured programming (Figure 12-13). Many manufacturers have begun to provide Pascal compilers for their computer systems.

```
FUNCTION
RADIUS (CIRCUMFERENCE:
        REAL): REAL;

CONST TWOPI=6.2831;
BEGIN
 IF CIRCUMFERENCE<0
  THEN RADIUS:=0
 ELSE
  RADIUS:=CIRCUMFERENCE/TWOPI;
END
```

Figure 12-13 The Pascal program above calculates the radius of a circle, given the circumference. Pascal is finding many supporters among microcomputer users.

A-2 & A-3	BACAIC	Commercial	FORTRAN	LISP 2	PILOT	SOAP
ADAM	BASEBALL	Translator	FORTRANSIT	MAD	PL/I	SOL
AED	BASIC	CORAL	FSL	MADCAP	PRINT	Speedcoding
AESOP	C-10	CPS	GAT	Magic Paper	Protosynthex	STRESS
AIMACO	CLIP	DEACON	GPSS	MAP	QUIKTRAN	TMG
ALGOL	CLP	DYNAMO	GRAF	MATHLAB	RPG	TRAC
ALTRAN	COBOL	473L Query	ICES	MATH-MATIC	RPG II	TRANDIR
AMBIT	COGENT	EASYCODER	IPL-V	META 5	RPG III	TREET
AMTRAN	COGO	FACT	IT	MILITRAN	Short Code	UNICODE
APL	COLASL	FLAP	JOSS	MIRFAC	SIMSCRIPT	
ASSEMBLER	COLINGO	FLOW-MATIC	JOVIAL	NEAT	SIMULA	
AUTOCODER	COMIT	FORMAC	LISP 1.5	PASCAL	SNOBOL	

Figure 12-14 A partial list of the many languages developed for programming computers is shown above.

Other programming languages

There are numerous other programming languages that have been developed over the past thirty years. Some of these languages with special names are nothing more than assembler languages that have been developed for specific computer systems.

There have, however, been a number of specialized programming languages that have been implemented. These languages were developed, for example, to program manufacturing machines, to provide for authoring computer-assisted learning programs, and to allow special manipulation of alphabetic data for information retrieval applications. As specialized application areas are placed on the computer, specialized software is frequently developed to assist in the programming of the computer for these areas. A chart of some of the languages which have been developed in the past three decades is shown in Figure 12-14.

INTERACTIVE SYSTEMS

The following RPGII Systems are available for the IBM System/32, System/34, HP300, HP3000, and TI990

- — CLINICAL ACCOUNTING
- — HOSPITAL MANAGEMENT (Not avail for Sys/32)
- — G/L WRITE-UP for CPA's
- — PRACTICE MANAGEMENT for Professionals

REGIONAL DISTRIBUTORS ARE WANTED

RPGII SUBROUTINES

- — Convert any Dollar Amount to its English Equivalent. $25.00
- — Julian Date Subroutines—convert to/from Julian Date. (Indicator Independent) $25.00

Figure 12-15 The advertisement above is typical of those found from software vendors.

Application packages

In addition to the standard and specialized programming languages that are available to use for writing programs, there are numerous application "packages" which can be purchased from software vendors to solve application problems (Figure 12-15). For example, many vendors have produced generalized systems for the common accounting functions.

The advantage of these systems, of course, is that they do not have to be developed or programmed in-house. The prime disadvantage is that these systems frequently do not meet the existing requirements of a company, and they have to be modified.

A close analysis must be performed to determine whether a generalized system will perform the task better and less expensively than a series of programs coded in one of the languages just discussed.

PROGRAM DEVELOPMENT

After the program has been designed, it must be coded, tested, and documented. The following paragraphs discuss these aspects of the program development cycle.

Coding the program

The programming language used to code an application will normally be determined by the systems analyst or project manager based upon the software available, the knowledge of the programming staff, and the standards established within the data processing department.

Coding begins after the program has been designed. Coding the program involves the actual writing of the detailed programming statements on a coding form. The code in the program must implement the program which has already been designed. Therefore, the programmer will use the program design as a guide in coding the program.

Coding is a very exact skill. The programmer must not only implement the program design in code, but must also be precise in using the language. Each programming language has its own syntax, or coding rules, which must be followed. The programmer must follow these rules explicitly or the program will not compile and execute as intended.

After the program has been coded (or in large programs, as the program is coded), the program code should be subjected to a walkthrough by other members of the staff for completeness, accuracy, and readability.

Once it is agreed that the program is well-written and correctly implements the design of the program, the source program must be prepared for processing on the computer. This requires that each line of the program either be placed on a machine readable medium such as cards, floppy disk, or tape, or that it be entered directly into the computer system via a terminal. When it is entered via terminal, the source program will normally be stored on disk or tape for future processing.

Translating a source program

A computer can only execute machine language instructions. Therefore, the source statements must be translated into machine language before they can be executed. For example, the COBOL verb ADD must be converted to a machine language instruction before it can be executed.

There are two major tools used to translate a source program into executable machine language: compilers and interpreters.

Compilers

A compiler is a program that translates source program statements into machine language instructions and produces an object program. An object program is the entire program expressed as machine language instructions. It is the object program which is loaded into main computer storage for actual execution of the program. Compilers are supplied by manufacturers of the computer systems and also by some software vendors.

On most computer systems, the compiler program is stored on disk. To compile a source program, the following events occur (Figure 12–16):

1. The compiler program stored on disk is read into main computer storage.
2. The source program is read into main computer storage by the compiler. The source program is data on which the compiler operates. In the example, a COBOL source program is read into main computer storage from a terminal.
3. The compiler analyzes each COBOL statement and produces the following output:
    a. The object program, which consists of machine language instructions generated from the source statements in the program. The object program is normally stored in a "library" on disk where it can be retrieved for use when necessary.
    b. A source listing of each COBOL statement in the program.
    c. As the compiler analyzes each source statement, it checks for errors in the use of the language. If any errors are found, the compiler prints a diagnostic listing which identifies those statements in error and the reason for the error.

After the program is compiled, the programmer will normally examine the source listing and any diagnostics to determine if there are any errors. In those organizations using modern programming methodologies, a walkthrough will be conducted on the code to ensure that the code is written to conform with department standards and that the code will work properly when executed.

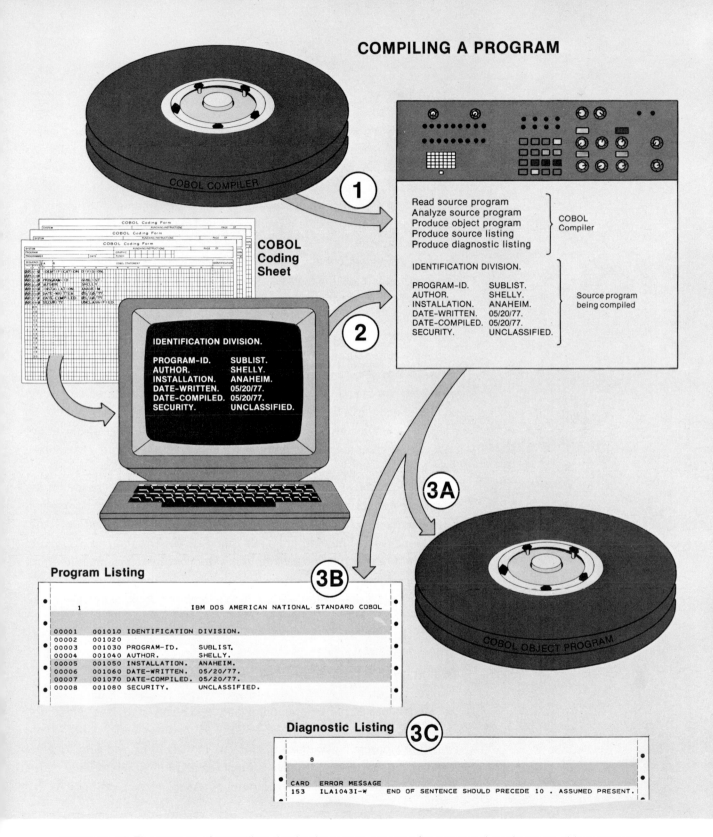

COMPILING A PROGRAM

COBOL COMPILER

COBOL Coding Sheet

Read source program
Analyze source program
Produce object program
Produce source listing
Produce diagnostic listing
} COBOL Compiler

IDENTIFICATION DIVISION.

PROGRAM-ID.   SUBLIST.
AUTHOR.   SHELLY.
INSTALLATION.   ANAHEIM.
DATE-WRITTEN.   05/20/77.
DATE-COMPILED.   05/20/77.
SECURITY.   UNCLASSIFIED.
} Source program being compiled

IDENTIFICATION DIVISION.

PROGRAM-ID.   SUBLIST.
AUTHOR.   SHELLY.
INSTALLATION.   ANAHEIM.
DATE-WRITTEN.   05/20/77.
DATE-COMPILED.   05/20/77.
SECURITY.   UNCLASSIFIED.

3A

COBOL OBJECT PROGRAM

Program Listing   **3B**

```
        1                    IBM DOS AMERICAN NATIONAL STANDARD COBOL

  00001   001010  IDENTIFICATION DIVISION.
  00002   001020
  00003   001030  PROGRAM-ID.      SUBLIST.
  00004   001040  AUTHOR.          SHELLY.
  00005   001050  INSTALLATION.    ANAHEIM.
  00006   001060  DATE-WRITTEN.    05/20/77.
  00007   001070  DATE-COMPILED.   05/20/77.
  00008   001080  SECURITY.        UNCLASSIFIED.
```

Diagnostic Listing **3C**

```
        8

 CARD   ERROR MESSAGE
 153    ILA1043I-W      END OF SENTENCE SHOULD PRECEDE 10 . ASSUMED PRESENT.
```

Figure 12-16 The process of compiling checks the source program for errors and produces an object program.

Interpreters

When a program is compiled, an object program is produced which contains the executable machine language instructions. These instructions can be placed in main computer storage to process the data according to the program requirements.

Another approach when processing source statements is the use of an interpreter. An interpreter is a program stored in main computer storage or, in many computers, in Read Only Memory (ROM), which will read a source program one statement at a time and cause the execution of that statement. The interpreter reads the source statements in a program on a statement-by-statement basis, identifies the function of the statement, and carries out the function to be performed. It then reads the next statement, which is analyzed and executed.

Since the source program is executed directly when using an interpreter, an object program is not generated. Instead, the interpreter generates the machine language code from the source statement as the source statement is encountered, and causes the source statement to be executed immediately. When utilizing an interpreter, many errors in the coding of the source program are not found until the program is actually executed.

Since an object program is not generated, disk storage space for the object program is not required. Only the source program must be retained for subsequent execution. The biggest disadvantage of interpreters is that they normally execute a program at a much slower rate than an object program could be executed on a computer system because they must interpret each instruction.

Interpreters are commonly found on microcomputers, especially where BASIC is the primary language used on the machine.

Coding quality programs

Regardless of the programming language being used, it is very important to produce a program which is easy to read and understand. Proper coding of a program can make the task of implementing and subsequently maintaining a program a relatively simple task, while an improperly coded program can be almost impossible to understand, correct, or modify.

Poor coding

SEQUENCE (PAGE)	(SERIAL)	CONT.	A	B	COBOL STATEMENT
010	010			IF	SLS > QUOTA MOVE QUOT-O TO QUOT-R ADD SLS
010	020				TO COUNT-O ELSE MOVE QUOT-U TO QUOT-R ADD
010	030			SLS TO COUNT-U.	

Good coding

SEQUENCE (PAGE)	(SERIAL)	CONT.	A	B	COBOL STATEMENT
010	010			IF	SALES-AMOUNT-INPUT IS GREATER THAN SALES-QUOTA
010	020				MOVE OVER-QUOTA-MESSAGE TO QUOTA-MESSAGE-REPORT
010	030				ADD SALES-AMOUNT-INPUT TO OVER-QUOTA-SALES-ACCUM
010	040			ELSE	
010	050				MOVE UNDER-QUOTA-MESSAGE TO QUOTA-MESSAGE-REPORT
010	060				ADD SALES-AMOUNT-INPUT TO UNDER-QUOTA-SALES-ACCUM.

The examples in Figure 12–17 illustrate poor coding and good coding to accomplish the same processing. The processing to be accomplished is as follows: If the sales amount in an input record is greater than the sales quota, a message indicating the salesperson is over quota is to be moved to the report output area and the sales amount is to be added to an accumulator containing the total sales for those sales people over quota. If the sales amount in the input record is not greater than the sales quota amount, a message indicating the sales person is under quota is to be moved to the report output area and the sales amount is to be added to an accumulator containing the total sales for those people under quota.

Both of the examples in Figure 12–17 accomplish this processing. The important point is that the example of poor coding is difficult to read and it is difficult to relate its coding to the statement of the problem to be solved.

The good coding, on the other hand, uses data names which reflect the data being processed, places the statements to be executed in an easy-to-read format, and allows the reader of the program to relate the coding directly to the specifications for the problem.

The principle of writing a legible, quality program applies to all programming languages, even though the example illustrates COBOL coding. Standards can be established for all programming languages which will result in programs that are easy to read and understand. It is the responsibility of the programmer to write code in a clear, easily understood manner.

Figure 12-17 The two examples of COBOL coding above illustrate poor coding and good coding to solve the same logical problem. The programmer has the responsibility of developing clear, concise code which is easily read and understood.

Testing the program

After the program has been coded, it must be tested to ensure that it produces the correct output. The basic procedures for testing a program are:

1. The program is compiled and all diagnostic errors are removed.
2. Test data is created with which to test the program.
3. The program is tested.
4. Any errors which are found in the program are corrected and the testing continues until the program is certified as error-free.
5. The program can be used in a system test to ensure that all programs within a system work properly together.

Creating test data

The development of test data with which to test a program is an important responsibility of a programmer. The development of adequate test data, together with good program design and coding, are the most important tasks accomplished by a computer programmer.

There are several elements to developing test data. These are: 1) What type of data should be developed; 2) Who should develop the test data; 3) Who will check the test data.

Test data should be designed to find errors in the program. Although it has been shown that testing, no matter how extensive, cannot be used to show that a program is entirely error-free, it has been found that properly designed test data can be used to show a high probability that errors do not exist.

Therefore, the task of developing test data should be approached with the same seriousness as designing or coding a program. Test data should be developed which requires the program to execute all the instructions within the program at least one time. To do this, test data will normally fall into two major areas: data which is in the correct format and which will cause the instructions processing correct data to be executed; data which contains predefined errors, causing the error routines within the program to be executed. For example, if a field is supposed to contain numeric data, one set of test data should have the correct numeric data in the field. Another set of test data, however, should place non-numeric data in the field. In this way, both the normal processing routines and the error routines are tested.

Testing sequence

A program will not normally be tested by being executed just one time. The programmer should develop a test plan which, among other things, specifies how many test runs of the program are to be executed, and what portions of the program are to be tested on each run. For example, a payroll program which calculates an employee's weekly earnings and prints the payroll check might first be tested to ensure that the payroll calculations were being performed properly, without regard to the ability of the program to print checks. After it is ensured that the calculations are done correctly, the portion of the program which prints the checks can be tested.

Stub testing

Testing only a portion of a program to ensure that it works properly is normally good testing strategy. A variation of this is found when structured design is used for a program and the program consists of a hierarchy of program modules. This strategy, called stub testing, allows a program to be partially coded and tested before the entire program is coded.

When using stub testing, one or more modules in the higher levels of the hierarchy of the program are coded. Those modules which are submodules will be coded as "stubs" when the program is tested. A stub contains merely a few statements of code which allows it to be referenced by those modules actually being tested. For example, in the hierarchy chart shown in Figure 12–18, there are five modules in the program. Using stub testing techniques, the modules which create the sales report, process detail records, and print final totals could be coded and tested. The two lower level modules which determine the lowest sales person and determine the highest sales person would be coded as stubs.

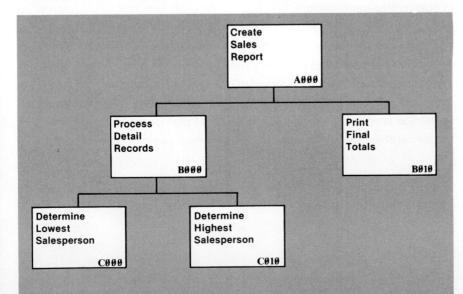

Figure 12-18 In the hierarchy chart on the left, the top three modules can be coded and tested without the bottom two modules being coded when stub testing is used.

12.23

The important concept to be understood is that the programmer can test the high-level modules, assure that the three modules tested are operational, and know that the program is 60% completed. The only tasks remaining are the coding and testing of the modules to determine the highest and lowest sales people.

Stub testing is an important testing technique in complex programs which may consist of hundreds of modules. Without stub testing, the entire program might have to be coded before testing could be started. With stub testing, testing can begin shortly after coding is begun; with the result that program testing is spread more evenly across the project time, and management can review the progress of completed portions of the program.

Assuring program correctness

There are several points in testing that must be recognized in order to have valid tests. First, the programmer who coded a program should not normally be the person who creates the test data. Many times the programmer who coded the program will not want, subconsciously, to find all the possible errors and, therefore, may not be completely diligent in preparing the test data.

Additionally, someone other than the programmer who coded the program should review the test results to determine if the correct output is produced. It has been found that when the person who coded the program checks the results, sometimes the programmer sees not what is there but what is supposed to be there. In large data processing departments, one group may be completely responsible for testing all programs which are produced.

Program documentation

The implementation of any system or program involves a considerable expenditure of both time and company resources. It is essential, therefore, that the facts regarding each program in a system be carefully recorded in a fashion that can be easily interpreted and understood. This information, called the program documentation, is a vital part of any program which is written; and is one of the most neglected areas in all of data processing.

The programmer writing a program is responsible for two levels of documentation: documentation within the program itself and documentation to be used by users of the program and operations personnel.

Most programming languages provide for comments within the listing itself (Figure 12–19). The comments may be identified by a special code, such as an asterisk at the start of the comment. Comments within the source program are used to explain to a reader of the program what processing is taking place. In most cases, programs which are commented are easier to read. It is important, however, that the comments be an accurate reflection of what is occurring. If they are misleading, they can do more harm than good.

The documentation of each program for users and operations personnel should include the following: 1) An abstract and general description of the purpose of the program; 2) Record layouts for report output, terminal output, files on auxiliary storage, subschemas of data bases used, and any other data which is necessary in the execution of the program; 3) A system flowchart, illustrating where the particular program fits within the system; 4) A detailed description of the processing which occurs within the program; 5) The structure or hierarchy chart of the modules within the program; 6) The logic utilized within each module of the program. This logic should be illustrated either through the use of flowcharts or through the use of pseudocode; 7) A listing of the source program; 8) A listing of the test data used to test the program and the results of the testing; 9) A console run form which includes the job control statements and any other information necessary to specify how the program is to be run on the computer system; 10) A user guide on how to use the program. This guide may include what data is used in the system; the way to prepare source documents; and, in transaction-oriented systems, the manner in which to establish contact with the computer system and interact with the program.

Most documentation "packages" prepared for a program will also include a page which can be used to record any changes or revisions to the original program which occur. Since program maintenance and modification is an on-going activity, it is important to keep a good record of what changes have been made to a program, when the changes were made, by whom they were made, and why they were made.

Program documentation is an important but often neglected part of the programming process. In an organization with many hundreds or even thousands of programs, the lack of documentation can cause significant problems when programs must be changed. It is an important responsibility of a programmer to properly document programs.

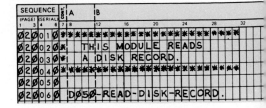

Figure 12-19 The sample of COBOL coding shown above illustrates the use of comments in a source program. The comments are identified by an asterisk in column 7 of the coding form. A line with an asterisk in column 7 is treated as a comment and is not compiled into machine language instructions by the compiler.

OPERATING SYSTEMS

In early computer systems, an operator had to perform initial start-up procedures for each program which was to be executed on the computer system. Typically, after a program had been run and the output had been removed from the system, the operator would load the next program to be executed into the system and this job would run until completion. This process would continue throughout the day.

In analyzing the efficiency of computer operations in these early systems, it was found that the computer was idle 50–60% of the time because of the manual operations required to run the programs. To improve the efficiency of computers, operating systems were widely implemented in the middle 1960's.

An operating system is a collection of programs that allows a computer system to supervise its own operations, automatically calling in programs, routines, languages, and data as needed for continuous throughput of a series of jobs. Thus, instead of performing start-up procedures for each job, the operator need only start-up the operating system and it handles all jobs which are to be run on the computer system.

An operating system is composed of basically three elements: control programs, processing programs, and data management programs (Figure 12–20). The control programs provide automatic control of the computer resources. Because of the control programs, there is a minimum of operator intervention as an orderly and efficient flow of jobs is facilitated.

The processing programs consist of language translators, which compile or interpret source programs; and service programs, which perform many of the common types of functions which must be accomplished in a data processing installation.

The data management programs are used to control the organization and access of data used by programs on the computer system.

Working together, the programs comprising the operating system provide significant advantages both in terms of the operating efficiency of the computer system and in terms of aiding the programmer by providing compilers, diagnostic aids, and libraries where frequently used modules or subroutines can be stored for ready access.

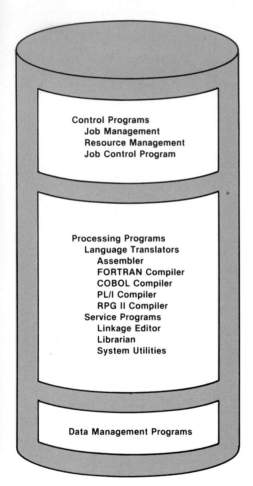

Control Programs
Job Management
Resource Management
Job Control Program

Processing Programs
Language Translators
Assembler
FORTRAN Compiler
COBOL Compiler
PL/I Compiler
RPG II Compiler
Service Programs
Linkage Editor
Librarian
System Utilities

Data Management Programs

Figure 12-20 The operating system is composed of control programs, processing programs, and data management programs.

Control programs

The control programs of an operating system interact with one another to provide automatic control of the computer resources and control of the jobs being run on the computer. The control programs can be roughly divided into three functional areas: job management, resource management, and job control.

The job management programs are concerned primarily with initiating and controlling the work to be accomplished on the computer system. They do this by performing the following types of functions: reading and analyzing control statements; scheduling jobs for execution on the computer system; initiating the actual processing of jobs; handling the termination of a job on the computer; and communicating with the operator of the computer.

The resource management programs are concerned primarily with allocating the resources of the computer system — main computer storage usage, CPU time, input/output operations, device assignments, communications network resources, and other system resources.

Both the tasks of job management and resource management are handled primarily by a set of programs called an executive, or supervisor (sometimes also called a monitor). This supervisor will normally be resident in main computer storage during the time the computer system is operating (Figure 12-21). As programs execute on the computer system, they interact with the supervisor when the functions performed by it are required. For example, when a record is to be read from a disk device, in most systems it is the supervisor program which issues the physical I/O statement that actually causes the transfer of data.

The supervisor in most systems is also responsible for error recovery. For example, if for some reason a disk channel becomes inoperative, the supervisor is responsible for attempting to correct, through software, the problem; and, if it cannot, for logging as much information as possible about the problem.

Working very closely with the supervisor are the job control programs. Job control provides continuity between jobs on the computer system. At the same time, it allocates physical devices, provides the mechanics for scheduling jobs on the computer system, loads programs for execution, and is available when programs terminate to take over control.

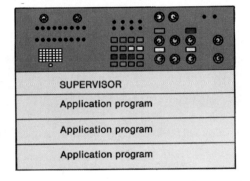

Figure 12-21 The supervisor portion of the operating system is loaded into main computer storage when the operation of the computer is begun. It remains in storage so long as the system is running. The application programs illustrated here are being run in a multiprogramming environment under control of the supervisor.

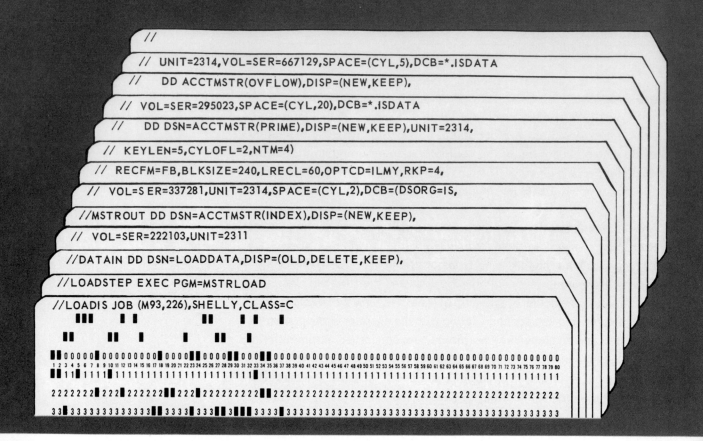

Figure 12-22 The job control language shown above is used with the IBM Operating System. The job control language for other operating systems can vary significantly from this example.

Communication with the job control programs is through the use of job control language (Figure 12-22). Job control language differs considerably, depending upon the operating system. Its major function, regardless of the operating system, is to define jobs to be processed on the computer system, identify programs which are to be executed, and provide a job-to-job transition on the system.

In most cases, programmers must be familiar with the use of job control language because it is the means to cause execution of the programs they write.

Through the use of the control programs, the computer system becomes a self-operating machine as far as job execution is concerned. The ability of the control programs to communicate with the computer operator in order to specify the needs of the system, such as mounting a disk or tape on a particular drive or placing paper in a printer, allows a smooth operating environment in which a maximum of work is accomplished on the system.

Processing programs

The processing programs found as a part of an operating system provide a number of commonly required functions of the computer. The processing programs include language translators and service programs.

The language translators are those compilers and interpreters which translate source programs written by programmers into a machine language format that can be executed on the computer system. The languages mentioned previously in this chapter commonly are found on medium and large computer systems. Through the use of job control language, the programmer can specify that a particular source program is to be translated by one of the translator programs.

The service programs are programs which are supplied as a part of the operating system to perform tasks which are required by programmers and operations personnel. They fall into three major categories: linkage editor, librarian, and system utilities.

The linkage editor programs are used to transform the object programs generated from the language translators into load modules which are ready for execution on the computer system. The output from the language translators is an object program which consists of machine language instructions. In most systems, however, this object program is not yet in a form which can be loaded into main computer storage for execution. For example, a program which performs any input/output operations requires routines from the data management programs to be included in the final load module. These routines are not included in the program when the program is compiled. One of the tasks of the linkage editor programs is to include the data management routines in the load module.

In addition, the linkage editor may have to determine certain addresses in the load module which must be resolved prior to loading the program into main computer storage for execution. After the object program is processed by the linkage editor programs, it is in a form ready to be executed on the computer system.

The librarian programs create and maintain system libraries. A library is nothing more than an area on a direct access device in which certain types of programs and modules are stored. With most computer systems, there are at least three types of libraries. One library will contain load modules which have been processed by the linkage editor and which are available to be loaded into main computer storage for execution. The load modules stored in this library (commonly called the core image library, program library, load module library, or a variety of other names) can be referenced in job control statements which indicate they should be loaded into storage for execution.

A second type of library contains object programs or subroutines which have been processed by a language translator and placed in machine language but have not yet been processed by the linkage editor. These programs and subroutines are commonly used routines which may be included in many different programs by the linkage editor. For example, the data management programs which provide for storing and accessing data are included in this library. They are included in the load module of a program when the program is link edited.

The third type of library contains source statements. These statements have not yet been processed by the language translators. These source statements generally are commonly used statements which can be included in a source program without requiring the programmer to recode them. For example, there may be twenty programs which reference a master file. Instead of each programmer writing the source coding which defines the record format for the file, the record format can be coded once and stored in the library. When a programmer requires the coding for the record format, it can be copied into the source program from the library.

In addition to the linkage editor and the librarian programs, the processing programs available with the operating system include system utility programs. These utility programs consist of file-to-file utility programs and sort/merge programs.

The file-to-file utility programs are used to copy data from one file to another. For example, a utility program would be available which copies data from a disk file onto magnetic tape. This utility program could be used to back up a file stored on disk. The file-to-file utility programs relieve the programmer of the need to write new programs whenever file-to-file processing is required.

The sort/merge programs which are normally a part of the processing programs available with an operating system are designed to sort or merge all files. These programs find great use in most installations because file sorting, particularly in batch processing systems that do not use data bases, consumes a significant portion of the processing time of the computer.

Data management programs

The third major element of an operating system is the series of programs which controls the organization and access of data used in the programs run on the computer system.

Data management routines are normally incorporated into the application program by the linkage editor to provide for the necessary processing to be accomplished. The data management programs relieve the programmer from having to code the detailed instructions necessary to perform such tasks as record blocking and deblocking, index maintenance, and so on. They are an important part of any operating system.

Virtual storage

One problem which programmers have frequently encountered is that the program they write requires more main computer storage than is available on the computer system. Although this problem persists on small computer systems, it has been overcome on some larger computer systems through the use of virtual storage.

When virtual storage is used, segments of a program which are not immediately required for processing are not stored in main computer storage. Instead, they are stored on a direct access device. Through control of the supervisor and other hardware and software features, the portion of a program stored on the direct access device is called into main computer storage when required.

Main computer storage is divided into a series of areas called page frames. When a portion of a program is called into main computer storage, the process is called paging. The page frames used for a given program do not have to be contiguous within main computer storage. Thus, as shown in Figure 12-23, a segment of a program can be stored in different, non-adjacent areas of main computer storage.

The major advantage of virtual storage is that since the entire program need not be in main computer storage at the same time, the program can be of any length. The operating system will ensure that the portion of the program required for program execution is in storage when required.

The major disadvantage of virtual storage is that since segments of a program must be retrieved from a direct access device when they are needed for execution, the overall speed of execution of the program is slower than if the entire program were stored in main computer storage. Indeed, it is possible that much of the time of a computer system can be spent in retrieving portions of programs. When this condition, called thrashing, occurs, the computer system may not effectively be accomplishing any processing. Portions of the program must usually be redesigned to eliminate thrashing.

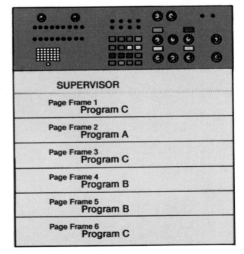

Figure 12-23 This diagram illustrates a possible main computer storage configuration of six page frames used for virtual storage. Segments of program C are found in page frame 1, page frame 3, and page frame 6. A segment of program A is found in page frame 2, while segments of program B are found in page frame 4 and page frame 5. The allocation of main computer storage and bringing pages into storage takes place under the control of the supervisor and other operating system software.

Chapter summary

The following points have been discussed and explained in this chapter.

1. The major programming languages in use today are: a) Assembler Language; b) FORTRAN; c) COBOL; d) PL/I; e) RPG; f) BASIC; g) Pascal.

2. Symbolic programming languages that are closely related to machine language are called low-level languages.

3. Assembler languages are low-level languages. Most assembler language statements generate a single machine language instruction.

4. Assembler language is quite efficient and requires a minimum of main storage usage.

5. A high-level programming language is one in which the program statements are not closely related to the internal characteristics of the computer system.

6. FORTRAN was developed by IBM to be used by scientists, engineers, and mathematicians.

7. FORTRAN allows the expression of complex mathematical calculations using arithmetic operators.

8. FORTRAN has limited file processing capabilities and limited ability to process alphabetic data. Therefore, it is not widely used as a business applications language.

9. COBOL, one of the most widely used programming languages for business applications, is designed to be written using English-like statements such as READ, WRITE, IF, ADD, SUBTRACT, MULTIPLY, and DIVIDE in sentences which express the operation to be performed.

10. Every COBOL program is divided into four divisions: 1) The Identification Division; 2) The Environment Division; 3) The Data Division; 4) The Procedure Division.

11. COBOL is designed to be machine-independent and has strong file handling capabilities.

12. PL/I was developed by IBM to serve both scientific and business users. The strongest characteristic of PL/I is its breadth and detail.

13. RPG (Report Program Generator) was designed to be a simplified business language for small-scale business users. RPG programs are written on special forms. Commonly used forms are the File Description Specifications, Input Specifications, Calculation Specifications, and Output Specifications.

14. The principal advantage of RPG is the ability to generate routine business reports quickly and easily.

15. BASIC is widely used with microcomputers and small business computer systems.

16. Pascal is one of the first major programming languages developed which offers ease of use with structured programming.

17. There are many specialized programming languages which have been developed.

18. The language to be used to code an application will be determined by the analyst or project manager based upon the software available, the knowledge of the programming staff, and the standards established within the data processing department.

19. Coding is an exact skill. A programmer must follow the precise rules of the programming language.

20. A computer can only execute a program which consists of machine language instructions. Therefore, the source statements in the programming language must be translated into machine language instructions.

21. A compiler is a program that translates source program statements into machine language instructions. An object program is the entire program expressed as machine language instructions.

22. The output of a compiler is: a) An object program containing the machine language instructions, which is normally stored on disk in a library; b) A source listing of the source statements in the program; c) A diagnostic listing of any statements in the program which contain errors in the use of the programming language.

23. An interpreter is a program stored in main computer storage or in Read Only Memory (ROM) which will read a source program one statement at a time and cause the execution of that statement. No object program is generated when an interpreter is used.

24. It is important that a programmer produce a program which is easy to read and understand.

25. The basic procedures when testing a program are: a) The program is compiled and diagnostic errors are removed from the program; b) Test data is created; c) The program is tested; d) Any errors which are found are corrected; e) The program is used in a system test.

26. Stub testing allows a program to be partially coded and tested before the entire program is coded.

27. It is essential that the facts regarding each program in a system be carefully recorded in a fashion that can be easily understood.

28. An operating system is a collection of programs that allows a computer system to supervise its own operations for continuous throughput of a series of jobs.

29. The operating system is composed of control programs, processing programs, and data management programs.

Student Learning Exercises

Review questions

1. List the most widely used programming languages.

2. What is meant by a low-level language? A high-level language? Give examples of each.

3. Explain the basic characteristics of assembler language. What are the advantages and disadvantages of assembler language?

4. Why was FORTRAN developed?

5. Why is FORTRAN not widely used as a business application programming language?

6. COBOL is derived from what words? Explain the basic characteristics of the COBOL language.

7. List the advantages and disadvantages of COBOL.

8. Why was PL/I developed? Briefly explain the major characteristics of the language.

9. For what does RPG stand? Where is RPG normally used?

10. Explain how programming occurs in RPG.

11. In what areas is BASIC commonly used?

12. List some of the considerations when evaluating a programming language.

13. Briefly explain the process that occurs when compiling a program.

14. What is the difference between a compiler and an interpreter?

15. Why is it important to write clear, readable code?

16. Explain the steps that should occur when testing a program.

17. What is an operating system? Briefly describe the parts of an operating system and their functions.

Controversial issues in data processing

1. Some data processing managers insist that all programming be done in a single programming language regardless of the type of application. Others argue that a programming language should be selected that "fits" the problem. For example, RPG should be used for routine business reports because it is easier and faster to write than COBOL. COBOL should only be used for more complex processing requirements. Discuss the advantages and disadvantages of a "one language shop" versus a data processing department that utilizes a variety of languages to fit the needs of the problem.

2. Copyright laws have been established to protect the rights of authors of textbooks, so that their works cannot legally be plagiarized. Should a programmer be able to copyright a program? Defend your position.

Research projects

1. Contact some of the large business organizations in your community to determine the type of programming languages used for business applications. Also contact some of the smaller companies to determine the type of programming languages they use. Report to class the results of your investigation.

2. Some have predicted that computer programming is a "dead-end" profession; for they say, in the near future, programming as we know it today will no longer be in existence. Prepare a research report on the future of computer programming as a profession.

Chapter 13
The Future of Computers in Society

Objectives

- To provide an insight into problems faced by the data processing profession in the years ahead

- To develop an awareness of some of the ethical considerations confronting those in data processing

- To point out some of the problems facing society with the utilization of data banks and electronic funds transfer systems

- To develop an awareness of the potential threat posed to freedom and privacy by computer systems

Chapter 13

Figure 13-1 These shiny surfaces which are used as the platters in disk packs could, in the future, contain data about every citizen in the world. Society faces a significant challenge to ensure that computer systems are used for the benefit of all mankind.

The Future of Computers in Society

"If every computer in the world were to suddenly go dead, planes would not fly, trains would not run, traffic lights would not change, banks would have to close, space projects would be aborted, and department stores and grocery stores would not be able to sell . . . If computers were suddenly silenced the world would be thrown into instant chaos.."[1]

Introduction

There is little doubt, as expressed above, that the computer is an integral part of the world's activities. With computers in the office, computers used to aid in decision making, computers used to control the manufacture of products, computers in schools, and computers in the home, it is easy to stand in awe of the tremendous technological achievements which have been made during the last forty years.

Some have begun to question, however, whether these remarkable advances in computer technology will ultimately contribute to the quality of life for the next generation. Indeed, some people assert that a "monster" has been created whose use will result in mass unemployment and whose misuse will threaten many basic freedoms which free people enjoy.

The burden of managing and controlling this rapidly expanding and changing technology falls upon members of the data processing industry and also those who will directly or indirectly be affected by its use.

Some of the important issues facing the data processing profession and some of the problems related to the impact of computers in society will be reviewed in this chapter.

Problems in the data processing industry

Although the data processing industry is one of the most dynamic industries in the world, in the next few years serious problems must be faced relative to the continued growth and progress of the profession.

---

1 David F. Webber, Rev. Noah Hutchings, THE COMPUTERS ARE COMING, The Southwest Radio Church, 1978.

These problems center around the difficulty of managing rapid technological change, improving methods for software development, and establishing standards of ethics within the data processing profession.

Advances in technology

One of the most significant effects of the advances in computer technology has been the great decrease in the cost of computer hardware and the resultant increase in the number of computer systems in use. Computers costing hundreds of thousands of dollars a decade ago can now be obtained for less than $10,000.00

It has been estimated that the market for computers selling for $50,000.00 or less is about 500,000 systems. Many such computers are available today. It has further been estimated that the market for very small computer systems, costing less than $10,000.00 is over three million machines. These systems are also currently available.

With this tremendous potential for the use of computers, a question arises concerning who will design the systems and write the programs that will allow these inexpensive computer systems to be used effectively in business and education. There is a critical shortage of programmers and analysts now; what will it be like in a few years with all of these new systems? Indeed, it has been argued that technological advances and improved hardware has far exceeded the ability of the industry to use them.

Problems with computer software

Although computer hardware has progressed amazingly during the past forty years, the ability to program these machines has not changed radically. The introduction of high-level languages was a significant improvement; but modern COBOL, the most widely used programming language for business applications is very similar to the first version introduced over 20 years ago.

It has been estimated that the "typical" programmer produces eight to ten debugged lines of code per day when working on a programming project. Although structured design and structured programming are aimed at improving programmer productivity, there is still much improvement to be made. Most projects are not implemented on schedule with all of the features promised in the system. Much of the reason for this is related to the problem of relatively low programmer productivity.

In addition, the industry continues to be plagued by unreliable software. In the past, unreliable software has been treated as a "joke" in local newspapers; but with today's sophisticated data communications networks servicing thousands of users, an error in a billing system or an error in a payroll system could conceivably affect thousands of individuals. Life and death may also be affected by computer failure; indeed, outages of computer systems controlling airport traffic have led to near mid-air collisions on more than one occasion. Today and in the future, the reliability of software is of paramount concern not only to the data processing industry, but also to those who are affected by computer use.

The need for professional standards

When a computer issues an inaccurate credit rating for a customer and the customer is denied credit based upon the response from the system, the computer is blamed for the error. Similarly, when a police officer stops a motorist for a traffic violation, makes an inquiry into a criminal network data base system, receives a message that there are outstanding arrest warrants for the person, and places the person under arrest only to find out later that the message was in error, the computer receives the blame.

To those knowledgeable in data processing, it is obvious the computer was not to blame. Rather, the errors were made because of the incompetencies or carelessness of the programmers and system analysts who did not provide safeguards to prevent these types of actions from occurring.

In each of the examples, an element of public safety and welfare was involved. In many areas of life where public safety and welfare is a consideration, society has seen fit to authorize governmental agencies to license personnnel prior to allowing them to practice their profession. Thus, doctors must be licensed to practice medicine, attorneys to practice law, nurses to practice nursing, and others such as real estate agents and barbers must be licensed as well.

Some have suggested that because much of what is done in the data processing world has an effect on public safety and welfare, data processing professionals should be licensed by governmental agencies. This area is one that generates strong emotions and is still highly debated within the data processing industry. Some of the issues are: should programmers and systems analysts be required to pass a rigid examination and be licensed before being allowed to practice their skills; or should programmers be required to carry malpractice insurance and be legally liable for errors in their programs that adversely affect public safety and welfare.

These are issues which the data processing industry faces within the coming years.

Professional ethics and crime

As an occupational area progresses to a professional level, ethics often becomes a consideration of the profession. Ethics refers to the standard of moral conduct practiced within the profession.

Even more important today, society is becoming increasingly concerned not only with the ethics of the data processing profession but with the relationship between ethical behavior and criminal behavior. The attitude test in Figure 13–2 illustrates some of the ethical/criminal considerations which those in the data processing profession must encounter daily. Take the test, being able to justify each answer.

A major problem facing the data processing industry is the prosecution for computer crimes because there has been little definition of what behavior constitutes a computer crime.

To remedy this situation, some states and the federal government have recently enacted a series of computer crime laws aimed at defining criminal activity as related to the computer and data processing. Although the content of such bills is extensive, the California crime bill passed in the latter part of 1979 is typical. It outlaws the use of data processing equipment for fraud and extortion; and forbids the malicious use or alteration of computing hardware, software, or data. Individuals convicted under this law would be guilty of a felony, punishable by a sixteen-month to three-year prison sentence, a fine of $2,500.00 to $5,000.00, or both. Such laws will become increasingly important as computer usage spreads.

COMPUTERS IN SOCIETY

The computer will have a significant influence on the way in which society functions in the future. One of the more pressing issues facing society is that modern computer systems have made it technically and economically feasible to store large volumes of data about citizens in the society in such a way that this data can be readily accessed and analyzed. Some feel that the establishment of these data banks offers a great potential for the loss of privacy and that misuse of this data threatens many of the basic freedoms found in society.

ATTITUDE TEST

ETHICS IN DATA PROCESSING

Instruction: Place a check in the space provided which best reflects your opinion.

1. A computer operator runs a program at work for a friend and uses 10 minutes of computer time. The program was run when the computer was idle; that is, not being used for company business.

   Ethical _____   Unethical _____   Computer Crime _____

2. A student gives out a password to another student not enrolled in a computer class for which a laboratory fee is charged. The password allows access to the school computer. The unauthorized student uses 3 hours of computer time in a timesharing environment.

   Student enrolled in class: Ethical _____   Unethical _____   Computer Crime _____
   Unauthorized student: Ethical _____   Unethical _____   Computer Crime _____

3. A copy of a payroll program developed by a programmer on the job is given to a friend at a different company.

   Ethical _____   Unethical _____   Computer Crime _____

4. Utilizing a terminal, an individual breaks a security code and reviews confidential company salaries of corporate executives. No use is made of the information . . . . "I was just curious" is the response when caught.

   Ethical _____   Unethical _____   Computer Crime _____

5. A bank teller electronically transfers money from a relatively inactive customer account to his own personal account and then transfers the money to a credit card account to pay current credit card charges. On pay day, money is deposited into his personal account, and then he electronically transfers the money back to the customer's account. No money changes hands, and no interest is lost to the customer's account.

   Ethical _____   Unethical _____   Computer Crime _____

6. A programmer is asked to write a program which she knows will generate inaccurate information for stockholders of the company. When she questions her manager about the program, she is told she must write it or lose her job. She writes the program.

   Company: Ethical _____   Unethical _____   Computer Crime _____
   Programmer: Ethical _____   Unethical _____   Computer Crime _____

Figure 13-2 The ethical issues in the Attitude Test above are representative of the types of ethical problems facing the data processing industry.

Data banks

In the early 1970's, the concept of a national data bank arose. The national data bank, it was reasoned, could be developed to serve as a central repository for as much information as could be obtained about the citizens of the country. It would contain name, address, marital status, income, medical history, education, credit rating, criminal records, social security information, tax data, and other types of information. This information is now available in a number of separate files throughout the country. Why not, it was asked, have a single data base containing all these separate files?

With this national data bank, economists, social workers, the FBI, or other authorized users could make inquiries to determine information such as the average income in New York City, the divorce rate in California, or the average age of people in Texas. In order to implement this data bank, a universal identifier, which would be assigned at birth, was required. This identifier would serve as a personal identification number for social security purposes, payroll records, student number, driver license number and even, it was suggested, as a personal telephone number.

The outcry was strong, both from those within the data processing profession and from other concerned citizens. The potential for misuse of such information was very great. Therefore, the national data bank has never been implemented. However, data about citizens is being gathered and stored in files at an astounding rate (next page). If these files were interconnected by means of a nationwide data communications network, some people feel that a national data bank would, in fact, result.

Electronic funds transfer systems

In the late 1960's, there was much discussion about the cashless society, where money would not be needed and all goods and services would be bought through the use of a universal cash card. On payday, the amount of an individual's paycheck would be electronically transferred from the company's account to the employee's account. To purchase groceries, gasoline, or any other products or services, the universal cash card would be used to transfer money from the purchaser's account to the vendor's account.

The benefits are obvious. At the end of the month, a complete record of each individual's expenditures would be available; there would be a tremendous reduction in paperwork; and bad checks would be eliminated.

THE MAIN DATA BANKS[2]

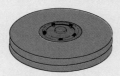

Department of Health, Education and Welfare: 693 data systems with 1.3 billion personal records including marital, financial, health and other information on recipients of Social Security, social services, medicaid, medicare and welfare benefits.

Treasury Department: 910 data systems with 853 million records that include files on taxpayers, foreign travelers, persons deemed by the Secret Service to be potentially harmful to the President, and dealers in alcohol, firearms and explosives.

Justice Department: 175 data systems with 181 million records including information on criminals and criminal suspects, aliens, persons linked to organized crime, securities-laws violators and "individuals who relate in any manner to official FBI investigations."

Defense Department: 2,219 data systems with 321 million records pertaining to service personnel and persons investigated for such things as employment, security or criminal activity.

Department of Transportation: 263 data systems with 25 million records including information on pilots, aircraft and boat owners, and all motorists whose licenses have been withdrawn, suspended or revoked by any state.

Veterans Administration: 52 data systems with 156 million records, mostly on veterans and dependents now receiving benefits or who got them in the past.

Department of Housing and Urban Development: 58 data systems with 27.2 million records including data on applicants for housing assistance and federally guaranteed home loans.

Department of Commerce: 95 data systems with 447 million records, primarily Census Bureau data, but including files on minority businessmen, merchant seamen and others.

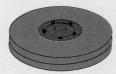

Civil Service: 14 data systems with 103 million records, mostly dealing with government employees or applicants for government jobs.

Department of Labor: 97 data systems with 23 million records, many involving people in federally financed work and job-training programs.

2 U. S. NEWS AND WORLD REPORT, April 10, 1978.

Today, under the term Electronic Funds Transfer (EFT), this concept is being implemented in what may become one of the largest communications networks in existence. The question posed by EFT is similar to the problem of national data banks — who is to have access to this financial information and what protection do citizens have in ensuring their rights of privacy.

Some authorities feel that EFT offers one of the greatest threats to freedom that currently exists in society. For, when carried to its fullest extent, EFT would provide governmental agencies with a complete record of every facet of each person's life. Little could be done, from eating to traveling, without a record's being recorded in a computer system. Some feel that a system such as this could lead to complete governmental control over society.

Others argue, however, that the benefits far outweigh the possible dangers; and all that is needed are safeguards built into the legal system that will protect individual rights and freedoms in the emerging computerized society.

The society as a whole and the data processing industry in particular face a challenging and exciting future. The problem of using computer power for beneficial purposes must be addressed and solved as the entire world becomes affected by the marvel of the twentieth century.

Controversial issues in data processing

1. Data banks and electronic funds transfer systems are very controversial issues in the data processing industry. Do you feel these systems offer serious threats to your privacy and basic freedoms?

Research projects

1. Determine the characteristics of the commonly accepted professions of medicine and law. Relate these characteristics to the current status of personnel in the data processing industry. Do you think data processing is a profession?

2. Prepare a report for the class on recently enacted computer crime laws. Include the acts defined as criminal, the punishments specified, and the results of any trials where people have been tried for computer crimes.

Picture credits

Figure 13–1   Sperry Univac

APPENDIX A
Programming in Basic

Introduction

The purpose of this appendix is to provide an introduction to the principles of program design and computer programming using the BASIC language. This appendix consists of a series of sample programs illustrating basic input/output operations, arithmetic operations, accumulating final totals, comparing, control breaks, and the use and searching of tables.

The programming concepts presented in each of the sample problems should provide an insight into the programming process and establish a foundation for further study in the field of data processing and computer science.

The programming process

It is extremely important that the task of computer programming be approached in a professional manner, for programming is one of the most precise of all human activities. Just as it is the job of the accountant, the mathematician, the engineer, and the scientist to produce correct results, so it is the job of the computer programmer to produce a program that will be reliable and give accurate results.

Programming is not "naturally" an error-prone activity. Errors will only enter into the design and coding of a computer program through carelessness or lack of understanding of the programming process. With careful study and attention to detail, both types of errors can be avoided.

It has been found that when using a careful approach to program design and coding, there is no reason why programs cannot be developed that will execute the first time on the computer and will never fail subsequently.

Problem 1 — Basic input/output operations

To illustrate some of the principles of computer programming, a program will be designed and coded in BASIC that will read a series of input records and produce displayed output.

Input

The input data to be processed consists of a series of input records that contain the employee number, the employee's current pay rate, and the employee name. The chart below illustrates the data to be processed.

EMPLOYEE NUMBER	PAY RATE	EMPLOYEE NAME
105	5.75	BETTY ALLEGRO
125	6.33	WILMA BRADLEY
140	7.52	HARRY LANGLEY
332	4.95	ALLEN CESARIO
999	9.99	END OF FILE
Variable Names E	P	N$

Figure A–1

In the chart above, the last record contains a 999 in the employee number field, the value 9.99 in the pay rate field, and the words END OF FILE in the employee name field. This is called a "trailer" record and is used to indicate when all of the records have been processed. For example, when a record is read that contains the value 999 in the employee number field, it is then known that all of the data records have been processed and the program can be terminated.

Variable names

When programming in BASIC, each field that is to be referenced in the program must be assigned a unique name, called a "variable name." With most BASIC languages, a variable name to be used for fields that contain numeric data may consist of up to two characters. The first character must be one of the letters of the alphabet, A–Z. The second character, if used, must be one of the digits 1–9. In Figure A–1, the variable name assigned for the employee number field is the letter of the alphabet "E." The variable name for the pay rate field is "P."

When processing alphabetic data or alphanumeric data (fields containing letters of the alphabet, numbers, or special characters), the variable name must begin with a letter of the alphabet and be followed by a dollar sign ($). Thus, the employee name field has been assigned the variable name "N$" (Figure A–1). Variable names that reference alphabetic or alphanumeric fields are called string variables.

In summary, variable names are names assigned to fields which will be referenced in a BASIC program. In the example, the variable name "E" will reference the employee number field; the variable name "P" will reference the pay rate field; and the variable name "N$" will reference the employee name field.

The flowchart, BASIC program, and output

The flowchart, BASIC program, and output for the sample problem, which reads a series of input records containing the employee number, pay rate, and employee name and displays these fields, are illustrated in Figure A–2. Note on the output that the fields are displayed in a format different from that contained in the input records. The output contains the employee number, the employee name, and then the pay rate.

BASIC INPUT/OUTPUT

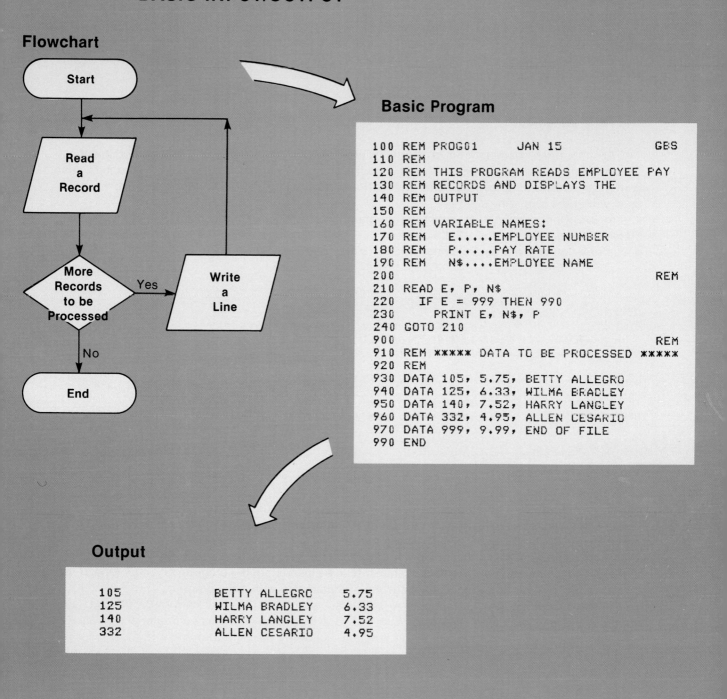

Figure A–2

The flowchart in Figure A–2 illustrates a basic loop in which a record is read; a check is made to determine if there are more records to be processed; and if there are more records to be processed, the record just read is displayed and another record is read. When there are no more records to be processed, the execution of the program is terminated.

The BASIC program

As previously discussed, it is important when writing computer programs to approach the task in a professional manner and develop a program that will be easy to read and easy to modify and maintain. For these reasons, the sample programs are written using a set of standards designed to teach professional programming techniques.

The REM statement

An important characteristic of a quality program is that the program is well documented. Documentation within the program should include a program identification, the date the program was written, an author identification, a brief description of the program, and a listing of the variable names used within the program.

In BASIC, documentation within the program is accomplished through the use of the remark statement (identified by the REM statement in BASIC). The segment of the coding containing the documentation of the program using remarks is illustrated below.

```
100 REM PROG01      JAN 15              GES
110 REM
120 REM THIS PROGRAM READS EMPLOYEE PAY
130 REM RECORDS AND DISPLAYS THE
140 REM OUTPUT
150 REM
160 REM VARIABLE NAMES:
170 REM    E.....EMPLOYEE NUMBER
180 REM    P.....PAY RATE
190 REM    N$....EMPLOYEE NAME
200                                     REM
```

Figure A-3

In BASIC, all statements begin with a line number, followed by the operation to be performed. The line numbers serve to identify each statement. Statements can begin with the number 1. The programs in this textbook always begin with the number 100, and the numbers are incremented by 10 for each of the subsequent statements in the program. This is to provide for uniformity in coding and readability. Incrementing by 10 allows statements to be inserted in the program at a later time, if required, and still retain the ascending sequence of statements within the program.

Following line number 100 in Figure A-3 is a blank space and the entry Rem. In BASIC, the Rem identifies a remark statement. It causes no operation to be performed by the computer and is merely used to provide documentation within the program. Following the Rem Statement is a blank space and the words to document the program.

The first remark statement on line 100 contains the program identification (PROG01), followed by the date the program was written and the identification of the author of the program.

Line 110 is a blank Rem Statement. It is used to cause a blank line to appear in the program. The blank line is included to increase the readability of the program.

On lines 120, 130, and 140 is a brief description of the program. These lines are again followed by a blank Rem Statement at line 150.

Beginning at line 160, the variable names used within the program are identified. Notice the format and indentation used in this section of the program. It is suggested that this format be used whenever a BASIC program is written.

On line 200, the Rem Statement is made in the rightmost positions. This entry is used to separate the introductory remarks portion of the program from the rest of the program. By placing the Rem Statement in the rightmost positions, the blank line is even more apparent and serves to separate major segments of the program.

The proper use of remarks, blanks, and indentation can substantially improve the readability of a program. With BASIC, blank spaces are ignored, so there is great flexibility in writing a BASIC program. It is suggested that the format illustrated in the sample program be used when coding all BASIC programs.

The READ, IF, PRINT, and GOTO statements

The executable statements in the BASIC program are illustrated below. This is the portion of the program that causes the processing to occur.

```
210 READ E, P, N$
220   IF E = 999 THEN 990
230     PRINT E, N$, P
240 GOTO 210
250                                         REM
```

Figure A–4

This segment of the program consists of four types of statements; the Read Statement, the If Statement, the Print Statement, and the Goto Statement.

The Read Statement is used to read the data to be processed. Specified in the Read Statement are the variable names of the fields where the data is to be placed. In the example, the Read Statement is followed by the variable names E (employee number); P (pay rate); and N$ (employee name). Upon execution of the Read Statement, the data will be placed in the fields referenced, ready for processing. In the sample problem, the data to be processed is defined in the last segment of the program.

After the Read Statement is the If Statement. The If Statement is a comparing statement used here to check if the last record has been read. The statement IF E = 999 THEN 990, causes the data stored in the field referenced by the variable name E to be compared to the value 999. If the fields are equal, then control is passed to statement 990, which is a statement to terminate execution of the program. If E is not equal to 999, then the next statement in sequence (230) is executed. Thus, in BASIC the If Statement is used to check for end of file. Note that the If Statement is indented two spaces.

If there are records to process, the Print Statement is executed. The Print Statement is further indented to make it easy to visualize the statement that is executed when it is not end of file. In the Print Statement, the variable names are listed in the sequence in which the fields are to be printed or displayed. In the example, the employee number (E) is to be displayed followed by the employee name (N$), and then the pay rate (P).

Each of the variable names in the Print Statement is separated by a comma. When the comma is used to separate variables in a Print Statement, each field will automatically be displayed in a predetermined location on the CRT screen. To simplify horizontal space control, BASIC divides the output area into a series of zones or columns. Each zone consists of a predetermined number of positions, depending upon the system used. Fields referenced in the Print Statement are placed in the leftmost positions of each of these zones.

The last statement in this segment of the program is the Goto Statement. As the name implies, this statement causes program control to be transferred to the statement specified in the Goto Statement. In the example, control returns to Statement 200, the Read Statement. Note that the Goto Statement is in the same vertical positions as the Read Statement. This is done to allow the processing loop to more easily be seen in the program listing.

The Rem Statement on line 250 in the rightmost positions places a blank line after this portion of the program.

DATA statements

The final segment of the program consists of a series of Data Statements (Figure A–5). Data Statements can be used in BASIC to define the data to be processed. The statements in this section of the program begin with statement number 900. This numbering is not required by BASIC but is used in the sample programs as a standard for numbering the Data Statements.

```
900 REM ***** DATA TO BE PROCESSED *****
910 REM
920 DATA 105, 5.75, BETTY ALLEGRO
930 DATA 125, 6.33, WILMA BRADLEY
940 DATA 140, 7.52, HARRY LANGLEY
950 DATA 332, 4.95, ALLEN CESARIO
960 DATA 999, 9.99, END OF FILE
990 END
```

Figure A–5

The first two Rem Statements are used to document this portion of the program. Following these statements are the Data Statements, containing the actual data comprising the records to be processed. In the example, each Data Statement contains an employee number, employee pay rate, and employee name. Each field is separated by a comma. The last Data Statement contains the end of file record.

In this program, when the Read Statement is executed the first time, the data read is contained in the first Data Statement. Thus, the first employee number is 105, the first pay rate is 5.75, and the first employee name is Betty Allegro. When the Read Statement is executed the second time, the data in the second Data Statement is read. This process continues until the last data record is read. Since it contains an employee number of 999, the program is terminated because the If Statement following the Read Statement tests for the value 999 (Figure A-4).

The last statement in the program is the End Statement. The End Statement terminates the execution of the program.

The complete BASIC program and the output produced by the program are again illustrated below. It is important to review each portion of this program and thoroughly understand the purpose and function of each statement prior to undertaking the student assignments.

Program

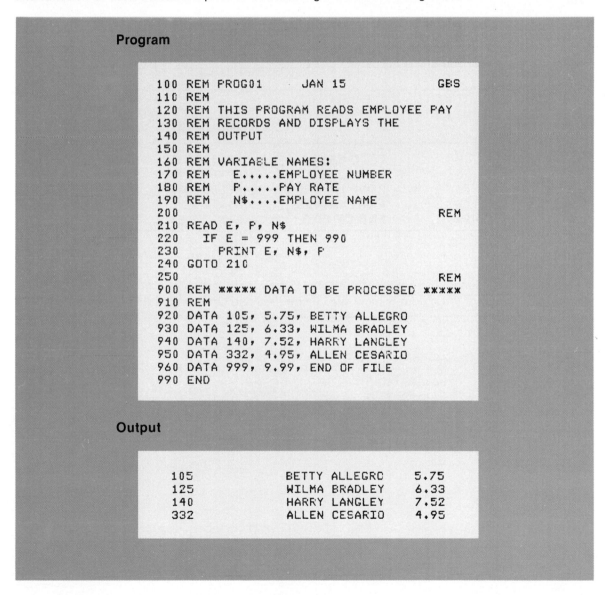

```
100 REM PROG01      JAN 15            GBS
110 REM
120 REM THIS PROGRAM READS EMPLOYEE PAY
130 REM RECORDS AND DISPLAYS THE
140 REM OUTPUT
150 REM
160 REM VARIABLE NAMES:
170 REM    E......EMPLOYEE NUMBER
180 REM    P......PAY RATE
190 REM    N$.....EMPLOYEE NAME
200                                   REM
210 READ E, P, N$
220    IF E = 999 THEN 990
230       PRINT E, N$, P
240 GOTO 210
250                                   REM
900 REM ***** DATA TO BE PROCESSED *****
910 REM
920 DATA 105, 5.75, BETTY ALLEGRO
930 DATA 125, 6.33, WILMA BRADLEY
940 DATA 140, 7.52, HARRY LANGLEY
950 DATA 332, 4.95, ALLEN CESARIO
960 DATA 999, 9.99, END OF FILE
990 END
```

Output

```
105           BETTY ALLEGRO    5.75
125           WILMA BRADLEY    6.33
140           HARRY LANGLEY    7.52
332           ALLEN CESARIO    4.95
```

Figure A-6

PROGRAMMING ASSIGNMENT 1

BASIC INPUT/OUTPUT OPERATIONS

Instructions

A list of personnel is to be prepared. A program should be designed and coded in BASIC to produce the list.

Input

Input consists of personnel input records containing a department number, the employee name, the social security number, and the pay rate. The input data is illustrated below. Department 99 should be used as the end of file indicator.

DEPARTMENT NUMBER	EMPLOYEE NAME	SOCIAL SECURITY NUMBER	PAY RATE
10	OTTO BAKER	551-52-5838	7.95
20	BILL KASEL	380-88-8811	3.39
30	ROSE HOWEL	871-86-5535	4.98
40	ANNE ONNES	844-22-9870	8.66
99	END OF FILE	999-99-9999	9.99

Output

Output is a personnel list containing the social security number, the employee name, and the pay rate. The format of the output is illustrated below. Spacing between the fields should be based upon the standard zones provided by the BASIC language being utilized.

```
551-52-5838     OTTO BAKER      7.95
380-88-8811     BILL KASEL      3.39
871-86-5535     ROSE HOWEL      4.98
844-22-9870     ANNE ONNES      8.66
```

BASIC ARITHMETIC OPERATIONS — ACCUMULATING FINAL TOTALS

To perform the basic arithmetic operations of addition, subtraction, multiplication, division, and raising a value to a power, a series of arithmetic operators are provided in BASIC that are similar to those used in ordinary mathematics. These symbols are illustrated in the chart below.

MATHEMATICAL OPERATION	BASIC OPERATION SYMBOL	EXAMPLE
Addition	+	100 LET T = D1 + D2
Subtraction	—	100 LET P = S - C
Multiplication	*	100 LET G = H * R
Division	/	100 LET A = D / 5
Raising to a Power	↑	100 LET M = A ↑ 4

Figure A-7

The column on the right illustrates the use of the arithmetic operators in a Let Statement. The Let Statement has a variety of uses in the BASIC language. One of its most important functions is its use in arithmetic operations.

When performing arithmetic operations, the calculations to be performed are specified on the right side of the equal sign, using the appropriate arithmetic operators. The area where the answer is to be stored is specified as a variable name on the left side of the equal sign. Thus, the statement LET T = D1 + D2 will cause the value in the field referenced by the variable D1 to be added to the value in the field referenced by the variable D2 and the answer will be stored in the field referenced by T. This concept is illustrated below.

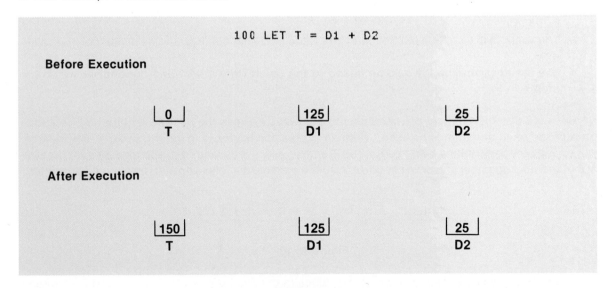

Figure A-8

In the example above, after execution of the instruction, the calculation has been performed and the answer 150 is stored in the area referenced by the variable name T. The values stored in the areas referenced by D1 and D2 have not been altered.

From the chart in Figure A-7, it can be seen that numeric values as well as variable names can be specified in an arithmetic calculation. For example, the divide statement illustrated specifies LET A = D / 5. This statement would cause the value stored in the area referenced by D to be divided by the value 5, with the answer stored in the area referenced by A.

Arithmetic operators can be combined to perform more complex operations. For example, to calculate a new balance in an account by adding the old balance and the purchases, and subtracting the returns, the following statement could be written:

```
200 LET N = O + P - R
```

Figure A-9

Thus, BASIC provides a very convenient way of expressing mathematical calculations that must be performed.

Hierarchy of operations

When performing more complex calculations that might require both addition and subtraction as well as multiplication and/or division, a problem is encountered in determining which calculations are to be performed first. When programming in BASIC, calculations are performed in accordance with the following hierarchy of operations: 1) Raising to a power; 2) Multiplication and division; 3) Addition and subtraction.

When evaluating an arithmetic expression, calculations are performed from left to right according to the hierarchy of operations. Thus, the statement LET F = A ↑ 2 * C / L + Q * T / M would be evaluated as follows:

1. The value in A would be raised to a power of 2.
2. The result of step 1 would be multiplied by the value in C. This result would be divided by the value in L.
3. The value in Q would be multiplied by the value in T. This result would be divided by the value in M.
4. The result from step 2 would be added to the result from step 3 and the answer would be stored in F.

Because this hierarchy of operations will not always express the desired arithmetic operation, parentheses must sometimes be used. When an expression is placed in parentheses, it is evaluated prior to any other operations being performed. For example, if it is desired to add the sales for the five days of the week together and divide by 5 to obtain the average, the following statement could be written.

```
220 LET A = (M + T + W + H + F) / 5
```

Figure A-10

In the example above, the addition of the values in the five fields — M, T, W, H, and F — would take place first. After they are added, the sum will be divided by the value 5 and the answer will be placed in the variable field A. If parentheses were not used, the value in the field F would be divided by the value 5 (since all division takes place before any addition), and then the result of that division would be added to the variables M, T, W, and H. Clearly, parentheses are required here to obtain the proper calculations.

Problem 2 — Basic arithmetic operations and accumulating final totals

Many applications require accumulating values and writing the totals after all records have been processed. In addition, it is desirable to write identifying information in the form of headings. These operations can easily be performed when programming in BASIC.

To illustrate the programming techniques necessary to write headings and to accumulate and write final totals, the logic and BASIC program to prepare a production listing will be explained.

Input

Input consists of weekly production records containing an employee number, employee name, and the number of units manufactured by the employee for the four weeks of the work month. A sample of the input is illustrated below.

	EMPLOYEE NUMBER	EMPLOYEE NAME	WEEK 1	WEEK 2	WEEK 3	WEEK 4
	108	T. JAMES	25	33	43	56
	110	B. BEARS	23	43	22	55
	198	E. MILES	44	56	76	44
	999	END FILE	99	99	99	99
Variable Names	N	N$	W1	W2	W3	W4

Figure A-11

To process the input data, the weekly production figures must be added together to obtain the total monthly production for each employee. The total production for each employee must then be added into an accumulator to obtain the total production for all employees. In addition, a count is to be obtained of the total number of employees.

Output

The production listing that is to be produced is illustrated below. Headings are to appear on the report. The listing is to contain the employee number, employee name, and the total monthly production. After all records have been processed, the total number of employees and the total production of all employees are to be displayed.

```
            PRODUCTION LISTING

    NUMBER          NAME          TOTAL

     108          T. JAMES         157
     110          B. BEARS         143
     198          E. MILES         220

 TOTAL EMPLOYEES 3
 TOTAL PRODUCTION 520
```

NOTE:
In the output report, the numeric fields are indented one space. This space is automatic and allows for the minus sign if present.

Figure A-12

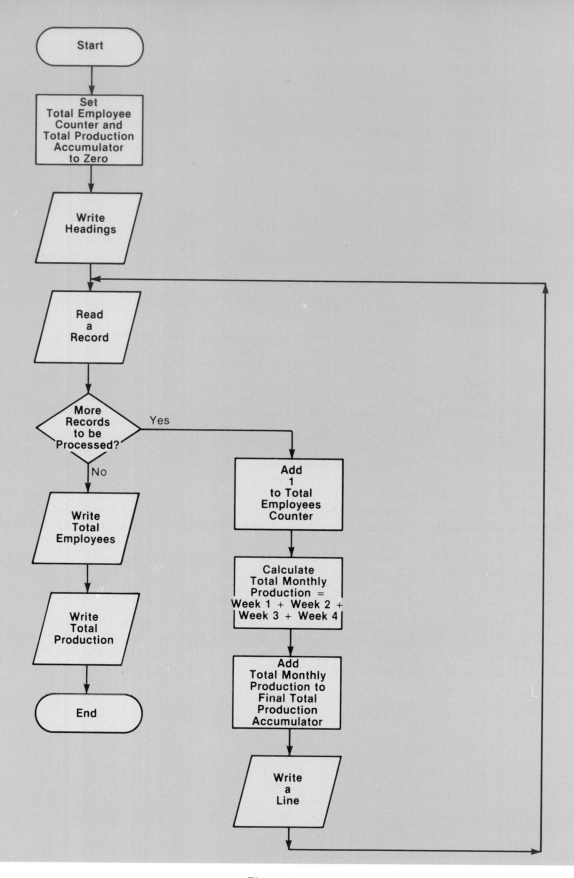

Figure A-13

A.12

The flowchart

The flowchart for the program to produce a production listing and accumulate and display final totals is illustrated in Figure A-13.

When counting records and accumulating totals, it is necessary to reserve an area of main computer storage for these totals. In addition, before processing begins, these areas must be set to zero. The process of establishing an area in storage for the two total areas in the sample program and setting these areas to zero should be indicated in the flowchart. In Figure A-13, the first entry "set total employee counter and total production accumulator to zero" is used for this purpose. A notation is then made in the flowchart to print the headings.

Next, a record is read and a test is performed to determine if there are more records to be processed. When there are records to be processed, a "1" is added to the total employees counter; total monthly production for each employee is calculated and added to a final total production accumulator; and a line is printed. The loop then returns to read another record.

At end of file, the values in the total employees counter and the final total production accumulator are displayed and the program is terminated.

The BASIC program

The BASIC program to create the production report is illustrated on the following page. As with all programs, the Rem Statements are used for program documentation. These statements are illustrated below.

```
100 REM PROG02      JAN 15              GBS
110 REM
120 REM THIS PROGRAM READS PRODUCTION
130 REM RECORDS AND PRODUCES A LISTING.
140 REM TOTAL MONTHLY  PRODUCTION IS
150 REM CALCULATED BY ADDING THE WEEKLY
160 REM PRODUCTION OF EACH EMPLOYEE.
170 REM AFTER ALL RECORDS ARE PROCESSED
180 REM THE NUMBER OF EMPLOYEES ARE
190 REM PRINTED AND THE TOTAL PRODUCTION
200 REM OF ALL EMPLOYEES IS DISPLAYED.
210 REM
220 REM VARIABLE NAMES:
230 REM    N.....EMPLOYEE NUMBER
240 REM    N$....EMPLOYEE NAME
250 REM    W1....WEEK 1 PRODUCTION
260 REM    W2....WEEK 2 PRODUCTION
270 REM    W3....WEEK 3 PRODUCTION
280 REM    W4....WEEK 4 PRODUCTION
290 REM    T.....TOTAL MONTHLY PRODUCTION
300 REM    F1....FINAL TOTAL - EMPLOYEES
310 REM    F2....FINAL TOTAL - PRODUCTION
320                             REM
```

Figure A-14

The complete program is illustrated in Figure A-15. The statements on lines 330 and 340, LET F1 = 0 and LET F2 = 0, are used to set the total employees counter (F1) and the final total production accumulator (F2) to zero.

To display the top heading, the Print Statement with the Tab Entry is used. The heading to be displayed is enclosed in quotation marks. In the example, the heading to be displayed is PRODUCTION LISTING. The Tab Entry followed by a number in parentheses indicates the beginning position of the heading. In the example, the heading will be indented 10 spaces in from the leftmost zone.

The Print Statement on line 360 with blanks following the word, Print, causes a blank line to be printed. This is used to cause a blank line to appear after the first heading. The second headings to be printed are specified on line 370. By enclosing the headings to be printed in quotation marks with a comma separating each entry, these headings will print over the first three zones. Note the blanks following the quotation marks enclosing the word NAME. This is another technique that may be used to control spacing on the heading. In this example, because of the two blank spaces following the quotation marks, the heading NAME will be indented 2 spaces from the leftmost position in the second zone.

The Read Statement on line 400 specifies the fields that are to be used to store the data which is read. These fields include the employee number (N), the employee name (N$), and the production for each week as identified by the variable names W1, W2, W3, W4.

If end of file has not been detected, the required calculations are performed.

The statement on line 420 is used to count the number of records processed. To add one to the counter, the statement LET F1 = F1 + 1 is specified. Each time the statement is executed, the value 1 is added to the value contained in the F1 field. Since F1 is set to zero before the first record is read, the value in F1 after the first record is read and processed will be 1. When the second read is read, the value 1 will be added to the 1 already in F1, making the value in F1 equal to 2. This counting will continue until all of the records have been read and processed. After they have all been read, the value in F1 will reflect the total number of records read and processed.

The total monthly production for each employee is obtained by adding together the weekly production of each employee. This is done by the statement at line 430. This total production is then added to the accumulator which will contain the final total of all production from all employees (line 440). As illustrated previously, the field F2 is initialized to a value of zero prior to processing the first record. When the production for the first employee is added to the field, it will contain just the value for the first employee. When the production for the second employee is added to the F2 field, it will then contain the total for both the first and second employee. This accumulation of a total will continue for all of the records which are read.

After the calculations are performed, a line is displayed and another record is read for processing. This sequence continues until there are no more records to be processed.

After all records have been processed, control is transferred to statement 800. This Print statement causes a blank line to be displayed. The statements on line 810 and 820 display the total employees counter (F1) and total production accumulator (F2). Note the use of the semicolon in the Print Statement following the strings "TOTAL EMPLOYEES" and "TOTAL PRODUCTION." A semicolon is used in the Print Statement to control the spacing of data on an output line. When a semicolon follows an alphanumeric variable or a string constant (such as in the program), the data specified following the semicolon will be displayed immediately adjacent to the string variable or constant. If the semicolon follows a numeric variable or constant, there will be a single space generated between the numeric value and the data which follows it. In the sample program, there is a space between the string constants "TOTAL EMPLOYEES" and "TOTAL PRODUCTION" and the numeric fields following them because each numeric value displayed is indented one position to allow for a sign (see Figure A-12).

If a comma were used instead of a semicolon, the values in the fields F1 and F2 would appear in the next print zone, leaving a large gap in the output line.

The last segment of the program defines the data to be processed through the use of the Data Statement. The End Statement terminates the program.

```
100 REM PROG02      JAN 15           GES
110 REM
120 REM THIS PROGRAM READS PRODUCTION
130 REM RECORDS AND PRODUCES A LISTING.
140 REM TOTAL MONTHLY  PRODUCTION IS
150 REM CALCULATED BY ADDING THE WEEKLY
160 REM PRODUCTION OF EACH EMPLOYEE.
170 REM AFTER ALL RECORDS ARE PROCESSED
180 REM THE NUMBER OF EMPLOYEES ARE
190 REM PRINTED AND THE TOTAL PRODUCTION
200 REM OF ALL EMPLOYEES IS DISPLAYED.
210 REM
220 REM VARIABLE NAMES:
230 REM    N......EMPLOYEE NUMBER
240 REM    N$....EMPLOYEE NAME
250 REM    W1....WEEK 1 PRODUCTION
260 REM    W2....WEEK 2 PRODUCTION
270 REM    W3....WEEK 3 PRODUCTION
280 REM    W4....WEEK 4 PRODUCTION
290 REM    T.....TOTAL MONTHLY PRODUCTION
300 REM    F1....FINAL TOTAL - EMPLOYEES
310 REM    F2....FINAL TOTAL - PRODUCTION
320                                  REM
330 LET F1 = 0
340 LET F2 = 0
350 PRINT TAB(10) "PRODUCTION LISTING"
360 PRINT
370 PRINT "NUMBER", "  NAME", "TOTAL"
380 PRINT
390                                  REM
400 READ N, N$, W1, W2, W3, W4
410   IF N = 999 THEN 800
420     LET F1 = F1 + 1
430     LET T = W1 + W2 + W3 + W4
440     LET F2 = F2 + T
450     PRINT N, N$, T
460 GOTO 400
470                                  REM
800 PRINT
810 PRINT "TOTAL EMPLOYEES"; F1
820 PRINT "TOTAL PRODUCTION"; F2
830                                  REM
900 REM ***** DATA TO BE PROCESSED *****
910 REM
920 DATA 108, T. JAMES, 25, 33, 43, 56
930 DATA 110, B. BEARS, 23, 43, 22, 55
940 DATA 198, E. MILES, 44, 56, 76, 44
950 DATA 999, END FILE, 99, 99, 99, 99
990 END
```

Figure A-15

PROGRAMMING ASSIGNMENT 2

BASIC ARITHMETIC OPERATIONS — ACCUMULATING FINAL TOTALS

Instructions

A bowling score summary is to be prepared. Design and code a program in BASIC to produce the summary.

Input

Input consists of a series of bowling score records which contain a player identification, player name, and three scores. The input data is illustrated below.

PLAYER I.D.	PLAYER NAME	SCORE GAME 1	SCORE GAME 2	SCORE GAME 3
15	TOM RICE	166	165	185
19	DON JETT	225	175	200
29	SAM LUOS	152	138	178
57	SUE ZINN	192	180	180

Output

The output is a bowling score summary, listing the player I.D., player name, and the average score for the three games. After all records have been processed, the total number of bowlers and the team average is to be displayed. The team average is obtained by totaling scores of each of the individual bowlers and dividing by the number of bowlers times the number of games they bowled (3). The format of the output is illustrated below.

```
              BOWLING SCORES

    I.D.              NAME            AVERAGE

     15             TOM RICE            172
     19             DON JETT            200
     29             SAM LUOS            156
     57             SUE ZINN            184

   TOTAL BOWLERS 4
   TEAM AVERAGE 178
```

COMPARING

The ability to compare letters of the alphabet or numbers and perform alternative operations based upon the results of that comparison is one of the more powerful features of any programming language. When comparing, six types of operations can be performed. These operations include comparing to determine if: 1) One value is equal to another; 2) One value is less than another; 3) One value is greater than another; 4) One value is less than or equal to another; 5) One value is greater than or equal to another; 6) One value is not equal to another.

Relational operators

In BASIC, there are six relational operators that may be used with the If Statement to perform comparing operations. Relational operators are symbols that may be used to express the comparing operations. The chart below summarizes these relational operators and how they are used in an If Statement.

RELATIONAL OPERATOR	INTERPRETATION	EXAMPLE
=	equal to	300 IF M = 100 THEN 420
<	less than	300 IF M < 100 THEN 420
>	greater than	300 IF M > N THEN 510
<=	less than or equal to	300 IF M <= 100 THEN 560
>=	greater than or equal to	300 IF M >= G THEN 430
<>	not equal to	300 IF M <> T THEN 500

Figure A-16

When using the relational operators, if the condition is true, then the statement or line number following the THEN is executed. If the condition is false, the next statement in sequence is executed.

Comparing strings

Alphanumeric data, or "strings," can also be compared using the If Statement. To compare alphanumeric data, one alphanumeric variable is placed to the left of the relational operator. Another alphanumeric variable or an alphanumeric literal is placed on the right side of the relational operator. This is illustrated in the two examples below.

Example 1   200 IF N$ = A$ THEN 430

Example 2   400 IF N$ = 'END OF FILE' THEN 800

Figure A-17

In example 1, if the value in the field N$ is equal to the value in the field A$, then control will be passed to statement 430. Otherwise, the next statement in sequence will be executed. The If Statement in example 2 will compare the value in N$ to the string value END OF FILE. If this value is contained in N$, then control will be passed to statement 800.

Problem 3 — Comparing

To illustrate a comparing operation, a problem requiring the preparation of an Auto Rental Summary will be designed and coded in BASIC.

In this application, the charges for the rental of an automobile are based upon the days used and the number of miles driven. If the automobile is driven 100 miles or less, the charge is $16.95 per day. If the automobile is driven more than 100 miles, the charge is $16.95 per day plus 22 cents per mile for each mile driven over 100 miles.

Input

Input consists of records containing a customer name, the miles driven, and the number of days the automobile was used. A sample of the input is illustrated below.

CUSTOMER	MILEAGE	DAYS
J. WHEELER	100	1
B. RESELEL	100	2
K. NGUYENS	233	2
R. LOPEZAT	099	3
Variable Names N$	M	D

Figure A-18

Output

The output is an auto rental summary that lists the customer name, the days the automobile was used, the miles driven, and the total charge to the customer. After all records have been processed, the total number of customers and the total charges for all customers are to be printed. The format of the output is illustrated below.

```
                    AUTO RENTAL SUMMARY

NAME                DAYS              MILES            CHARGE

J. WHEELER           1                100              16.95
B. RESELEL           2                100              33.9
K. NGUYENS           2                233              63.16
R. LOPEZAT           3                99               50.85

TOTAL CUSTOMERS 4
TOTAL CHARGES 164.86
```

Figure A-19

The flowchart

The flowchart below illustrates the logic required to produce the auto rental summary. This flowchart should be carefully reviewed to analyze the logic associated with the comparing operation.

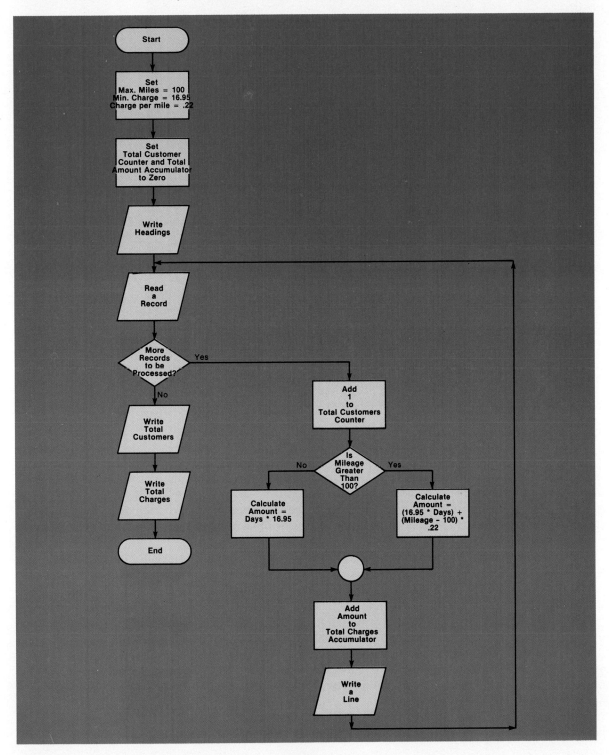

Figure A-20

The BASIC program

The documentation and the first portion of the BASIC program is illustrated in Figure A-21.

```
100 REM PROG03      JAN 15                GBS
110 REM
120 REM THIS PROGRAM PRODUCES AN AUTO
130 REM RENTAL SUMMARY. FOR AUTOS USED
140 REM 100 MILES OR LESS THE CHARGE IS
150 REM $16.95 PER DAY. FOR AUTOS
160 REM USED OVER 100 MILES, THE
170 REM CHARGE IS $16.95 PER DAY
180 REM PLUS .22 CENTS FOR EACH MILE
190 REM OVER 100. AFTER ALL RECORDS
200 REM ARE PROCESSED THE TOTAL
210 REM CUSTOMERS AND TOTAL CHARGES
220 REM ARE DISPLAYED.
230                                       REM
240 REM VARIABLE NAMES:
250 REM    N$....CUSTOMER NAME
260 REM    M.....AUTO MILEAGE USED
270 REM    D.....DAYS AUTO RENTED
280 REM    A.....AUTO RENTAL CHARGE
290 REM    F1....FINAL TOTAL - CUSTOMERS
300 REM    F2....FINAL TOTAL - CHARGES
310 REM    F.....FREE MILES - 100 MILES
320 REM    C.....MINIMUM CHARGE - $16.95
330 REM    P.....CHARGE PER MILE - .22
340                                       REM
350 LET F = 100
360 LET C = 16.95
370 LET P = .22
380 LET F1 = 0
390 LET F2 = 0
400                                       REM
```

Figure A-21

Although actual numeric values can be used to perform comparing and calculation operations, it is better programming technique to define the constants used in a program with variable names and use the variable names in the comparing and calculation statements. For example, in the sample program the free mileage (100 miles) is assigned the variable name F; the minimum charge amount (16.95) is assigned the variable name C; and the charge per mile constant (.22) is assigned the variable name P (lines 310–330).

Values are assigned to variable names by the Let Statements on lines 350–370. With these Let Statements, the value on the right side of the equal sign is stored in the area referenced by the variable name on the left side of the equal sign. After these Let Statements are executed, the variable names F, C, and P can be used in the comparing and calculation statements instead of the actual values.

The reason for programming in this manner is to assist in the maintenance of the program. If a change is ever made in any of the constant values, the change can be made in this section of the program. All references to the variable will use the new values in subsequent runs of the program. For example, if the minimum mileage charge is changed from 16.95 to 18.95, the Let Statement on line 360 could be changed rather than searching through the entire listing to find all occurences of the constant 16.95 that have to be changed.

The final statements in this portion of the program on lines 380 and 390 initialize the final total counter for the total number of customers and the final total accumulator for the total charges to zero.

The portion of the program to display the headings and read and process the data is illustrated below.

```
410  PRINT TAB(17) "AUTO RENTAL SUMMARY"
420  PRINT
430  PRINT "NAME", "DAYS", "MILES", "CHARGE"
440  PRINT
450                              REM
460  READ N$, M, D
470    IF N$ = "END OF FILE" THEN 800
480      LET F1 = F1 + 1
490      IF M > F THEN 530
500        LET A = C * D
510        GOTO 540
520                              REM
530      LET A = (C * D) + (M - F) * P
540      LET F2 = F2 + A
550      PRINT N$, D, M, A
560  GOTO 460
570                              REM
800  PRINT
810  PRINT "TOTAL CUSTOMERS"; F1
820  PRINT "TOTAL CHARGES"; F2
830                              REM
900  REM ***** DATA TO BE PROCESSED *****
910  REM
920  DATA J. WHEELER, 100, 1
930  DATA B. RESELEL, 100, 2
940  DATA K. NGUYENS, 233, 2
950  DATA R. LOPEZAT, 099, 3
960  DATA END OF FILE, 999, 99
990  END
```

Figure A-22

The statements on lines 410 to 440 are used to display the headings.

A record is then read and a check is made to determine if it is end of file. Note in the example that the string constant END OF FILE is used in the If Statement. The string constant END OF FILE is contained in the last Data Statement on line 960.

If it is not end of file, a 1 is added to the total customer counter (F1) by the Let Statement on line 480. A comparison is then made to determine if the mileage (M) is greater than the free mileage (F) by the statement IF M > F THEN 530.

If the mileage is less than or equal to the free mileage, the statement following the If Statement on line 490 is executed; in which case, the amount of the charge is calculated by multiplying the minimum charge (C), which contains 16.95, by the number of days the automobile was used (D). Control is then transferred to statement 540.

If the mileage used is greater than the free mileage allowed, the Let Statement at line 530 is executed. When this occurs, the amount of the charge is calculated by multiplying the minimum charge (C) by the number of days the automobile was used (D); and adding this amount to the value calculated by multiplying the charge per mile (P) times the difference between the mileage used (M) and the free mileage (F).

Regardless of which method is used to calculate the charge, the amount calculated (A) is added to the final total accumulator (F2) by the Let Statement on line 540. A line is then written and control is passed back to statement 460, where another record is read.

After all of the records have been read and processed, the total number of customers and the total charges for all customers are displayed by the statements on lines 800–820. The program is then terminated.

The complete program is illustrated below.

```
100 REM PROG03     JAN 15             GBS
110 REM
120 REM THIS PROGRAM PRODUCES AN AUTO
130 REM RENTAL SUMMARY. FOR AUTOS USED
140 REM 100 MILES OR LESS THE CHARGE IS
150 REM $16.95 PER DAY. FOR AUTOS
160 REM USED OVER 100 MILES, THE
170 REM CHARGE IS $16.95 PER DAY
180 REM PLUS .22 CENTS FOR EACH MILE
190 REM OVER 100. AFTER ALL RECORDS
200 REM ARE PROCESSED THE TOTAL
210 REM CUSTOMERS AND TOTAL CHARGES
220 REM ARE DISPLAYED.
230                                   REM
240 REM VARIABLE NAMES:
250 REM    N$.....CUSTOMER NAME
260 REM    M......AUTO MILEAGE USED
270 REM    D......DAYS AUTO RENTED
280 REM    A......AUTO RENTAL CHARGE
290 REM    F1....FINAL TOTAL - CUSTOMERS
300 REM    F2....FINAL TOTAL - CHARGES
310 REM    F.....FREE MILES - 100 MILES
320 REM    C.....MINIMUM CHARGE - $16.95
330 REM    P.....CHARGE PER MILE - .22
340                                   REM
350 LET F = 100
360 LET C = 16.95
370 LET P = .22
380 LET F1 = 0
390 LET F2 = 0
400                                   REM
410 PRINT TAB(17) "AUTO RENTAL SUMMARY"
420 PRINT
430 PRINT "NAME", "DAYS", "MILES", "CHARGE"
440 PRINT
450                                   REM
460 READ N$, M, D
470   IF N$ = "END OF FILE" THEN 800
480     LET F1 = F1 + 1
490     IF M > F THEN 530
500       LET A = C * D
510       GOTO 540
520                                   REM
530     LET A = (C * D) + (M - F) * P
540     LET F2 = F2 + A
550     PRINT N$, D, M, A
560 GOTO 460
570                                   REM
800 PRINT
810 PRINT "TOTAL CUSTOMERS"; F1
820 PRINT "TOTAL CHARGES"; F2
830                                   REM
900 REM ***** DATA TO BE PROCESSED *****
910 REM
920 DATA J. WHEELER, 100, 1
930 DATA B. RESELEL, 100, 2
940 DATA K. NGUYENS, 233, 2
950 DATA R. LOPEZAT, 099, 3
960 DATA END OF FILE, 999, 99
990 END
```

Figure A-23

PROGRAMMING ASSIGNMENT 3

COMPARING

Instructions

A loan payment listing is to be prepared. Design and code a program in BASIC to produce the listing.

Input

Input consists of loan approval input records that contain a customer name and loan amount. The format of the input records is illustrated below.

CUSTOMER NAME	LOAN AMOUNT
T. WANN	496.00
G. LANG	602.00
C. LOVE	392.00
B. YETT	598.00

Output

Output is a loan payment listing that contains the customer name, loan amount, interest charge, and the monthly payments. For loans in excess of $500.00, the flat interest rate is 10%. For loans $500.00 or less, the flat interest rate is 15%. All loans are for a period of ten months. The monthly payment is obtained by adding the amount of the loan to the flat interest charge and dividing the result by 10 months. After all records have been processed, the total number of customers and the total amount of the loans are to be displayed. The format of the output listing is illustrated below.

```
                 LOAN PAYMENT LISTING

     NAME           AMOUNT          INTEREST          PAYMENTS

   T. WANN           496             74.4              57.04
   G. LANG           602             60.2              66.22
   C. LOVE           392             58.8              45.08
   B. YETT           598             59.8              65.78

   TOTAL CUSTOMERS 4
   TOTAL LOAN AMOUNT 2088
```

A.23

CONTROL BREAKS — PROBLEM 4

As discussed in Chapter 11, taking a control break and performing special processing when there is a change in a control field is a common application in many business problems. Control break processing can be implemented when using the BASIC language. To illustrate the programming of control breaks in BASIC, a program will be developed which prepares an order register.

Input

Input for the sample problem is a series of records indicating orders received from customers. These records contain the customer number, item description, and sales amount. A sample of the input is illustrated below.

CUSTOMER NUMBER	ITEM DESCRIPTION	SALES AMOUNT
2000	BAND AIDS	15.35
2000	TAPE	12.13
2010	ASPIRIN	14.87
2010	EAR DROPS	22.46
N	**I$**	**A**

Variable Names

Figure A-24

Output

The output is an order register which lists the customer number, the item description, and the sales amount. When there is a change in customer number, a total is taken for all sales to that customer. After all records have been processed, a final total is printed of the total sales to all customers. The output is illustrated below.

```
              ORDER REGISTER

CUSTOMER          ITEM              AMOUNT

  2000            BAND AIDS         15.35
  2000            TAPE              12.13
                                    27.48 *

  2010            ASPIRIN           14.87
  2010            EAR DROPS         22.46
                                    37.33 *

                  FINAL TOTAL       64.81 **
```

Figure A-25

Flowchart

The flowchart in Figure A-26 illustrates the control break logic for the sample problem. In this program, if end of file is detected by the first Read Statement, the output will consist of headings and totals of zero.

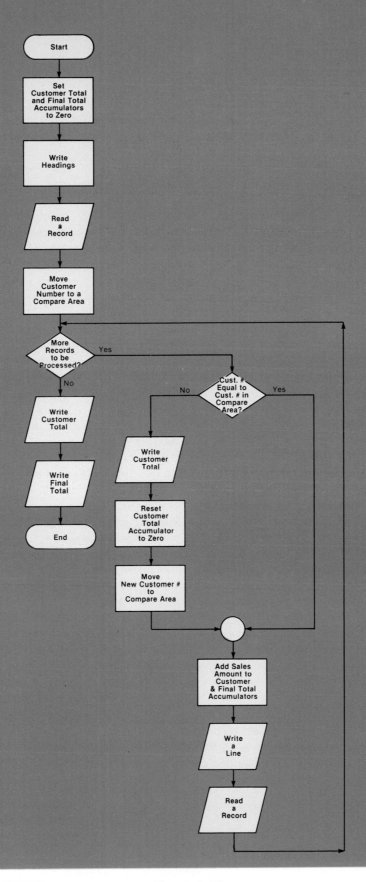

Figure A-26

The BASIC program

The BASIC program is illustrated on the following page. It is extremely important when programming any application that the programmer implement the logic developed in the design of the program. The program in Figure A–27 implements the control break logic as defined by the flowchart in Figure A–26.

The first segment of the program documents the program and the variable names. The statements on lines 290 and 300 set the customer total accumulator (T1) and the final total accumulator (F1) to zero. Headings are then written.

The Read Statement on line 370 is used to read the first record. The customer number from the input record is then placed in a compare area so that subsequent records may be compared with the first record. This is accomplished through the statement LET C = N on line 380. This statement takes the value stored in N (which is the customer number in the input record) and places it in the area referenced by the variable name C.

A check is then made to determine if there are more records to be processed. If there are records to be processed, then the statement on line 410 is executed. This statement is used to compare the customer number in the input record (N) to the customer number in the compare area (C). When processing the first record, an equal condition will always occur; therefore, control will transfer to statement 470.

Line 470 contains the statement to add the sales amount from the input record into the customer total accumulator. This is followed by a statement to add the sales amount into the final total accumulator (line 480).

A line is then written and another record is read. Control is returned to statement 400 where a check is performed to determine if there are more records to be processed.

If there is a record to be processed, statement 410 is executed again; and if the customer number in the input record is equal to the customer number in the compare area, the sequence of operations is repeated.

When a record is read in which the customer number (N) is not equal to the customer number in the compare area (C), a control break has occurred. Statements 420 through 450 will be executed. The customer total (T1) is written by statement 420. The two commas in the Print Statement will cause the total to be displayed in the third zone established by BASIC. Whenever a comma appears in a Print Statement with no data preceding it, a zone will be skipped. After the total is displayed, a blank line is written (statement 430), the customer total accumulator is reset to zero (statement 440), and the new customer number is moved to the compare area (statement 450).

When the control break processing is completed, the amount in the record for the new customer is added to the customer total (statement 470), the amount is added to the final total (statement 480), a line is displayed (statement 490), and another record is read (statement 500). Control is then passed to the If Statement on line 400 to check if the loop should continue.

When end of file is detected by the If Statement on line 400, control is transferred to statement 800. It displays the customer total. A blank line is then written, followed by the final total for all sales. The program is then terminated.

This program illustrates a single level control break. Multiple level control breaks are also commonly found in business applications programming. In these applications, more than one control field is compared to determine if their values changed. Even though there are more control breaks, the same basic logic illustrated in this program can be applied to solve the problem.

```
100 REM PROG04      JAN 15              GES
110 REM
120 REM THIS PROGRAM READS CUSTOMER
130 REM SALES RECORDS AND PRODUCES A
140 REM LIST OF ORDERS RECEIVED FOR THE
150 REM DAY.   WHEN THERE IS A CHANGE IN
160 REM CUSTOMER NUMBER, CUSTOMER TOTALS
170 REM ARE PRINTED. AFTER ALL RECORDS
180 REM ARE PROCESSED A FINAL TOTAL IS
190 REM PRINTED OF ALL ORDERS.
200 REM
210 REM VARIABLE NAMES:
220 REM    N......CUSTOMER NUMBER
230 REM    I$....ITEM DESCRIPTION
240 REM    A.....AMOUNT
250 REM    T1....CUSTOMER TOTAL
260 REM    F1....FINAL TOTAL
270 REM    C.....COMPARE AREA
280                                     REM
290 LET T1 = 0
300 LET F1 = 0
310                                     REM
320 PRINT TAB(15) "ORDER REGISTER"
330 PRINT
340 PRINT "CUSTOMER", "ITEM", "AMOUNT"
350 PRINT
360                                     REM
370 READ N, I$, A
380 LET C = N
390                                     REM
400 IF N = 9999 THEN 800
410    IF N = C THEN 470
420       PRINT ,, T1; "*"
430       PRINT
440       LET T1 = 0
450       LET C = N
460                                     REM
470    LET T1 = T1 + A
480    LET F1 = F1 + A
490    PRINT N, I$, A
500    READ N, I$, A
510 GOTO 400
520                                     REM
800 PRINT ,, T1; "*"
810 PRINT
820 PRINT , "FINAL TOTAL", F1; "**"
830                                     REM
900 REM ***** DATA TO BE PROCESSED *****
910 REM
920 DATA 2000, BAND AIDS, 15.35
930 DATA 2000, TAPE, 12.13
940 DATA 2010, ASPIRIN, 14.87
950 DATA 2010, EAR DROPS, 22.46
960 DATA 9999, END OF FILE, 99.99
990 END
```

Figure A-27

PROGRAMMING ASSIGNMENT 4

CONTROL BREAKS

Instructions

A sales summary listing is to be prepared for a group of retail stores. The report is to be group-printed; that is, there is to be one line displayed for each group of input records. Design and code a program in BASIC to produce the listing.

Input

Input consists of a series of daily sales records for each store. The records contain the store number, the store location, and the total daily sales. The format of the input is illustrated below.

STORE NUMBER	STORE NAME	SALES AMOUNT
10	LOS ANGELES	997.26
10	LOS ANGELES	842.49
10	LOS ANGELES	956.87
10	LOS ANGELES	740.12
22	LONG BEACH	926.82
22	LONG BEACH	564.91
22	LONG BEACH	838.46
22	LONG BEACH	798.43

Output

Output is a group-printed listing in which one line is displayed containing the total sales for each store. Thus, there will be one line on the listing for the Los Angeles store and one line on the listing for the Long Beach store. After all records have been processed, the final total of all sales should be displayed.

```
                 SALES SUMMARY

    NUMBER              NAME              SALES

      10             LOS ANGELES         3536.74
      22             LONG BEACH          3128.62

    TOTAL SALES 6665.36
```

TABLES AND TABLE SEARCHES

The use of tables and searching of tables to extract data for processing is easily accomplished in the BASIC language. The following problem is developed to illustrate the use of tables in BASIC.

Problem 5 — Tables and table searches

To illustrate the use of tables and table searching, a problem similar to that illustrated in Chapter 11 involving the use of a payroll table will be programmed in BASIC. In this problem, two tables, one containing a paycode and the other containing a corresponding pay rate, will be created. These tables will then be displayed. A payroll listing will then be prepared, using the data in the tables as required.

Input

The input records contain an employee name, a pay code, and the hours worked. On the basis of the pay code, a pay rate will be extracted from the pay rate table. The pay rate will be used to calculate the gross pay (hours times pay rate). The data for the two tables and the data to be processed are shown below.

PAY CODE TABLE		PAY RATE TABLE	
17	49	5.25	7.75
24	52	6.25	8.05
29	57	6.45	8.25
41	69	7.11	6.75
43	70	7.50	4.92
	90		8.57

NAME	PAY CODE	HOURS
SMITH, R. A.	24	33
ONEAL, D. E.	41	39
ELLIS, M. L.	52	25
LOGUE, R. G.	75	25
N$	C1	H

Variable Names

Figure A-28

Output

The following is an illustration of a portion of the output of the pay code and pay rate tables that are printed and also the payroll listing. If an input record does not contain a valid pay code, an error message is displayed.

```
        PAY RATE TABLE

PAY CODE            PAY RATE                              PAYROLL LISTING

  17                  5.25           NAME            CODE            HOURS              PAY
  24                  6.25
  29                  6.45        SMITH, R. A.        24              33              206.25
  41                  7.11        ONEAL, D. E.        41              39              277.29
  43                  7.5         ELLIS, M. L.        52              25              201.25
  49                  7.75        LOGUE, R. G.     INCORRECT PAY CODE
  52                  8.05
  57                  8.25
   :                   :
   :                   :
```

Figure A-29

Flowchart

The flowchart for the table search program is illustrated below.

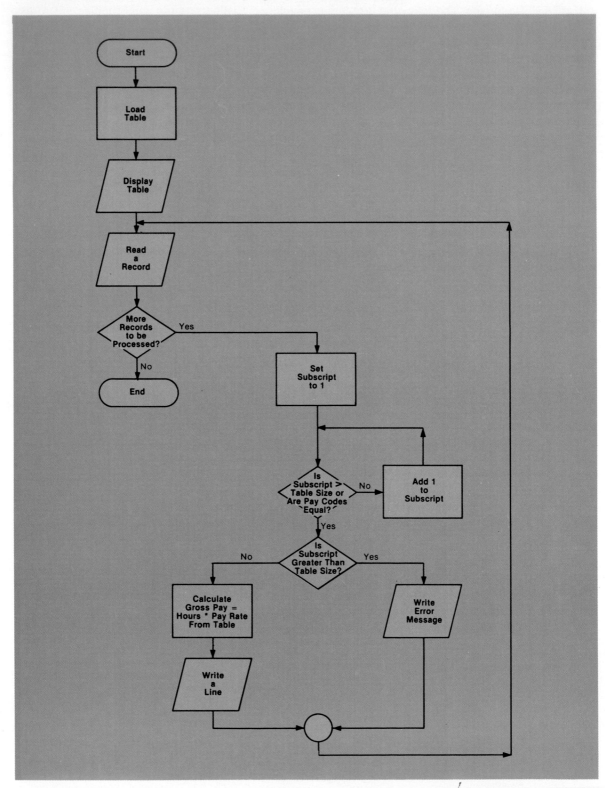

Loading the table

To load the pay code table and the pay rate table requires the use of the Dim Statement (Dimension Statement) and the For-Next Statement. The segment of the program which loads the table and the related data to be loaded are illustrated below.

```
350 REM ***** LOAD PAY RATE TABLE *****
360                                    REM
370 DIM C(11), R(11)
380                                    REM
390 FOR L = 1 TO 11
400    READ C(L), R(L)
410 NEXT L
420                                    REM
430 REM ***** DATA FOR TABLE *****
440 REM
450 DATA 17, 5.25, 24, 6.25, 29, 6.45
460 DATA 41, 7.11, 43, 7.50, 49, 7.75
470 DATA 52, 8.05, 57, 8.25, 69, 6.75
480 DATA 70, 4.92, 90, 8.57
```

Figure A-30

The data to be loaded into the pay code table consists of eleven pay codes. The data for the pay rate table is eleven pay rates. The first pay code in the pay code table corresponds to the first pay rate in the pay rate table, the second pay code in the pay code table corresponds to the second pay rate in the pay rate table, and so on.

When there are more than ten elements in a table, most BASIC interpreters and compilers require the use of the Dimension Statement. The Dim Statement specifies the number of storage areas to be reserved for the elements of the table. In the example on line 370, the statement DIM C(11), R(11), reserves eleven storage areas for the paycodes (C), and eleven storage areas for the pay rates (R). The number of storage areas to be reserved are specified in parentheses following the appropriate variable names.

The diagrams below illustrate the reserved storage areas after the Dim Statements are executed.

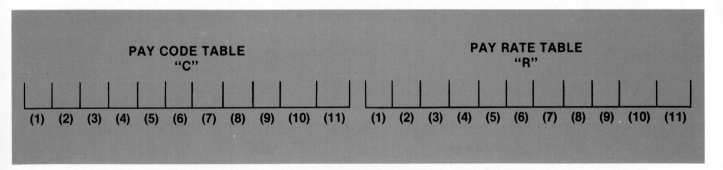

Figure A-31

To reference each element in the tables, a subscript is used. A subscript is a value specified within parentheses which identifies the element to be used. For example, the variable and subscript C(1) references the first element in the pay code table, the entry C(2) references the second element in the pay code table, and so on. Similarly, the entry R(1) references the first element in the pay rate table, etc.

A variable can also be used as a subscript. Thus, the entry C(L) will reference the element in the table corresponding to the value found in the variable L. If L contains the value 1, then the first element of the pay code table will be referenced. If L contains the value 2, then the second element of the pay code table will be referenced. This same technique can be used for the pay rate table.

The Dimension Statement reserves areas of storage but does not place any values in the area. Therefore, the next step is to place the pay codes in the pay code table and the pay rates in the pay rate table. When the exact number of elements in a table are known, the For-Next Statement is normally used to place the data in the table.

The For-Next Statement provides a looping capability that allows the execution of a group of statements a specified number of times. The general format for the For-Next Statement is illustrated in Figure A–32.

```
                                        ──── Initial value of counter
    300  FOR  L  =  1  TO  11 ◄──── Top limit of counter
                            ┐├── Statements to be executed
    320  NEXT  L
```

Figure A-32

Following the word FOR is a variable name followed by an equal sign and values used to control the number of times the loop is executed. In the example, the entry, FOR L = 1, sets the storage area referenced by L to 1. This storage area is used as a counter for the number of times the loop will be executed. The last portion of the statement (TO 11) indicates the top limit of the counter. Upon execution, the statements following the For Statement and ending with the Next Statement will be executed eleven times.

Each time through the loop, the counter L is automatically incremented by 1 until the top level of the counter is exceeded. At that time, the loop is terminated and the statements following the Next Statement are executed. The variable name in the Next Statement must be the same as the variable name in the For Statement. In the example, this variable name is L.

To place the data in the table, the Read Statement is used (Figure A–33). The entry C(L) in the Read Statement specifies that the first data read from the Data Statement is to be placed in the element of the C Table identified by the value in the subscript L. When the value in L is equal to 1, the data read will be placed in the first element of C. The same is true for the entry R(L). Thus, as can be seen, the first elements of each table will be loaded by the Read Statement executed when L is equal to 1.

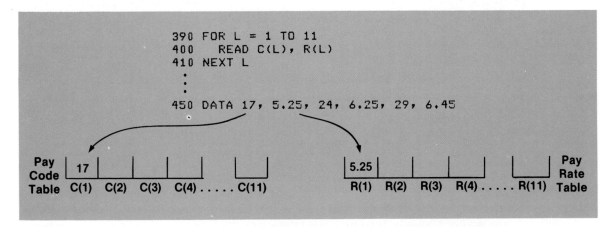

Figure A-33

When the loop is repeated a second time, the value in L will be automatically increased to 2 by the For Statement. Since the loop has not been executed eleven times, the Read Statement will be executed. The next data from the Data Statement will be placed in the second elements of the pay code table and the pay rate table. This process continues for eleven passes through the For-Next loop. When the looping is complete, the remaining statements in the program are executed.

When the Read Statement in Figure A–33 is executed, it takes the data from the Data Statement. After the first Read, the first two numbers from the Data Statement have been placed in the tables. The second execution of the Read Statement does not cause data to be taken from the second Data Statement. The Read Statement takes the next data in the first Data Statement. Thus, the value 24 is placed in the second element of the pay code table and the value 6.25 is placed in the second element of the pay rate table. Throughout a program, any Read Statement which is executed will take the next available data from a Data Statement. Therefore, it is important that the data be precisely defined in the Data Statement so that the correct data is used by the Read Statements in the program.

The segment of the program to display the table that has just been loaded is illustrated in Figure A–34.

```
500 REM ***** LIST PAY RATE TABLE *****
510                                        REM
520 PRINT TAB(5) "PAY RATE TABLE"
530 PRINT
540 PRINT "PAY CODE", "PAY RATE"
550 PRINT
560                                        REM
570 FOR P = 1 TO 11
580    PRINT C(P), R(P)
590 NEXT P
```

Figure A-34

After the headings for the tables are displayed, the For-Next Statement is used to display the eleven elements that comprise the pay code table and the pay rate table. The basic structure of the For-Next Statement is the same in this example as in Figure A–33; except that a Print Statement is used to display the table rather than a Read Statement to load the table. The variable names C(P) and R(P) are used to reference the elements in the table. The table variable names are C and R, and the subscript used is the variable P, which is also specified in the For and Next Statements.

The first time through the For-Next loop, the subscript P will contain the value 1; therefore, the first elements of the pay code table and the pay rate table will be printed. The second time through the loop, the subscript will contain the value 2 and the second elements in the tables will be displayed. This process will continue until all elements in the tables have been displayed.

The segment of the program to read the input payroll records, extract the proper pay rate from the pay rate table based upon the pay code, calculate the gross pay, and display a line on the payroll listing is illustrated below.

```
630 REM ***** PRODUCE PAYROLL LISTING *****
640                                         REM
650 PRINT TAB(20) "PAYROLL LISTING"
660 PRINT
670 PRINT "   NAME", "CODE", "HOURS", "  PAY"
680 PRINT
690                                         REM
700 READ N$, C1, H
710    IF N$ = "END OF FILE" THEN 990
720       LET S = 1
730                                         REM
740       IF S > 11 THEN 790
750       IF C1 = C(S) THEN 790
760          LET S = S + 1
770       GOTO 740
780                                         REM
790       IF S > 11 THEN 840
800          LET G = H * R(S)
810          PRINT N$, C1, H, G
820          GOTO 850
830                                         REM
840       PRINT N$, "INCORRECT PAY CODE"
850 GOTO 700
```

Figure A-35

The statement on line 700 reads the first record containing the employee name, the pay code, and the hours worked. A test is then performed for end of file. If there is a record to process, the subscript S is set to the value 1. The If Statement on line 740 checks if the subscript is greater than 11. If it is, it indicates that the entire pay code table has been searched and there is no pay code in the table equal to the pay code in the input record.

If the subscript is still within table range, the If Statement on line 750 checks if the code in the input record is equal to the code in the pay code table (C). If it is, control is passed to line 790. If it is not, the value in the subscript (S) is incremented by 1 and control is passed back to line 740 where the loop is begun again. This loop will continue until either the subscript is greater than the number of elements in the table or until the pay code in the input record is equal to the pay code in the pay code table. In either case, control is passed to line 790.

On line 790, the If Statement checks if the subscript value is greater than the number of elements in the table. If it is, control is passed to statement 840, where an error message is displayed. If it is not, the gross pay is calculated by the Let Statement on line 800 and a line is written on the listing. Control is then passed to statement 850, which causes control to be sent to line 700, where another input record is read.

This loop will continue until there are no more records to be processed, at which time the program will be terminated.

The BASIC program

The complete program for the sample problem is illustrated on this and the following page. Note on page A.36 that the names in the Data Statements (Statements 920–960) are contained within quotation marks. Quotation marks must enclose string constants that contain commas, such as the ones used in this program (i.e. "SMITH, R. A.").

```
100 REM PROG05      JAN 15              GBS
110 REM
120 REM THIS PROGRAM READS DATA TO LOAD
130 REM A TABLE WITH A PAY CODE AND A
140 REM PAY RATE. THE PAY TABLE IS
150 REM THEN LISTED. PAY RECORDS
160 REM ARE THEN READ AND THE TABLE
170 REM IS SEARCHED TO EXTRACT THE
180 REM THE PAY RATE FROM THE TABLE
190 REM BASED UPON A PAY CODE IN
200 REM THE INPUT RECORD. THE PAY
210 REM RATE IS USED TO CALCULATE
220 REM PAY AND A LINE IS DISPLAYED.
230 REM
240 REM VARIABLE NAMES:
250 REM    C(.)..PAY CODE IN TABLE
260 REM    R(.)..PAY RATE IN TABLE
270 REM    N$....EMPLOYEE NAME
280 REM    C1....PAY CODE IN INPUT RECORD
290 REM    H.....HOURS
300 REM    G.....GROSS PAY
310 REM    L.....SUBSCRIPT TO LOAD TABLE
320 REM    P.....SUBSCRIPT TO LIST TABLE
330 REM    S.....SUBSCRIPT TO SEARCH TABLE
340                                    REM
350 REM ***** LOAD PAY RATE TABLE *****
360                                    REM
370 DIM C(11), R(11)
380                                    REM
390 FOR L = 1 TO 11
400    READ C(L), R(L)
410 NEXT L
420                                    REM
430 REM ***** DATA FOR TABLE *****
440 REM
450 DATA 17, 5.25, 24, 6.25, 29, 6.45
460 DATA 41, 7.11, 43, 7.50, 49, 7.75
470 DATA 52, 8.05, 57, 8.25, 69, 6.75
480 DATA 70, 4.92, 90, 8.57
490                                    REM
```

Figure A-36 (Part 1 of 2)

```
500 REM ***** LIST PAY RATE TABLE *****
510                                 REM
520 PRINT TAB(5) "PAY RATE TABLE"
530 PRINT
540 PRINT "PAY CODE", "PAY RATE"
550 PRINT
560                                 REM
570 FOR P = 1 TO 11
580    PRINT C(P), R(P)
590 NEXT P
600                                 REM
610 PRINT
620                                 REM
630 REM ***** PRODUCE PAYROLL LISTING *****
640                                 REM
650 PRINT TAB(20) "PAYROLL LISTING"
660 PRINT
670 PRINT "    NAME", "CODE", "HOURS", "  PAY"
680 PRINT
690                                 REM
700 READ N$, C1, H
710    IF N$ = "END OF FILE" THEN 990
720       LET S = 1
730                                 REM
740       IF S > 11 THEN 790
750       IF C1 = C(S) THEN 790
760         LET S = S + 1
770       GOTO 740
780                                 REM
790       IF S > 11 THEN 840
800         LET G = H * R(S)
810          PRINT N$, C1, H, G
820          GOTO 850
830                                 REM
840       PRINT N$, "INCORRECT PAY CODE"
850 GOTO 700
860                                 REM
900 REM ***** DATA TO BE PROCESSED *****
910 REM
920 DATA "SMITH, R. A.", 24, 33
930 DATA "ONEAL, D. E.", 41, 39
940 DATA "ELLIS, M. L.", 52, 25
950 DATA "LOGUE, R. G.", 75, 25
960 DATA "END OF FILE", 99, 99
990 END
```

Figure A-36 (Part 2 of 2)

PROGRAMMING ASSIGNMENT 5

TABLES AND TABLE SEARCHES

Instructions

A daily medical charge listing is to be prepared. Design and code a program in BASIC to produce the listing.

Input and table

Input consists of patient records containing the patient identification number, patient name, and a code indicating the type of treatment and related charges. The input records and the related table containing the code, service rendered, and the charge for the service are shown below.

PATIENT I.D.	PATIENT NAME	CHARGE CODE
1998	GRIGGS, B.	10
2372	LAYRNX, T.	50
4443	SMALES, L.	30
6093	VERRYL, D.	68
7204	ZITCHE, D.	40
8795	ZOPZKE, E.	20

SPECIAL SERVICES	
Code 10 — EXAMINATION	$20.95
Code 20 — INJECTION	$12.95
Code 30 — BLOOD TEST	$25.75
Code 40 — X-RAY	$35.25
Code 50 — MEDICATION	$15.95

Codes in the input record not contained in the table are to be considered errors.

Output

Output is a listing of the patient's identification number, the patient's name, the charges, and an explanation of special services. Charges and services are obtained by extracting them from the tables based upon the charge code in the input record. After all records have been processed, the total number of patients and the total charges are to be displayed.

```
                    MEDICAL CHARGES

    NUMBER              NAME            CHARGE          SERVICE

     1998              GRIGGS, B.       20.95          EXAMINATION
     2372              LAYRNX, T.       15.95          MEDICATION
     4443              SMALES, L.       25.75          BLOOD TEST
     6093              VERRYL, D.     INVALID CHARGE CODE
     7204              ZITCHE, D.       35.25          X-RAY
     8795              ZOPZKE, E.       12.95          INJECTION

    TOTAL PATIENTS 6
    TOTAL CHARGES 110.85
```

ADDITIONAL BASIC STATEMENTS

In addition to the BASIC Statements illustrated in the previous programming examples, there are other statements that are useful for various applications. Some of the more widely used of these statements are summarized below and on the following pages.

INPUT statement

To enter data directly into storage, the Input Statement is used. An example of the Input Statement is illustrated below.

```
100 INPUT N
200 INPUT M$
300 PRINT N, M$
```

Figure A-37

The Input Statement includes a line number and the word INPUT followed by a variable name. The variable name can be a numeric variable (such as the variable N in Figure A-37) or an alphanumeric variable (such as the variable M$ in Figure A-37).

When the Input Statement is executed, the computer will display a question mark (?) on the terminal screen. This indicates the program is ready to accept data from the terminal. The operator then enters the appropriate data and depresses the required key to return control to the program. The data that is entered on the terminal keyboard may then be used for processing as required. In the example in Figure A-37, the data entered is displayed.

The Input Statement may have more than one variable name. This is illustrated in Figure A-38.

```
100 INPUT N, M$
200 PRINT N, M$
```

Figure A-38

When more than one variable is used with the Input Statement, the variable names must be separated by a comma. The Input Statement will accept one variable at a time. Thus, when the Input Statement is encountered, the computer will display a question mark and the operator would enter a value for the first variable (in the example, N). After the first value is entered, the operator would return control to the program by depressing the appropriate key. The computer would again display a question mark and the value for the second variable would be entered by the operator. The program can then use the values entered as required.

RESTORE statement

The Restore Statement causes the next Read Statement to read the first data specified in the first Data Statement in the program. This allows the program to reuse the same data. The Restore Statement is often used in search operations. An example of the Restore Statement is illustrated in Figure A-39.

```
200 READ X
210 READ Y
    .
    .
    .
300 RESTORE
310 GOTO 200
320 DATA 10, 20
```

Figure A-39

When the Read Statement on line 200 is first executed, the value 10 from the Data Statement on line 320 would be placed in the variable field X. The second Read Statement on line 210 would cause the value 20 to be placed in variable field Y. After processing, the Restore Statement on line 300 will cause the first piece of data in the Data Statement on line 320 to again be used when a Read Statement is executed. Thus, when the Read Statement on line 200 is executed a second time, it would again cause the value 10 to be placed in the variable X. The Read Statement on line 210, when executed a second time, would cause the value 20 to be placed in the variable Y. If the Restore Statement were not used in the coding in Figure A-39, the error message "Out of Data" would be displayed when the Read Statement is executed a second time.

ON GOTO statement

The On Goto Statement is a multi-way branching statement. An example is illustrated in Figure A-40.

```
150 ON C GOTO 200, 300, 400
```

Figure A-40

When the statement above is executed, if the value in the variable referenced by C is equal to 1, control will be transferred to statement 200. If the value in C is 2, then control is transferred to statement 300; while if the value in C is equal to 3, control is passed to line 400. If C does not contain 1, 2, or 3, then control passes to the statement following the On Goto Statement. The On Goto Statement is valuable when a comparing type of operation must be performed on a sequence of values beginning with 1.

GOSUB-RETURN statement

The Gosub Statement, in conjunction with the Return Statement, is used in BASIC to transfer control to a subroutine and then return control back to the point where the subroutine was called. The example on the next page illustrates the use of the Gosub and Return Statements.

```
100 READ N, N$, P
110 GOSUB 500
120 PRINT N, N$, P, T
             .
             .
             .


500 LET T = P/N
             .
600 RETURN
```

Figure A-41

When the Gosub Statement is executed, control is passed to the statement number specified in the statement. In the example, the statement at line 500 receives control. The statements following statement 500 are executed until a Return Statement is encountered. At that time, control is returned to the statement following the Gosub Statement.

Functions

BASIC includes a number of functions as a part of the language. Functions are prewritten subprograms for common problems that can be called by a single statement. Functions supplied as a part of the BASIC language are called library functions. Some of the commonly available functions are listed below.

Function	Purpose
ABS(x)	Gives the absolute value of x.
INT(x)	Gives the greatest integer less than or equal to x.
SGN(x)	Returns the value 1 if x is positive, –1 if x is negative, and 0 if x is zero.
SQR(x)	Calculates the square root of x.
RND(x)	Returns a random number between 0 and 1.
SIN(x)	Calculates the sine of x where x is in radians.
COS(x)	Calculates the cosine of x where x is in radians.
TAN(x)	Calculates the tangent of x where x is in radians.
ATN(x)	Calculates the arctangent of x.
LOG(x)	Calculates the natural logarithm of x.
EXP(x)	Calculates the exponential e^x.

Figure A-42

The following example illustrates the use of the Square Root function.

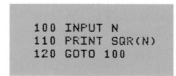

```
100 INPUT N
110 PRINT SQR(N)
120 GOTO 100
```

Figure A-43

The routine above will obtain a number from the operator and print the square root of the number.

Summary

The examples in this appendix have been designed to introduce many of the basic concepts and programming techniques associated with typical applications; and the means for implementing them in the BASIC language. For a further study of computer programming using BASIC and more assignments and examples, see the study guide and workbook which accompanies this textbook.

CASE STUDY

PROGRAMMING ASSIGNMENT 6

Instructions

A hospital patient entry system is to be designed and coded in BASIC. The basic operations to be performed are: 1) A menu is to be displayed explaining to the operator the functions available. The operator must be able to choose one of the options; 2) Upon request, a patient entry form should be displayed that allows for entering patients into the hospital; 3) Upon request, it should be possible to make an inquiry to determine the room and doctor for each patient entered in the hospital; 4) Upon request, it should be possible to obtain a listing of all patients, their room assignments, and their doctors.

The menu

Upon beginning operation, a menu should be displayed. An example of the menu is illustrated below. The menu lists the functions that can be performed.

```
        BELMONT HOSPITAL
             MENU

     CODE   FUNCTION

        1     PATIENT ENTRY
        2     PATIENT INQUIRY
        3     PATIENT SUMMARY
        4     END OF JOB

     ENTER 1, 2, 3, OR 4
     TO SELECT FUNCTION

     ENTER CODE
```

By entering a 1, 2, 3, or 4, the operator should be able to select the function to be performed.

Patient entry

If a code 1 is selected on the menu, a patient entry form should be displayed as illustrated below. All patients must be entered before other functions can be performed. For the purposes of this program, there should be five patients entered. After all patients have been entered, control should return to the menu.

The inquiry

After all patients have been entered, inquiries should be accepted. The operator enters the patient name and the inquiry response is patient name, room number, and doctor name. If a patient is not found, an error message should be displayed. After all inquiries have been processed, control should return to the menu. The format of the inquiry is illustrated below.

The patient summary

After all patients have been entered, it should be possible to obtain a patient summary. The format of the patient summary is illustrated below.

Variations

For a less complex assignment, the following variations can be programmed, moving from the simplest to more complex: 1) Patient entry and patient summary; 2) Patient entry and patient inquiry; 3) Patient entry, patient summary, menu; 4) Patient entry, patient inquiry, and menu; 5) The complete assignment.

```
        BELMONT HOSPITAL
        PATIENT ENTRY

ENTER PATIENT NAME
   LAST NAME:  ? SMITH
ENTER ROOM NUMBER:? 54
ENTER DOCTOR NAME
   LAST NAME:  ? JONES

MORE PATIENTS?
   ENTER Y (YES) OR N (NO):
```

```
        BELMONT HOSPITAL
        PATIENT INQUIRY

   ENTER PATIENT NAME:? SMITH

   ┌NAME           ROOM          DOCTOR
   │
   └SMITH           54           JONES
OR
   ┌
   └ PATIENT SMIT NOT ADMITTED

   MORE INQUIRIES?
      ENTER Y (YES) OR N (N):
```

```
        BELMONT HOSPITAL
        PATIENT SUMMARY

      NAME          ROOM          DOCTOR

   SMITH            54            JONES
   HONNY            55            YUNG
   REMMO            56            TANNY
   REYNOLDS         57            WILLEM
   VULTO            58            HANKSY

   WHEN FINISHED VIEWING
   SUMMARY, DEPRESS ENTER KEY
```

APPENDIX B

The Coding of the 80 Column Card

The standard punched card contains 80 columns in which numeric data, alphabetic data, or special characters may be punched. Numeric data is recorded by punching a hole in any selected card column. Alphabetic data is recorded by utilizing two punches in a single column, a zone punch (punching positions 0, 11, 12), and a numeric punch. Special characters are represented by a combination of two or three characters in a single column.

The following is an illustration of the 80 column card.

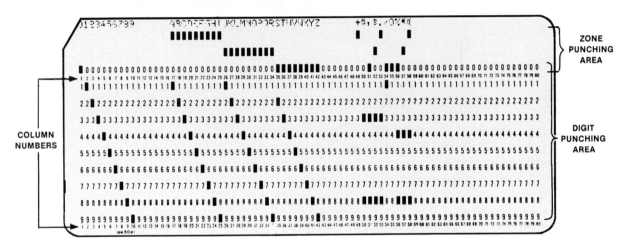

Figure B-1

The chart below summarizes the coding structure for the letters of the alphabet.

LETTER	ZONE	+	NUMERIC PUNCH	LETTER	ZONE	+	NUMERIC PUNCH	LETTER	ZONE	+	NUMERIC PUNCH
A	12	and	1	J	11	and	1	S	0	and	2
B	12	and	2	K	11	and	2	T	0	and	3
C	12	and	3	L	11	and	3	U	0	and	4
D	12	and	4	M	11	and	4	V	0	and	5
E	12	and	5	N	11	and	5	W	0	and	6
F	12	and	6	O	11	and	6	X	0	and	7
G	12	and	7	P	11	and	7	Y	0	and	8
H	12	and	8	Q	11	and	8	Z	0	and	9
I	12	and	9	R	11	and	9				

Figure B-2

APPENDIX C

Number Systems

Introduction

Data is stored in main computer storage as a series of bits being "on" or "off," symbolically represented as a "1" or "0." As these bits can only assume one of two possible states, the representation of data in main computer storage is based upon the binary number system — a number system in which only two symbols are used to represent values.

Although not required for a general understanding of how computers operate and store data, an understanding of the binary number system provides added insight into the operation of computer systems.

The decimal number system

A review of some of the basic concepts of the decimal number system is often useful in understanding other number systems.

The decimal system utilizes ten symbols to represent values. These symbols are: 0, 1, 2, 3, 4, 5, 6, 7, 8, and 9. Through the use of these ten symbols, any quantity can logically be represented.

To represent quantities greater than 9, two or more symbols must be used. The proper utilization of these symbols to represent quantities is based upon the concept of place values.

In the decimal number system, each place position from right to left is as follows: ones, tens, hundreds, thousands, etc. These place values are obtained by using a base of 10 (as there are ten symbols in the decimal number system) and raising this base to the next highest power each position to the left.

The example below illustrates the concept of place values and how decimal numbers derive their meaning.

0	1	1	0	
THOUSAND	HUNDRED	TEN	ONE	Place Value
10^3	10^2	10^1	10^0	Base

Figure C-1

In the example above, the number one hundred and ten is represented by the digits 110. The number 110 in the decimal number system derives its value from the place value of each digit. Thus, the number 110 in the decimal system really means 1 - one hundred, 1 - ten, and 0 - ones. Any decimal number can be analyzed in a similar manner. The place value concept can be applied to a number system with any base. The remainder of this appendix will examine number systems with a base 2 (binary), a base 16 (hexadecimal), and a base 8 (octal).

The binary number system

In the binary number system 0 and 1 are the only digits used. Thus, the binary number system uses a base of 2 to establish the place value for each digit. In the binary number system, each place position is assigned the following values: one, two, four, eight, etc. The place value is established by raising the base of 2 to the next highest power each place position to the left. The following charts illustrate the place values for the first four positions in the binary number system and the decimal numbers 1, 2, and 3 represented in the binary number system.

	0	0	0	1	
NUMBER 1 =	EIGHT	FOUR	TWO	ONE	Place Value
	2^3	2^2	2^1	2^0	Base

	0	0	1	0	
NUMBER 2 =	EIGHT	FOUR	TWO	ONE	Place Value
	2^3	2^2	2^1	2^0	Base

	0	0	1	1	
NUMBER 3 =	EIGHT	FOUR	TWO	ONE	Place Value
	2^3	2^2	2^1	2^0	Base

Figure C-2

As can be seen from the illustration above, the decimal number 1 is represented in binary as 0001, the decimal number 2 as 0010, and the decimal number 3 as 0011.

The following chart summarizes the binary equivalents of the decimal numbers 0 – 9.

Decimal	Binary
0	0000
1	0001
2	0010
3	0011
4	0100
5	0101
6	0110
7	0111
8	1000
9	1001

Figure C-3

By relating these binary numbers to the place value chart, it is easy to see how these zeros and ones derive their related decimal values.

The diagram from Chapter 4 illustrating the decimal number 2317 stored in a binary format is shown in Figure C-4. Note the use of the place values to derive the decimal value.

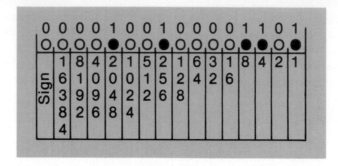

Figure C-4

The hexadecimal number system

On some computer systems, machine language instructions, storage locations, and data in main storage are referenced in a number system using the base 16. This number system is called the hexadecimal number system.

The hexadecimal number system represents the decimal values 0–15 by means of 16 individual symbols. The representation of the digits 0–9 are the same in the hexadecimal number system as in the decimal number system. To represent the decimal values 10–15, however, the hexadecimal system uses the letters of the alphabet A–F. Thus, the decimal value 9 is represented in hexadecimal as 9, the decimal value 10 is represented in hexadecimal as the character A, the decimal value 11 as the character B, etc. The chart below illustrates the decimal values 0–15 and their equivalent hexadecimal notation.

DECIMAL VALUE	HEXADECIMAL NOTATION	DECIMAL VALUE	HEXADECIMAL NOTATION
0	0	8	8
1	1	9	9
2	2	10	A
3	3	11	B
4	4	12	C
5	5	13	D
6	6	14	E
7	7	15	F

Figure C-5

Understanding the use of the hexadecimal number system requires an understanding of the place value concept as it relates to hexadecimal numbers. The hexadecimal number system uses the base 16 with sixteen different symbols. By raising the base 16 to the next highest power when moving from right to left, the place values become 1, 16, 256, 4096, and so on.

The diagram in Figure C-6 illustrates the first four place positions of the hexadecimal number system, with the digits one and zero recorded in the first 2 positions.

0	0	1	0	
4096	256	16	1	Place Value
16^3	16^2	16^1	16^0	Base

Figure C-6

Using the place value chart, it can be seen that the right-most position represents the units position. Thus, a 1 recorded in this position would represent the decimal value 1. An A recorded in this position would represent the decimal value 10 because the symbol A in hexadecimal represents the decimal quantity 10. The symbol F represents the decimal value 15, which is the highest value that can be represented by a single character in hexadecimal. In order to represent the decimal value 16, two digits are required. The entry 10 in hexadecimal represents the value 16 in decimal. This is because in hexadecimal, the 1 in the second place position to the left represents the decimal value 16. In hexadecimal, the value 11 would represent the decimal value 17, hexadecimal 12 the decimal value 18, and so on. The chart below summarizes the representation of the decimal values 0–47 in hexadecimal.

DECIMAL	HEXADECIMAL	DECIMAL	HEXADECIMAL	DECIMAL	HEXADECIMAL
0	0	16	10	32	20
1	1	17	11	33	21
2	2	18	12	34	22
3	3	19	13	35	23
4	4	20	14	36	24
5	5	21	15	37	25
6	6	22	16	38	26
7	7	23	17	39	27
8	8	24	18	40	28
9	9	25	19	41	29
10	A	26	1A	42	2A
11	B	27	1B	43	2B
12	C	28	1C	44	2C
13	D	29	1D	45	2D
14	E	30	1E	46	2E
15	F	31	1F	47	2F

Figure C-7

Use of hexadecimal number system

As previously mentioned, on some machines storage addresses and data in main computer storage are referenced in a hexadecimal form. This is done because a representation in binary form is difficult to interpret.

For example, the number 5 recorded in main computer storage in the extended binary coded decimal interchange code would be displayed in a binary form as 11110101. This type of notation is difficult to interpret, especially if long sequences of digits were to be read.

If, however, the binary notation 11110101 is separated into four bits and each of the four bits is converted to a hexadecimal value, the results would appear as illustrated in Figure C-8.

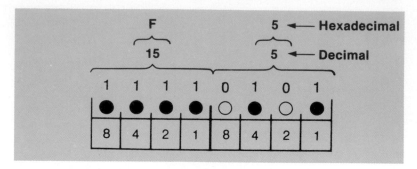

Figure C-8

In the drawing above, the leftmost four bits contain a binary 1111. This is the equivalent of decimal value 15, which is represented in hexadecimal as an "F."

The next four bits contain 0101. This is a decimal 5 and a hexadecimal 5. Thus, the number 5 in the extended binary coded decimal interchange code recorded in a binary form as 11110101 is displayed in hexadecimal as F5.

Addition using hexadecimal numbers

Data is often displayed for use by the programmer in hexadecimal form. This includes machine language instructions, storage addresses, and the data in storage. Because of this fact, it is sometimes necessary to add and subtract hexadecimal numbers. A simplified technique for adding and subtracting hexadecimal values is explained in the paragraphs below.

The following examples illustrate typical problems.

Figure C-9

An easy way to add hexadecimal numbers is to mentally convert the hexadecimal value to decimal, add in decimal, and then mentally convert the answer back to hexadecimal. Using this technique, the mental reasoning to add the hexadecimal values above would be as follows:

Example 1: Hexadecimal A is added to hexadecimal 3: 1) Hexadecimal A is equivalent to decimal 10; 2) Hexadecimal 3 is equivalent to decimal 3; 3) Decimal 10 plus decimal 3 is equal to decimal 13; 4) Decimal 13 is equivalent to hexadecimal D; therefore, the answer is hexadecimal D.

Example 2: Hexadecimal 2C is added to hexadecimal 1B: 1) Hexadecimal C is equivalent to decimal 12; 2) Hexadecimal B is equivalent to decimal 11; 3) The sum of decimal 12 and decimal 11 is decimal 23; 4) The sum 23 is 7 greater than decimal 16, which is the base of the hexadecimal number system. Therefore, the result is hexadecimal 7 with a carry of 1; 5) The value 2 plus the value 1, plus 1 carry equals 4. Thus, the answer is hexadecimal 47.

Subtraction using hexadecimal numbers

A similar approach is taken when subtracting hexadecimal values. Several examples are illustrated below.

Figure C-10

To subtract, each hexadecimal value should be converted to its decimal value, subtraction should take place, and the answer should be converted back to hexadecimal.

Example 1: Hexadecimal 1D is subtracted from hexadecimal 4F: 1) Hexadecimal F is equivalent to decimal 15; 2) Hexadecimal D is equivalent to decimal 13; 3) Decimal 13 subtracted from decimal 15 is equal to 2; thus, 2 becomes the rightmost digit in the answer; 4) Hexadecimal 1 is subtracted from hexadecimal 4, giving a 3. Thus, the final answer is hexadecimal 32.

Example 2: Hexadecimal 2F is subtracted from hexadecimal C1E: 1) Hexadecimal E is decimal 14 and hexadecimal F is decimal 15, so a one must be borrowed. Therefore, the first two characters of the minuend C1E become C0. When a 1 is borrowed in hexadecimal, it is in reality the decimal value 16. Therefore, the total value becomes 30 (E + 16 = decimal 30); 2) Decimal 15 from 30 leaves a value of decimal 15 or a hexadecimal value of F. Hence, the rightmost value in the answer is F; 3) The problem now becomes C0 minus 2; 4) Once again, a 1 must be borrowed from the digit to the left (the C). Decimal 2 is subtracted from decimal 16, and the answer is decimal 14 which is hexadecimal E; 3) When the 1 was borrowed from the hexadecimal C, it became hexadecimal B. The final answer is, therefore, hexadecimal BEF.

Using this approach, hexadecimal values can be added and subtracted rapidly and accurately.

The octal number system

With the extended binary coded decimal interchange code (EBCDIC), the hexadecimal number system is normally used to provide an easy method to read storage addresses which are in a binary form.

Some computers display storage using the octal number system, which is a number system based upon the use of 8 symbols to represent values. The symbols are 0, 1, 2, 3, 4, 5, 6, and 7.

The octal number system uses the base of eight. The place values in the octal number system use powers of eight. The rightmost position represents 8^0, the next position is 8^1, the next position to the left is 8^2, and so on (Figure C-11). Thus, even though the base number is changed, the octal system operates in the same manner as the decimal, binary, and hexadecimal number systems.

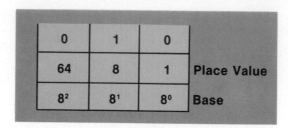

0	1	0	
64	8	1	Place Value
8^2	8^1	8^0	Base

Figure C-11

Since the octal number system uses eight numeric symbols, the largest decimal number that can be represented by a single digit is the value 7. The decimal number eight is represented in octal by the value 10. The chart below summarizes the decimal values 1–16 and their octal equivalents.

DECIMAL	OCTAL	DECIMAL	OCTAL
1	1	9	11
2	2	10	12
3	3	11	13
4	4	12	14
5	5	13	15
6	6	14	16
7	7	15	17
8	10	16	20

Figure C-12

For ease of reading, the ASCII code is often displayed in octal. When displaying data in octal, the bits are separated into groups of three bits starting at the right. Each three bits are treated as a unit and converted from their binary value to their respective octal value. The leftmost bit is considered as a bit by itself when interpreting the 7-bit ASCII code.

In the example below, the number 1 in ASCII code is illustrated in both a binary and octal form. In binary, the value is 0110001. The equivalent value using the octal number system is 061.

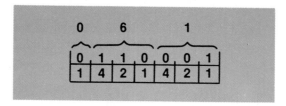

Figure C-13

The chart below summarizes the ASCII bit pattern for the numbers 0 – 9 and their related octal value.

ASCII Character	Meaning	ASCII Bit Pattern							Octal Value
0	Zero	0	1	1	0	0	0	0	60
1	One	0	1	1	0	0	0	1	61
2	Two	0	1	1	0	0	1	0	62
3	Three	0	1	1	0	0	1	1	63
4	Four	0	1	1	0	1	0	0	64
5	Five	0	1	1	0	1	0	1	65
6	Six	0	1	1	0	1	1	0	66
7	Seven	0	1	1	0	1	1	1	67
8	Eight	0	1	1	1	0	0	0	70
9	Nine	0	1	1	1	0	0	1	71

Figure C-14

Addition using octal numbers

When adding in octal, it must be kept in mind that 7 is the greatest decimal value that can be represented by a single character and that the base of eight is used in the octal number system. The following examples illustrate adding in octal.

Example 1:		**Example 2:**	
	5		376
	+ 4		+ 233
	11		631

Figure C-15

Example 1: Octal 4 is added to octal 5: 1) The two values are added as decimal numbers; 2) Since the result, 9, is greater than the base 8, the base 8 must be subtracted from 9, obtaining the value 1 with a carry of 1; 3) As there is only a single column of numbers to be added, the answer is octal 11.

Example 2: Octal 376 is added to octal 233: 1) Add the numbers in the rightmost column as decimal numbers. The result is 9; 2) Since 9 is greater than the base 8, the base 8 must be subtracted from 9, resulting in the value 1 with a carry of 1; 3) Add the next column. The 7 plus the 3 plus the carry of 1 yields decimal 11 as the result; 4) Since decimal 11 is greater than the base 8, the base 8 must be subtracted from decimal 11, giving the answer 3 with a carry of 1; 4) Add the 3 plus the 2 plus the carry of 1, giving a value 6. Since 6 is less than 8, there is no carry. Thus, the answer is 631 in octal.

Subtraction using octal numbers

When subtracting using octal numbers, a value 1 borrowed from a column to the left is equivalent to the decimal value 8 being borrowed. The following examples illustrate subtraction when using octal numbers.

Figure C-16

Example 1: Octal 07 is to be subtracted from octal 16: 1) Beginning with the rightmost column, the value 7 cannot be subtracted from 6. Therefore, a value must be borrowed from the column to the left; 2) When a value is borrowed in octal, the value borrowed is decimal 8. Thus, the borrowed value 8 plus the 6 equals 14; 3) Subtracting the value 7 from the value 14 gives an octal 7.

Example 2: Octal 176 is to be subtracted from octal 525: 1) The digits in the rightmost columns are subtracted. As a 6 cannot be subtracted from a 5, a value is borrowed from the column to the left. A decimal value 6 from 13 gives a 7; 3) The next column is then subtracted. As a 7 cannot be subtracted from a 1, a value from the next column is borrowed; 4) The 7 is now subtracted from a decimal 9 (8 + 1) and the answer is 2. The last column is subtracted and the answer is a 3. Thus, the answer is 327.

Using the techniques presented provides an easy method for performing calculations in number systems other than the decimal number system.

Glossary / Index

Binary Number System A number system with a base 2 that uses two symbols (0 and 1) to represent values. **C.2**

Bit (Binary Digit) The smallest unit for storing data in main computer storage. **4.2**

Blocking The storing of two or more logical records on magnetic tape or disk to form a physical record for the purpose of more efficiently storing and processing the records. **7.4**

Bubble Memory A type of memory which is composed of small magnetic domains formed on a thin crystal film of synthetic garnet. **7.10**

Bursting The process of separating each page of continuous forms. **1.16**

Byte A given number of bits considered as a unit to form a storage location. **4.2**

C **Card Reader** A device capable of reading the data stored in a punched card and transmitting it to main computer storage. **1.11, 3.2, 5.7**

Cards, Punched See punched cards. **1.7, 5.4, B.1**

Cathode Ray Tube Terminal A device used as a computer terminal which contains a television-like screen for displaying data. Most CRT terminals also have a typewriter-like keyboard. **1.11, 1.20, 3.2, 5.15, 6.6**

Central Processing Unit Electronic components which cause processing on a computer to occur by interpreting instructions, performing calculations, moving data in main computer storage, and controlling the input/output operations. It consists of the arithmetic/logic unit and the control unit. **1.5, 3.3, 4.1, 4.9**

Centralized Departments An organizational structure in which computer power is concentrated in a single location. **9.11**

Certificate in Data Processing (CDP) A professional certificate awarded by the ICCP to individuals who have passed a comprehensive examination. **2.14**

Chain Printer A type of high-speed printer which contains characters on a rotating chain. **6.17**

Channel An electronic device associated with a computer system that controls the physical transfer of data between the input/output device and main computer storage. **8.26**

Channels, Communication The lines or data links over which data is transmitted including standard telephone lines, coaxial cables, microwave transmission, satellite, and fiber optics. **8.7**

Check Digit A calculated digit appended to a numeric field to assure validity when referenced in the future. **5.22**

Classify To separate data into different categories according to some specification. **3.22**

Coaxial Cables High-quality communication lines normally laid underground or under the ocean. **8.7**

COBOL Common Business Oriented Language: one of the most widely used business programming languages. **2.12, 12.6**

Coding The process of writing instructions for a computer. **12.17**

COM (Computer Output Microfilm) A technique used to record output from a computer as very small images on roll or sheet film. **6.19**

Common Carrier A company or organization which contracts with state or federal governments to carry the property of others. **8.28**

Communications, Data See data communications. **2.25, 8.1**

Comparing, Logical Operations The ability of the computer to compare data and perform alternative actions based upon the results of the comparison. **3.10, 11.18-11.21, A.17**

Compiler A program that interprets computer statements written in a symbolic form and converts the statements to machine language instructions. **2.11, 12.18**

Computer A device which can perform computations, including arithmetic and logic operations, without intervention by a human being. **1.1**

Computer Center The area in a company that is used to house the computer system and the people who program and operate the computer system. **1.7**

Computer Crime See crime, computer. **2.26, 13.4**

Computer Operator An individual who operates the computer system. **1.11, 10.3**

Computer Program A series of instructions which directs the computer to perform a sequence of tasks that produce a desired output. **1.6, 11.1, 12.1**

Computer Programmers People who design, write, test, and implement the programs which process data on a computer system. **1.17, 10.3**

Computer System The actual computer hardware, which consists of the processor unit, operator console, input devices, output devices, and auxiliary storage devices. **1.15, 3.4**

Computer Users The people who utilize the output from a computer system in their daily activities. **1.19**

Computers in Banking See banking, computers in. **2.36, 3.18, 5.24**

Computers in Education See education, computers in. **2.34**

Computers in Manufacturing See manufacturing, computers in. **2.43**

Computers in the Office See office, computers in. **2.33**

Computers in Retailing See retailing, computers in. **2.38**

Computers in Society See society, computers in. **13.1**

Computers in Transportation See transportation, computers in. **2.40**

Concentrator A device which accepts information from many terminals over slow-speed lines and transmits the data to the main computer over a high-speed line. **8.23**

Console Terminal A device through which the computer operator communicates with the processor unit. **1.11**

Constantine, Larry Early leader in the development of structured design concepts. **11.9**

Control Break The change that occurs when a record is read in which the control field is different from the control field in the previous record. **11.24, A.24**

Control Programs Programs that are a part of an operating system that provide for automatic control of computer resources. **12.27**

Control Unit That part of the central processing unit that directs and coordinates the entire computer system. **4.10**

Controls, System The method used to assure that only valid data is accepted and processed on a computer. **10.20**

Conversion See parallel or direct. **10.27**

Core Dump See dump, core. **2.18**

Core Storage See storage, magnetic core. **4.14**

CPU See central processing unit. **1.5, 3.3, 4.1, 4.9**

Crime, Computer The use of a computer system to steal, embezzle, or maliciously access or destroy data or files used with computer systems. **2.26, 13.4**

CRT Terminal See cathode ray tube terminal. **1.11, 1.20, 3.2, 5.15, 6.6**

Cylinder The amount of data that can be read with a single positioning of an access arm on a magnetic disk. **7.8**

D **Daisy Wheel Printer** A printing device consisting of rotating spokes or arms which contain embossed characters. **6.16**

Data A representation of facts, concepts, or instructions in a formalized manner suitable for communication, interpretation, and processing by humans or machines. **1.5**

Data, Storage and Retrieval The process of recording and extracting data from auxiliary storage devices using a computer. **3.15**

Data Banks A collection of data which is stored on auxiliary storage devices. **3.17, 13.6**

Data Base A collection of interrelated data stored together with a minimum of redundancy to serve multiple applications. **9.1, 9.5**

Data Base, Hierarchical A data base in which there is a fixed relationship between the elements in the hierarchy. **9.6**

Data Base, Network A data base in which each of the elements is linked to each other through pointers. **9.6**

Data Base Administrator The person who is responsible for creating, updating, and controlling access to a data base. **1.17, 9.6, 10.6**

Data Base Management System A series of programs which is used to establish a data base, update the data base, and query the data base. **9.5**

Data Collection Those operations to obtain data in an uncontrolled environment from those doing the work being reported on. **5.31**

Data Communications The transmission of data from one location to another using communications channels such as telephone lines, coaxial cables, microwaves, or other means. **2.25, 8.1**

Data Communications, Line Speed The speed at which data is transmitted over communications channels. **8.12**

Data Definition Language A language that is a part of a data base system which allows for the definition of files and records, and their relationships. **9.7**

Data Entry The process of preparing data in some machine-processable form or entering data directly into a computer system. **1.16, 2.24, 5.1**

Data Entry Department The department where data is prepared for processing on a computer system. **1.16, 5.1**

Data Flow Diagram A diagramming technique used to graphically illustrate the flow of data through a system. **10.11**

Data Management Programs Programs supplied as a part of a system's software that handle such operations as the blocking and deblocking of records, accessing files, etc. **7.22, 9.8, 12.26, 12.30**

Data Processing Department The department in a company that is commonly made up of systems, programming, and operations. **10.3**

Data Processing Manager The individual who is in charge of and manages a data processing department. **1.17, 10.3**

Data Statement In BASIC, the statement that is used to define data. **A.6**

Decision Tables Graphical representations of logical decisions that must be made concerning conditions that can occur within a program. **11.30**

Decollating The process of removing carbon and separating the multiple copies of a report. **1.16**

Desk Top Computers Computer systems which are small enough to be placed on the top of a desk for use. **1.23**

Detail Printed Reports A report in which each input record is examined to determine if it will be printed on the report. **6.9**

Digitizer A data entry device which can scan images and transmit those images as digital impulses to a computer. **5.32**

Dim Statement In BASIC, the statement used to reserve areas of storage for tables or arrays. **A.31**

Dinosaur A term given to large computer systems by minicomputer and microcomputer supporters. **1.27**

Direct Access Storage Device An auxiliary storage device on which data can be stored and retrieved in any order, sequentially or randomly. **7.6, 7.23-7.27**

Direct Conversion At a given date, the old system ceases to be operational and the new system is placed into use. **10.27**

Direct or Relative File Organization A file in which records are stored in a location based upon the key found in the record. **7.18**

Disk, Floppy See floppy disk. **1.12, 3.2, 5.10, 7.27**

Disk Cartridge A type of removable disk storage commonly containing a single disk for recording and retrieving data. **7.27**

Disk Drive A device consisting of a spindle on which a disk pack can be mounted for electronically storing data. **1.13, 7.5, 7.24-7.27**

Disk Pack A unit which consists of multiple metal platters connected to a common hub. Each platter is coated with a metal oxide on which data can be electronically stored. **1.13, 7.5, 7.24-7.27**

Distributed Data Base The concept of distributing portions of a data base at remote sites where the data is most frequently referenced. **9.13**

Distributed Data Processing The distribution of computing power and data using minicomputers at locations where processing is required. **9.11, 10.6**

Do While A basic control structure used in structured programming to implement a loop. **11.7**

Documentation, Program The detailed recording of the facts about a program through supporting materials and within the program itself. **10.26, 12.24**

DPMA Data Processing Management Association: a professional association of data processing managers, programmers and systems analysts. **2.14**

Drum Printer A type of high-speed printer that features a cylindrical drum which rotates to position characters for printing. **6.17**

Dump, Core A printout of the contents of main storage. **2.18**

E

EBCDIC See extended binary coded decimal interchange code. **4.2, 7.3**

Eckert, J. Presper Working with Dr. John W. Mauchly, designed the ENIAC computer. **2.3**

Editing Input Data The process of checking to assure the validity of input data. **5.20, 10.21**

EDSAC The first computer which was operational using the stored program concept. **2.6**

Education, Computers in In education, computers are now used for computer-assisted instruction, as an area of specialized study, or as a tool to support classes in all disciplines. **2.34**

EDVAC An early computer developed by John von Neumann that utilized the stored program concept. **2.6**

Egoless programming Programming attitude based upon the concept that a program is not one's personal possession but open to all to view. **11.13**

Electrographic printer A non-impact printer that uses specially coated paper on which the image is "burned" or formed by various means. **6.16**

Electronic Funds Transfer A method of receiving and paying for goods and services by which funds are transferred from one account to another electronically under control of one or more computer systems. **13.6**

ENIAC The first large-scale electronic digital computer. **2.3**

Ethics Standards of conduct within a profession. **13.4**

Exception Report A report in which only unusual situations are displayed. **6.10**

Executing Instructions The process of analyzing machine language instructions on a computer and carrying out the functions to be performed. **4.10**

Extended Binary Coded Decimal Interchange Code (EBCDIC) A widely used coding system for representing data in computer storage and on auxiliary storage devices. **4.2, 7.3**

F   **Fiber Optics** Technology based upon light-weight, smooth hair-like strands of transparent material used for transmission of data and sound at high rates of speed. **8.8**

Fields A unit of data within a record. **3.2, 5.5**

File A collection of one or more records. **3.1, 3.2, 7.5, 7.14, 9.2**

File Organization The methods used to organize records so that they are accessible by computers. **7.1, 7.17**

File Updating The processing of additions, deletions, and changes against a master file. **7.14**

Fixed Word Length Computers Computers using a representation of data in main storage in which all values are stored in a fixed number of bits regardless of the size of the number. **4.12**

Flat Files Single files which exhibit no relationship to other files. **9.9**

Floppy Disk An oxide-coated plastic disk about 8" in diameter enclosed in a protective covering that can be used for magnetically storing data. **1.12, 3.2, 5.10**

Floppy Disk Reader A device which can read data stored on a floppy disk. **1.12, 3.2, 5.10**

Flowchart Symbols Standard symbols used to flowchart programming logic. **11.4**

Flowcharting The process of graphically depicting the detailed steps in the solution of a problem. **11.4, 11.14**

FORTRAN A high-level language designed for scientists, mathematicians, and engineers. **2.11, 12.4**

Front-end processor A sophisticated, programmable communications control unit consisting of a computer designed to handle communication functions to relieve the main computer of these tasks. **8.10**

Full-Duplex Line A data communications channel that allows data to be sent in both directions at the same time. **8.15**

G   **Gantt Chart** A charting technique used to illustrate schedule deadlines and milestones. **10.24**

General Ledger System The system used to provide a complete historical record of all financial transactions of a company. **10.32**

General Purpose Computers Computers which can perform any task by changing the application program in main computer storage. **1.28**

GIGO Garbage in, garbage out. **5.1**

GoTo Statement In BASIC, the statement that provides for unconditional transfer of control. **A.6**

Graphic Display Terminals CRT terminals capable of displaying not only letters of the alphabet and numbers but graphs and drawings as well. **6.6, 6.20**

H   **Half-Duplex Line** A channel that allows data to be sent in both directions, but not in both directions at the same time. **8.15**

Hexadecimal Number System A number system with a base 16 that uses 16 individual symbols to represent values. **2.18, C.4**

Hierarchical Data Base See data base, hierarchical. **9.6**

Hierarchy Chart A chart used in structured design to show the relationship of modules within a program. **11.11**

Hierarchy of Operations In BASIC, the sequence in which calculations are performed. **A.10**

High-level programming language A programming language far removed from the internal characteristics of the machine. **2.11, 12.4**

Hoff, Dr. Ted One of the first electronic engineers to design an entire central processing unit on a single silicon chip. **2.30**

Hollerith Code The coding system used to record data on punched cards. **5.4, B.1**

If Statement In BASIC, the statement that causes comparing operations to take place. **A.5**

If-Then-Else A basic control structure used with structured programming that implements conditional statements. **11.7**

Impact Printers Printing devices which print by some print mechanism striking paper, ribbon, and characters together. **6.2, 6.16**

Indexed File Organization A file organization method in which records are stored in ascending or descending sequence and are referenced by an index which permits sequential or random retrieval. **7.20**

Input Data used for processing on a computer system. **5.1**

Input Errors Errors that occur when data is converted to a machine-readable form or when data is entered into the computer for processing. **5.3**

Input/Output Operations A basic data processing function that requires the reading of data and producing some output from the data read. **3.5, 11.14**

Input/Processing/Output The sequence of events that occurs when data is processed on a computer system. **1.7, 3.4, 5.7**

Input Units Units that are a part of a computer system which present data to the processor unit for processing. **1.5, 1.11, 3.2, 5.1–5.17**

Inquiry A request from a terminal operator to a computer system for information. **3.16, 6.12**

Instruction Register An area of storage in the central processing unit where machine-language instructions are stored and analyzed prior to execution. **4.10**

Instructions, Computer The unique numbers, letters of the alphabet, or special characters that, when interpreted by the computer's circuitry, cause a particular operation to be performed. **2.10, 4.9, 11.1**

Intelligent Computer Terminal A terminal with the ability to process data using the electronic components within the terminal without the need to access the power of a large computer. **2.30, 5.16**

Interblock Gap A blank space typically .6 inch wide that separates records or groups of records on magnetic tape. **7.4**

Interpreter A program that reads source statements and immediately causes the statements to be executed one at a time. **12.20**

Interrupt An electronic signal which indicates to the central processing unit that the transfer of data between an input or output device and storage has been completed. **8.26**

Inventory Control The method used to keep track of merchandise available for sales. **10.30**

IPO Chart Input/processing/output chart used in structured design to assist in designing the structure of a program. **11.10**

J   Jackson, Michael The developer of a program design theory in which design is based upon the structure of the data to be processed. **11.12**

Job Control Language (JCL) A language that serves as a link between the operating system and the application programs to define jobs being processed, programs to be executed, and provide for job-to-job transition. **12.28**

K   Kemeny, Dr. John J. Early advocate of the use of computers in education; President of Dartmouth College; developed the BASIC language. **2.34, 12.14**

Keypunch A device used to punch holes in cards. **5.6**

Key-to-Disk Shared Processor System A data entry system in which multiple key stations are used to enter source data into a minicomputer for storage on disk. **5.11**

Key-to-Diskette A data entry device used to manually record data onto a floppy disk. **5.9**

Key-to-Tape Data Recorder A data entry device used to manually record data onto magnetic tape. **5.9**

Kurtz, Dr. Thomas In cooperation with Dr. John Kemeny, he developed the BASIC language at Dartmouth College. **12.14**

L   Large Scale Integration (LSI) Method of constructing electronic circuits in which many thousands of circuits can be stored on a single chip of silicon. **2.30, 4.16**

Laser Printers Very high-speed printers, printing in excess of 20,000 lines per minute. **6.5**

Leased Line A permanent communications channel used to connect a terminal with a computer system. **8.18**

Millisecond One thousandth of a second. **7.8**

Minicomputer A computer system which has smaller computer storage, slower processing speeds, and lower cost than large computer systems. **1.24, 2.22, 5.11, 7.27, 8.22, 9.11**

Modems A device which accepts a digital signal and converts it to an analog signal or accepts an analog signal and converts it to a digital signal. **8.3, 8.6**

MPU Microprocessor unit. **4.19**

Multidrop Lines A communication network in which more than one terminal is on a single line connected to the computer. **8.17**

Multiplexer An electronic device which divides a channel of a certain speed into a series of channels of a slower speed. **8.22**

Multiprogramming The concurrent execution of two or more computer programs on one computer system. **8.26**

Myers, Glenford Early leader in the area of structured design. **11.9**

N **Nanosecond** One billionth of a second. **4.15**

Network Data Base See data base, network. **9.6**

Networks, Data Communications A system composed of one or more computers and terminals. **8.21**

Nonimpact Printers Printers which use a specially coated or sensitized paper that responds to stimuli to cause an image to appear on a form. **6.3, 6.16**

O **Object Program** The machine language instructions resulting from a compilation of source statements. **12.18**

OCR See optical character recognition. **5.24, 5.27**

Octal Number System A number system with a base 8 that uses eight symbols to represent values. **C.6**

Office, Computers in the Computers are widely used in word processing activities for inquiry and updating files. Computer terminals are replacing the typewriter as an office tool in many companies. **2.33**

Operand That portion of a computer instruction that commonly indicates the address of data to be processed. **4.9, 12.2**

Operation Code That portion of a computer instruction which indicates the operations to be performed. **4.9, 12.2**

Operating System A collection of programs that allows a computer system to supervise its own operations. **12.26**

Operations Department The department that is responsible for carrying out the day-to-day processing on a computer once a system is operational. **1.8-1.11, 10.3**

Optical Character Recognition (OCR) The reading of data by scanning the location or shape of the data on a document. **5.24, 5.27**

Optical Scanning Devices Devices that read or otherwise sense data on forms for processing on a computer. **5.24-5.27**

Order Entry System The system which defines the procedures used when processing an order. **10.29**

Output Information that is produced as a result of processing input data. **1.5, 6.1**

Output, External Output used outside a company. **6.8**

Output, Internal Output used within an organization. **6.8**

Output, Transaction-Oriented See Transaction-oriented output. **6.12**

Output Units Units which are a part of a computer system that can display, print or otherwise make available to people the results of processing data. **1.5, 1.12, 3.3, 6.4-6.7, 6.19-6.23**

P **Paging** The ability to display an entire screen full of data on a CRT terminal under terminal control. **6.7**

Parallel Conversion Processing data in both the old system and the new system and comparing results. **10.27**

Parity Check A checking method in which a bit is associated with each character stored so that all characters will contain an odd (or even) number of bits. **7.3**

Pascal A programming language designed to make it easy to write programs using structured techniques. **12.15**

Payroll System The system used to pay employees for services rendered. **10.33**

Physical Record A group of records placed together on an auxiliary storage device. **7.4**

PL/I A programming language developed by IBM for use as a general-purpose language in both business and scientific applications. **12.10**

Plotter A device capable of producing drawings as hard copy output from a computer. **6.22**

Point of Sale Terminals (POS) Terminals placed at locations where business transactions occur. **5.28**

Point-to-Point Line A direct communication line between a terminal and a computer system. **8.16**

Polling A method used in data communications networks in which each terminal is interrogated in sequence to determine if there is data to be sent. **8.19**

Preliminary Investigation That phase of a system project undertaken to determine if a problem warrants further study. **10.8**

Print Statement In BASIC, the statement used to cause data to be displayed as output. **A.5**

Printed Reports Reports which are printed by printers attached to the computer system. **1.12, 6.9-6.11**

Printer Spacing Chart A preprinted form to assist in designing output reports. **10.14**

Printers Devices which are connected to the computer system and which can prepare printed reports under the control of a computer program. **1.12, 6.2-6.5, 6.16, 6.17, 10.14**

Privacy Act of 1974 A law enacted in 1974 to protect rights of citizens from invasion of privacy. **2.26**

Procedures A series of logical steps by which all repetitive actions are initiated, performed, controlled, or completed. **10.1**

Processing Programs Those programs that are a part of the operating system which perform commonly required functions; they include the language translator and the service programs. **12.26, 12.28**

Processor Unit The unit which stores the data and contains the electronic circuitry necessary to carry out the processing of the stored data. It consists of the central processing unit and main computer storage. **1.5, 3.3, 4.1, 4.10**

Program See computer program. **1.6, 11.1**

Program Design The process of developing the structure of a program and the detailed steps required for the solution of a problem. **11.3**

Program Development Cycle The well-defined sequence of steps in writing a program that includes review of specifications, design, code, test, and document. **10.25, 12.1**

Program Documentation See documentation, program. **16.26, 12.24**

Programmers See computer programmers. **1.17, 10.3**

Programming The process of writing instructions for a computer. **2.10, 10.25, 12.1**

Programming, Automatic An early term used to describe writing a computer program in a notation other than machine language. **2.10**

Programming Language, High-Level See high-level programming language. **2.11, 12.4**

Programming Language, Low-Level See low-level programming languages **12.2**

Programming Languages The software supplied as a part of the computer system that provides a means of instructing the computer to perform operations. **2.10, 12.1, 12.16**

Programming, Machine-Language The writing of instructions for a computer by means of numbers, letters of the alphabet, and special characters that can be understood by the electronic circuitry. **2.10, 4.9, 12.2**

Programming Manager The person in charge of the programming group in a data processing department. **1.17, 10.3**

Programming, Structured See structured programming. **11.6**

Programming, Symbolic Programming using simple words or abbreviations to express the operations to be performed. **2.11, 12.2**

Programs, Unreliable Programs that do not always produce consistent results. **2.23**

PROM See memory, programmable read only. **4.19**

Pseudocode A method used to express the logic required in the solution of a problem using English-like phrases. **11.8**

Punched Cards A piece of lightweight cardboard capable of storing data in the form of punched holes recorded in predefined locations. **1.7, 1.11, 5.4, B.1**

Punched Card Reader See card reader. **1.7, 1.11, 5.7**

Q **Query Language** A language provided as a part of data base management systems that provides for easy access to data in a data base. **9.5, 9.9**

R **RAM** See memory, random access. **4.19**

RAMAC One of the first magnetic disk storage devices introduced by IBM in the mid-1950's. **7.5**

Random Access The ability to retrieve records in a file without reading any previous records. **7.11**

Random Access Storage Devices See direct access storage devices. **7.6, 7.23-7.27**

Random File Updating The process of updating files in which each master record is individually retrieved without searching through each master record sequentially. **7.16**

Storage, Vacuum Tubes One of the first methods used to store data electronically in main storage. **2.3, 4.14**

Stored Program Concept The concept in which instructions are stored internally in the main storage unit of the computer. **2.5**

Strings In BASIC, alphanumeric data. **A.2**

Structured Design A method of designing programs in which a large program is decomposed into small modules, each of which performs a given function. **11.9**

Structured Programming A method of programming in which three basic control structures are used to develop programs. **11.6**

Structured Walkthroughs The process of reviewing program design and program coding with other programmers. **11.13**

Stub Testing The process of testing a program one module at a time. **12.23**

Subroutine A group of instructions which are used a number of times in a program and can be called as needed. **11.9**

Summarizing The process of accumulating and printing values contained in records. **3.22**

Summary Reports A report in which one line is printed for each group of records. **3.23, 6.9**

Supervisor A program that is part of the operating system that controls and schedules the resources of a computer system. **8.26, 12.27**

Switched Line A type of data communications line in which connection is established with a computer over a regular telephone network. **8.18**

Symbolic Programming See programming, symbolic. **2.11, 12.2**

Synchronous Transmission Transmission of data based upon a timing mechanism in which data is transmitted at fixed intervals. **8.14**

System Project, Conducting The steps in conducting a systems project can be broken down into a series of phases including: initiation of the project; detailed investigation; design; development; implementation and evaluation. **10.7**

System A series of related procedures designed to perform a specific task. **1.17, 10.1**

Systems Analysis The process of analyzing existing systems for the purpose of evaluating possible improvements in methods and procedures. **10.1**

Systems Analysts People who design and develop systems which will be implemented on a computer system. **1.17, 10.3**

System Design That phase of a system project in which the new system is created. **10.12**

System Development That phase of a system project concerned with scheduling, programming, and documenting a system. **10.24**

System Flowchart A series of symbols designed to graphically illustrate the procedural steps in a system. **10.18**

System Implementation and Evaluation That phase of a system project that is concerned with the conversion to the new system. **10.27**

System Investigation That phase of a system project concerned with fact gathering and analyzing the existing system. **10.10**

Systems Manager The person who is in charge of the systems analysis and design group within a data processing department. **1.17, 10.3**

T **Tab Statement** In BASIC, the statement used to cause output to be displayed beginning at a specific location. **A.14**

Tape, Magnetic A 1/2" wide piece of mylar on which data can be stored electronically. Typical lengths for tape are 600 feet, 1200 feet, and 2400 feet. **1.13, 3.2, 5.9, 7.2–7.5**

Tape Coding, Magnetic The coding structure used to represent data on magnetic tape. **7.3**

Tape Density, Magnetic The number of characters per inch that can be recorded on magnetic tape; common densities include 800, 1600, or 6250 bytes per inch. **7.4**

Tape Library An area in a data processing department where tape reels are stored when not being used on the computer system. **1.15**

Tape Reels A plastic container on which magnetic tape is stored for processing on a computer system. **1.15, 7.3**

Terminals, CRT See cathode ray tube terminals. **1.11, 3.2, 5.15, 6.6**

Terminals, Data Communication A terminal used in a data communication system for the transmission and reception of data. These terminals may consist of CRT terminals, small computer systems, or other types of I/O devices. **8.4**

Terminals, Dumb A terminal that is used to accept keyed data and transmit that data to a computer with no other processing capabilities. **5.16**

Terminals, Hard Copy A computer terminal that can produce printed output. **5.16**

Terminals, Intelligent See intelligent computer terminals. **2.30, 5.16**

Test Data Data created to test the reliability of a program. **10.26, 12.22**

Testing, Program The process of checking to assure that a program produces reliable and accurate results. **10.26, 12.22**

Track, Magnetic Disk The concentric recording positions on magnetic disk. **7.7**

TRADIC The first transistorized computer. **2.13**

Transaction-Oriented Processing System That type of system in which data is entered into the computer at the time the transaction occurs. **2.25, 5.2, 5.14, 5.18, 6.12**

Transaction-Oriented Output Output, normally displayed on a CRT terminal in a transaction-oriented processing system. **6.12**

Translator See compiler. **2.11, 12.18**

Transportation, Computers in Computers are widely used in airline and hotel reservation systems, as well as in the guidance systems of aircraft, training systems, and other support areas. **2.40**

TRS-80 A microcomputer system made by Radio Shack. **1.20**

U **Unbundling** The separate pricing of hardware, software, and related services. **2.21**

UNIVAC I The first electronic computer dedicated to data processing applications. **2.6**

Universal Product Code A code placed on many consumer products to facilitate check out at retail stores. **5.24**

Updating The process in which files are changed, with additions, deletions, and changes, to reflect the latest information. **3.18, 7.14, 7.16**

Utilities, System Programs that are a part of an operating system that are used to perform frequently used applications such as file-to-file conversion and sort-merge operations. **12.26, 12.30**

V **Variable Names** In BASIC, symbolic fields and areas of storage. **A.2**

Variable Word Length A method of storing data in which each digit, letter of the alphabet or special character is stored in a single storage location; the number of storage locations required will vary with the size of the field. **4.12**

Verifier A machine used to check the accuracy of cards by rekeying the data which has already been punched. **5.6**

Virtual Storage A storage method in which portions of a program are stored on auxiliary storage until needed, giving the illusion of unlimited main storage. **12.31**

Voice Input A device that allows vocal input to be accepted and interpreted in a form processable by a computer. **5.32**

Voice Output An output device which converts data in main storage to vocal response understandable by humans. **6.22**

von Neumann, Dr. John Prepared the first written documentation of the "stored program" concept: a pioneer in the use of program flowcharts. **2.5. 11.4**

W **Walkthroughs, Structured** See structured walkthroughs. **11.13**

Warnier Design Methodology A method of program design based upon the structure of the data to be processed. **11.12**

Watson, Thomas J., Jr. Led IBM in the 1950's and 1960's during the time it became the world leader in electronic computers. **2.8**

Watson, Thomas J., Sr. Chairman of the Board of IBM for 40 years and a guiding force in its early years of growth. **2.8**

Weinberg, Dr. Gerald Author of "The Psychology of Computer Programming" and advocate of egoless programming and structured walkthroughs. **11.13**

Wilkes, Maurice V. A student of John von Neumann who designed the EDSAC computer. **2.6**

Word Processing The storage, manipulation, and processing of data as needed in the preparation of letters and reports using terminals and related devices. **3.14**